CELESTIAL FORECASTER ®

2007

EVERYONE'S

DAILY ASTROLOGY GUIDE

FEATURING:

- Daily forecasts based on planetary alignments
- Monthly overview of significant aspects
- Time zone adjustments chart
- Daily table of aspect influences
- Full year calendar, and
- Built-in ephemeris

Loon Feather Publications
Box 47031 Victoria, B.C.
V9B 5T2 Canada
www.metaphysical.ca/forecaster
email: loonfeather@metaphysical.ca

Acknowledgements:

Thanks to all of you for continuing to make the Celestial Forecaster
a success. Your enthusiasm is what keeps the Forecaster going.
Special thanks to Soror SSH for the great work editing,
and to Frater 72 for production.

Printing and Binding: Worzalla
Production & cover: Frater 72
Editing: Soror SSH
Inside Graphics: Merx Toledo International
ISBN: 0-9731518-4-6

TABLE OF CONTENTS

2007 calendar . . . . inside front
Time zone adjustment chart 5
Definition of terms 6
Glossary of symbols 7
How to use this book 7
Mercury retrograde periods 8
Overview – aspects at a glance 9
Table of aspect influences 18
Detailed forecasts 22
Ephemeris 248
Ordering information 255
Horoscope blank . . . . inside back

TIME ZONE ADJUSTMENTS

In the *Celestial Forecaster* we show Pacific Time and Eastern Time. Most poeple in North America are familiar with adjusting to one of those two zones. If you use **Central Time**, add two hours to Pacific Time. For **Rocky Mountain Time**, add one hour to Pacific Time. To get **Greenwich Mean Time**, add 8 hours to Pacific Time (PST) or seven hours to Pacific Daylight Time (PDT). If you live outside North America, you can refer to the Time Zone Map below.

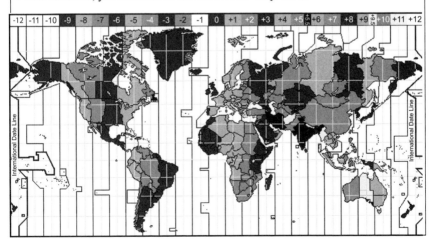

Definitions of Terms

Aspect: Planets are said to be "in aspect" with each other when their location in the sky forms particular angles with the earth which are deemed significant. The main aspects and angles used in this book are as follows:

✳ **Sextile (60°):** The sextile aspect is considered to be favorable, and opens up possibilities and opportunities to work energies out between the two planetary influences.

☐ **Square (90°):** The square aspect indicates a struggle or stress between two planetary influences. This aspect often brings obstacles, or difficulties in our ability to learn and understand. A positive way to address this aspect is to see it as a time when we need to work through our challenges. In these blocks or obstacles a great deal of energy is concentrated. If one acts with caution and care, the energy released by dealing with our challenges can be harnessed, and overcoming the obstacle becomes a personal triumph that leads to growth and the strengthening of character.

△ **Trine (120°):** The most advantageous and harmonious aspect. It is considered to bring the most positive effects. A trine aspect brings gifts, and talents are often realized and acted upon.

☍ **Opposition (180°):** The opposition is the furthest apart the two planets are able to be in their orbits. This aspect brings an acute awareness of the energies that two planetary influences have upon us. It can also bring an overwhelming effect, and handling the polarity often requires awareness and caution.

☌ **Conjunction (0°):** Conjunction is the act of joining, or the state of being joined. When two planets have reached the same degree in the sky this is called a conjunction. It represents the direct confrontation of these energies which will be positive or negative depending on the nature of the planets which are in conjunction.

The Orb: The orb is the area of influence before and after an exact aspect, measured in degrees. The smaller the orb, the closer we are to an exact aspect, and the more strongly we feel the planetary influences. Orbs are divided into two parts: applying and separating. **Applying** — the part of the orb when the planetary aspect is approaching the exact time of reaching its peak. **Separating** — the part of the orb when the planetary aspect is moving away from the peak point of the aspect. Orbs in this book have been calculated using an orb of 6° applying, and 3° separating for all aspects except the sextile, for which 4° applying and 2° separating have been used.

V/C **Void-of-course Moon:** As it travels through a zodiacal sign, the Moon is in aspect with a number of planets. The final major aspect it reaches in a sign marks the time when the Moon goes void-of-course (v/c), meaning it will undergo no further aspects while in that zodiac sign. The Moon will remain void-of-course until it enters the next zodiac sign. While the Moon is void-of-course is a time of less direction and more confusion, particularly on the emotional or mood level.

R **Retrograde:** This occurs when the orbit of a planet causes it to appear to move backward through the sky. It represents a time of moving back over old ground, and inverting influences. The section on Mercury retrograde (next page) gives examples of how retrogrades work. The Sun and Moon, not being planets, do not go retrograde.

D **Direct:** After a period of retrograde motion, the planet ceases its backward motion and moves forward again through the zodiacal signs. It represents a time of release and forward movement, though the old ground that was just covered in retrograde fashion must be gone over again before any new progress can be made.

Glossary of Astrological Symbols

Aries	♈	Sun	☉
Taurus	♉	Moon	☽
Gemini	♊	Mercury	☿
Cancer	♋	Venus	♀
Leo	♌	Mars	♂
Virgo	♍	Jupiter	♃
Libra	♎	Saturn	♄
Scorpio	♏	Neptune	♆
Sagittarius	♐	Uranus	♅
Capricorn	♑	Pluto	♇
Aquarius	♒		
Pisces	♓		

How to Use this Book

To adjust for time zones other than Pacific or Eastern USA, use the *Time Zone Adjustments* table on page 5.

For planetary aspectarian and for the phases of the Moon: use the *Overview of Significant Aspects in 2007* found on pages 9 – 17.

For major daily influences at a glance: look at the *Table of Aspect Influences* on pages 18 - 21.

For exact zodiacal position of a planet: use the *Ephemeris* on pages 248-254.

For daily commentary and analysis: see the main section pages 22-247, including:

<u>Sun Signs:</u> The glyph for the current sun sign is shown in the upper right margin on each page of the daily commentary.

<u>Headers:</u> The date headers at the top of each day show the date, the day of the week, and a selection of notable holidays.

<u>Moon signs and void-of-course periods:</u> Below the date header is the Moon's sign. The Moon's void-of-course period and entry to the next sign is shown chronologically with the day's planetary aspects. The numerous lunar aspects are included this year, and are often interpreted in the *Mood Watch* section.

<u>Aspects:</u> Below the Moon's sign in the header is a list of the day's exact planetary and lunar aspects, together with their time of occurrence. Also listed are aspects whose orb of influence is just beginning, and the aspect's date of exact occurrence. Occasionally the aspect information is followed by quotes from famous people.

<u>Mood Watch:</u> Each day features a *Mood Watch* section. This commentary examines key lunar aspects of the day, and explains their likely influence on our moods. Like our moods, these lunar aspects are generally short-lived.

<u>Aspect Analysis:</u> Below the *Mood Watch* section are shown the day's main planetary aspects, the dates their orb of influence occurs, and an in-depth aspect analysis.

Mercury retrograde periods: 2007

BEGINS (Mercury goes retrograde)
Feb. 13 in Pisces
June 15 in Cancer
October 11 in Scorpio

ENDS (Mercury goes direct)
March 7 in Aquarius
July 9 in Cancer
November 1 in Libra

Mercury Retrograde through the Water Signs and through two Air Signs

Mercury represents how we process information and communicate. Mercury retrograde is a term that describes an orbital shift as it moves backwards through a sign. Technically it only appears to move backwards through the degrees of the zodiac from our geocentric view. Astrologically, this is a time of communication related setbacks, reiterations, or inconsistencies. Mercury retrograde periods take place for an average of three weeks at a time, and will occur on the average of three times a year.

Mercury retrograde is a time of going back over various topics, and repeating or correcting, a lot of information. General misinformation is the most common symptom, and people may be afflicted with bouts of dyslexia – the switching around of numbers, thought forms, and words. Those who are not so adept at, or inclined towards paying attention to important details and communicating accurately, are highly affected by Mercury retrograde, and in a more difficult way.

Mercury retrograde periods affect business, media, and news casting. They also affect anyone who relies on the accuracy of information. While Mercury is retrograde, the professionals work hard to correct communication mistakes, no matter how thick the stratosphere is with misinformation.

This year Mercury will go retrograde mainly in the water signs of the zodiac (Pisces, Cancer, Scorpio) with the exception of Mercury being retrograde in the air sign, Aquarius February 13 – 26, and it will also be retrograde in the air sign Libra, October 23 – November 1.

As Mercury goes retrograde through the water signs, communications of an emotional nature are likely to be easily misinterpreted. It may be very difficult to accurately describe emotionally stirring experiences. It is best to mind the emotional sensitivity of others when attempting to communicate during Mercury retrograde in the water signs. In turn, expect to be confused or perplexed by the emotional rants of others while receiving messages. While Mercury is retrograde in Pisces it may be best to avoid being too complex with religious or spiritual topics. While Mercury is retrograde in Cancer, beware of the tendency to overstress the morals and dogma of home related or domestic points of interest. While Mercury is retrograde in Scorpio, it may be dangerous to joke about tender subjects like, birth, sex, jealousy, or death.

While Mercury is retrograde in the air sign, Aquarius, communication mistakes and mishaps will be apparent and highlighted in Aquarius related topics such as technology, science, inventions, experiments, and politics. While Mercury is retrograde in the air sign, Libra, miscommunications between friends and loved ones are likely to occur quite frequently, and there may be several delays, and re-scheduling, occurring in the courts and within various levels of the justice system.

Overview of Significant Aspects in 2007

January

2	Sun sextile Uranus	1:17 am	4:17 am	
3	**Full Moon in Cancer**	5:58 am	8:58 am	
	Venus enters Aquarius	7:32 pm	10:32 pm	
	Mercury sextile Uranus	9:20 pm	12:20 am	(Jan. 4)
6	Sun conjunct Mercury	10:06 pm	1:06 am	(Jan. 7)
8	Mars trine Saturn	10:06 am	1:06 pm	
11	**Last QTR Moon in Libra**	4:46 am	7:46 am	
12	Venus sextile Jupiter	4:46 am	7:46 am	
13	Mars conjunct Pluto	2:03 am	5:03 am	
15	Mercury enters Aquarius	1:26 am	4:26 am	
16	Mars enters Capricorn	12:55 pm	3:55 pm	
18	Venus conjunct Neptune	6:49 pm	9:49 pm	
	New Moon in Capricorn	8:02 pm	11:02 pm	
20	Sun enters Aquarius	3:02 am	6:02 am	
22	Venus opposite Saturn	7:40 am	10:40 am	
	Mercury sextile Jupiter	8:14 am	11:14 am	
	Jupiter square Uranus	1:44 pm	4:44 pm	
25	**First QTR Moon in Taurus**	3:03 pm	6:03 pm	
26	Venus sextile Pluto	3:00 am	6:00 am	
	Mercury conjunct Neptune	5:21 am	8:21 am	
27	Venus enters Pisces	7:33 pm	10:33 pm	
28	Mercury opposite Saturn	10:08 am	1:08 pm	
31	Mercury sextile Pluto	6:34 pm	9:34 pm	

February

1	**Full Moon in Leo**	9:46 pm	12:46 am	(Feb. 2)
2	**Candlemas – Groundhog Day**			
	Mercury enters Pisces	1:21 am	4:21 am	
3	Mars sextile Uranus	2:42 am	5:42 am	
	Sun sextile Jupiter	7:48 am	10:48 am	
7	Venus conjunct Uranus	10:58 am	1:58 pm	
8	Sun conjunct Neptune	7:53 am	10:53 am	
9	Venus square Jupiter	3:32 am	6:32 am	
10	**Last QTR Moon in Scorpio**	1:52 am	4:52 am	
	Sun opposite Saturn	10:43 am	1:43 pm	
13	Venus sextile Mars	2:48 pm	5:48 pm	
	Mercury goes retrograde	8:39 pm	11:39 pm	

February (Cont'd)

17	Sun sextile Pluto	5:08 am	8:08 am	
	New Moon in Aquarius	8:15 am	11:15 am	
18	Sun enters Pisces	5:10 pm	8:10 pm	
19	Venus square Pluto	7:58 pm	10:58 pm	
21	Venus enters Aries	12:22 am	3:22 am	
22	Sun conjunct Mercury	8:47 pm	11:47 pm	
23	**First QTR Moon in Gemini**	11:57 pm	2:57 am	(Feb. 24)
25	Mars enters Aquarius	5:33 pm	8:33 pm	
26	Mercury enters Aquarius	7:02 pm	10:02 pm	
28	Saturn opposite Neptune	4:03 am	7:03 am	
	Mercury sextile Pluto	5:10 am	8:10 am	

March

3	**Full Moon in Virgo**	3:18 pm	6:18 pm
5	Sun conjunct Uranus	7:40 am	10:40 am
7	Mercury goes direct	8:46 pm	11:46 pm
8	Venus trine Jupiter	3:17 am	6:17 am
9	Venus trine Saturn	12:42 am	3:42 am
	Sun square Jupiter	6:20 am	9:20 am
	Venus sextile Neptune	7:42 pm	10:42 pm
11	**DAYLIGHT SAVINGS TIME BEGINS –**		
	Turn clocks ahead one hour at	2:00 am	2:00 am
	Last QTR Moon in Scorpio	8:55 pm	11:55 pm
16	Jupiter trine Saturn	3:44 pm	6:44 pm
	Mercury sextile Pluto	4:35 pm	7:35 pm
	Venus trine Pluto	5:19 pm	8:19 pm
	Mercury sextile Venus	6:24 pm	9:24 pm
17	Venus enters Taurus	3:02 pm	6:02 pm
	Mercury enters Pisces	2:36 am	5:36 am
	New Moon in Taurus	7:44 pm	10:44 pm
19	Sun square Pluto	3:15 pm	6:15 pm
20	**Vernal Equinox**		
	Sun enters Aries	5:09 pm	8:09 pm
23	Mars sextile Jupiter	9:02 am	12:02 pm
25	**First QTR Moon in Cancer**	11:17 am	2:17 pm
	Mars conjunct Neptune	10:40 am	1:40 pm
31	Venus sextile Uranus	1:23 am	4:23 am
	Pluto goes retrograde	3:47 pm	6:47 pm

April

1	Mercury conjunct Uranus	11:31 am	2:31 pm	
2	Venus square Saturn	12:02 am	3:02 am	
	Full Moon in Libra	10:16 am	1:16 pm	
4	Mercury square Jupiter	12:18 am	3:18 am	
	Venus square Neptune	11:17 am	2:17 pm	
	Mars sextile Pluto	5:23 pm	8:23 pm	
5	Jupiter goes retrograde	6:24 pm	9:24 pm	
6	Mars enters Pisces	1:50 am	4:50 am	
7	Mercury sextile Venus	9:11 am	12:11 pm	
8	Sun trine Saturn	4:57 am	7:57 am	
9	Sun trine Jupiter	5:08 pm	8:08 pm	
10	Mercury square Pluto	12:26 am	3:26 am	
	Last QTR Moon in Capricorn	11:05 am	2:05 pm	
	Mercury enters Aries	4:08 pm	7:08 pm	
11	Sun sextile Neptune	12:34 pm	3:34 pm	
	Venus enters Gemini	7:16 pm	10:16 pm	
17	**New Moon in Aries**	4:37 am	7:37 am	
19	Sun trine Pluto	12:36 am	3:36 am	
	Saturn goes direct	2:25 pm	5:25 pm	
20	Sun enters Taurus	4:08 am	7:08 am	
21	Mercury trine Saturn	12:10 am	3:10 am	
	Mercury trine Jupiter	3:40 pm	6:40 pm	
22	Mercury sextile Neptune	9:12 pm	12:12 am	(Apr. 23)
	Venus square Mars	10:31 pm	1:31 am	(Apr. 23)
23	**First QTR Moon in Leo**	11:37 pm	2:37 am	(Apr. 24)
26	Mercury trine Pluto	10:07 am	1:07 am	
	Venus square Uranus	8:21 pm	11:21 pm	
27	Mercury enters Taurus	12:17 am	3:17 am	
	Venus sextile Saturn	1:08 pm	4:08 pm	
28	Venus opposite Jupiter	5:45 am	8:45 am	
	Mars conjunct Uranus	9:38 pm	12:38 am	(Apr. 29)
30	Mars square Jupiter	3:22 pm	6:22 pm	
	Venus trine Neptune	6:35 pm	9:35 pm	

May

1	**Beltane / May Day**		
2	**Full Moon in Scorpio**	3:11 am	6:11 am
	Sun conjunct Mercury	9:06 pm	12:06 am
5	Mercury sextile Uranus	8:54 am	11:54 am
	Mercury square Saturn	3:56 pm	6:56 pm
6	Jupiter trine Saturn	12:12 am	3:12 am
	Venus opposite Pluto	7:06 pm	10:06 pm
7	Mercury square Neptune	7:29 am	10:29 am
8	Venus enters Cancer	12:29 am	3:29 am
	Sun sextile Uranus	1:26 pm	4:26 pm
	Mercury sextile Mars	5:40 pm	8:40 pm
9	Sun square Saturn	5:06 am	8:06 am
	Last QTR Moon in Aquarius	9:28 pm	12:28 am	(May 10)
10	Jupiter square Uranus	8:33 pm	11:33 pm
11	Mercury enters Gemini	2:18 am	5:18 am
12	Sun square Neptune	7:57 pm	10:57 pm
13	Mars square Pluto	8:16 am	11:16 am
15	Mars enters Aries	7:07 am	10:07 am
16	**New Moon in Taurus**	12:28 pm	3:28 pm
19	Mercury opposite Jupiter	10:31 pm	1:31 am	(May 20)
20	Mercury square Uranus	4:27 pm	7:27 pm
21	Sun enters Gemini	3:13 am	6:13 am
	Mercury sextile Saturn	3:49 am	6:49 am
23	Mercury trine Neptune	12:48 am	3:48 am
	First QTR Moon in Virgo	2:04 pm	5:04 pm
24	Neptune goes retrograde	6:08 pm	9:08 pm
	Venus trine Uranus	11:42 pm	2:42 am	(May 25)
27	Mercury opposite Pluto	8:14 am	11:14 am
28	Mercury enters Cancer	5:57 pm	8:57 pm
31	**Full Moon in Sagittarius**	6:05 pm	9:05 pm

June

4	Mars trine Jupiter	7:59 am	10:59 am
5	Venus enters Leo	11:00 am	2:00 pm
	Sun opposite Jupiter	4:14 pm	7:14 pm
8	**Last QTR Moon in Pisces**	4:44 am	7:44 am
9	Sun square Uranus	1:09 pm	4:09 pm
11	Sun sextile Mars	3:28 am	6:28 am
	Sun sextile Saturn	12:41 pm	3:41 pm
	Mars trine Saturn	3:44 pm	6:44 pm

June (Cont'd)

13	Sun trine Neptune	12:31 am	3:31 am	
	Mars sextile Neptune	1:36 pm	4:36 pm	
14	**New Moon in Gemini**	8:14 pm	11:14 pm	
15	Mercury goes retrograde	4:41 pm	7:41 pm	
18	Sun opposite Pluto	11:50 pm	2:50 am	(June 19)
19	Venus trine Jupiter	3:49 pm	6:49 pm	
21	Mars trine Pluto	6:37 am	9:37 am	
	Summer Solstice			
	Sun enters Cancer	11:08 am	2:08 pm	
22	**First QTR Moon in Libra**	6:16 am	9:16 am	
23	Uranus goes retrograde	7:44 am	10:44 am	
24	Mars enters Taurus	2:28 pm	5:28 pm	
25	Saturn opposite Neptune	8:55 am	11:55 am	
28	Sun conjunct Mercury	11:41 am	2:41 pm	
30	**Full Moon in Capricorn**	6:50 am	9:50 am	
	Venus opposite Neptune	8:32 am	11:32 am	

July

1	Venus conjunct Saturn	7:39 am	10:39 am	
	Mercury sextile Mars	12:09 pm	3:09 pm	
7	**Last QTR Moon in Aries**	9:55 am	12:55 pm	
8	Venus trine Pluto	6:10 pm	9:10 pm	
9	Mercury goes direct	7:16 pm	10:16 pm	
10	Sun trine Uranus	10:34 pm	1:34 am	(July 11)
14	**New Moon in Cancer**	5:05 am	8:05 am	
	Venus enters Virgo	11:25 am	2:25 pm	
20	Mars sextile Uranus	3:14 pm	6:14 pm	
21	**First QTR Moon in Libra**	11:30 pm	2:30 am	(July 22)
22	Sun enters Leo	10:01 pm	1:01 am	(July 23)
24	Mars square Neptune	4:11 pm	7:11 pm	
27	Venus goes retrograde	10:29 am	1:29 pm	
28	Mercury trine Uranus	8:26 pm	11:26 pm	
29	**Full Moon in Aquarius**	5:49 pm	8:49 pm	
31	Mars square Saturn	5:00 pm	8:00 pm	

August

1	**Lammas / Lughnassad**		
2	Sun trine Jupiter	8:13 am	11:13 am

August (Cont'd)

3	Mercury sextile Mars	2:54 am	5:54 am	
4	Mercury enters Leo	10:16 am	1:16 pm	
5	**Last QTR Moon in Taurus**	2:21 pm	5:21 pm	
6	Saturn trine Pluto	3:36 am	6:36 am	
	Jupiter goes direct	7:06 pm	10:06 pm	
	Mars enters Gemini	11:02 pm	2:02 am	(Aug. 7)
7	Venus square Mars	4:37 pm	7:37 pm	
8	Venus enters Leo	6:11 pm	9:11 pm	
9	Mercury trine Jupiter	8:37 am	11:37 am	
12	**New Moon in Leo**	4:04 pm	7:04 pm	
13	Sun opposite Neptune	11:26 am	2:26 pm	
	Venus conjunct Saturn	12:17 pm	3:17 pm	
14	Mercury opposite Neptune	1:10 pm	4:10 pm	
15	Venus trine Pluto	6:45 am	9:45 am	
	Sun conjunct Mercury	12:57 pm	3:57 pm	
16	Mercury conjunct Venus	10:28 pm	1:28 am	(Aug. 17)
17	Mercury trine Pluto	10:24 am	1:24 pm	
	Sun conjunct Venus	8:42 pm	11:42 pm	
18	Mercury conjunct Saturn	6:45 am	9:45 am	
19	Mercury enters Virgo	6:02 am	9:02 am	
	Sun trine Pluto	11:15 am	2:15 pm	
20	**First QTR Moon in Scorpio**	4:55 pm	7:55 pm	
21	Sun conjunct Saturn	4:29 pm	7:29 pm	
23	Sun enters Virgo	5:09 am	8:09 am	
	Mars opposite Jupiter	9:04 am	12:04 pm	
24	Mercury square Jupiter	6:04 pm	9:04 pm	
25	Mercury square Mars	9:00 am	12:00 pm	
	Venus opposite Neptune	2:49 pm	5:49 pm	
28	**Full Moon in Pisces**	3:36 am	6:36 am	
	Mercury opposite Uranus	12:40 pm	3:40 pm	

September

2	Saturn enters Virgo	6:50 am	9:50 am	
	Mercury square Pluto	10:05 pm	1:05 am	(Sept. 3)
3	Mars square Uranus	1:10 pm	4:10 pm	
	Venus sextile Mars	4:37 pm	7:37 pm	
	Sun square Jupiter	5:05 pm	8:05 pm	
	Last QTR Moon in Gemini	7:33 pm	10:33 pm	

September (Cont'd)

5	Mercury enters Libra	5:03 am	8:03 am	
7	Pluto goes direct	7:56 am	10:56 am	
8	Venus goes direct	9:15 am	12:15 pm	
	Mars trine Neptune	9:06 pm	12:06 am	(Sept. 9)
9	Sun opposite Uranus	11:47 am	2:47 pm	
11	**New Moon in Virgo**	5:45 am	8:45 am	
13	Mercury sextile Jupiter	3:44 am	6:44 am	
17	Sun square Mars	1:50 pm	4:50 pm	
	Mercury sextile Venus	2:29 pm	5:29 pm	
18	Mercury trine Neptune	7:01 pm	10:01 pm	
19	Sun square Pluto	9:00 am	12:00 pm	
	First QTR Moon in Sagittarius	9:49 am	12:49 pm	
21	Mars opposite Pluto	1:41 am	4:41 am	
	Venus opposite Neptune	1:04 pm	4:04 pm	
23	**Autumnal Equinox**			
	Sun enters Libra	2:52 am	5:52 am	
24	Mercury sextile Pluto	3:56 am	6:56 am	
26	Mercury trine Mars	10:54 am	1:54 pm	
	Full Moon in Aries	12:46 pm	3:46 pm	
27	Mercury enters Scorpio	10:19 am	1:19 pm	
28	Mars enters Cancer	4:56 pm	7:56 pm	
30	Mercury sextile Saturn	11:17 pm	2:17 am	(Oct. 1)

October

3	**Last QTR Moon in Cancer**	3:07 am	6:07 am	
	Venus trine Pluto	6:17 am	9:17 am	
7	Venus enters Virgo	11:54 pm	2:54 am	(Oct. 8)
8	Mars sextile Saturn	8:45 pm	11:45 pm	
	Sun sextile Jupiter	9:05 pm	12:05 am	(Oct. 9)
9	Jupiter square Uranus	11:25 am	2:25 pm	
10	**New Moon in Libra**	10:02 pm	1:02 pm	(Oct. 11)
11	Mercury goes retrograde	9:01 pm	12:01 am	(Oct. 12)
12	Sun trine Neptune	6:41 pm	9:41 pm	
13	Venus conjunct Saturn	9:29 pm	12:29 am	(Oct. 14)
16	Venus sextile Mars	10:38 am	1:38 pm	
	Mercury sextile Venus	8:19 pm	11:19 pm	
17	Mercury trine Mars	1:38 am	4:38 am	
19	**First QTR Moon in Capricorn**	1:34 am	4:34 am	
	Mercury sextile Saturn	6:55 am	9:55 am	

October (Cont'd)

20	Sun sextile Pluto	6:40 am	9:40 am	
23	Sun enters Scorpio	12:16 pm	3:16 pm	
	Sun conjunct Mercury	4:56 pm	7:56 pm	
	Mercury enters Libra	8:38 pm	11:38 pm	
25	Full Moon in Taurus	9:53 pm	12:53 pm	
	Venus opposite Uranus	2:09 am	5:09 am	
26	Mercury sextile Pluto	10:53 am	1:53 pm	
29	Venus square Jupiter	2:09 am	5:09 am	
	Sun sextile Saturn	8:43 pm	11:43 pm	
	Jupiter sextile Neptune	9:00 pm	12:00 am	(Oct. 30)

31 All Hallows (Halloween) / Samhain / Witches' New Year

	Neptune goes direct	1:06 pm	4:06 pm	

November

1	Last QTR Moon in Leo	2:19 pm	5:19 pm	
	Mercury goes direct	4:00 pm	7:00 pm	
4	DAYLIGHT SAVINGS TIME ENDS			
	Turn clocks back one hour at	2:00 am	2:00 am	
	Sun trine Mars	3:20 am	6:20 am	
5	Venus square Pluto	10:01 pm	1:01 am	(Nov. 6)
7	Sun trine Uranus	8:50 am	11:50 am	
8	Venus enters Libra	1:06 pm	4:06 pm	
	Mercury sextile Pluto	2:28 pm	5:28 pm	
9	New Moon in Scorpio	3:04 pm	6:04 pm	
11	Mercury enters Scorpio	12:42 am	3:42 am	
	Sun square Neptune	5:43 pm	8:43 pm	
15	Mars goes retrograde	12:26 am	3:26 am	
16	Mercury sextile Saturn	3:23 pm	6:23 pm	
17	First QTR Moon in Aquarius	2:34 pm	5:34 pm	
19	Venus square Mars	6:20 pm	9:20 pm	
	Mercury trine Mars	6:54 pm	9:54 pm	
21	Mercury trine Uranus	9:59 am	12:59 pm	
22	Sun enters Sagittarius	8:51 am	11:51 am	
24	Uranus goes direct	2:14 am	5:14 am	
	Full Moon in Gemini	6:31 am	9:31 am	
	Mercury square Neptune	9:50 am	12:50 pm	
26	Venus trine Neptune	1:56 am	4:56 am	
30	Sun square Saturn	12:24 pm	3:24 pm	

December

1	Mercury enters Sagittarius	4:22 am	7:22 am	
	Last QTR Moon in Virgo	4:45 am	7:45 am	
2	Venus sextile Jupiter	12:15 am	3:15 am	
3	Venus sextile Pluto	2:35 pm	5:35 pm	
5	Venus enters Scorpio	5:30 am	8:30 am	
6	Mercury square Saturn	1:17 pm	4:17 pm	
7	Sun square Uranus	12:35 am	3:35 am	
8	Mars sextile Saturn	8:00 pm	11:00 pm	
9	**New Moon in Sagittarius**	9:42 am	12:42 pm	
10	Mercury square Uranus	4:26 pm	7:26 pm	
11	Jupiter conjunct Pluto	11:37 am	2:37 pm	
	Venus trine Mars	3:17 pm	6:17 pm	
	Sun sextile Neptune	7:49 pm	10:49 pm	
12	Venus sextile Saturn	11:34 am	2:34 pm	
13	Mercury sextile Neptune	7:03 pm	10:03 pm	
17	**First QTR Moon in Pisces**	2:19 am	5:19 am	
	Sun conjunct Mercury	7:28 am	10:28 am	
	Venus trine Uranus	10:44 pm	1:44 am	(Dec. 18)
18	Jupiter enters Capricorn	12:13 pm	3:13 pm	
19	Saturn goes retrograde	6:10 am	9:10 am	
	Mercury conjunct Pluto	10:51 am	1:51 pm	
20	Mercury enters Capricorn	6:44 am	9:44 am	
	Mercury conjunct Jupiter	1:55 pm	4:55 pm	
	Sun conjunct Pluto	4:18 pm	7:18 pm	
21	**Winter Solstice**			
	Sun enters Capricorn	10:09 pm	1:09 am	(Dec. 22)
22	Venus square Neptune	2:23 am	5:23 am	
	Mercury opposite Mars	10:30 am	1:30 pm	
	Sun conjunct Jupiter	9:57 pm	12:57 am	(Dec. 23)
23	**Full Moon in Cancer**	5:17 pm	8:17 pm	
24	Sun opposite Mars	11:48 am	2:48 pm	
25	Mercury trine Saturn	3:11 pm	6:11 pm	
26	Mars opposite Jupiter	11:54 am	2:54 pm	
29	Mercury sextile Uranus	8:11 pm	11:11 pm	
30	Sun trine Saturn	5:24 am	8:24 am	
	Venus enters Sagittarius	10:03 am	1:03 pm	
	Last QTR Moon in Libra	11:52 pm	2:52 am	(Dec. 31)
31	Mars enters Gemini	8:01 am	11:01 am	

TABLE OF ASPECT INFLUENCES

JANUARY 2007

| 1 | 2 | 3 | 4 | 5 | 6 | 7 | 8 | 9 | 10 | 11 | 12 | 13 | 14 | 15 | 16 | 17 | 18 | 19 | 20 | 21 | 22 | 23 | 24 | 25 | 26 | 27 | 28 | 29 | 30 | 31 |

2□♅
♂♂♀   ♂＊♅
♂△♄
♀＊2   ♀♂♄
☿＊♅   ♀♂Ψ   ♀＊♀   ☿＊♀
☉＊♅   ☿＊2   ☿♂♄
☉♂♀   ☿♂Ψ
☉＊2

FEBRUARY 2007

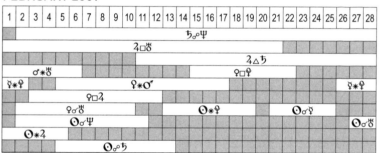

MARCH 2007

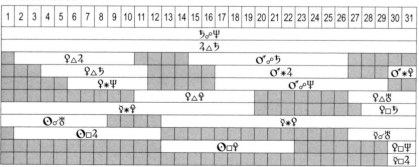

18

TABLE OF ASPECT INFLUENCES

APRIL 2007

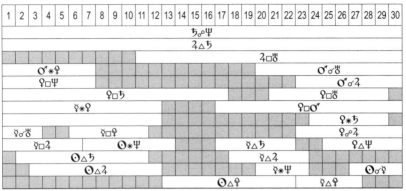

MAY 2007

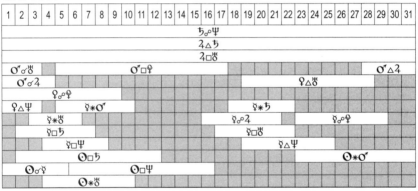

JUNE 2007

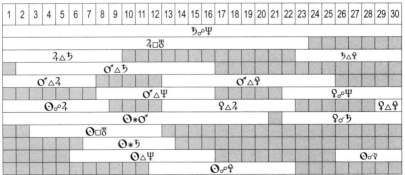

19

TABLE OF ASPECT INFLUENCES

JULY 2007

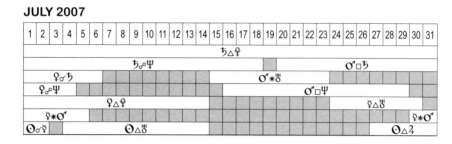

AUGUST 2007

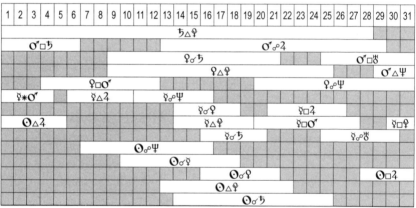

SEPTEMBER 2007

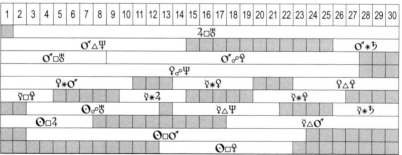

TABLE OF ASPECT INFLUENCES

OCTOBER 2007

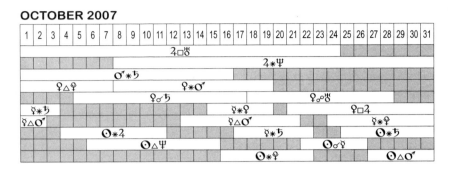

NOVEMBER 2007

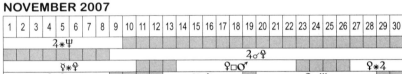

DECEMBER 2007

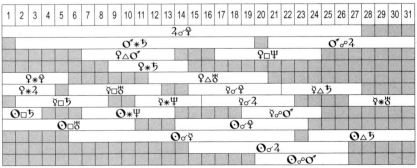

CAPRICORN

Key Phrase: "I USE"

Cardinal Earth Sign

Symbol : The Goat

December 21st, 2006

through January 20th, 2007

January 1st Monday
New Year's Day
Moon in Gemini

	PST	EST	
Moon trine Neptune	10:32 AM	1:32 PM	
Moon opposite Mars	12:05 PM	3:05 PM	
Moon sextile Saturn	9:26 PM	12:26 AM	(January 2)
Mercury sextile Uranus begins (see January 3)			

Mood Watch: Gemini Moon keeps our minds busy and curious. A new year begins with the harmonious lunar aspect of Moon trine Neptune, kicking off this festive day with moods that are in harmony with our beliefs and spiritual perspectives on life. Moods will be pleasant and very accepting of the way the day begins. This is followed by Moon opposite Mars, bringing moods which are bursting with energy and aggressiveness, and some folks may be overwhelmed or affronted by the activities and actions occurring around us. We can be sure to experience a somewhat raucous and outgoing level of energy on this first day of the year. Later tonight, Moon sextile Saturn brings moods of duty and responsibility.

January 2nd Tuesday
Moon in Gemini / Cancer

	PST	EST
Sun sextile Uranus	1:17 AM	4:17 AM
Moon opposite Pluto goes v/c	2:07 AM	5:07 AM
Moon enters Cancer	7:15 AM	10:15 AM

Mood Watch: Long before sunrise, Moon opposite Pluto may be the cause of some sleepless energy for some folks, particularly due to the fact that at this late hour our moods may seem opposed to intense subjects. Many folks may be annoyed by their struggles with the nature of those super powers that are at work, affecting our lives in big ways. Meanwhile, the Moon also goes void-of-course before the break of day, bringing the potential for mixed feelings and mental complexities. It's no wonder that by the time the day begins, many folks may find themselves somewhat tired or disoriented. Soon enough, however, the Moon enters Cancer, and our moods enter into the need for nurturing and emotional security. The Cancer Moon is almost full, and our moods will be highlighted with emotional concerns which are often worked out at home or in domestic settings where the nurturing spirit of Mother Moon brings responsive and sympathetic conscientiousness.

Sun sextile Uranus (occurring December 29, 2006 – January 4, 2007) This occurrence of Sun sextile Uranus particularly affects those Capricorn folks celebrating birthdays from December 29, 2006 through January 4, 2007. These birthday people are being given an opportunity to blow off some chaotic steam and to reach for qualities of freedom that may have been absent in their recent past. This will be your time to make radical breakthroughs, birthday Capricorn; your natal Sun is currently sextile Uranus for a good reason – to find a liberating balance in the midst of the chaos. Once you've done this, you'll be ready to take the next step. Right now, there is no holding back, so go for it; discover your freedom. The victory of creative change will bring a more optimistic outlook on life. This aspect will repeat on May 8, affecting the lives of people born early in the sign of Taurus.

January 3rd Wednesday

FULL MOON in CANCER	PST	EST	
Moon opposite Mercury	1:33 AM	4:33 AM	
Moon trine Uranus	3:52 AM	6:52 AM	
Moon opposite Sun goes v/c	5:58 AM	8:58 AM	
Venus enters Aquarius	7:32 PM	10:32 PM	
Mercury sextile Uranus	9:20 PM	12:20 AM	(January 4)

Mood Watch: Long before dawn, Moon opposite Mercury brings an overwhelming feeling of being affronted by mental activity, causing insomnia for some folks and busy dream states for others. A little later, Moon trine Uranus brings a sense of freedom and our moods will be carefree, or blithely reckless, probably occurring in the course of our dreams. **Full Moon in Cancer** (Moon opposite Sun) reaches its peak just as it also goes void-of-course this morning, bringing moods which are likely to distract us, and in some cases will bring excessive, or obsessive, moodiness. The Moon will remain void-of-course throughout the entire day, causing a tendency for delays and minor set backs. The need for nurturing and care is strong now, as the energy and vitality of the mood begins to recede in a more self-reflective way. As a general rule, productivity will run slowly today. The archetypal image of Mother and her nurturing care is magnified. As we muddle though the mundane world, emotional currents are strong everywhere. Take time to rest and to ward off winter fatigue with warm and nurturing foods.

Venus enters Aquarius (Venus in Aquarius: January 3 - 27) Venus in Aquarius creates a fondness for invention, eccentric pleasures, and social life. Venus in Aquarius puts the focus of attraction and adoration on illuminating kinds of knowledge and on brilliant humanitarian causes and exploits. There is an especially strong attraction to invention – all types of invention – and to new technologies. It is likely to be a beneficial time for the love life of Aquarius people, whose affections and aesthetic pleasures can be enhanced now. By contrast, Scorpio and Taurus people may notice that love related focuses are causing tension in their personal lives – too many complex issues. Leo people, as a general rule, can never get enough love and affection, and they may be particularly aware of their own personal needs for love

23

and beauty while Venus is opposing their natal Sun this month. Venus in Aquarius is a prime time to perfect and enhance our love of humanity, and to break down the barriers of useless and destructive prejudice and stereotyping.

Mercury sextile Uranus (occurring January 1 - 5) Mercury in Capricorn is sextile to Uranus in Pisces. Serious investigations may lead to sensational conclusions. This aspect represents an opportunistic position for the voices of rebels and revolutionaries to be heard. Here is a time when our thoughts and ideas may be enhanced in a very colorful way. Some may act on this aspect with wild abandon, creating an effect of repelling and offending, while for others, this radical communication will represent freedom from a particular kind of slavery that holds them back. This may be a good time for authors to make a breakthrough in writing. Mercury sextile Uranus gives us the opportunity to freely speak our minds and to address the chaos and turmoil that exists in our lives. This aspect will repeat on May 5, when Mercury will be in Taurus, and finally, it will repeat again on December 29, when Mercury will be in Capricorn once again.

January 4th Thursday

Moon in Leo

	PST	EST
Moon enters Leo	1:15 PM	4:15 PM
Moon opposite Venus	3:09 PM	6:09 PM
Mars conjunct Pluto begins (see January 13)		

Mood Watch: Throughout the morning and into the afternoon, the void-of-course post full Moon energy brings a general sense of disorientation. While many folks are still adjusting to the close of the holidays, most folks are definitely adjusting to the tiring aftermath of yesterday's Full Cancer Moon. The pace picks up this afternoon as the Leo Moon brings a strong sense of self-awareness, and a focus on our personal needs. The overall mood of the day is friendly, outgoing, and playful. This afternoon's Moon opposite Venus may bring overwhelming or obsessive desires for beauty and pleasure. The Leo Moon wanes and many folks will seek a token of acceptance: public recognition, encouragement or appreciation. Be aware of the tendency for people to tackle too much at once. Waning Moon reminds us to let go of overtaxing aspirations and desires, and to center in on the self in a way that preserves and protects vital energy levels.

January 5th Friday

Moon in Leo

	PST	EST
Moon trine Jupiter	6:16 AM	9:16 AM
Moon opposite Neptune	11:39 PM	2:39 AM (January 6)

Mood Watch: Moon in Leo puts the focus of our moods on the need for entertainment, the company of friends, or on personal hobbies and practices. There will also be a strong emphasis placed on family related matters. Early this morning, the Moon trine Jupiter brings moods which will be in harmony with a sense of prosperity or adventure. Jovial moods bring playfulness. Although the Moon wanes and the exuberance of our playfulness may be somewhat reserved, there is a definite need for people to interact and be creative with each other. Much later tonight, Moon opposite Neptune brings moods which may be overwhelmed by addictive tendencies or spiritual beliefs. However daunting the task may seem for some folks, late night is a good time to attempt to get some rest and relaxation.

♑

January 6th Saturday

Moon in Leo / Virgo	PST	EST	
Moon trine Mars	7:49 AM	10:49 AM	
Moon conjunct Saturn	10:59 AM	1:59 PM	
Moon trine Pluto goes v/c	4:57 PM	7:57 PM	
Sun conjunct Mercury	10:06 PM	1:06 AM	(January 7)
Moon enters Virgo	10:19 PM	1:19 AM	(January 7)

Mood Watch: The waning Leo Moon brings self-absorbed moods and there is also a strong focus on family and friends this weekend. This morning, Moon trine Mars harmoniously energizes our moods. This is followed by Moon conjunct Saturn, instilling a sense of duty and responsibility to our moods. Later today, Moon trine Pluto allows for a feeling of harmony with regard to matters of fate and the unchangeable factors of life. The Moon also goes void-of-course in the evening, causing our moods to be distracted by laziness, and the need for glitz and glamour. By the close of night, the Moon enters Virgo, focusing our moods on meticulousness and careful forethought.

Sun conjunct Mercury (occurring December 27, 2006 – January 11, 2007) This is a very common aspect, which will create a much more thoughtful, communicative, and expressive year ahead for those Capricorn people celebrating birthdays from December 27, 2006 through January 11, 1007. This is your time (birthday Capricorns) to record ideas, relay important messages, and pay close attention to your imaginative thoughts as they are touched by Mercury, creating the urge to speak and be heard. Birthday Capricorns, your thoughts will reveal a great deal about who you are, now and in the year to come.

January 7th Sunday

Moon in Virgo	PST	EST	
Moon square Jupiter	5:17 PM	8:17 PM	
Moon opposite Uranus	9:38 PM	12:38 AM	(January 8)

Mood Watch: The waning Virgo Moon brings the need to get a handle on practical matters through communications. The Capricorn Sun and Virgo Moon bring an emphasis on earthly practicalities and necessities. This afternoon's Moon square Jupiter may cause our moods to be less generous, and we may find we are less willing to extend ourselves beyond our limits. Waning Virgo Moon is an excellent time to clean up and organize our lives. Ironically, later tonight, Moon opposite Uranus challenges our moods with an overwhelming feeling of chaos and disorder. It is wise to remember that before a sense of order can be achieved, a whole lot of chaos and disruption are likely to occur in the process. Tomorrow is another Virgo Moon day.

January 8th Monday

Moon in Virgo	PST	EST	
Mars trine Saturn	10:06 AM	1:06 PM	
Moon trine Sun	10:11 AM	1:11 PM	
Moon trine Mercury	12:20 PM	3:20 PM	
Moon square Mars	11:02 PM	2:02 AM	(January 9)
Venus sextile Jupiter begins (see January 12)			

Mood Watch: Today's Virgo Moon brings a strong resolve to get a handle on practical matters and there is likely to be a strong focus on organization and communication. Waning Virgo Moon also brings a fair dollop of doubt and scrutiny as to how to best proceed at this early stage of the year. This morning's Moon trine Sun usually ensures our moods will be in harmony with the current focuses of the season. Moon trine Mercury brings the gift of thoughtfulness, and communications will be very harmonious. Much later, Moon square Mars challenges our energy levels, and for some, the temper may be challenged. Virgo says: "I analyze" and this may not be the best time to draw any hasty conclusions.

Mars trine Saturn (occurring December 31, 2006 – January 12, 2007) Mars in Sagittarius trine Saturn in Leo brings brazen enthusiasm and a quality of adventure to the act of achievement. Our actions bring gifts with this aspect, provided there is an application of discipline and timing. This may be a time for those who are affected by this aspect to become noticed or actively acknowledged. Activities will be naturally work oriented. At best, Mars trine Saturn provides a sense of good timing. This may be a good time to apply diligent practice with one's favorite sport, especially those physical activities which demand precision and perfect timing. Cultivate those physical activities that demand precision and perfect timing. Offensive and defensive forces will tend to work harmoniously now. IT is always important to pay attention to those aspects of one's life that hold the potential to receive recognition. A timely gift of will-power and the rewards of hard work harmonize to bring positive results. To fully benefit from this aspect, one must use the energy (Mars) responsibly (Saturn.) This is a time of transition when endings and new beginnings are harmoniously and naturally merged.

January 9th Tuesday

Moon in Virgo / Libra	PST	EST
Moon square Pluto goes v/c	4:52 AM	7:52 AM
Moon enters Libra	10:16 AM	1:16 PM

Mood Watch: Overnight, the waning Virgo Moon goes void-of-course and simultaneously, Moon square Pluto brings moods that are challenged by the unforeseeable factors of life. At times throughout the morning, our moods are distracted by doubt or uncertainty. By the time the Moon enters Libra, our moods enter into the need for harmony in relationships and for a sense of balance or justice. Libra Moon emphasizes the need to clear up any troubling imbalances that exist between friends. This is a good time to drop grudges and attempt diplomacy with others.

January 10th Wednesday

Moon in Libra

	PST	EST	
Moon trine Venus	2:15 AM	5:15 AM	
Moon sextile Jupiter	6:51 AM	9:51 AM	
Moon trine Neptune	11:47 PM	2:47 AM	(January 11)

Mood Watch: This is the eve of the Last Quarter Moon in Libra. It's a splendid time to drop grudges and to enjoy the company of our loved ones. With the exception of Saturn now traveling through the summer constellation, Leo, the other planets are now traveling in the autumn and winter signs of the zodiac. This brings a strong sense of the need for preservation and perseverance. The days of Capricorn bring the occasional quiet lulls of winter, and this teaches us how to pace ourselves and to more wisely distribute our energies in the face of nature's demands. Libra Moon energies create the need for harmony and balance with others. When we learn how to harmoniously work together, mountains are moved, and we have achieved the perfect Sun in Capricorn with Moon in Libra experience. Much later tonight, Moon trine Neptune brings the gift of tranquility and our dreams will be filled with harmonious receptivity.

January 11th Thursday

Moon in Libra / Scorpio - LAST QUARTER MOON in LIBRA

	PST	EST	
Moon square Sun	4:46 AM	7:46 AM	
Moon sextile Saturn	10:47 AM	1:47 PM	
Moon square Mercury	11:01 AM	2:01 PM	
Moon sextile Mars	3:56 PM	6:56 PM	
Moon sextile Pluto goes v/c	5:57 PM	8:57 PM	
Moon enters Scorpio	11:09 PM	2:09 AM	(January 12)

Mood Watch: Moods will be ever shifting today with five lunar aspects at work. With so many of them occurring today, it may be best to intermittently stop and center yourself, to be sure that all is balanced from within. Morning kicks off the day with the **Last Quarter Moon in Libra** (Moon square Sun) reminding us of the need to continue working on the imbalances in our relationships and in the halls of justice. Moon sextile Saturn inspires discipline and focus. Moon square Mercury brings challenging communications. Moon sextile Mars tends to bring energetic moods which are motivated by force and activity. Moon sextile Pluto brings moods which are inspired by vigilant efforts in the face of intensity and strife. The Libra Moon goes void-of-course at this point in the evening and we may find ourselves easily distracted by the imbalances of indecision for awhile. When the Moon enters Scorpio, clairvoyance abounds.

January 12th Friday

Moon in Scorpio

	PST	EST	
Venus sextile Jupiter	4:46 AM	7:46 AM	
Moon square Venus	9:55 PM	12:55 AM	(January 13)
Moon trine Uranus	11:08 PM	2:08 AM	(January 13)

Mood Watch: The waning Scorpio Moon focuses our moods on the powerful and astonishing quality of the 21st century events which have occurred up to this date.

These are dangerous times in the world and quite often the waning Scorpio Moon puts us in touch with our sensibilities, our suspicions and our deeper concerns. There's a surreal sense of mood-play occurring, giving the occasional impression that this dangerous world is utterly incompetent. We may feel constantly affronted by mini-dramas and the audacity of life's unexpected surprises. Our moods instinctively will rise to the occasion of every real life encounter with a sense of Scorpio-like urgency. Late tonight, Moon square Venus brings moods which are challenged by matters of love and attraction. Moon trine Uranus brings liberating moods which are often in harmony with chaos and disorder — a good aspect for smashing things in our dreams.

Venus sextile Jupiter (occurring January 8 - 14) Venus is in Aquarius, the place of humanitarian exploits and love play. Jupiter is in Sagittarius, bringing a powerful sense of adventure and a joyful outreach towards the need to discover love's capabilities. Unusual and intellectually inspired attractions and pleasures (Venus in Aquarius) lead us to prosperous opportunities in philosophy, world travel, treasure hunting, extreme sports, and international business (Jupiter in Sagittarius.) It is here that love and beauty are potentially found in the experience of going beyond the limits. This is an excellent time to shower loved ones with gifts and compliments. A lovers' getaway may be just the ticket to recapture some romance. This is the time to allow expansion to occur in love matters, and to take the next step towards enlivening and enhancing life. A greater opportunity for increasing skills or augmenting your livelihood is available, especially if your focus remains on doing what you love most. This aspect will repeat on December 2, when Venus will be in Libra.

January 13th Saturday

Moon in Scorpio

	PST	EST	
Mars conjunct Pluto	2:03 AM	5:03 AM	
Moon square Neptune	12:00 PM	3:00 PM	
Moon sextile Sun	10:01 PM	1:01 AM	(January 14)
Moon square Saturn	10:07 PM	1:07 AM	(January 14)
Venus conjunct Neptune begins (see January 18)			

Mood Watch: Today's Moon in Scorpio puts us in touch with Mars conjunct Pluto (see below.) Before the discovery of Pluto in 1930, Mars was the ruling planet of Scorpio; these days, Pluto is Scorpio's ruling planet. This tells us the nature of Scorpio is power-oriented, since Mars and Pluto are known for being aggressive forces that tackle both the daily and the long term effects of the flow of life's energy. This afternoon, Moon square Neptune brings struggles with regard to our beliefs and in spiritual matters. Moon sextile Sun inspires our moods to accept and be at peace with the seasonal factors of this time. Moon square Saturn brings moods which are challenged by deadlines, responsibilities, and limitations. Scorpio Moon keeps us passionate, as well as tolerant, through the overall course of our affairs.

Mars conjunct Pluto (occurring January 4 - 17) Powerful forces are likely to take some form of disruptive and very possibly destructive action with fiery Mars conjunct Pluto in Sagittarius. The philosophical viewpoints of different generations are being activated, and there may be some forcefulness and heat between them.

This is an especially important time to take precautionary measures in dealing with authorities. Expect some definite social and political tension to escalate around this time. There is no use in worrying. It is wisest to be vigilant and clear about what is happening in our lives during abrupt challenges, and to use caution in all that we do. Like a catalyst, Mars conjunct Pluto is simply giving the fiery energy of unsettled warring countries an outlet for confrontation.

January 14th Sunday

Moon in Scorpio / Sagittarius	PST	EST
Moon sextile Mercury goes v/c	7:51 AM	10:51 AM
Moon enters Sagittarius	10:12 AM	1:12 PM

Mood Watch: There is always some element of a waning Scorpio Moon that reminds us to keep our guard up. Most of what takes place with regard to our moods is a reaction to whatever tension exists in the air or in the deeper regions of the heart. In some cases, intense feelings must be handled and addressed immediately — or anxiety, suffering, violence, disaster, and any number of exceedingly useless and ugly old patterns may surface. This morning, Moon sextile Mercury brings the potential for inspiring news and communications. At the same time, the Moon goes void-of-course for a couple of hours, and disruptive moods are likely to distract us from making any kind of constructive progress. Fortunately, for most of the day and into the night, Moon in Sagittarius brings conscientiousness, optimism, and hopefulness. It's a good time to spread hope.

January 15th Monday

Dr. Martin Luther King Junior Day

Moon in Sagittarius	PST	EST	
Mercury enters Aquarius	1:26 AM	4:26 AM	
Moon conjunct Jupiter	7:12 AM	10:12 AM	
Moon square Uranus	9:06 AM	12:06 PM	
Moon sextile Venus	1:58 PM	4:58 PM	
Moon sextile Neptune	9:10 PM	12:10 AM	(January 16)

" A nation that continues year after year to spend more money on military defense than on programs of social uplift is approaching spiritual doom."   – Dr. Martin Luther King Junior (1929 – 1968)

Mood Watch: The waning Sagittarius Moon brings an internal process of hope and reflection. As the morning Moon is conjunct with Jupiter, our moods are jovial and enthusiastic. Moon square Uranus brings moods challenged by chaos and rebellion. Moon sextile Venus brings moods inspired by beautiful attractions. Much later, Moon sextile Neptune inspires tranquility and peace. In light of Dr. King's quote above, it is never too late to encourage social uplift and to spread brotherly and sisterly love in every way possible.

Mercury enters Aquarius (Mercury in Aquarius: January 15 – February 2) Mercury in Aquarius is a time when we explore the power of knowledge through our communications. Mercury is the planet that represents the thought processes, as well as the means by which we communicate the message we are sending out into the world. Today, Mercury enters Aquarius, the *fixed air* sign of the zodiac, which represents humanity's knowledge. As the force of communication (Mercury) travels through the constellation of fixed thought and meditation (Aquarius), there are great opportunities for us to share and to empower each other through our knowledge. This is a splendid time to communicate ideas and investigate the latest in technology, science, and the world of invention. Mercury in Aquarius is also a special time to speak out on humanitarian issues and the rights of freedom. Eccentric talk and unusual subjects will fill the airwaves while Mercury is in Aquarius.

January 16th Tuesday

Moon in Sagittarius/Capricorn	PST	EST
Moon trine Saturn	6:13 AM	9:13 AM
Mars enters Capricorn	12:55 PM	3:55 PM
Moon conjunct Pluto goes v/c	1:30 PM	4:30 PM
Moon enters Capricorn	5:50 PM	8:50 PM
Moon conjunct Mars	6:07 PM	9:07 PM

Mood Watch: This morning's Moon trine Saturn brings harmonious moods with regard to our approach to discipline. The waning Sagittarius Moon of winter is the time to prepare for the days ahead, to focus on our visions, to shed old pretenses, and to gather our courage. This is the time to broaden our awareness through exploration, and to do so with enthusiasm and wit. This afternoon's Moon conjunct Pluto brings intensity to our moods as the Moon also goes void-of-course. For a fair portion of the day, our moods may be distracted by forgetfulness or hastiness. Tonight, when the Moon enters Capricorn, our moods enter a phase of determination. Moon in Capricorn brings serious moods, and Moon conjunct Mars activates our moods with a strong surge of determined force.

Mars enters Capricorn (Mars in Capricorn: January 16 – February 25) Now through February 25, the planet Mars, known to many as "the god of war," is in the sign of Capricorn. The main thrust of activities will be inspired by the industrious push of Capricornian persistence. Mars in Capricorn is the place where it's exalted. Activities will shift towards dynamic, ambitious and enterprising endeavors. With Mars in Capricorn a sense of duty is instilled. Activities, if successfully managed, will produce long lasting results. This is *not* a good time to create enemies; the inherent difficulties will also produce long lasting results, and long standing enemies are not a good thing to have when trying to create a sense of forward moving progress. The last time Mars was in Capricorn was February through March 2005, a difficult time for our ruthlessly warring planet. Before that, Mars entered Capricorn in March 2003, when the U.S. war on Iraq began. Interestingly enough, the time Mars entered Capricorn before that was the week of September 11th, 2001. It appears that here in the beginning of the 21st century, the guns of war are activated in no uncertain terms when Mars is in Capricorn. Keep your eyes open!

January 17th Wednesday

Moon in Capricorn	PST	EST
Moon sextile Uranus	3:30 PM	6:30 PM
Venus opposite Saturn begins (see January 22)		

Mood Watch: Today will be a good day to focus on completing goals and tying up loose ends. The darkly waning Capricorn Moon brings serious introspection and determination. There is a strong emphasis on the need to accomplish what we set out to do today, but by the time Moon sextile Uranus rolls around, our moods lean more prone towards rebelliousness and reckless activities. The need to break out of old trends is competing with the desire to stay on track and be focused. This is a good time to keep goals simple and to do what comes naturally.

January 18th Thursday
Moon in Capricorn / Aquarius - NEW MOON in CAPRICORN

	PST	EST	
Venus conjunct Neptune	6:49 PM	9:49 PM	
Moon conjunct Sun goes v/c	8:02 PM	11:02 PM	
Moon enters Aquarius	10:17 PM	1:17 AM	(January 19)

Mood Watch: Throughout today, the waning Capricorn day brings a smooth but somewhat monotonous process of focusing on our duties and the tasks at hand. **New Moon in Capricorn** (Moon conjunct Sun) brings down-to-earth determination to our moods. New beginnings happen on the physical plane with the Moon and Sun conjunct in Capricorn. Whew! It was dark there for awhile, but the stiff upper lip now begins to hint the curve of a contented smile. We are ready to begin raising some light again. New Moon in Capricorn urges us to create new goals and set new heights for ourselves. The Moon goes void-of-course at same time it reaches the new mark. Evening moods might seem a little macabre and misdirected for awhile. Later on, the Aquarius Moon brings hope, spontaneity, and a little bit of ingenuity which will boost our morale for the coming day.

Venus conjunct Neptune (occurring January 13 - 21) These two very feminine planets are currently aligned as a higher and lower octave of each other, creating a very fluid and open expression of femininity. Venus represents love, magnetism, and attraction, while Neptune (the higher octave of Venus) represents spiritual love, and the melding of spiritual energies. Venus is conjunct with Neptune in the sign of Aquarius. Here the cohesive and melding forces of Venus and Neptune manifest with original, idealistic, and inventive expressions. Beauty and art (Venus) are linked with spirituality and belief (Neptune), mucho of it focused around humanitarian causes and issues (Aquarius.) Science and technology are given more acceptable and aesthetic appearances with this aspect. Venus conjunct Neptune can be utilized to reach a higher vibration of feminine, spiritual love. This aspect allows beauty, femininity, and personal attraction to be connected with the higher spiritual vibrations of the universe. This is an ideal time to connect with one's own guardian angel and spirit guide. Venus conjunct Neptune, if utilized, will bring great wisdom.

January 19th Friday
Moon in Aquarius

	PST	EST
Moon conjunct Mercury	10:57 AM	1:57 PM
Moon sextile Jupiter	6:31 PM	9:31 PM
Mercury sextile Jupiter begins (see January 22)		

Mood Watch: Today begins with the newly waxing Moon in Aquarius. Our moods are open to new discoveries and to social events and galas. Moon conjunct Mercury reminds us of our need to stay on top of communications. This is a time when our moods are one with our thoughts and we are not likely to spend too much time explaining what we already intuitively know. Aquarius Moon gives us the inclination to exercise our knowledge and our expertise. Scientific knowledge and innovative breakthroughs are often highlighted during Aquarius Moon. Moon sextile Jupiter brings moods inspired by a sense of prosperity and adventure. Today will be a good day to explore new ideas and to share them with others.

AQUARIUS

Key Phrase: "I KNOW"

Fixed Air Sign

Symbol : The Water Bearer

January 20th through February 18th

January 20th Saturday

Moon in Aquarius	PST	EST	
Sun enters Aquarius	3:02 AM	6:02 AM	
Moon conjunct Neptune	6:03 AM	9:03 AM	
Moon conjunct Venus	9:19 AM	12:19 PM	
Moon opposite Saturn	1:34 PM	4:34 PM	
Moon sextile Pluto goes v/c	9:02 PM	12:02 AM	(January 21)

Mood Watch: The Aquarius Moon is conjunct with Neptune, bringing peaceful and spiritual moods. The Moon is also conjunct with Venus, bringing a focus on art and those places, people, and things that attract us. This afternoon, Moon opposite Saturn brings moods which may appear opposed to — or overwhelmed by — restrictions and limitations. This evening, Moon sextile Pluto brings moods which are likely to be affected by life's unchangeable circumstances. The void-of-course Moon, which begins later tonight, brings moods which may be easily puzzled or distracted by eccentrics, soothsayers, know-it-alls, and the like.

Sun enters Aquarius (Sun in Aquarius: January 20 – February 18) *Happy Birthday Aquarians!* Aquarius represents the *water bearer* -- perhaps this is why it is often mistaken as a water sign. Aquarius is actually the *"fixed air"* sign of the zodiac, and it deals specifically with human intelligence, hence the phrase: *"I Know"*. The Aquarius influence emphasizes reaching out towards a body of light and information, the raising up and enhancement of human consciousness which will benefit everyone. This is a time for opening up new ideas and possibilities. We started out the calendar year with the Sun in Capricorn emphasizing the crystallization of goals and the fulfillment of duty and responsibility. Now the Sun in Aquarius inspires changes in our concepts, ideas, and work ethics. We begin to see how much easier we can make life and our workload through innovative approaches. Aquarius calls for the need to break through outmoded methods of achieving progress and set new precedents for what we accept as fixed or scientific knowledge. Freedom is the real key behind what inspires Aquarians most. Abraham Lincoln, who fought against slavery in America, is a primary example of an Aquarius freedom fighter. Despite the established systems, we are free as humans to influence the wave of the future. Aquarius is a large contributor to the progress of scientific discovery. Aquarians are often eccentric and dynamic, and even when they are common and complacent in their outlook they manage to surprise us on many levels. They are usually adept in some unexpected way. They're often knowledgeable about complex systems, or have a keen understanding of bureaucracy and how to approach the unimaginable puzzles of human existence. Aquarians know – they know all – and to dispute anything with them is to be duly tested, if not surprised in a manner least expected.

Aquarians are usually clever people who enjoy a challenge. The Aquarian wave of the future will continue to battle the unfeeling aspects of scientific research. This is called humanitarianism; it is the key to human survival and also a very big part of the Aquarian drive. Human rights issues are Aquarian issues, and these days of the Sun in Aquarius will help us to differentiate between true humanitarianism and the posturing that is actually a deceitful ploy to gain political and economic control. This is why we must adhere to the Aquarian concept of learning to think and act for ourselves and not to rely exclusively on scientific methods, government authority, or the brainwashing of political propaganda to establish the facts. This also means that we must speak up for our rights whenever necessary and resolve those controversies concerning our chosen ways of living or dying.

The important thing to realize is that we *do have a choice* concerning the directions our lives take. Today's celebrated inventors and visionaries were yesterday's heretics and heathens. The voice of modern day heretics, eccentrics and rebels will continue to challenge and awaken our understanding. Future generations will dismiss our current fears as outmoded forms of ignorance. Aquarius is ruled by the enigmatic planetary force of Uranus -- often the strange villain that forges new clarity and hope through the storms of chaos and disruption. Freedom fighters will remind us always that we must find a solution to every great atrocity that dampens the human spirit. We must always take measures to prevent tomorrow's human crisis, to insure the perpetuity of our species. Aquarius, the fixed sign of air, represents the sum of human knowledge used to determine the direction humanity will take.

The price of freedom is uncommonly high, and the Aquarian age viewpoint increasingly defines us in this very young century. Over the past decade, major planetary influences have been gracing the skies of Aquarius. Uranus and Neptune are stimulating changes that reflect our overall global awareness. It is time for us to turn our minds to the vision of utopia – to create a positive picture of the future, while we face up to and vigorously protest the oppression that makes our lives difficult and inhumane. It is an old world oppression that we must address in this Aquarian time; through knowledge we will succeed. This is the time for Aquarians to apply their brilliance and be heard.

January 21st Sunday

Moon in Aquarius / Pisces	PST	EST	
Moon enters Pisces	12:49 AM	3:49 AM	
Moon sextile Mars	6:39 AM	9:39 AM	
Moon square Jupiter	9:21 PM	12:21 AM	(January 22)
Moon conjunct Uranus	9:30 PM	12:30 AM	(January 22)

Mood Watch: Overnight, the newly waxing Moon enters Pisces and our moods are met by a calm, curious, and flirtatious spirit. Moon sextile Mars kicks off the day with active and outgoing moods. Positive vibrations are often qualities of the youthfully waxing Pisces Moon, though sometimes Pisces Moon puts us in touch with our addictive tendencies. Temptations abound, yet they also empower us when we resist them. This is not a good time to side with old habits that aren't beneficial. Pisces Moon reminds us that everything we do in our life is special, no matter how insignificant an action or task may seem. We must therefore make an art out of all of our movements, and find within ourselves the special qualities of each waking hour. Later tonight, Moon square Jupiter brings slightly less generous or adventurous moods. Moon conjunct Uranus puts us in touch with the many aspects of chaos that exist in our lives.

January 22nd Monday

Moon in Pisces	PST	EST	
Venus opposite Saturn	7:40 AM	10:40 AM	
Mercury sextile Jupiter	8:14 AM	11:14 AM	
Jupiter square Uranus	1:44 PM	4:44 PM	
Moon square Pluto goes v/c	11:12 PM	2:12 AM	(January 23)
Mercury conjunct Neptune begins (see January 26)			
Venus sextile Pluto begins (see January 26)			

Mood Watch: It is often true that the imagination likes to roam on a Pisces Moon day. Pisces Moon puts us in touch with our belief systems and the personal trials we must endure concerning our own particular or individual beliefs. For some there is a creative process unfolding; for others there is a battle going on with addictive behavior or the need to escape. For most, the dreamlike quality of this time drifts in a timeless fashion connecting us with our past as well as showing us the future as we open ourselves up in the *now*. Late tonight, Moon square Pluto brings moods which may be challenged by intensity and, at the same time, the void-of-course Moon brings moods which will be distracted by temptations.

Venus opposite Saturn (occurring January 17 - 24) Love, beauty, and magnetism are opposed to restrictive discipline. While there is a very strong need to attain a sense of beauty, to stop and smell the roses, there is a constantly compelling and obsessive compulsion to press on with work and vital responsibilities. This may be particularly so because Saturn is currently retrograde (Dec. 5, 2006 – April 19, 2007.) Love matters are subjected to unavoidable trials and restrictions. There will be folks among us thrust into the challenge of facing jealousy, guilt, offensive outbreaks, anguish, oppression, defeat or despair. There are always lessons where our sheltered passions lie. We must be careful how our passions are stirred or handled. To stir up such passion at this time, one is likely to be quickly confronted by his or her own personal turmoil. Hold steadfast to all principles of wisdom. Be careful not to bite off more than you can chew, especially with regard to irresistible attractions and restrictive love matters.

Mercury sextile Jupiter (occurring January 19 - 23) This aspect offers the potential for good news of growth and prosperity, especially for those who are open to broadening their awareness. Mercury brings news and talk, while Jupiter brings wealth and prosperous advancement. The money flows where our attention goes. It may be an advantageous time to ask for a job or a loan. Communicating our knowledge (Mercury in Aquarius) brings opportunities and the potential for success (the sextile aspect) in the expanding fields of Sagittarius related affluence such as travel, space exploration, extreme sports, philosophical endeavors, international trade and business exploits and, treasure hunting (Jupiter in Sagittarius.) Opportunity exists for both the employer and the employee. Mercury sextile Jupiter brings joyful and mind expanding conversations. This aspect will repeat on September 13, when Mercury will be in Libra.

Jupiter square Uranus (occurring December 17, 2006 – February 21, 2007) Jupiter in the square position to Uranus is likely to focus our energies on radical economic difficulties, and is bound to bring real economic trouble and disruption. Jupiter in Sagittarius is square to Uranus in Pisces. Jupiter expands energies, while Uranus explodes and disrupts them. Our senses will be awakened swiftly, causing the realization of how great and how vast the universe really is and how limitless the possibilities of life are. This is an aspect that may cause a notable, and no doubt radical, shift in the stock market. For some folks, this aspect is stirring up a frightful threat to the existence of their livelihoods and investments. For the next month, this is certainly *not* a good time to take any chances experimenting with the market, or to try anything new or inventive with money matters and skill advancement. Businesses born under this aspect are not likely to be successful. This is a good time to keep careful records of financial events as they occur. This aspect will reoccur on two separate occasions this year; first, on May 10, when Jupiter will be retrograde, and second, on October 9, when Uranus will be retrograde.

January 23rd Tuesday

Moon in Pisces / Aries	PST	EST
Moon enters Aries	2:53 AM	5:53 AM
Moon sextile Sun	8:23 AM	11:23 AM
Moon square Mars	11:27 AM	2:27 PM

Mood Watch: Before dawn, the Moon enters Aries and our moods begin a phase of confidence. Moon sextile Sun brings moods which are inspired by the seasonal factors of this time. Moon square Mars usually brings challenging moods with regard to masculine energies, making this a time to watch the temper. Overall, we can expect to get a lot of things accomplished on this Aries Moon Tuesday. Aries Moon generates energy and gives many of us the impetus to tend to personal needs and projects requiring attention.

January 24th Wednesday

Moon in Aries	PST	EST	
Moon trine Jupiter	12:11 AM	3:11 AM	
Moon sextile Mercury	5:04 AM	8:04 AM	
Moon sextile Neptune	10:44 AM	1:44 PM	
Moon trine Saturn	5:33 PM	8:33 PM	
Moon sextile Venus	11:29 PM	2:29 AM	(January 25)

Mood Watch: The Aries Moon motivates us and moves our moods into an active phase of expression. There are positive and upbeat lunar aspects occurring today. Moon trine Jupiter brings moods that are in harmony with adventure and exploration. Moon sextile Mercury brings moods which will be inspired by communications. Moon sextile Neptune brings accepting and flexible kinds of moods. Moon trine Saturn brings moods that are likely to be in harmony with our responsibilities and, as a result, basic duties and tasks may be carried out much more smoothly than expected. Lastly, the close of the day is nicely balanced by Moon sextile Venus, which brings moods that will be responsive to, and inspired by, love and affection.

January 25th Thursday

Moon in Aries / Taurus - FIRST QUARTER MOON in TAURUS

	PST	EST
Moon trine Pluto goes v/c	1:51 AM	4:51 AM
Moon enters Taurus	5:30 AM	8:30 AM
Moon square Sun	3:03 PM	6:03 PM
Moon trine Mars	5:02 PM	8:02 PM
Mercury opposite Saturn begins (see January 28)		

Mood Watch: Overnight, Moon trine Pluto brings moods which will be in harmony with matters of fate. At the same time, the Aries Moon goes void-of-course and it's a good time to rest. This morning, as the Moon enters Taurus, the general outlook on life becomes more pragmatic and oriented towards material tasks and goals. **First Quarter Moon in Taurus** (Moon square Sun) brings the pressure to take care of essential needs. Taurus is the *fixed earth* sign, and the nature of Taurus Moon leads many folks to watch their pocketbook and make sure they're getting the most value possible out of all expenditures. There is also a need to let the beauty of our surroundings be accented and appreciated. Somewhere in between the processes of earning and reaping rewards, a happy medium is struck. The Moon is *exalted* in the place of Taurus, and positive harmony brings satisfaction. Moon trine Mars bring moods that will be in harmony with masculine forces. It's a good time to put some muscle into the work and accomplish something beautiful.

January 26th Friday

Moon in Taurus	PST	EST
Venus sextile Pluto	3:00 AM	6:00 AM
Moon sextile Uranus	3:03 AM	6:03 AM
Mercury conjunct Neptune	5:21 AM	8:21 AM
Moon square Neptune	2:07 PM	5:07 PM
Moon square Mercury	3:18 PM	6:18 PM
Moon square Saturn	8:40 PM	11:40 PM

Mood Watch: The waxing Taurus Moon brings good, down-to-earth efforts and vibrations. Before dawn, Moon sextile Uranus brings freedom-loving rebelliousness and our dreams are likely to be explosive and colorful. Later today, Moon square Neptune brings moods which may be challenged by passivity, resignation, or perhaps even laziness. Moon square Mercury brings moods that may be challenged by intellectual debates and discussions. Tonight, Moon square Saturn brings moods challenged by work, disciplines, and responsibilities. After a number of challenges posed by the lunar squares of today, a relaxing and comfortable way to escape from worries may be best. Wherever there is no option but work, persistent and stubborn effort is the way of the waxing Taurus Moon. Hang in there!

Venus sextile Pluto (occurring January 22 - 27) Venus is in Aquarius where our vision of beauty and art is captured by practical knowledge, and by humanitarian and civil rights issues. Venus sextile Pluto implies that even in the midst of hardship, opportunities are arising with regard to the things we treasure and are attracted to, and also in matters of love and affection (Venus.) These opportunities often are born out of fate or destiny (Pluto), or sometimes are a result of an unpredictable factor. For some, this aspect may be teaching them the lessons of acceptance, of learning to let go of attachments, as well as finding liberation through the transformative process of acceptance, particularly in matters of love. This is a good time to reinforce the love of humanity, by placing affection and care in areas of life that will make a difference in the long run, and by trusting in the outcome. For more information on Venus sextile Pluto, see December 3, when Venus will be in Libra.

Mercury conjunct Neptune (occurring January 22 - 28) This aspect inspires communications on the hypersensitive issues of people's belief systems and the domain of spirituality. Aquarius represents humanity. Neptune in the sign of Aquarius focuses on the essential need for belief in humankind; that is, we must believe in ourselves and our own capabilities in order to survive spiritually. Mercury in Aquarius focuses news, talk, and discussion on human rights issues. Many people, especially Aquarians, are deeply moved to speak about their convictions. This aspect also presents a good time to learn from the talk concerning humanitarian issues and the news going on around us, to pray, meditate, and connect with that higher spirit that dwells within.

January 27th Saturday

Moon in Taurus / Gemini	PST	EST	
Moon square Venus goes v/c	8:09 AM	11:09 AM	
Moon enters Gemini	9:11 AM	12:11 PM	
Venus enters Pisces	7:33 PM	10:33 PM	
Moon trine Sun	11:08 PM	2:08 AM	(January 28)

Mood Watch: This morning, Taurus Moon square Venus brings moods that are likely to be challenged by the effort to maintain beauty and comfort. The Moon then goes void-of-course too, bringing a very brief period of impractical distractions. As the Moon enters Gemini, our moods enter into a period of curiosity and wonder. Moon trine Sun brings moods that will be harmonious and in tune with the spirit of the season. Gemini says: "I think" and the Gemini Moon brings talkative, thoughtful, and communicative expressions of mood. The Sun and Moon are both in air signs; it's a good time to communicate with others and to share thoughts and ideas.

Venus enters Pisces (Venus in Pisces: January 27 – February 21) Venus, the planet of magnetism and love, will be focusing our attraction on Pisces related subjects. From today through February 21, music, poetry, the arts, psychic phenomena, and spiritual and religious practices will all be endearing and lively pursuits. Over the next few weeks, as Venus crosses over their natal Sun sign, it will touch the personal realms of our Pisces friends with an awareness of the need for love and beauty in their lives. Venus is the feminine planet of love, and Pisces is an extremely feminine, dreamy, and spiritual placement for the love force of Venus. Matters of the heart will emphasize passivity, tenderness, sensitivity and the need for a gentle approach towards love's expression.

January 28th Sunday

Moon in Gemini

	PST	EST
Moon square Uranus	7:29 AM	10:29 AM
Moon opposite Jupiter	8:47 AM	11:47 AM
Mercury opposite Saturn	10:08 AM	1:08 PM
Moon trine Neptune	6:48 PM	9:48 PM
Mars sextile Uranus begins (see February 3)		

Mood Watch: The Moon in Gemini brings a curiosity to our moods, with lively conversation and interaction. Sun in Aquarius with the Moon in Gemini is often a time when research is highlighted and innovative new approaches to problem solving are available. This is a particularly good time to study, to memorize, to examine important decisions more closely, and to investigate the well being of the working systems that we depend on. This morning, Moon square Uranus brings challenging disorder. Moon opposite Jupiter brings moods which will be opposed to overextension or exploration. People will not appreciate being brought out on any kind of limb. This evening's Moon trine Neptune brings harmonious peace, and people will be inclined to kick back, relax and to accept their beliefs as they stand.

Mercury opposite Saturn (occurring January 25 - 30) This aspect brings a very strong awareness of the need to speak out on serious and important subjects. News, talk, discussions and media tend to revolve around matters of closure, deaths, endings, and the establishment of control. There may be an overwhelming tone of command or restriction in some of the more serious subjects being communicated. While Mercury opposes Saturn, be careful where you choose to draw the lines and what you agree to when negotiating. Mercury is in Aquarius, where articulate precision is usually simplified to suit everyone's needs. Saturn is in Leo, where it emphasizes the perimeters and security of the family and other Leo-like issues such as personal goals and the need for entertainment. It also represents responsibilities to the family and to the self. At this time we may be especially aware of the delicate subject of how rules and laws are affecting family life and entertainment.

January 29th Monday

Moon in Gemini / Cancer	PST	EST
Moon sextile Saturn	1:06 AM	4:06 AM
Moon trine Mercury	3:17 AM	6:17 AM
Moon opposite Pluto goes v/c	10:41 AM	1:41 PM
Moon enters Cancer	2:17 PM	5:17 PM
Moon trine Venus	6:42 PM	9:42 PM
Mercury sextile Pluto begins (see January 31)		
Sun sextile Jupiter begins (see February 3)		

Mood Watch: Throughout the morning, the Gemini Moon keeps our minds busy. Overnight, Moon sextile Saturn brings moods that will be inspired by disciplines. Moon trine Mercury brings harmonious thoughts and positive dreams. As the Moon goes void-of-course, Moon opposite Pluto brings moods that are likely to be opposed to the influences of super powers. For a number of hours, our scattered Gemini Moon moods will be easily distracted by mental interjections and interruptions. As the Moon enters Cancer, our moods will enter into a better awareness of our emotions. Tonight's Moon trine Venus brings peace and harmony in love related matters. Beauty and pleasure will be much more attainable as the evening unfolds.

January 30th Tuesday

Moon in Cancer	PST	EST
Moon opposite Mars	8:46 AM	11:46 AM
Moon trine Uranus goes v/c	1:32 PM	4:32 PM

Mood Watch: The Moon is in Cancer today, and carries the demand for some form of nurturing or care to occur. The listening ear is a helpful tool as a form of nurturing. Food and flowers are also nurturing and empower the magic of Cancer Moon. The morning may seem rocky with the Moon opposite Mars creating moods which are likely to be overwhelmed by forcefulness and brazen activity. A little later today, Moon trine Uranus brings a blast of liberated feelings. The Cancer Moon is also void-of-course at this point, and for the rest of the day, our moods are likely to be easily distracted by various kinds of emotional concerns. Tonight, it may be best to avoid being in a position that would compromise your emotional stability or your best judgment.

January 31st Wednesday

Moon in Cancer / Leo	PST	EST	
Mercury sextile Pluto	6:34 PM	9:34 PM	
Moon enters Leo	9:16 PM	12:16 AM	(February 1)

Mood Watch: Strongly the Moon waxes and throughout today the void-of-course Cancer Moon impedes on our ability to get very much work done. There will be a great tendency towards worry, defensiveness, or selfishness. In those situations where we need to focus on our work, it may be best to avoid getting involved in other people's dramas, particularly while there is such a strong drive to maintain some sense of security and control. On the other hand, some situations will be just plain moody, and there may be no avoiding the powerful sentiments of this time. Oh well, they don't call it a Full Moon Eve for nothin'. When the Moon finally enters

Leo, there will be a strong desire for entertainment — a lively and heartwarming escape from the daunting woes.

Mercury sextile Pluto (occurring January 29 – February 2) Last year this aspect occurred twice, as it commonly does during a solar year, but this year Mercury sextile Pluto will visit us six times over, going through its retrograde cycles during the commencement of this aspect. That means that the messenger planet (Mercury) is focusing a great deal of our talk and discussion on important power issues. The persistent repetition of this aspect determines how we will use media focuses, talk, social interplay, and communications to transform our understanding of life's course and to handle power issues and fateful matters (Pluto) in an opportunistic and positive manner (the sextile aspect). Mercury is now in Aquarius, ensuring that there is a scientific explanation for the matters at hand, while Pluto is forcing us to see beyond our expectations, creating a virtual transformation of our views and how we understand our lives. Vital information regarding treatments for illness or disease may frequent the news, and news in general may well have some critical impact. This is a good time to reach out to those of another generation and make an attempt to communicate something essential. Mercury in Aquarius focuses a lot of our discussions on human rights and humanitarian issues, and those who are in positions of power are listening, so don't hesitate – speak out wisely. This aspect will repeat again on February 28, when Mercury will be retrograde in Aquarius, and again on March 16, with Mercury direct in Aquarius. For the final triple-round this year, Mercury sextile Pluto will occur during a Mercury in Libra retrograde cycle on the following dates: September 24, October 26, and November 8.

February 1st Thursday
FULL MOON in LEO

	PST	EST
Moon opposite Sun	9:46 PM	12:46 AM (February 2)

Mood Watch: **Full Moon in Leo** (Moon opposite Sun) captivates our moods today with a wild and instinctual push. There may be an opportunity here to enhance and harmonize friendships and family situations in a fulfilling and enriching manner. Moon in Leo puts us in touch with those places, people, and things to which we feel loyal. Many folks may find themselves feeling somewhat courageous and confident about this new month ahead of us. Moon in Leo brings out the playful, imaginative, and creative side of our moods. Most of us are easily drawn towards the need to find warmth and affection, or just plain attention.

February 2nd Friday
Candlemas – Groundhog Day

Moon in Leo	PST	EST
Moon trine Jupiter	12:07 AM	3:07 AM
Mercury enters Pisces	1:21 AM	4:21 AM
Moon opposite Neptune	9:48 AM	12:48 PM
Moon conjunct Saturn	3:35 PM	6:35 PM
Venus conjunct Uranus begins (see February 7)		
Sun conjunct Neptune begins (see February 8)		
Saturn opposite Neptune begins (see February 28 and June 25)		

Mood Watch: Overnight, Moon trine Jupiter brings moods which are at peace with a sense of well being and prosperity. The energy of last night's full Moon in Leo is still upon us, although now the energy begins to wane. Overall, this will be a high energy day. Full Leo Moon unleashes our wild side. Meanwhile, when the animal nature isn't looking for excuses to play and frolic in an instinctual way, the need to face family related mayhem and/or personal identity issues will be strong. Moon opposite Neptune brings moods that will be stimulated by spiritual encounters and experiences. Moon conjunct Saturn brings moods that are serious and responsive to our duties and obligations.

Mercury enters Pisces (Mercury in Pisces: February 2 – 26) Today Mercury enters Pisces and this brings the emphasis of news, media, and communications on our beliefs, spiritual growth, cultural expression, and our tendencies towards escapism and drug use. For an extended period of time, Mercury will be in Pisces, as the planet Mercury will go retrograde in Pisces on February 13, resuming its forward course on March 7. Today through February 26, Mercury in Pisces brings out the mystic in all of us and adds quite a bit of color and flare to the imagination in relayed messages. This is also a good time to immerse one's self in creative writing and music or to open up the channels to the spirit world, allowing for messages from the other side to penetrate our psyches. Listen and learn from the priests, holy teachers, loved ones, and spirit guides of your choice. Sometimes the voice of sense and reason needs to give over to the simplicity of just listening in silence. Mercury goes retrograde, it will re-enter the sign of Aquarius on February 26, then on March 18, Mercury will return to the sign of Pisces. For more information on Mercury retrograde in Pisces, see the introduction in this book on *"Mercury retrograde periods: 2007."*

Today is Candlemas: a celebration of the return of the light. Out of the darkness and into the light -- this represents a time of blossoming knowledge and a time to acknowledge one's own growth. We are now one half of the way through winter season. This holiday is also known as **Imbolc**, the breakthrough of winter's darkness. The Sun's light reaches a point at the 14 degree mark of Aquarius, beginning the process of bringing more noticeable light into our homes. The days to come bring prismatic sparkling color through crystals suspended from windows. The light awakens and stirs the seeds of hope, and touches us from within. The legendary Irish Saint, Bridget, dons a crown of candles. Light candles, celebrate the return of the light! Today is also Groundhog Day, when the absence or presence of the groundhog's shadow predicts the course of the final half of winter season.

February 3rd Saturday

Moon in Leo / Virgo

	PST	EST
Mars sextile Uranus	2:42 AM	5:42 AM
Moon trine Pluto goes v/c	2:56 AM	5:56 AM
Moon enters Virgo	6:35 AM	9:35 AM
Sun sextile Jupiter	7:48 AM	10:48 AM
Moon opposite Mercury	10:27 AM	1:27 PM
Venus square Jupiter begins (see February 9)		

Mood Watch: In the pre-dawn hours, the waning Leo Moon brings dreams of summer fields. Moon trine Pluto puts our moods in harmony with the forces of fate and at the same time, the void-of-course Moon distracts our moods with personal concerns. Soon enough, the Moon enters Virgo, setting the overall tone for the day, and our moods enter into a discerning quality of expression. Moon opposite Mercury brings moods that will tend to be overwhelmed by — or opposed to — communications. Beware of exhausting arguments. Virgo Moon influences our powers of discernment and it also represents our ability to care for ourselves through practical means. Waning Virgo Moon is an excellent time to apply good health and diet practices.

Mars sextile Uranus (occurring January 28 – February 6) Mars in Capricorn is sextile to Uranus in Pisces. Serious forces of combat are ignited in unanticipated ways. Mars governs all activities and forces of action. The sextile aspect puts this exalted Capricornian Mars energy into a position of opportunity and hope with regard to the explosive, unpredictable and chaotic energies of Uranus in Pisces. Both of these planets are charged with forceful energy and vitality as well as being violent and unsettled at times. Masculine forces are forging ahead abruptly and loudly right now, and the outlook is very fiery, although not necessarily completely destructive. It is important to look for the opportunity and potential in all sources of raw masculine energy. This aspect will occur once more this year on July 20, when Mars will be in Taurus.

Sun sextile Jupiter (occurring January 29 – February 5) This aspect brings those Aquarius people celebrating birthdays from January 29 – February 5 into a favorable natal Sun position to Jupiter. This represents a time of opportunity and expansion for these birthday folks, if they act on their desires and work towards their goals. Skills learned throughout this year will support their overall plans for career advancement and fortune building. This aspect will repeat again on October 8, and will have a similar affect on the birthday Librans of that time.

February 4th Sunday

Moon in Virgo	PST	EST
Moon opposite Venus	12:10 AM	3:10 AM
Moon opposite Uranus	8:20 AM	11:20 AM
Moon trine Mars	10:08 AM	1:08 PM
Moon square Jupiter	11:24 AM	2:24 PM

Mood Watch: The waning Virgo Moon brings cautious and curious moods. The pre-dawn effects of Moon opposite Venus bring moods easily stirred by love related matters and feelings of affection. Come morning, Moon opposite Uranus brings agitation, inspired by tyrannical types of disruption. Moon trine Mars brings moods in harmony with masculine forces taking action. Moon square Jupiter often brings moods that are challenged by matters of expenses and wealth. Overall, Virgo Moon keeps us communicative, resourceful, and somewhat oriented towards cleanliness and organization.

February 5th Monday

Moon in Virgo / Libra	PST	EST
Moon square Pluto goes v/c	2:38 PM	5:38 PM
Moon enters Libra	6:16 PM	9:16 PM
Sun opposite Saturn begins (see February 10)		
Venus sextile Mars begins (see February 13)		

Mood Watch: The Moon continues to wane in Virgo, and the start of our day will be pragmatic and focused with an emphasis on organization and accuracy. A little later today, Moon square Pluto brings moods that are likely to be challenged by matters of fate and by difficult transformations. The Virgo Moon also goes void-of-course at this point, creating a tendency for folks to be easily distracted by skepticism or doubt. By the time the Moon enters Libra, our moods enter into the need for balance, and our energies become more focused on creating harmony among friends and partners.

February 6th Tuesday
Moon in Libra

Mood Watch: There are no significant exact aspects occurring today between any of the planets or with the Moon to any of the planets. This does not always mean that we are in for an uneventful day. There are always non-exact aspects at work which may create unexpected turns in the course of our affairs. The waning Libra Moon emphasizes our need to create harmony and to put a sense of balance into our lives. This is a good time to encourage others, apply good team-work practices, and to enjoy quality time with friends and loved ones.

February 7th Wednesday

Moon in Libra	PST	EST
Moon sextile Jupiter	12:43 AM	3:43 AM
Moon square Mars	2:42 AM	5:42 AM
Moon trine Sun	7:47 AM	10:47 AM
Moon trine Neptune	9:46 AM	12:46 PM
Venus conjunct Uranus	10:58 AM	1:58 PM
Moon sextile Saturn	2:40 PM	5:40 PM

Mood Watch: Throughout today, the waning Libra Moon continues to place an emphasis on the need to encourage partnerships, friendships, and professional groups to work harmoniously together. Overnight, Moon sextile Jupiter brings moods that will be inspired by travel and adventure. Moon square Mars brings moods challenged by masculine forces or energies. Moon trine Sun always reminds us of the aspects of the current season that are inspiring and uplifting. Moon trine Neptune brings easygoing attitudes and spiritual inclinations. Libra is the Venus ruled sign emphasizing harmony. Despite the Venus conjunction with Uranus (see below) which often causes chaos in love related matters, the Libra Moon reminds us that love conquers all. Later today, Moon sextile Saturn brings moods inspired by work, particularly teamwork.

Venus conjunct Uranus (occurring February 2 – 10) It's no wonder that love matters seem wild or chaotic – this conjunction brings an element of shock value to the expression of love. Venus conjunct Uranus in Pisces creates the potential for lively encounters with spiritual love and affection, wherein there is sometimes an exceedingly wise, though often unusual, counsel of love. A radical or explosive attraction or fascination may occur with this conjunction, opening our senses to a more artistic understanding of chaos. For those who are strongly affected, mischievous, brilliant, outgoing and challenging modes of love and affection now occur.

Hang in there. Chaos is often considered a true test of love. Be positive and open to the challenge of love with chaos.

February 8th Thursday

Moon in Libra / Scorpio	PST	EST	
Moon sextile Pluto goes v/c	3:40 AM	6:40 AM	
Moon enters Scorpio	7:11 AM	10:11 AM	
Sun conjunct Neptune	7:53 AM	10:53 AM	
Moon trine Mercury	11:47 PM	2:47 AM	(February 9)

Mood Watch: Moon sextile Pluto occurs at the start of the day causing our moods to be preoccupied with the need for trouble-shooting and problem solving. The Libra Moon goes void-of-course simultaneously bright and early, causing our moods to be distracted by indecisiveness. As the Moon enters Scorpio this morning we feel the need to let go, and to face or drop emotional build-ups which have occurred up to this point. Scorpio Moon encourages us to confront important matters with a sense of urgency. Much later tonight, Moon trine Mercury eases our minds in a more positive fashion and our moods are likely to be receptive and thoughtful.

Sun conjunct Neptune (occurring February 2 – 11) This occurrence of Sun conjunct Neptune particularly affects Aquarius people celebrating birthdays February 2 – 11 with intuitive inclinations and spiritual desires. Your visions (Aquarius birthday folks) will inspire great feats, and the higher, more spiritually refined parts of the soul are going to be speaking to you throughout the upcoming year. Listen! This may be a time to let go of personal attachments and outmoded desires that appear to be going nowhere. Your highly complex Aquarian idealism will work up your spiritual beliefs into a kind of peak performance level, even if you don't believe you have such a thing as spiritual beliefs. Birthday Aquarians, you will continue to encounter a kind of spiritual catharsis and, by the time you've come through this, you'll know what that means. This is all magnified by your ruling planet, Uranus, which has been traveling through the Neptune-ruled sign of Pisces since March 2003. Integrate a listening pattern concerning the Great Spirit in your life: focus on the spiritual part of the self (or higher self) that rules over personal destiny and guides the true desires of the soul. Can you handle that, birthday folks?

February 9th Friday

Moon in Scorpio	PST	EST	
Venus square Jupiter	3:32 AM	6:32 AM	
Moon trine Uranus	10:04 AM	1:04 PM	
Moon trine Venus	3:15 PM	6:15 PM	
Moon sextile Mars	7:23 PM	10:23 PM	
Moon square Neptune	10:29 PM	1:29 AM	(February 10)

Mood Watch: Waning Moon in Scorpio allows us to face emotional build-ups with incisive and intuitive clarity. Moon trine Uranus lets our moods be in harmony with the chaos around us. Moon trine Venus brings moods in harmony with feminine energies. Moon sextile Mars brings moods inspired by high energy levels and by activiy in general. Much later, Moon square Neptune brings moods which will be challenged by nebulousness or vagueness, but then again, no one is likely to be especially clear or coherent by late, late evening. We are now on the brink of the

Last Quarter Moon in Scorpio, set to occur before dawn tomorrow.

Venus square Jupiter (occurring February 3 – 12) Venus in Pisces is square to Jupiter in Sagittarius. A love for art, music, and the pursuits of comforting beauty and affection are challenged by the need to handle escalating economic obligations or social debts. Our experiences of beauty and affection may be tested by the difficulty of attracting or acquiring prosperity. Some might say that the act of appreciating beauty is a form of prosperity in itself. Unfortunately, this aspect may create an obstacle to acknowledging the expenses incurred by our attractions and love-needs. This aspect reminds us that something more than love's blindness is required in order for us to fully realize our riches and the value of what we care about most. This aspect will repeat on October 29, when Venus will be in Virgo.

February 10th Saturday
Moon in Scorpio / Sagittarius - LAST QUARTER MOON in SCORPIO

	PST	EST
Moon square Sun	1:52 AM	4:52 AM
Moon square Saturn goes v/c	2:40 AM	5:40 AM
Sun opposite Saturn	10:43 AM	1:43 PM
Moon enters Sagittarius	7:02 PM	10:02 PM

Mood Watch: The **Last Quarter Moon in Scorpio** (Moon square Sun) occurs before dawn and it focuses our attention on issues of passion and compassion. It is likely that the dark secrets of our life will be touched on somehow. This Moon urges us to release stored up tension, and to find release for our emotions without imposing them on others. Physical workouts are excellent for this, provided safety consciousness is maintained. Safety consciousness of any kind is particularly important during Scorpio Moon. Don't forget to keep an eye out for suspicious activity -- beware of thieves, smooth talkers, and the potential for violent outbreaks. Moon square Saturn causes challenges with our abilities to concentrate, stay focused and handle pending deadlines. This is especially true as the void-of-course Moon in Scorpio takes over for the entire day. Overall, our moods will be distracted by emotional quandaries, both hidden and on the surface. This is no time to let your guard down. This evening as the Moon enters Sagittarius, various philosophical views are revealed to give us a better perspective on matters.

Sun opposite Saturn (occurring February 5 – 13) This occurrence of Sun opposite Saturn particularly affects those Aquarius people celebrating birthdays from February 5 – 13. These birthday folks are undergoing personal challenges with regard to patience, leaving them strongly aware of who and what is in control. These people are mindful of the crucial factors of time, limitations, and timing. Work demands may be overwhelming, but most Aquarians have what it takes to apply discipline and determination in order to achieve success. Work that requires self motivation may be the most challenging part of applying discipline while Saturn is in Leo. Aquarius birthday folks, this is a most important time in your life to persist! Endure! Keep up the Great Work! This may well be your year, Birthday Aquarians, to accomplish something astounding.

February 11th Sunday

Moon in Sagittarius	PST	EST
Moon square Mercury	1:55 PM	4:55 PM
Moon square Uranus	8:58 PM	11:58 PM
Jupiter trine Saturn begins (see March 16 and May 6)		

The waning Sagittarius Moon of winter is the time to prepare for the days ahead, to focus on our visions, to shed old pretenses, and to gather our courage. This is the time to broaden our awareness through exploration, and to do so with enthusiasm and wit. Moon square Mercury brings moods that are often challenged by communications and it may be difficult to get the message across. Perhaps this is a prelude to the upcoming phase of Mercury retrograde, set to begin in a couple of days *(see Feb. 13)* and bound to cause nerve racking miscommunications. This evening's Moon square Uranus is likely to challenge our moods with regard to disorder and chaos. Sagittarius Moon, although waning, is always a good time to encourage optimism.

February 12th Monay

Moon in Sagittarius	PST	EST
Moon conjunct Jupiter	1:17 AM	4:17 AM
Moon square Venus	7:53 AM	10:53 AM
Moon sextile Neptune	8:36 AM	11:36 AM
Moon trine Saturn	12:01 PM	3:01 PM
Moon sextile Sun	4:32 PM	7:32 PM

Mood Watch: The Moon wanes in Sagittarius bringing an outgoing and free flowing expression of creativity. Moods are especially optimistic with Moon conjunct Jupiter. However, Moon square Venus challenges our feelings in the sphere of love and attraction. Fortunately, moods will be inspired by a sense of tranquility brought to us by Moon sextile Neptune. The progress of the day will go well with Moon trine Saturn bringing harmonious and work-oriented moods. Overall, we can expect to make the most of the day and enjoy the optimism brought to us by the Sagittarius Moon sextile the Aquarius Sun. Now is the time to hold off on making a lot of changes in your plans over the next few days as complexities loom with Mercury retrograde, starting tomorrow.

February 13th Tuesday

Moon in Sagittarius / Capricorn	PST	EST	
Moon conjunct Pluto goes v/c	12:46 AM	3:46 AM	
Moon enters Capricorn	3:43 AM	6:43 AM	
Venus sextile Mars	2:48 PM	5:48 PM	
Mercury goes retrograde	8:39 PM	11:39 PM	
Moon sextile Mercury	10:09 PM	1:09 AM	(February 14)
Sun sextile Pluto begins (see February 17)			

Mood Watch: Overnight, moods are intense but therapeutic with Moon conjunct Pluto. The Sagittarius Moon also goes void-of-course and our dream world may go off course, giving some light sleepers the sense of being lost, or confused. Soon enough, the Moon enters Capricorn and our moods awaken to a serious phase of expression throughout the day. Capricorn Moon keeps our moods focused on important matters and the need to accomplish necessary duties and tasks. Later tonight, Moon sextile Mercury inspires our moods with informative talk and information, but with Mercury now retrograde (see below) it would be wise to follow-up on any new information with careful research.

Venus sextile Mars (occurring February 5 – 17) Venus in Pisces emphasizes spiritual and artistic love. Mars in Capricorn represents an unyielding and uncompromising force of action. This aspect is favorable, bringing opportunities to situations that involve love and beauty. It is here that feminine (Venus) and masculine (Mars) forces have an opportunity (the sextile aspect) to support each other. The Mars influence emphasizes the awareness and application of action, movement, involvement, and also harnesses focuses of strength and energy. Venus reminds us to draw towards ourselves the pleasures we desire. Here we have the incentive to apply action with love. Venus sextile Mars will repeat on September 3, when Venus will be retrograde in Leo and Mars will be in Gemini. Venus sextile Mars will occur for the third time this year on October 16, when Venus will be in Virgo and Mars will be in Cancer.

Mercury goes retrograde (Mercury retrograde: February 13 – March 7) Mercury goes retrograde today in the sign of Pisces; it will travel back to the end of Aquarius before going direct at the twenty-five degree mark of Aquarius on March 7. Mercury retrograde in Pisces is likely to disrupt communications with topics that cover our beliefs and religion, as well as music and the arts. Despite strong instinctual impulses to articulate abstract or profound subjects, Mercury retrograde in Pisces will leave us stuttering and tongue tied. A real test of everyone's patience occurs; this leaves us susceptible to arguments and confusion regarding spiritual development. While Mercury is retrograde in Aquarius (February 26 – March 7,) there may be a number of irritating miscommunications over technology related subjects or situations. At first it may be difficult to sit through everyone's excuses and misinformation, but eventually a logical explanation will emerge despite Mercury retrograde setbacks. Expect to repeat yourself more than once or twice, and to be persistent as well as patient. For more information on Mercury retrograde, see the section in the introduction about *Mercury retrograde periods.*

February 14th Wednesday
Saint Valentine's Day

Moon in Capricorn	PST	EST
Moon sextile Uranus	4:08 AM	7:08 AM
Moon conjunct Mars	6:22 PM	9:22 PM
Moon sextile Venus goes v/c	7:25 PM	10:25 PM

Mood Watch: A Capricorn Moon on a Valentine's Day does not give a whole lot of flexibility to the overall sense of humor of this time, nor does it help our ability to take things lightly. This is a good time to mean what you say and to follow through with flying colors. Avoid making idle promises of any kind. Moon sextile Uranus kicks off the day with moods that are inspired by rebellion and freedom. While Moon conjunct Mars occurs, our moods are active, hot, and eager to take action. Moon sextile Venus brings moods that will be inspired by beauty and feminine expressions. This occurs at the same time the Moon also goes void-of-course in Capricorn. Tonight's romances will best succeed wherever there are no great expectations riding on the need for a specific performance to be carried out, or wherever there is a non-mutual lust for results. Avoid having grand expectations or making high demands — pleasant surprises may occur.

February 15th Thursday
Moon in Capricorn / Aquarius PST   EST

	PST	EST
Moon enters Aquarius	8:35 AM	11:35 AM
Venus square Pluto begins (see February 19)		

Mood Watch: Throughout the night and into part of the morning, a darkly waning Capricorn Moon brings out serious moods. While there is a great emphasis on fulfilling work tasks and completing projects, the void-of-course Capricorn Moon keeps our sense of progress moving at a slow clip — or in some cases, coming to a grinding halt. Soon enough, the Moon enters Aquarius, bringing a much more intelligent and logical approach to life. Our moods enter into a state of know-how and a greater sense of confidence can be felt. The insightful intelligence which is shared during the Aquarius Moon helps to ease the burden of miscommunications which commonly occurr while Mercury is retrograde (since February 13).

February 16th Friday
Moon in Aquarius – New Moon Eve

		PST	EST
Moon sextile Jupiter	12:06 PM	3:06 PM
Moon conjunct Neptune	5:49 PM	8:49 PM
Moon opposite Saturn	7:58 PM	10:58 PM

Mood Watch: The darkness of this waning winter Moon brings internal reflection, and now is certainly a time to preserve our energies. This may also be an excellent time for researchers, and for scientific studies to lead to important discoveries and lessons. This afternoon's Moon sextile Jupiter brings moods that will be inspired by generous joviality. This evening, Moon conjunct Neptune connects our moods with our beliefs and our spirituality. Also tonight, Moon opposite Saturn brings moods that are likely to be overwhelmed by work-related matters or responsibilities. Aquarius Moon beckons to humankind to look within and find solutions.

February 17th Saturday
Moon in Aquarius / Pisces - NEW MOON in AQUARIUS

	PST	EST
Sun sextile Pluto	5:08 AM	8:08 AM
Moon sextile Pluto	8:03 AM	11:03 AM
Moon conjunct Sun goes v/c	8:15 AM	11:15 AM
Moon enters Pisces	10:31 AM	1:31 PM

Mood Watch: Early this morning, Moon sextile Pluto brings adaptable moods, good for facing challenges. **New Moon in Aquarius** (Moon conjunct Sun) is a good time to begin new social and philanthropic endeavors, and to learn something new about ourselves or our ever changing world. New Aquarius Moon moods may be daring, with a flare for experimenting with life. This is the time to open up to new feelings and greater comprehension of science and technology and of these changing times, adding to our power. The Moon will go void-of-course at the same time it reaches the new mark; this morning's final hours of the Moon in Aquarius are likely to bring distractions over glitches in technology and in various public systems. When the Moon enters Pisces, our moods will appear more tranquil and introspective in nature. Pisces Moon brings out intuitive, artistic, and imaginative perspectives on life.

Sun sextile Pluto (occurring February 13 – 19) Sun in Aquarius is sextile Pluto in Sagittarius, bringing opportunities that appear both vast and demanding to Aquarians celebrating birthdays this year between February 13 – 19. These birthday people are experiencing the sextile aspect of their natal sun to Pluto, giving them opportunities to take charge, to step into positions of power, and to accept and embrace permanent change in their lives. These are powerful transformations which provide opportunities to embody what has been learned from the personal trials of the past. Go thee forth and conquer, master Aquarians! Persist with diligence to resolve the conflicts of your life with self-respect and assurance. Your time to triumph is always available when your will to achieve is balanced by knowledge and hard work. This holds true for all signs of the zodiac. This aspect will repeat again on October 20 when the Sun will be in Libra.

PISCES

Key Phrase: "I Believe"

Mutable Water Sign

Symbol : The Fishes

February 18th through March 20th

February 18th Sunday

Chinese New Year: Pig (Year 4705) *Fire Pig*

Moon in Pisces	PST	EST
Moon conjunct Mercury	12:44 AM	3:44 AM
Moon conjunct Uranus	8:59 AM	11:59 AM
Moon square Jupiter	1:31 PM	4:31 PM
Sun enters Pisces	5:10 PM	8:10 PM

Mood Watch: Overnight, Moon conjunct Mercury allows us to drop nervous tension in our sleep, and allows those who can't sleep to work through relevant mental processes. As Moon conjunct Uranus occurs this morning, our moods may go through abrupt or chaotic change, and we may find ourselves being somewhat counterproductive. Moon square Jupiter brings moods which will be challenged by expenditures and the handling of large productions. As a general rule, Pisces Moon is the time to kick back, to enjoy spiritual endeavors, and to be artistic and open minded.

Happy Chinese New Year! - Year of the Pig (occurring: February 18, 2007 – February 6, 2008). Pigs are somewhat earthy in nature, as they are pragmatic and enjoy material luxuries like the earth signs. They are studious, thorough, and often quiet. The Pig personality is notorious for chivalrous gallantry and great inner strength. Pigs are generally very kind, have impeccable manners and taste, although sometimes they are nice to a fault. With unwavering concentration, people born in the year of the Pig (or Boar) apply all their strength to whatever they do. They are honest, loyal, and they don't talk over much — but they do have a great hunger for knowledge. Pig people are often well informed, prone to perfection, and usually willing to do the work. Pigs love to serve and be served and they often make wonderful life-long partners due to their love of family and their golden hearts. They don't like to argue with others but they can be quick tempered. Pigs love people, make great lifetime friends and they often prosper when they open up their lives to a diverse group of people. This year marks the year of the Fire Pig – Fire Pigs are boldly adventurous, cleverly witty, and are often well-rounded and successful in many aspects of life.

Sun enters Pisces (Sun in Pisces: February 18 – March 20) *Happy Birthday to our Pisces friends!* The Piscean symbol of the fishes is a prehistoric representation of long term experience or incarnation, and of age old wisdom. Pisces is the last sign of the zodiac, representing the completion of a cycle. This mutable water sign is adaptive and Pisceans can absorb all kinds of influence. However, bogged down by oppressive influences, the Piscean becomes burnt out, oversensitive, and depressed. It is essential therefore that the Pisces character finds ways to vent heavy feelings of oppression, especially to overcome oppression by choosing a path other than the misuse of addictive substances, one of Pisces' weaknesses. Pisces is the mutable water sign, very capable of taking on a challenge with the ability to adapt and change very quickly – like water it takes on many forms. The whole Piscean character can meld and blend in to become intuitively aware of any belief system that exists around them. It is that psychic touch, that quality of being able to absorb knowledge or awareness of something on those unseen levels that makes Pisces the most spiritually adaptive character in the zodiac.

Aquarius, the sign through which the Sun has just passed, is the eccentric, whereas Pisces, the sign in which the Sun now travels, is the artist. The one expression melds into the other: brilliant, creative, sublime and even divine art and music take the stage as the emerging Pisces energy shows us how to celebrate, and how to develop some kind of belief in the arts of life. All of this is especially true now that rabble-rousing Uranus is in the sign of Pisces as of March 2003, and will remain there until March 2011. Uranus forges radical awareness in the realms of Pisces. This will cause deep, unimaginable spiritual disruption or rebellion, which notoriously leads to a revolutionary process in our beliefs and, consequently, our systems of belief. Out of Aquarius we take the extraordinary knowledge and experience of humanity, and in Pisces we purify that experience and seek further insight by getting in touch with divinity.

Pisces is ruled by Neptune, the planet of least resistance. Neptune, one of the three outer planets along with Uranus and Pluto, is currently traveling through Aquarius, and will return to its native sign, Pisces, in the spring of 2011. Sometimes the Piscean character is like a conduit, able to take in and facilitate any influence that comes along. The art of channeling spirits is very Piscean, and the three outer planets are said to be the voice, or influence, of the gods. They travel through the further reaches of space and because they are the furthest away from planet Earth in our solar system, these planets take the longest time to travel through the signs of the zodiac. The shifts of these planets through our lives and our history have been very profound influences which span through the generations and affect us all.

February 19th Monday
Washington's Birthday, USA

Moon in Pisces / Aries	PST	EST
Moon sextile Mars	3:03 AM	6:03 AM
Moon conjunct Venus	7:45 AM	10:45 AM
Moon square Pluto goes v/c	8:44 AM	11:44 AM
Moon enters Aries	11:07 AM	2:07 PM
Venus square Pluto	7:58 PM	10:58 PM

"Labor to keep alive in your breast that little spark of celestial fire called conscience."   - George Washington (1732 – 1799)

Mood Watch: Overnight, Moon sextile Mars brings active dreams and moods that are inspired by action. This morning, Moon conjunct Venus brings moods connected to the need for beauty and love. Moon square Pluto brings moods that will be challenged by transformations. The Pisces Moon then goes void-of-course for a couple of hours, bringing a morning of distractions and a lack of concentration. By the time the Moon enters Aries our moods will be much more confident and forthright. Aries Moon brings a sense of newness to life, especially now that the Moon newly waxes. This will be a good day to get things done.

Venus square Pluto (occurring February 15 – 22) Venus in Pisces is square Pluto in Sagittarius. The intuitive, instinctual and hypersensitive side of our affections is likely to take a pretty good beating. Our concepts of beauty may be challenged as the corruption of superpowers prompts action which threatens or alters the beauty and pleasure in our lives. Venus square Pluto usually involves such difficulties as loss or death of a loved one, the obstacles of rejection, and general oppression for those aspects of life to which we are undeniably attached and which we hold dear. If something of this nature is occurring for you, it is best to recognize that love will triumph in every dimension, despite the pain of separation, or the disease and strife of the beloved. Be both strong and gentle in matters of love. Let the obstacles of love's pain become the building blocks of a better outlook, and a stronger love will supersede these current trials of the heart. This aspect repeats on November 5, when Venus will be in Virgo.

February 20th Tuesday
Mardi Gras, USA

Moon in Aries	PST	EST
Moon trine Jupiter	2:33 PM	5:33 PM
Moon sextile Neptune	7:34 PM	10:34 PM
Moon trine Saturn	8:56 PM	11:56 PM

Mood Watch: Activating our moods, this waxing Aries Moon and Mardi Gras, will be a perfect day for having fun and for frolicking about. There may be a bit of anxiety in the air — possibly the need to get out and about is affecting our moods and this is a common syndrome of what we call "winter fever." Restless and anxious souls are not always willing to be patient and, as a result, may be somewhat accident prone in their haste. This afternoon, Moon trine Jupiter brings harmoniously generous moods. This evening, Moon sextile Neptune brings moods inspired by spiritual perspectives. Moon trine Saturn brings moods that will be agreeably work-oriented. Overall, another excellent workday paves the way for progress.

February 21st Wednesday

Ash Wednesday

Moon in Aries / Taurus	PST	EST
Venus enters Aries	12:22 AM	3:22 AM
Moon square Mars	6:30 AM	9:30 AM
Moon trine Pluto goes v/c	9:43 AM	12:43 PM
Moon enters Taurus	12:04 PM	3:04 PM
Moon sextile Sun	5:05 PM	8:05 PM
Moon sextile Mercury	8:48 PM	11:48 PM
Sun conjunct Mercury begins (see February 22)		

Mood Watch: The Aries Moon sets the tone of the morning starting with Moon square Mars; this brings moods that may be challenged by the masculine forces around us. Later, Moon trine Pluto brings moods that will be, for the most part, in harmony with transformation. The Aries Moon also goes void-of-course early in the day, creating distractions brought on by pushy energy, bouts of impatience — and there may be delays due to various forms of hastiness. As the Moon enters Taurus, our moods beckon to the call of practicality, and also the desire and need for beauty. As the early days of Pisces continue to unfold in the final throes of winter, Moon sextile Sun brings moods inspired by the seasonal factors currently at work. Moon sextile Mercury brings the potential for inspiration through thoughts and ideas, and all this is possible despite the travails of Mercury retrograde occurring February 13 – March 7.

Venus enters Aries (Venus in Aries: February 21 – March 17) As Venus enters Aries the expression of beauty, love and attraction assumes a fascination for the warrior spirit. Venus represents magnetic draw and attraction, and now the planet of love and beauty focuses our attention on the force and fire of Aries related interests. This brings sheer love of and appreciation for such activities as competition, rights (or rites) of selfhood, and initiation into new endeavors. Venus in Aries brings out the warrior and conqueror quality in people, and a new sense of life and vitality will be evident. Venus in Aries emphasizes ardent, open and forthright expressions and proposals of love, especially from our Aries friends who may be blinded by the lust for beauty. New hobbies, crafts and talents will spring forth. Remember, Aries rules the head; there are numerous ways you can use your head before plunging head first into love matters. Try not to be too militant in the display of personal defenses and in the expression of true feelings of affection. New love is inspired with Venus in Aries.

February 22nd Thursday

Moon in Taurus

	PST	EST	
Moon sextile Uranus	11:32 AM	2:32 PM	
Sun conjunct Mercury	8:47 PM	11:47 PM	
Moon square Neptune	9:40 PM	12:40 AM	(February 23)
Moon square Saturn	10:41 PM	1:41 AM	(February 23)

Mood Watch: The Taurus Moon brings practical, amicable, business-like awareness. This morning, Moon sextile Uranus brings moods that will be inspired by freedom, and this may be perceived as rebellious. Taurus Moon keeps us focused on practical needs as well as the desire for luxurious quality. Much Later, Moon square Neptune brings spiritual challenges – on the physical level, these spiritual challenges sometimes have to do with drug and/or alcohol related problems. Moon square Saturn slips into the night and into our dreams bringing moods often challenged by the need for discipline; with any luck, this is a time to rest and not to worry.

Sun conjunct Mercury (occurring February 21 – 25) This is a very common aspect, which will create a much more thoughtful, communicative, and expressive year ahead for those Pisces born people celebrating birthdays from February 21 – 25. Despite the fact that Mercury is retrograde (February 13 – March 7,) this is your time (birthday Pisces) to record ideas, relay important messages, and pay close attention to your imaginative thoughts as they are touched by Mercury, creating the urge to speak and be heard. Your thoughts will reveal a great deal about who you are, now and in the year to come.

February 23rd Friday

FIRST QUARTER MOON in GEMINI

	PST	EST	
Moon trine Mars goes v/c	11:48 AM	2:48 PM	
Moon enters Gemini	2:43 PM	5:43 PM	
Moon square Mercury	8:06 PM	11:06 PM	
Moon sextile Venus	8:48 PM	11:48 PM	
Moon square Sun	11:57 PM	2:57 AM	(February 24)

Mood Watch: The Taurus Moon trine Mars brings moods in harmony with force and energy. The Moon also goes void-of-course at this early stage of the day bringing moods that are easily distracted, probably with regard to financial matters. A series of afternoon corrections are likely to take place, and there will be a lot of directing and re-directing our facts and figures. As the Moon enters Gemini, our moods will enter into thoughtful deliberations. Moon square Mercury brings challenging thoughts and discussions. Moon sextile Venus brings moods inspired by beauty and the feminine touch. **First Quarter Moon in Gemini** (Moon square Sun) brings the necessity for our moods to be changeable and adaptable. Our moods are easily affected by the busy buzz of intellectual focuses and pursuits, and this may be tiresome to some folks due to Mercury retrograde (Feb. 13 – March 7). The emphasis of covering many details at once becomes the primary objective, but not necessarily the answer to our insatiable curiosity. The act of processing information becomes essential. Do not let gossip and idle chatter be the cause of disruption in your day – thoughtlessness is also a symptom of the Gemini Moon atmosphere. As it waxes towards the first quarter mark later tonight, the Gemini Moon puts us in touch with how we feel about our thoughts, If you don't like how you feel about your thoughts; endeavor to alter your way of thinking. Omit thoughts which attempt to defeat your sense of purpose; encourage thoughts that uplift and inspire your spirit. Be careful not to overdo the caffeine.

February 24th Saturday

Moon in Gemini	PST	EST	
Moon square Uranus	3:30 PM	6:30 PM	
Moon opposite Jupiter	9:12 PM	12:12 AM	(February 25)

Mood Watch: A Pisces Sun and a Gemini Moon bring a creative, bubbling well of mixed thoughts and ideas. Emotional images blend with the mind to create an intuitive understanding of our beliefs. Moon square Uranus brings moods that are likely to be challenged by chaos and disruption. Moon opposite Jupiter brings moods which may seem overwhelmed by overextension, either on a financial or a psychological level. Too much prosperity at once can seem overwhelming; be cautious with late-night travel schedules, with expenditures, and with the potential to do an overkill job on a celebration. Today will have a bigger-than-life quality to it all by itself.

February 25th Sunday

Moon in Gemini / Cancer	PST	EST	
Moon trine Neptune	2:03 AM	5:03 AM	
Moon sextile Saturn	2:40 AM	5:40 AM	
Moon opposite Pluto goes v/c	5:23 PM	8:23 PM	
Mars enters Aquarius	5:33 PM	8:33 PM	
Moon enters Cancer	7:49 PM	10:49 PM	
Moon trine Mercury	9:27 PM	12:27 AM	(February 26)

Mood Watch: A busy schedule of lunar aspects is about to occur. First, long before most North Americans are fully awake, Moon trine Neptune brings harmonious spiritual moods. Moon sextile Saturn brings dreams that inspire a sense of discipline. Throughout the day, the Gemini Moon brings thoughtful interactions and exchanges between people. This evening, Moon opposite Pluto brings moods which will be strongly affected by the generation gaps, or the cultural gaps that exist between different folks. As the Gemini Moon goes void-of-course, our moods will be easily distracted by mixed feelings. A couple of hours later the Moon enters Cancer as our moods enter into a nurturing phase. Moon trine Mercury brings harmony in communications, a welcomed boon during this challenging time of Mercury retrograde.

Mars enters Aquarius (Mars in Aquarius: February 25 – April 6) As Mars, the red warrior planet, moves through Aquarius over the next couple of weeks, a surge of energy and vitality takes place in the lives of Aquarius people. Now the fixed signs of the zodiac go into an activity mode, for as Mars goes through Aquarius, Scorpio and Taurus people will experience Mars squaring with their natal Sun signs, causing their lives to be more prone towards accidents, fights, fevers, and unyielding activities of great challenge. Mars in Aquarius will be opposing the fixed sign Leo, making our Leo friends realize that the activities in their lives are a challenge to keep up with; occasional bouts of exhaustion will be common. Mars in the air sign of Aquarius shows that activities will emphasize science, technology and computer data banks, as well as humanitarian endeavors. Watch out for the tendency of electrical equipment to overheat and fry during this time of Mars in Aquarius.

February 26th Monday

Moon in Cancer

	PST	EST	
Moon square Venus	7:43 AM	10:43 AM	
Moon trine Sun	9:58 AM	12:58 PM	
Mercury enters Aquarius	7:02 PM	10:02 PM	
Moon trine Uranus goes v/c	10:04 PM	1:04 AM	(February 27)
Mercury sextile Pluto begins (see February 28)			

Mood Watch: The Sun and Moon are in water signs, commonly bringing wet weather throughout most of North America. The Moon is trine with the Sun, which also brings harmonious feelings with regard to the seasonal factors of this time. Cancer Moon keeps our moods focused on personal comfort zones, the nurturing spirit of motherly energies, and on the shifts taking place on the emotional level. Late tonight, Moon trine Uranus brings a feeling of wild and reckless abandon, and all is in harmony with the forces of chaos. The Cancer Moon goes void-of-course, making this a good time to rest the mind and to avoid emotional distractions that might infringe on a good night's sleep. For some folks, tomorrow's full-length void-of-course Cancer Moon may be emotionally challenging.

Mercury enters Aquarius (Mercury in Aquarius: February 26 – March 18) Retrograde Mercury re-enters Aquarius today and will continue to go back through the late degrees of Aquarius until March 7, when it goes direct at the 25 degree mark of Aquarius. On March 18, the forward moving Mercury will re-enter Pisces once again, bringing it right back to the place where it is today. For more information on Mercury in Aquarius, see January 15, when Mercury first entered Aquarius this year. As for this time of Mercury retrograde in Aquarius, occurring today through March 7, see the introduction in the beginning of this book about *Mercury retrograde periods.*

February 27th Tuesday

Moon in Cancer
Sun conjunct Uranus begins (see March 5)

Mood Watch: There will be no exact lunar aspects occurring today. In fact there are no exact aspects occurring at all. The Cancer Moon is void-of-course for the entire day and night and this may be challenging for many folks. This day will be filled with numerous distractions, usually of an emotional nature. Mood fluctuation is inescapable and this tends to slow down overall progress considerably. All of this moodiness is a natural process, but it can cause forgetfulness, oversensitivity, or defensiveness. For those who have a busy agenda, a conscious effort to practice a little extra tenderness and forgiveness will go a long way and, believe it or not, it will save a lot of time.

February 28th Wednesday

Moon in Leo	PST	EST	
Moon enters Leo	3:31 AM	6:31 AM	
Saturn opposite Neptune	4:03 AM	7:03 AM	
Mercury sextile Pluto	5:10 AM	8:10 AM	
Moon opposite Mars	7:12 AM	10:12 AM	
Moon trine Venus	10:04 PM	1:04 AM	(March 1)

Mood Watch: Yesterday's long void-of-course Cancer Moon comes to a close in the pre-dawn hours of today. As the Moon enters Leo, a much more playful and relaxed level of confidence fills our moods. A sense of loyalty and praise comes out with regard to the things in life that we value. Leo Moon is a good time to bond with family and friends, and it is also a good time to get in touch with personal needs and desires. Moon opposite Mars brings astounding energy into our moods and some folks may feel overwhelmed by forceful activities. Later tonight, Moon trine Venus harmoniously tempers all our hearts and puts us in touch with love and beauty.

Saturn opposite Neptune (occurring February 2 – July 18) Due to the retrograde processes of these two planets, this aspect will continue for a good portion of the year and will repeat once again on June 25. Today the retrograde Saturn in Leo is opposite the direct moving Neptune in Aquarius, emphasizing the need to review the restrictive qualities of current spiritual activities. Saturn represents the ability to focus, to keep track of time, to apply discipline, and to exercise authority. Saturn's influence also assists us to accurately determine our perimeters and limitations. Neptune, on the other hand, connects us with the higher and more spiritual realms of the universe, where there are no boundaries that can be compared to our saturnian world of harsh physical realities and the demands of time. While Saturn is in the alarming opposition to Neptune, the discipline of attempting to make a connection with the spirit world may seem overwhelming and somewhat daunting to our limited perspectives. This aspect brings out a focus on the restrictions and trials of religions and religious belief. Saturn opposite Neptune will be a valuable time to observe what occurs around leaders of religious sects, and there may be notable reactions to the dictates and enforcement of their religious customs. It may take longer than usual to prepare for spiritual ceremonies until this aspect fully dissipates. Time restraints and strict regulations will have a bearing on the planning of ceremonies and on our spiritual practices. Expect to work extra hard during this time to guard and maintain spiritual practices. Saturn opposite Neptune reminds us that this is a time of dying beliefs, as well as newly emerging beliefs. Religious persecution is historical disruption that is often reflected in this type of aspect. It also reflects on the struggle between the body and the spirit, and on our need to overcome the limitations posed on our belief structures. The struggle against, and resistance to, absolute surrender is also a symptom of this aspect. Many folks may seem incredibly hard on themselves with regard to their beliefs. Saturn is in Leo, creating the need for many to gain control and to work on personal goals, as well as tend to family needs and limitations. Neptune has been in Aquarius since the dawning of the 21st century (1998) stirring up a spiritual emphasis in humanitarian exploits. These are indeed interesting times. On June 25, this opposition will repeat, and by that time, Neptune will be retrograde and Saturn will be direct.

Mercury sextile Pluto (occurring February 26 – March 19) Today, the retrograde planet Mercury is sextile Pluto. While Mercury is retrograde, this aspect focuses our attention on power issues, but there also may be a tendency for communications to be challenging and even confusing, and difficult subjects may seem to be easily misinterpreted. For more information on Mercury sextile Pluto, see January 31.This aspect will also repeat on March 16, September 24, October 26, and November 8.

March 1st Thursday

Moon in Leo	PST	EST
Moon trine Jupiter	1:55 PM	4:55 PM
Moon conjunct Saturn	6:13 PM	9:13 PM
Moon opposite Neptune	6:33 PM	9:33 PM

Mood Watch: Throughout the month of March, the light of day increases more rapidly than any other month of the year. While we have a much brighter month to look forward to, the final weeks of winter are stirred by the restlessness of the coming of spring. There's no more hiding in the calm respite of winter's slumber – the time has come to greet the light, and what a better way to do it than on the day of Moon in Leo? The watchword for this playful tune of a Moon is "will." If one or more facets of your personal will is purposefully executed and gratefully achieved, you will have experienced a successful Leo Moon time. This afternoon's Moon trine Jupiter brings generous and outgoing moods. This evening, Moon conjunct Saturn brings a strong, guarded feeling to our moods. This is swiftly followed by Moon opposite Neptune; bringing the potential for escapist tendencies and a challenge to feel comfortable or spiritually in tune with others. Overall, the waxing Moon in Leo is a good time to assert some confidence, as it may well bring moods of self-assurance, amusement, and delight.

March 2nd Friday

Moon in Leo / Virgo	PST	EST
Moon opposite Mercury	7:54 AM	10:54 AM
Moon trine Pluto goes v/c	11:04 AM	2:04 PM
Moon enters Virgo	1:33 PM	4:33 PM
Venus trine Jupiter begins (see March 8)		
Sun square Jupiter begins (see March 9)		

Mood Watch: The morning Moon in Leo waxes towards fullness as it opposes Mercury, bringing moods which may appear overwhelmed by a common syndrome known as information overload. This is true particularly now, as Mercury is still in the throes of being retrograde (Feb. 13 – March 7). Moon trine Pluto brings moods in harmony with the fateful conditions of this time, while the Leo Moon also goes void-of-course, bringing delays due to family or personal related matters. Someone may be likely to steal the stage for awhile but eventually the Moon enters Virgo, and the scrutinizing qualities of the Virgo Moon atmosphere will direct us toward a more impelling need to organize, purify, and apply some cleanliness to our existence.

March 3rd Saturday
FULL MOON in VIRGO – Total Lunar Eclipse

	PST	EST
Moon opposite Sun	3:18 PM	6:18 PM
Moon opposite Uranus	6:29 PM	9:29 PM

Mood Watch: **Full Moon in Virgo** (Moon opposite Sun) reaches its peak today and reminds us of the need to organize, analyze, and constructively criticize our health and cleanliness practices. Virgo also puts the focus on organization, filing, accounting, preparing taxes, and handling all of life's mundane necessities. Virgo Moon energy purges and purifies our surroundings with sound resourcefulness and simple logic. Virgo rules the intestines of the body and represents the process of elimination, making this an excellent time to focus on eliminating toxins and purifying the body. This is also a good time to purge the useless, destructive, or outmoded habits of our life. Celebrate your existing health and do something good for your body on this Full Virgo Moon. This evening as the Moon opposes Uranus, volcanic and explosive kinds of energy may show signs of erupting. While the natives are restless, it's best not to add to the heat.

Total Lunar Eclipse in Virgo – This Full Virgo Moon marks a Total Lunar Eclipse event. Besides the scientific phenomenon of the visual effects in places where it is visible, what we are likely to observe are the darkening psychological affects and the shadowy emotional subtleties of the Virgo Lunar Eclipse. Depression is one commonly noticed symptom of this Virgo Moon phenomenon. Doubt, scrutiny, criticism, and uncertainty may also be the subtle shadows cast upon us. The death of prominent people may be notable. This somewhat hidden lunar extravaganza influences priests, divinatory practices, and the worship of gods. The quality of our intuition may seem compromised by doubt, confusion, or by confrontation. The mutable earth sign of Virgo in the ecliptic state also influences earthquakes, hurricanes, floods, storms, drought, thunder and lighting. This is the time to combat emotional doubts and fears, to calm and ease the nerves and the mind with diligent care. Gentle kindness helps.

March 4th Sunday
Purim
Moon in Virgo

	PST	EST	
Moon square Jupiter	1:38 AM	4:38 AM	
Moon square Pluto goes v/c	10:57 PM	1:57 AM	(March 5)
Venus trine Saturn begins (see March 9)			

Mood Watch: The effects of a post-full total eclipse Virgo Moon still ring with a buzz of information sharing and questioning. As we prioritize our personal needs and achieve success by cherry picking our way through numerous tasks, often physical in nature, we also pull in our reins and act with a great deal more subtlety and poise. The pre-dawn Moon square Jupiter aspect brings moods that are challenged by overextension — or perhaps, overexertion — especially in the dream world. We awake more reserved, and more prudent towards life. Tonight, Moon square Pluto brings intense moods challenged by matters of transformation. By then the late night void-of-course Moon casts shadows of doubt and may cause restless minds. Tonight, it would be best to concentrate on getting some rest and dropping nervous fears.

March 5th Monday

Moon in Libra	PST	EST
Moon enters Libra	1:26 AM	4:26 AM
Sun conjunct Uranus	7:40 AM	10:40 AM
Moon trine Mars	1:26 PM	4:26 PM

Mood Watch: Today's Libra Moon brings the stability of balance into our moods. We naturally focus on those areas of life that require the most attention, as well as the most diplomacy and tact. This is the time to share experiences with friends and working partners, to develop a sense of teamwork and togetherness. As our moods enter into the need for balance, Moon trine Mars brings harmony towards our sense of strength and confidence. Today will be a good day to exert some energy and accomplish some goals.

Sun conjunct Uranus (occurring February 27 – March 8) This occurrence of Sun conjunct Uranus especially affects people celebrating birthdays this year from February 27 – March 8. There will be a healthy dollop of disruption and chaos in their lives. Radical breakthroughs towards creating a sense of freedom will be apparent. Sun conjunct Uranus causes strong rebellious tendencies. There is a stronger than usual Piscean desire to roll with change and take life at a different pace, to fight oppression and injustice, possibly even with an entirely off-the-wall approach to deal with calamity. Where there is knowledge to back this radical new approach, there is a way to achieve a sense of freedom, and there is a good chance to make an impression in the year to come. This will be your year (birthday folks) to express yourselves and your innovative desires and ideas.

March 6th Tuesday

Moon in Libra	PST	EST
Moon opposite Venus	10:49 AM	1:49 PM
Moon sextile Jupiter	2:44 PM	5:44 PM
Moon sextile Saturn	5:31 PM	8:31 PM
Moon trine Neptune	6:57 PM	9:57 PM
Venus sextile Neptune begins (see March 9)		

Mood Watch: Over the course of the next couple of weeks, numerous aspects will be piling up and with them comes swift and daunting changes and challenges. This is partly the symptom of a notoriously busy month of seasonal changes and the return of solar light but, for the most part, we are really in for some relatively alarming shifts. Today's Libra Moon reminds us of the importance of applying logic to the structure of our lifestyle and our choices in life. Moon opposite Venus implies that our moods may be dominated by feminine types of expression or demands. Lady Justice is blind, but that doesn't mean that her logic is not sound. Moon sextile Jupiter brings moods which will be inspired by notions of travel, or by expansion of some nature. Moon sextile Saturn inspires our moods to concentrate and to apply discipline towards reaching goals. Moon trine Neptune brings moods which will be in harmony with spiritual energies.

March 7th Wednesday

Moon in Libra / Scorpio

	PST	EST
Moon trine Mercury	5:01 AM	8:01 AM
Moon sextile Pluto goes v/c	11:52 AM	2:52 PM
Moon enters Scorpio	2:18 PM	5:18 PM
Mercury goes direct	8:46 PM	11:46 PM

Mood Watch: Moon trine Mercury brings harmonious morning chatter. Moon sextile Pluto brings moods that will be inspired by transformation. The Libra Moon goes void-of-course for a couple of hours causing a short phase of afternoon indecisiveness. As the Moon enters Scorpio, our moods enter into a phase of instinctual awareness and some very astute perceptions may be revealed. The waning Scorpio Moon is an excellent time to carefully face emotional or psychological disturbances with a brave and conscientious effort.

Mercury goes direct (Mercury direct: March 7 – June 15) Since February 13, Mercury has been retrograde in the signs of Pisces, causing emotional communication mix-ups and confusion when relaying information. It has also been retrograde in the sign of Aquarius, causing communication mix-ups with regard to social engagements, charity efforts, and technological events. Today Mercury resumes course at the 25 degree mark of Aquarius. Now we can breathe a greatly needed sigh of relief as Mercury, the planet governing the realms of communication, becomes stationary and will soon begin to move forward. Take note that our faculties and manner of communicating will definitely improve within the next few days. Although perhaps not today, very soon our communications will run more smoothly; and this will be a good time to begin clearing up various misunderstandings that have occurred over the past few weeks. For more information on this recently completed phase of Mercury retrograde, see February 13. For more on Mercury retrograde patterns throughout this year, see the introduction on *Mercury retrograde periods.*

March 8th Thursday

Moon in Scorpio

	PST	EST
Venus trine Jupiter	3:17 AM	6:17 AM
Moon square Mars	6:31 AM	9:31 AM
Moon trine Uranus	8:25 PM	11:25 PM

Mood Watch: The Sun and Moon are both in water signs and this represents a very fluid and insightful time of adaptability and transformation. This morning's Moon square Mars brings moods challenged by forcefulness and, as a result, some folks may seem particularly prone towards angry and temperamental responses. Later tonight, Moon trine Uranus brings moods in harmony with radical expressions. This would be an especially good time to embrace safe and therapeutic outlets for emotional build-ups and fear. Beware of addictive or violent tendencies. There is also the potential here for breathtaking art and creativity.

Venus trine Jupiter (occurring March 2 – 10) Valuable and inspiring gifts of love and affection come with this aspect. Love (Venus) is harmoniously placed with prosperity and opportunity (Jupiter.) Venus in Aries trine Jupiter in Sagittarius brings confident love and affection, inspiring adventurous growth and prosperity.

This is a great time to give gifts of love, and for many, it offers an expansive outlook of love's power. Getting ahead in life, in this case, has everything to do with appreciating and loving those areas of life in which we want to expand and prosper. A positive outlook can indeed help make this happen. This year we will be graced with the presence of this delicious tango of Venus and Jupiter again on June 19, when Venus will be in Leo.

March 9th Friday

Moon in Scorpio	PST	EST
Venus trine Saturn	12:42 AM	3:42 AM
Moon trine Sun	3:43 AM	6:43 AM
Moon square Saturn	5:54 AM	8:54 AM
Sun square Jupiter	6:20 AM	9:20 AM
Moon square Neptune	7:50 AM	10:50 AM
Moon square Mercury goes v/c	5:52 PM	8:52 PM
Venus sextile Neptune	7:42 PM	10:42 PM

Mood Watch: The waning Scorpio Moon prepares us for a busy roller coaster of emotional responses. Moon trine Sun brings harmony and peace for starters, but Moon square Saturn intensifies a demanding focus on deadlines and responsibilities. Also this morning, Moon square Neptune brings challenging spiritual forces into the picture. The Scorpio Moon keeps us hypersensitive to the difficulties and dangers of life. Tonight, Moon square Mercury brings uncommunicative moods. The Scorpio Moon also goes void-of-course at this time, leaving some people in the dark. As our moods are distracted by various kinds of intensity this evening, the Scorpio Moon reminds us to work with our perceptions like a sixth sense that ties in all the other senses. The Scorpio Moon makes anything possible, especially miraculous transformations.

Venus trine Saturn (occurring March 4 – 11) Venus in Aries trine Saturn in Leo brings a fiery, creative, and willing expression of love and commitment to love. This aspect may assist in bringing some peace to the structure or the closure of a love relationship. Venus trine Saturn often brings the gift of responsive and enduring love. This is good time to initiate or enhance a love vow or oath, and to apply the values of devotion and responsive caring. Love is a gift and a responsibility. Genuine love, when given without expectations, will return naturally, bringing true love into your life.

Sun square Jupiter (occurring March 2 – 12) This occurrence of Sun square Jupiter will particularly affect those Pisces people celebrating birthdays during its influence. This aspect creates difficulties and obstacles to the personal joy and prosperous welfare of these birthday folks. Getting ahead financially or just staying on top of current trends or financial shifts may be personally challenging right now, requiring persistence and determination. Pisceans who are doing well financially may find that this aspect is challenging their sense of what makes them happy, or that advancement in the world brings too much complexity and requires a lot of management. Though not all Pisceans are living as prosperously as they may desire, they do have the ability to come through this and be much better for it. Obstacles create challenges, but do not necessarily dictate an end to efforts to improve our welfare. It is the Pisces personality (Sun) that is being challenged (square aspect) in matters of advancement (Jupiter), requiring Pisceans to make do with less assistance than they had anticipated. This may be a time to redefine and redirect personal goals. Pisces birthday folks must reexamine what truly brings prosperity for them in their lives. This aspect will repeat again on September 3 with the Sun in Virgo. Virgo birthday folks, some of you are next in line to experience this Jupiter square to your natal sun. See September 3 for more details.

Venus sextile Neptune (occurring March 6 – 11) Venus in Aries brings love, attraction, beauty, and the nature of feminine expression into prominence. Neptune in Aquarius is time to awaken human spirituality and to excel in creative expression through music, art, writing, etc. The sextile of Venus to Neptune also brings the opportunity for us to find spiritual enhancement in the adventure of love, and to spread its healing power around for all to share. This serves as an excellent aspect to reach out spiritually to those we love as well as to our spirit guides. It also holds the potential for one to realize the profound beauty and the depths of which true love is capable. Faith and belief in love matters may be rewarded at this time, and will be enhanced where similar beliefs are shared. This is a great time to take your love to a special place, or sanctuary of divine countenance, where the depth of tranquility can be accessed.

March 10th Saturday
Moon in Scorpio / Sagittarius

	PST	EST
Moon enters Sagittarius	2:38 AM	5:38 AM
Moon sextile Mars	10:21 PM	1:21 AM (March 11)

Mood Watch: The waning Scorpio Moon enters Sagittarius and our moods are drawn towards adventure and exploration. This is a reflective time when philosophical perspectives bring strong insights. Sagittarius Moon brings the ability for our moods to explore beyond the usual realms and to reach out towards creative new insights and visions. Often the moods brought on by the Sagittarius Moon become restless around tedium and stagnation. Creative urges are strong right now. With the Sagittarius Moon on our side, it usually isn't that difficult to push beyond the dull monotony of the daily grind in order to explore new possibilities. Much later tonight, Moon sextile Mars brings moods inspired by incisive action and by the affirmation of will — and at this late hour, this inspiration manifests mostly in the far reaches of our dream world.

March 11th Sunday
DAYLIGHT SAVING TIME BEGINS
(Turn clocks ahead one hour at 2:00 a.m.)
LAST QUARTER MOON in SAGITTARIUS

	PDT	EDT
Moon square Uranus	9:04 AM	12:04 PM
Moon conjunct Jupiter	4:22 PM	7:22 PM
Moon trine Saturn	5:35 PM	8:35 PM
Moon sextile Neptune	7:53 PM	10:53 PM
Moon square Sun	8:55 PM	11:55 PM
Venus trine Pluto begins (see March 16)		

Daylight Savings Time: No, it's not a mistake, and yes, it's true; instead of the time change occurring on the usual first Sunday in April and last Sunday in October, Daylight Savings Time will begin much earlier and end a bit later this year. Due to the United States' Energy Policy Act of 2005, Daylight Savings Time 2007 begins today and ends on Sunday, November 4.

Mood Watch: The Sagittarius Moon continues to wane and brings us visionary introspection. Moon square Uranus kicks off the day with moods that will probably be challenged by explosive energies. Later in the day, Moon conjunct Jupiter brings extravagant and optimistic moods. Moon trine Saturn brings moods in harmony with work and responsibility. Moon sextile Neptune brings spiritually open moods. The **Last Quarter Moon in Sagittarius** (Moon square Sun) is a good time to internalize your new wishes and thoughts about the upcoming season. At the same time, focus on healing disruptive feelings and make a sporting effort to let go of unsatisfactory habits. Sagittarius Moon focuses our attention on such things as fitness, philosophy and travel. This is the time to broaden the mind and allow yourself to go further than anticipated in realizing your vision for the future.

March 12th Monday
Moon in Sagittarius / Capricorn

	PDT	EDT
Moon trine Venus	12:48 AM	3:48 AM
Moon sextile Mercury	6:44 AM	9:44 AM
Moon conjunct Pluto goes v/c	11:28 AM	2:28 PM
Moon enters Capricorn	1:36 PM	4:36 PM

Mood Watch: Overnight, Moon trine Venus brings dreams that are in harmony with affections and beauty. This morning, Moon sextile Mercury brings moods by intelligence. Moon conjunct Pluto brings awareness of the influence of super powers and how these forces affect everyone. The Sagittarius Moon also goes void-of-course for a couple of hours, and our moods may be easily distracted by flamboyant means of travel, traffic, roadside attractions, and by meandering philosophers. As the Moon enters Capricorn, our moods enter into the need to tackle the work, and progress will finally show itself.

March 13th Tuesday
Moon in Capricorn

	PDT	EDT
Moon sextile Uranus	5:31 PM	8:31 PM
Mercury sextile Venus begins (see March 16)		
Sun square Pluto begins (see March 19)		

Mood Watch: Moon in Capricorn commonly decrees that our moods become distinctly more serious and more inclined towards efforts to be work conscious. Moon in Capricorn throughout the day gives our moods a sense of diligent, persistent, and disciplined focus. There is a need today to get things done, to face up to unfinished business and to handle whatever comes along with serious intent. This evening, Moon sextile Uranus brings inspired moods over explosive and brilliant kinds of energy. As the Moon wanes in Capricorn, be careful not to overdo the work. Pace yourself while the universe prepares us for a great deal of celestial activity at the end of the week. Keeping the foundation of our work strong and steady is the underlying theme of today.

March 14th Wednesday

Moon in Capricorn / Aquarius

	PDT	EDT
Moon sextile Sun	8:46 AM	11:46 AM
Moon square Venus goes v/c	1:22 PM	4:22 PM
Moon enters Aquarius	7:53 PM	10:53 PM

Mood Watch: Waning Capricorn Moon engages our sense of duty. Most folks will have little patience for emotional dawdling today, and it may be a necessary to give emotionality a rest and concentrate on other focuses such as work, discipline, and practical needs. The day starts off nicely – the Moon sextile Sun aspect brings out positive moods toward the late winter seasonal factors of this time. Things turn ugly by afternoon. Moon square Venus brings moods that will be challenged by the effort to show any affection, and not all flattery will be received well. The Moon goes void-of-course in Capricorn, too, and for the better part of the day and into the evening, our moods may drive us to perform, but with no incentive to work and no inclination to concentrate, not much is likely to get done. As the Moon enters Aquarius, innovative perspectives open our minds. Our moods will enter into a humanitarian kind of acceptance of all things past and present.

March 15th Thursday

Moon in Aquarius

	PDT	EDT
Moon conjunct Mars	7:26 PM	10:26 PM
Mars opposite Saturn begins (see March 22)		

Mood Watch: As the Moon wanes in Aquarius, our moods are sensing the ways in which large groups of people are being affected by the build up of celestial energies. Electrical, fiery, hot energy fascinates us. All of this is especially true as the Moon conjunct Mars aspect brings energized moods, and in some cases, incredulous force. A good sound explanation of life's great mysteries is difficult to find. The waning Aquarius Moon draws our attention to the need for logic, knowledge, and scientific wisdom. The Pisces Sun carries us through the final days of winter with the trepidation of storms, both internal and external. Our beliefs are always tested in the final throes of winter, particularly as the Moon wanes toward a Solar Eclipse (March 18).

March 16th Friday

Moon in Aquarius / Pisces

	PDT	EDT	
Moon sextile Jupiter	12:06 PM	3:06 PM	
Moon opposite Saturn	4:37 AM	7:37 AM	
Moon conjunct Neptune	7:19 AM	10:19 AM	
Jupiter trine Saturn	3:44 PM	6:44 PM	
Mercury sextile Pluto	4:35 PM	7:35 PM	
Venus trine Pluto	5:19 PM	8:19 PM	
Mercury sextile Venus	6:24 PM	9:24 PM	
Moon sextile Pluto	8:44 PM	11:44 PM	
Moon conjunct Mercury	8:57 PM	11:57 PM	
Moon sextile Venus goes v/c	9:02 PM	12:02 AM	(March 17)
Moon enters Pisces	10:31 PM	1:31 AM	(March 17)

Mood Watch: With a long list of lunar and planetary aspects at work today, this is not only a busy time for the shifts of our moods — it is also an important time for the shifting of events and the changing of the season. The Aquarius Moon will help to keep us mentally clear in order to handle so many mood shifts. Moon sextile Jupiter brings moods inspired by opportunity, generosity, and extravagance. Moon opposite Saturn brings moods that may be overwhelmed by responsibilities. Moon conjunct Neptune brings a stronger spiritual awareness and there is the general feeling of connectedness among people. Moon sextile Pluto brings moods inspired by the opportunities that are shaped by fate. Moon conjunct Mercury brings communicative moods and there will be a good level of responsiveness to the voice of reason and logic. This evening, Moon sextile Venus brings moods inspired by beauty and, at the same time, the Aquarius Moon will go void-of-course, creating moods that may be easily distracted by spontaneous or eccentric behavior. As the Moon enters Pisces tonight, our moods will enter into an instinctual phase, a place where we examine beliefs.

Jupiter trine Saturn (occurring February 11 – June 9) Good news! Economic conditions will be promising this late winter, and throughout the spring season. This time, the fruits of our labor will be rewarded with the enthusiasm and determination created by this most pleasant aspect. Jupiter and Saturn are the two social planets of our solar system. Jupiter represents joy, attainment, expansion, and the place where economic growth occurs. Saturn is the guard at the edge of time, and represents the work, discipline, timing, and responsibility that comes with prosperous growth. They have a natural relationship, as with each bountiful step of attainment there is always the restriction required to maintain it and the duty of labor necessary to keep it growing or expanding in value and quality. In June 2006, Jupiter was in the square position to Saturn, challenging our economic strengths and fiscal responsibilities. Now Jupiter is in the favorable trine position to Saturn, and this promising time of the pending spring season also brings the celestial promise of stable economic growth and well being. Jupiter is now in its native sign, Sagittarius, and Saturn is in the Sun-ruled sign, Leo. The favorable trine aspect brings harmonious strength to these two planets (both in fire signs,) boosting our economy with breakthroughs in enterprise and financial gifts, especially for the fire signs of the zodiac and for those who are interacting with them. This is a good time for business, and a good time to take positive steps towards the attainment of health, wealth, and happiness. Enjoy this boost of positive vibrations while you can: this aspect will reach its peak again this year on May 6, and will dissipate completely by June 9. Then for a final round this year, this aspect will begin occurring once again on December 29 and will reach another peak on January 21, 2008. By then, Jupiter will be in Capricorn and Saturn will be in Virgo, and the trine aspect of these two planets in the earth signs will bring bountiful and harmonious material wealth, as well as a wealth of material responsibility.

Mercury sextile Pluto (occurring February 26 – March 19) Communications and discussions are facilitated, with an opportunity to get your message across in negotiations with those in positions of power. Due to Mercury's retrograde phase (February 13 – March 7), this aspect reaches its peak today for the third time this year. It last occurred on February 28, while Mercury was retrograde. For more information on Mercury sextile Pluto, see January 31. This aspect will repeat three more times this year: September 24, October 26, and November 8.

65

Venus trine Pluto (occurring March 11 – 19) Venus in Aries is trine to Pluto in Sagittarius. Beauty can be found in all aspects of existence. Venus trine Pluto represents a love or fascination for the workings of fate and power. This aspect often allows a breakthrough to occur for those who are under stress from hardship. There is hope yet that we will acquire an appreciation for the not-so-glamorous aspects of existence. This is also an aspect that allows for adoration and loving energy to flow more easily between generations, despite all the differences that have separated us in these fast changing times. Due to the retrograde motion of Venus this year, this aspect will repeat three times: on July 8, August 15, and October 3, when Venus will be in Leo.

Mercury sextile Venus (occurring March 13 – April 12) Mercury in Aquarius sextile Venus in Aries brings opportunities for brilliant thoughts to be sparked over ardent love matters. This aspect will be helpful with regard to speaking up and communicating about our affections and our love for those things in life which give us pleasure. Mercury sextile Venus will repeat April 7, and by then, Mercury will be in Pisces and Venus will be in Taurus.

March 17th Saturday

Saint Patrick's Day
Moon in Pisces

	PDT	EDT	
Venus enters Taurus	3:02 PM	6:02 PM	
Moon conjunct Uranus	11:27 PM	2:27 AM	(March 18)
Mars sextile Jupiter begins (see March 23)			
Mars conjunct Neptune begins (see March 25)			

"I showed my appreciation of my native land in the usual Irish way by getting out of it as soon as I possibly could. " - George Bernard Shaw (1856 – 1950)

Mood Watch: Sensitivity levels are higher than usual with the waning Moon in Pisces. This is also a time when intuition becomes a particularly helpful tool for handling the ups and downs of our wild mood swings. Many folks are still reacting to the pile up of celestial activity which hit us yesterday, and a number of aspects will strike again throughout the coming week. The waning Pisces Moon can assist to keep us out of trouble if we use our intuition and listen to it very carefully. Beware: this may be an especially raucous Saint Patty's night with the Moon conjunct Uranus; moods will be crazy, chaotic, somewhat explosive, and unpredictable.

Venus enters Taurus (Venus in Taurus: March 17 – April 11) Venus in Taurus is the time of an extraordinary attraction to beauty. Here in Taurus, Venus is at home nurturing us with sensual pleasure and enhancing our appreciation of nature and earthly bounty, as well our as appreciation for quality and specialty craftsmanship. Venus in Taurus brings out aesthetic awareness, and places a greater emphasis on the love of having valuable items, wealth, and abundance. Venus attracts and draws, and Taurus represents material acquisition and attainment. Taurus people will be touched by the need for love and affection in their lives as Venus crosses over their natal Sun. Now is the time to acquire, polish, clean, and beautify things that give a sense of truly having something. To create beauty around oneself is to enhance one's sense of well-being. Beauty, of course, varies according to the eye of the beholder. Simple pleasures are the best – an effort to enjoy the beauties of life is not necessarily expensive.

March 18th Sunday
Moon in Pisces / Aries - NEW MOON in PISCES

Partial Solar Eclipse	PDT	EDT	
Mercury enters Pisces	2:36 AM	5:36 AM	
Moon square Jupiter	5:37 AM	8:37 AM	
Moon conjunct Sun	7:44 PM	10:44 PM	
Moon square Pluto goes v/c	9:00 PM	12:00 AM	(March 19)
Moon enters Aries	10:43 PM	1:43 AM	(March 19)

Mood Watch: We awaken to Moon square Jupiter bringing the feeling of being challenged by overabundant enthusiasm. **New Moon in Pisces** (Moon conjunct Sun) focuses our attention on the need to get in touch with our own beliefs and to inspire those beliefs with devotion and renewed faith. Tendencies towards escapism may be strong today, particularly for those who are unwilling to let go of the past. The New Moon in Pisces inspires a new spirit of outlook on our moods. This is a time of both emotional as well as spiritual purging. The spirit of what is now emerging and showing through our moods is a sense of renewed faith, in something divine and omnipotent. The world of magic exists in the melding mutable water of the Piscean expression. Crisp new psychic and intuitive inclinations lead to a spark of inspiration that carries us through the dwindling days of winter towards the renewed light of Spring Equinox. Let the intuitive and creative process begin! Let the spirit of renewed faith cleanse our beliefs. Tonight's Moon square Pluto brings the challenge of blocks between generations and, for a short while, the void-of-course Pisces Moon brings spacey moods. By late evening, the sprouting young Aries Moon, still very dark, inspires a youthful vigor to the mood.

A **Solar Eclipse in the sign of Pisces** brings an emphasis on controversies rooted in religion. This is particularly true since Uranus in Pisces (since March 2003) has been stirring up a revolutionary process in our belief systems. Eclipses are believed to threaten the lives and liberty of leaders and special figures in society. Every time there is a Solar Eclipse, there is always a Lunar Eclipse within two weeks — and it was just two weeks ago that one occurred. This Eclipse duo will have another Eclipse pair to follow at the opposite time of year, six months from now. Although this may not feel like a particularly easy time for starting anew, the Solar Eclipse touches our lives with a fluid and accepting kind of assertiveness to move through the greatest obstacles. Beware of the tendency for some people to lean towards substance abuse, depression, and emotional instability.

Mercury enters Pisces (Mercury in Pisces: March 18 – April 10) For the second time this year, Mercury enters the sign of Pisces. Mercury travels through Pisces for an extended period of time due to the retrograde period of Mercury from February 13 to March 7. For a recap of the story of Mercury's travels through Pisces, see February 2 when Mercury first entered this sign.

March 19th Monday

   Sun square Pluto   3:15 PM   6:15 PM

Mood Watch: There are no lunar aspects at work on this day of the newly waxing Aries Moon. The basic mood-setting for today focuses on the need to stand out and be in control of events. There is an eagerness about our moods as the Sun is on the brink of entering Aries. Today's moods will filled with determination and inspiration. Sometimes the Aries Moon causes too much inspiration, and the search for a good fight or release of raw aggression must come out. This may be a difficult time to ignore pushy aggressors; nonetheless, being aware of this behavior and attempting to avoid it by watching for the signs — before the oppressor gets out of hand — may well be in your favor today.

Sun square Pluto (occurring March 13 – 22) This aspect particularly affects Pisces and early Aries born people celebrating birthdays this month from March 13 – 22. For them, Pluto squaring their natal Sun brings disruptive changes and many challenges to overcome, such as the pain of loss and the severity of transformation. As well, Virgo people who are born at the exact opposite of this Pisces time of year must also change in order to progress through these necessary Pluto-inspired tests of transformation. These tests often involve dealing with illness and loss, irreparable damage, and dramatic life changes. December-born Sagittarians (Pluto conjunct natal Sun) and June-born Gemini people (Pluto opposite natal Sun) also know what these tests of Pluto are about, as Pluto continues to trace a slow moving path through the late degrees of Sagittarius. Trying to hold onto the regrets and the pain of the past will only bring greater destruction later. This is the time to persevere through the obstacles of hardship. Yet, the hardships that are taking place now will resurface in time, so do take note of the struggles going on in the life of Pisces, Virgo, Gemini, and Sagittarius people affected by Pluto's tests. Realize this trend will be repeated, and so necessitates finding methods of release and attitude changes in order to survive the anxiety and stress. Take it one day at a time and do not let fear and worry rule this condition. Know that you are not alone in facing these challenges. Move steadily through the required transformation, as stagnation and fear will only bring extended suffering. This aspect will repeat again on September 19, when the Sun will be in Virgo, affecting the Virgo birthday people of that time.

ARIES

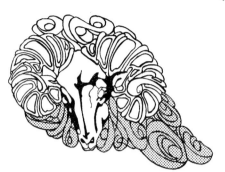

Key Phrase: "I AM"

Cardinal Fire Sign

Symbol: The Ram

March 20th through April 19th

March 20th Tuesday

Vernal Equinox

Moon in Aries / Taurus	PDT	EDT	
Moon sextile Mars	1:34 AM	4:34 AM	
Moon trine Saturn	4:44 AM	7:44 AM	
Moon trine Jupiter	5:21 AM	8:21 AM	
Moon sextile Neptune	7:50 AM	10:50 AM	
Sun enters Aries	5:09 PM	8:09 PM	
Moon trine Pluto goes v/c	8:34 PM	11:34 PM	
Moon enters Taurus	10:16 PM	1:16 AM	(March 21)

Mood Watch: Good vibes come with this Equinox day. In our overnight dreams, Moon sextile Mars brings inspiration through swift and intrepid action. Moon trine Saturn brings moods in harmony with disciplines and responsibilities. Moon trine Jupiter brings joyous generosity and optimism. Also on this busy morning of lunar aspects, Moon sextile Neptune brings moods that will be inspired by spiritual energies. Later, after the Sun has entered Aries this evening, Moon trine Pluto brings moods in harmony with matters of fate. The Aries Moon goes void-of-course for a couple of hours and our moods may be easily distracted by aggressive or domineering energies. As the Moon enters Taurus, our moods enter into the need for practicality and beauty, and, just as important – the need for comfort, too.

Sun enters Aries (Sun in Aries: March 20 – April 20) Today, the event classically called **Vernal Equinox**, also known as Spring Equinox, marks the start of a new season, and the beginning of the zodiac. Today the daylight hours are equal in length to the hours of the night. Spring arrives when the earth is tilted so that the Sun is directly over the equator. In the northern parts of the world, the first day of spring is on or about March 20. In the northern hemisphere we are on the side of the Equinox that returns toward the light, as opposed to Autumnal Equinox when the Sun enters Libra, the opposite of Aries. With Daylight Savings Time already underway, since March 11, we now celebrate the continued lengthening of the days.

Happy Birthday Aries! The Sun in Aries inspires courageous and bold new beginnings, as well as instilling confidence and forcefulness. Many Aries folks have an inherent desire to not only survive, but to exceed, and to make a lasting impression. Aries is the cardinal fire sign that doesn't give up easily. Arians are known for beginning projects with a pioneering zeal. However, they are also infamous for suddenly leaping into a new venture, leaving someone else to complete their original endeavor. Some Aries folks love to start up businesses, but continue into other ventures once the business has been established and requires the dull monotony of upkeep and maintenance. Aries does like to make things happen! Aries' character style expresses quality of leadership in the fiery realm of the cardinal signs, and is ruled by the active and vital planet, Mars. Aries boasts of being the first, and works earnestly to defy all who would mock, criticize, or misunderstand their drive to reach a certain self-appointed plateau of excellence. There is a strong sense of devotion to the self and the need to excel in the Arian's chosen field. The Mars ruled Aries person is loaded with fervor and a relentless fortitude that often, at best, motivates and inspires, or, at worst, repels and puts off others around them. Sun in Aries serves as a good time to initiate new projects and apply diligence with inspired ability. The youthful vigor that is characteristic of Arians is reflected in the season, and this springlike sprouting and growth is inspiration for us all.

March 21st Wednesday

Moon in Taurus	PDT	EDT	
Moon sextile Mercury	2:33 AM	5:33 AM	
Moon conjunct Venus	5:12 AM	8:12 AM	
Moon sextile Uranus	11:27 PM	2:27 AM	(March 22)

Mood Watch: The first full day of the Sun in Aries is upon us. The newly waxing Moon in Taurus fixes our moods on the need to stay grounded and practical. Many of us will have our eyes fixed on new things we need or want to have in our life. For that very reason, this is an excellent time to indulge in some early spring cleaning. Overnight, Moon sextile Mercury brings intellectually stimulating dreams. Moon conjunct Venus brings affectionate morning moods and many will be attracted to finding beauty. Later tonight, Moon sextile Uranus ends the day with radical notions, and our moods will be inspired by the pursuit of freedom.

March 22nd Thursday

Moon in Taurus / Gemini	PDT	EDT	
Moon square Mars	4:16 AM	7:16 AM	
Moon square Saturn	4:44 AM	7:44 AM	
Moon square Neptune goes v/c	8:13 AM	11:13 AM	
Mars opposite Saturn	12:35 PM	3:35 PM	
Moon enters Gemini	11:07 PM	2:07 AM	(March 23)

Mood Watch: Early on this Taurus Moon spring morning, our moods may be challenged by the irresistible need to become motivated during Moon square Mars. Moon square Saturn compounds the situation as the challenge of our moods demands greater work to reach deadlines and get around our limitations. Also this morning, the Taurus Moon goes void-of-course just as Moon square Neptune challenges our moods with regard to inactivity and passiveness. For the rest of the day and evening, nothing terribly progressive occurs — just a lot of mundane work that seems to be going nowhere, or isn't getting done. There may be delays due to laziness or drug related factors. For some, this time of "spring break" leads them to think of little else, and good service may be hard to find. By the time the Moon enters Gemini, our moods enter into the need to communicate intelligently and to set our minds on a whole new strategy for tomorrow's work. ♈

Mars opposite Saturn (occurring March 15 – 26) Mars opposite Saturn always makes us aware of the timeliness of our actions and the importance of acting in a timely manner, such as doing something about a problem before it's too late. Medical emergencies often crop up with this type of aspect. There will also be an awareness of the dynamic polarity between offensive and defensive forces. For opposing forces in battle, this aspect often brings fiery and sometimes tragic endings. Mars in Aquarius is opposing the retrograde Saturn in Leo. Saturn has been retrograde since December 5, 2006 and will go direct on April 19 this year. Saturn is the restrictive discipline behind every effort to contain, guard, and hold on to what matters to us. Mars in Aquarius brings technologically advanced force which may seem to oppose or overwhelm family structure, individuation, and personal achievement (Saturn in Leo). Saturn in Leo forces us individually to face our sense of security, particularly with regard to matters concerning personal skills and levels of confidence. Be careful and pay attention to those aspects of life that hold active potential for accidents. The popular old adage of "look before you leap" is a good meditation to apply during this crucial time of Mars opposite Saturn.

March 23rd Friday

Moon in Gemini	PDT	EDT
Moon sextile Sun	3:08 AM	6:08 AM
Moon square Mercury	7:22 AM	10:22 AM
Mars sextile Jupiter	9:02 AM	12:02 PM

Mood Watch: Overnight, Moon sextile Sun brings good vibrations. In the morning, Moon square Mercury makes it difficult for us to receive information or to further investigate our curiosities. The buzz and chatter of the new spring season awakens our thoughts. The conversation in which we have chosen to engage is thought provoking and sets the tone for how we will choose to make the lifestyle shift from one season to the next. Gemini says "I think" and, despite the urgent push of the Aries season to get out there and get a taste of life, our moods may determine that this is the time to step back, observe, and think about matters for awhile.

Mars sextile Jupiter (occurring March 17 – 26) Mars in Aquarius is sextile Jupiter in Sagittarius. Ingenious and knowledgeable actions, when taken, have the opportunity to go extraordinarily far and be very successful in the long run. Those who act on specific urges and impulses to achieve their heart's desire are more likely to make a breakthrough during this aspect. This is a time to make true efforts to promote career skills or to enhance a career move. Remember – action is required; mere good intentions will get you nothing while this aspect is in full force. This is a good time to go adventuring and exploring while Mars sextile Jupiter promotes opportunities, but be careful too. Mars is also opposite to Saturn (see yesterday,) and there is a good chance that activities may be overwhelming or risky – as well as successful – but isn't that usually the way?

March 24th Saturday

Moon in Gemini

	PDT	EDT
Moon square Uranus	1:50 AM	4:50 AM
Moon sextile Saturn	7:04 AM	10:04 AM
Moon opposite Jupiter	8:25 AM	11:25 AM
Moon trine Mars	9:43 AM	12:43 PM
Moon trine Neptune	11:03 AM	2:03 PM

Mood Watch: Overnight, Moon square Uranus brings explosive nightmares. The Gemini Moon gives us the feeling that there will be much to think about today. We will be more inclined to communicate what's been on our minds, as well as being more interested in setting the facts and records straight. Moon sextile Saturn kicks off the morning with a sense of duty, and we will be inspired by our work to get a handle on matters. Moon opposite Jupiter gives us the sense that we could be easily overwhelmed by overextending ourselves, or by indulging in costly affairs too greatly. It's okay to indulge a bit as Moon trine Mars indicates that this will be an easy time to rustle up some energy and to be very active. Moon trine Neptune brings harmonious spiritual energies. The upbeat side of the Gemini Moon makes this a good time to enjoy a party.

March 25th Sunday

Moon in Gemini / Cancer - FIRST QUARTER MOON in CANCER

	PDT	EDT
Moon opposite Pluto goes v/c	12:58 AM	3:58 AM
Moon enters Cancer	2:50 AM	5:50 AM
Mars conjunct Neptune	10:40 AM	1:40 PM
Moon square Sun	11:17 AM	2:17 PM
Moon trine Mercury	4:25 PM	7:25 PM
Moon sextile Venus	8:42 PM	11:42 PM

Mood Watch: Overnight, the waxing Gemini Moon opposes Pluto and, at the same time, the Moon goes void-of-course. Our dreams may be overwhelmed by decadence and troubling dual perspectives. The Moon enters Cancer and before most North Americans awaken, our moods are touched by a keen emotional awareness. **First Quarter Moon in Cancer** (Moon square Sun) occurs early in the day and, whatever is going on at this time, the emotional current tends to be magnified. Treating ourselves and others in a nurturing way becomes the key to enhancing or cleansing our emotional perspective. Be careful not to push the buttons of sensitive people; use words wisely while considering the feelings of yourself and others. This is a good time to share confessions as Moon trine Mercury brings moods in harmony with communications. Tonight, Moon sextile Venus brings the inspiration of love and affection.

Mars conjunct Neptune (occurring March 17 – 29) Mars, the planet of activity and action, is conjunct Neptune, the planet of mysticism and spiritual bounty. This aspect generally brings action to a fondness for the arts, and magnifies generosity, spiritual activity, and enthusiasm. There is mysticism, romance, and adventure in the air with this conjunction, which will also add a special and very spiritual quality to the activities of spring. Mars comes on very strong, directing the forces of our actions, while Neptune evokes a deeper, more dramatic spiritual awareness. This is a time to be especially careful not to overindulge in strong beverages, rich fatty foods, drugs, chemicals, anesthetics, etc. It's an important time to ensure one has the proper nutrients. Mars conjunct Neptune can also create busy activity in temples, churches or any kind of spiritual retreat. On the downside, there may be a militant flare of energy brewing in the sanctuaries of holy places. However, on a more positive note, it is an active time for folks on spiritual quests as well as artists, musicians, choreographers and designers. Mars conjunct Neptune in Aquarius activates an openness to rise above mundane concerns with heightened awareness and newly inspired spiritual strength.

March 26th Monday

Moon in Cancer

	PDT	EDT
Moon trine Uranus goes v/c	7:37 AM	10:37 AM

Mood Watch: This morning brings rebellious moods as Moon trine Uranus ignites a strong urge for freedom from oppression. At this point the Moon also goes void-of-course and remains so throughout the rest of the day and night. Delays, setbacks, and minor contingencies are likely to be the result of moody distractions and self-indulgences. Being truthful about what is occurring on an emotional level allows expression of the heart to take its rightful place. In troubling matters, be sure to embrace a noble and worthy depth of feeling. For example, empower and create feelings of self respect to fully replace destructive or useless feelings such as self pity. Positive efforts bring positive results. For the most part this will be a somewhat moody Monday.

March 27th Tuesday

Moon in Cancer / Leo

	PDT	EDT	
Moon enters Leo	10:05 AM	1:05 PM	
Moon trine Sun	11:54 PM	2:54 AM	(March 28)
Venus sextile Uranus begins (see March 31)			
Mercury conjunct Uranus begins (see April 1)			

Mood Watch: The lingering remains of a void-of-course Cancer Moon cloud our moods at times throughout the early part of the day. It may be difficult at first to determine which way our moods are headed. After a while it won't matter — the Moon will enter Leo and our moods will enter into a playful phase. Moon trine Sun brings moods in harmony with the season. Fiery, ambitious and creative energy abounds with the Sun and Moon both in fire signs. The waxing Leo Moon places an emphasis on family and friends, as well as personal hobbies and needs.

March 28th Wednesday

Moon in Leo

	PDT	EDT	
Moon square Venus	11:07 AM	2:07 PM	
Moon conjunct Saturn	9:56 PM	12:56 AM	(March 29)
Venus square Saturn begins (see April 2)			

Mood Watch: As a general rule, the Leo Moon brings upbeat, entertaining, and delightful moods. However, Moon square Venus may bring moods that are challenged by our attempts to seek beauty or love. Although the results of our affections may be less than what we were hoping for, the effort to appease our need for comfort, beauty, and harmony will be worth it. The Leo Moon energies demand a good performance and some showmanship. Tonight, Moon conjunct Saturn brings moods that will be inclined towards discipline and responsibility, and will appeal to our protective instincts.

March 29th Thursday

Moon in Leo / Virgo	PDT	EDT
Moon trine Jupiter	12:07 AM	3:07 AM
Moon opposite Neptune	3:04 AM	6:04 AM
Moon opposite Mars	8:46 AM	11:46 AM
Moon trine Pluto goes v/c	6:25 PM	9:25 PM
Moon enters Virgo	8:28 PM	11:28 PM

Mood Watch: Overnight, Moon trine Jupiter brings dreams in harmony with wealth and wellbeing. Moon opposite Neptune brings a special awareness of spiritual needs. This morning, Moon opposite Mars motivates us and brings the acute awareness of martial forces and masculine energies. Tonight, Moon trine Pluto brings moods that will be in harmony with the influences of superpowers, and with matters of fate. The Leo Moon also goes void-of-course for a couple of hours tonight, and our moods will be distracted by laziness and extravagance. A sensible mood occurs as the Moon enters Virgo, and our moods enter into a health-conscious phase. Whether we pay attention to the signs of our bodies or not, they are there.

March 30th Friday

Moon in Virgo
Mercury square Jupiter begins (see April 4)
Venus square Neptune begins (see April 4)
Mars sextile Pluto begins (see April 4)

Mood Watch: Waxing Moon in Virgo emphasizes the need for purity and perfection. This quality of mood is also inclined to meticulous thought and deep contemplation. Virgo Moon is a superb time to clean and purify our surroundings, and to organize, simplify, and weed out superfluous emotional baggage. Youthful, innocent, virginal purity and beauty stand out and attract many folks today during this early stage of spring season. Virgo Moon is an excellent time to get in touch with personal surroundings and physical health, and to make some effort to improve and preserve these things.

March 31st Saturday

Moon in Virgo	PDT	EDT
Moon opposite Mercury	12:56 AM	3:56 AM
Venus sextile Uranus	1:23 AM	4:23 AM
Moon opposite Uranus	4:43 AM	7:43 AM
Moon trine Venus	5:04 AM	8:04 AM
Moon square Jupiter	11:59 AM	2:59 PM
Pluto goes retrograde	3:47 PM	6:47 PM

Mood Watch: Overnight, Moon opposite Mercury brings overwhelming dreams, perhaps loaded with too much information. Moon opposite Uranus brings moods

that may seem overwhelmed by chaotic energies. It's no wonder chaos seems difficult — the waxing Virgo Moon impresses our moods with the need to get things
just right, to get our accounting in order and to get organized wherever necessary.
Love conquers all, however, and the energy of the morning is saved by the soothing
affects of Moon trine Venus, bringing harmony, beauty, and affection. Midday
brings Moon square Jupiter, and our moods may be challenged by inflation and the
act of overspending. Virgo Moon keeps us questioning and striving for perfection.

Venus sextile Uranus (occurring March 27 – April 1) Venus in Taurus is sextile
to Uranus in Pisces. There is an opportunity for the rebellious and aesthetically
challenging aspects of the arts to break through and be known. There is also an
opportunity here for people in love relationships to undergo an eccentric or unusual
and yet very memorable experience. This is the time to work out frustrations with
loved ones, and to reconcile differences by applying love and accepting variation
in your love. Try to give freedom and slack to loved ones without feeling oppressed
in the process. Now is the time to let go of false hopes and get back in touch with a
sense of personal freedom and self-reliance. Trust, in turn, that everything struc-
turing your love relationship up to this point is as strong as the foundation of love
itself. Stand by those who inspire you.

Pluto goes retrograde (Pluto retrograde: March 31 – September 7) Processes
governed by Pluto take the longest time to go through since, from our perspective, Pluto appears to move the slowest of all the planets because it's the furthest
away from us. Pluto goes retrograde today and when it resumes a forward moving
course late this summer, it will have traveled only a few degrees in the sky, which
is average for a Pluto retrograde period. This means the types of hardships that have
been created and brought to our attention in the past five months must be addressed
all over again, and that we must acknowledge the evolution of humankind's current
condition in order to survive the changes that are occurring on Earth.

Pluto deals with the changes that occur in attitude according to the overall group
consciousness of each of the generations. Each generation has its own insight as to
what hardship represents. This is a time to make life better by consciously transforming fear into determination and despair into belief in oneself, no matter what
condition of fate surrounds you. The destructive habits, prejudices, sufferings and
haunts of previous generations must be acknowledged and addressed, and of course
altered to enable us to tackle the world of the future. We will all face greater challenges and tests of epic proportions, and outdated concerns must be dealt with so
that we may find solutions to the new problems in front of us.

With Pluto's changes we must face tragedies, diseases, losses, shattered dreams,
and altered or unexpected doses of reality. Pluto retrograde forces us to look within;
this is a good time to confirm our greatest strengths by directing abusive patterns
into constructive and useful disciplines which will reshape and bring hope to the
emerging outlook on life.

Pluto represents the forces of power and control, which are always in a state of
flux due to our mortal tango with fate. Our old concepts and memories of how life
once was, or is supposed to be, are dying with the times. Reality and normality
are illusions that Pluto sweeps away as its traversal of Sagittarius opens up global

awareness and increases our foresight of world-wide struggles. There are aspects of life that are not meant to be controlled, but how we react to the shifts of this time is something we do control. Pluto retrograde is a time of re-addressing universal human problems that take decades to fix.

April 1st Sunday
Palm Sunday / April Fool's Day

Moon in Virgo / Libra	PDT	EDT
Moon square Pluto goes v/c	6:39 AM	9:39 AM
Moon enters Libra	8:44 AM	11:44 AM
Mercury conjunct Uranus	11:31 AM	2:31 PM

" The cure for boredom is curiosity. There is no cure for curiosity. "
– Dorothy Parker 1893 - 1967

Mood Watch: This morning, Moon square Pluto brings moods challenged by their own intensity. The Virgo Moon goes void-of-course for a couple of hours, bringing delays and distractions due to doubt or uncertainty. As the Moon enters Libra, the Full Moon Eve energy begins to captivate us. Libra Moon activities emphasize the need for sound logic and clear objectives. There may be a need to research or to investigate the feasibility of our plans. There is also a need for us to understand the current laws and rules of the situations we face. Libra Moon requires balanced thinking and acting, as well as benevolent and civilized approaches to creating harmony and camaraderie in the midst of carrying out our objectives. This task may be tricky, or at least entertaining, while Mercury is conjunct Uranus (see below) but as long as matters are conducted amicably, decisions and adjustments can be made successfully. Leadership is emphasized on this Libra Moon day, and true leaders must be patient as well as convincing. Certainly no one can do absolutely everything alone, for without the corroboration of others, even the decisions of the most assertive leaders have no staying power.

Happy **April Fool's Day**, also known as *All Fools' Day*. This is a holiday of uncertain origin, but just about everybody knows it as the day for practical joking. Before the adoption of the Gregorian calendar in 1564, April 1st was observed as New Year's Day by many cultures from the Roman to the Hindu. This holiday is considered to be related to the festival of the Vernal Equinox, when the Sun enters Aries, on or about March 20th. The English gave April Fool's Day its first widespread celebration during the 18th century, where it quickly spread to the American colonies. Remember the classic North American school prank of anonymously taping a sign on the back of a fellow classmate? The sign customarily reads something degrading such as: "Kick Me," or "April Fool." The French call April 1st *Poisson d'Avril,* (April Fish). French children tape a picture of a fish on the back of their schoolmates, crying "Poisson d'Avril," when the prank is discovered. Our Full Libra Moon moods allow us to take simple pranks in stride. If something fishy is occurring around you, remember to keep the jokes in perspective, and to watch the backs of those you care about.

Mercury conjunct Uranus (occurring March 27 – April 3) Mercury and Uranus are conjunct in Pisces giving birth to radical, bright, inspired and intuitive ideas. This may raise some very interesting and unusual questions about what we choose to believe in. Consciousness raising talk is prevalent. Mercury conjunct Uranus magnifies the volume of shocking or question-raising news, and stirs the minds and mouths of rebels and non-conformists who are inspired to speak out. Everyone is crying for some kind of freedom!

April 2nd Monday
FULL MOON in LIBRA

	PDT	EDT	
Venus square Saturn	12:02 AM	3:02 AM	
Moon opposite Sun	10:16 AM	1:16 PM	
Moon sextile Saturn	10:05 PM	1:05 AM	(April 3)
Sun trine Saturn begins (see April 8)			

Mood Watch: **Full Moon in Libra** (Moon opposite Sun) brings events that revolve around such things as law, the justice system, friends, and marital partners. Relationships are a balancing act. Friends will share their strengths as well as their weaknesses. Troubled times can strengthen even the weakest links in friendship. Refuse to contribute to the weakness of a friend; nurture friendship with patience, understanding, and encouragement. Use this full Libra Moon energy to empower your relationships. Diplomacy, peace and goodwill can be achieved among loved ones, but a definite effort is required. Later, Moon sextile Saturn brings serious and determined moods.

Venus square Saturn (occurring March 28 – April 4) Venus in Taurus is square to Saturn in Leo. It may be difficult to engage in romance, as it might seem that something is always getting in the way. Perhaps it is best not to get bent out of shape over some people's need to create restrictions in order to protect their own sense of security while love related troubles are being worked out. No matter how much one prioritizes their focuses of love, it is still likely to be misinterpreted on some level during Venus square Saturn. This is no time to take love dramas too seriously. The basic expression of love will flow more easily without the limitations of expectations or demands, though this advice may not work so well when it comes to making excuses. Give it your best and keep singing the praises of love, but expect some trouble nonetheless. Perseverance and patience are advisable, as Venus is also square to Neptune (see April 4,) creating spiritual complications in love matters. True love overcomes all obstacles.

April 3rd Tuesday
Passover
Moon in Libra / Scorpio

	PDT	EDT	
Moon sextile Jupiter	12:51 AM	3:51 AM	
Moon trine Neptune	4:01 AM	7:01 AM	
Moon trine Mars	6:00 PM	9:00 PM	
Moon sextile Pluto goes v/c	7:31 PM	10:31 PM	
Moon enters Scorpio	9:37 PM	12:37 AM	(April 4)
Sun trine Jupiter begins (see April 9)			

Mood Watch: Overnight, while most folks are dreaming, Moon sextile Jupiter brings moods which are hopeful and optimistic. Moon trine Neptune brings tranquil and passive energy. The Libra Moon emphasizes harmony in relationships, and today is a good day to work on all kinds of relationships. This evening, Moon trine Mars brings moods inspired by action. Moon sextile Pluto brings Moods that are intensi-fied by powerful situations, and by diversity. At this point the Libra Moon will be void-of-course, bringing indecisive moods. Finally, as the Moon enters Scorpio, a much more passionate perspective of life comes along.

April 4th Wednesday

Moon in Scorpio	PDT	EDT
Mercury square Jupiter	12:18 AM	3:18 AM
Venus square Neptune	11:17 AM	2:17 PM
Mars sextile Pluto	5:23 PM	8:23 PM

Mood Watch: Since yesterday, we have been going through a post-full moon period, also known as *Waning Gibbous*. This is a time of recovery from, and reflec-tion upon, the energies that built up to the full Moon. The *Waxing Gibbous* -- just before the moon is full -- represents the anticipation of energy build-up. After the luminous peak of the Moon's full energy, there is a certain amount of relief -- and sometimes grief -- that comes to us during the Waning Gibbous Moon of Scorpio. Intense tiredness or the strife of being confronted by mundane yet annoying distur-bances is sometimes characteristic of this moon. Be cautious and clear.

Mercury square Jupiter (occurring March 30 – April 6) During this aspect it may be best to hold off on a job request, asking for a raise, or signing any binding contracts concerning long term investment and payment schedules. This may be an especially difficult time to communicate during travels, and it may be best to double check travel schedules. This aspect has a tendency to create expensive mis-understandings when it comes to large scale investments. It may also be a tough time for sports coaches to communicate effectively. With Mercury now in Pisces square to Jupiter in Sagittarius, it may be difficult to raise money for charities – particularly with regard to endowments for the arts. Dig harder and investigate more thoroughly the details associated with long term investments. This aspect will repeat on August 24, when Mercury will be in Virgo.

Venus square Neptune (occurring March 30 – April 7) Venus in Taurus is square to Neptune in Aquarius. Earthy pleasures, love, and expressions of beauty and femininity run up against the obstacles represented by the higher, more refined goddess image that humanity expects. A conflict of beliefs about womanhood is common with this aspect, and sometimes women, artists, and very attractive people are placed on high pedestals. Despite this, the human element usually leads them to certain error and they suffer great delusions. It is here that beauty suffers a spiritual conflict. The expectation and conditioning of others has created a false image of beauty, and the person on whom it is imposed is likely to be suffocated by the beliefs of others. With Venus square to Neptune, what we want is challenged by what we know is best for us. Consequently, it may be difficult for some people to make a personal connection with spiritual teachings. Beliefs concerning love matters may be tested. Despite the conflicts, this is a time to rise to the challenge of believing in love and loving your own choice of spiritual path. As for the art of love, the influences of this aspect are not as harsh for those who understand that true beauty is found in the core of feminine wisdom, and that magnetic attraction goes beyond temporal beauty. This aspect will repeat again on December 22, when

Venus will be in Scorpio.

Mars sextile Pluto (occurring March 30 – April 7) Mars, the planet of action is in a favorable position to Pluto, the planet of the generations. This is a superb time to take up activities with people of a different culture, or with someone who is of a different level of maturity or experience. This is also potentially a good time to reconcile differences. Those who are not in accordance with others at this time are likely to stand out – quite obviously. This may be a beneficial aspect for successfully recuperating from an illness. Mars represents the masculine push of our personal lives, the area where we activate our will, strength, and vitality; this brings opportunity, optimism, and the added boost to face otherwise tense situations and predicaments. The activities of Mars sextile Pluto will teach us about hardships and what we can learn from other generations. Some will make breakthroughs during this time. Some may choose to be more forgiving of the destructive behaviors of previous generations. All around, tender care is advised in your efforts to create peace.

April 5th Thursday

Moon in Scorpio	PDT	EDT
Moon trine Uranus	6:44 AM	9:44 AM
Moon square Saturn	10:38 AM	1:38 PM
Moon square Neptune	4:46 PM	7:46 PM
Jupiter goes retrograde	6:24 PM	9:24 PM
Moon trine Mercury goes v/c	6:44 PM	9:44 PM

Mood Watch: The Scorpio Moon of spring is rich and vital — just bursting with raw, untamed energy. Moon trine Uranus brings moods inspired by rebellion. Moon square Saturn adds a feeling of being restricted. Later, Moon square Neptune brings moods challenged by passiveness and resignation. Moon trine Mercury makes it easy for us to talk, and our moods will be inclined to give explanations. Tonight, Moon opposite Venus brings obsessive moods with regard to loved ones. The waning Scorpio Moon also goes void-of-course; beware of the dangers of sexual offenses, violence, and theft.

Jupiter goes retrograde (Jupiter retrograde: April 5 – August 6) The planet of expansion and prosperity now begins to recede back through the degrees of the zodiac today through August 6. The planet Jupiter itself does not go backwards; it is only the apparent shift in our orbital position to Jupiter that makes it appear this way. Most planets orbiting around the Sun eventually go into a retrograde pattern from our geocentric view of planetary movement. Jupiter in Sagittarius brings prosperity and expansion to areas of life such as philosophy, travel, and sports. This is a time when marketing strategies often employ the themes of global trade and investments, and space exploration. Jupiter retrograde is not the best time for the growth of large scale funds and investments, but it is a good time to meditate, and to observe carefully, what truly makes us happy. A clearer sense of growth will occur through internal processing, and through personal skill development. It is an important time to apply wisdom and caution in this area of our lives, and in our livelihood, so that we may see future growth. While Jupiter is retrograde through Sagittarius this spring and summer, the economy may appear to be receding or to be progressing slowly at times, while unpredictable or volatile market trends may occur.

April 6th Friday

Good Friday

Moon in Scorpio / Sagittarius

	PDT	EDT	
Mars enters Pisces	1:50 AM	4:50 AM	
Moon enters Sagittarius	9:58 AM	12:58 PM	
Moon square Mars	10:31 AM	1:31 PM	
Mercury square Pluto begins (see April 10)			

Mood Watch: Throughout morning, the waning Moon in Scorpio is void-of-course. This is a good time to be cautious, observant, and to stay keenly aware of the dangers in the world. As the Moon enters Sagittarius, our moods enter into a time of optimism and adventurousness. The waning Sagittarius Moon also keeps us philosophical about matters, particularly in an introspective way. Moon square Mars challenges our moods with offensive and defensive forces. This is a good time to beware of the possibility for angry or turbulent responses in our moods. Overall, it's a Good Friday.

Mars enters Pisces (Mars in Pisces: April 6 – May 15) Mars represents the heated energy in our lives. Force, vitality, energy, and action are influenced by Mars. While Mars traverses Pisces, much activity is taking place with regard to music and the arts, not to mention some heated action concerning the politics of our spiritual and religious beliefs. As Mars crosses over their natal Sun during the next several weeks, Piscean people will feel lots of hot and busy energy entering their realm. The nature of Pisces is fluid, passive, and dreamy – this is the spiritual realm of the zodiac. Mars in Pisces opens the gates to active visions and dreams. Intuitive strength is realized. This is a time to activate our creativity, and to work out hot feelings, such as anger, in an artful and healthy manner. Mars is also the famed god of war, reminding us to be especially cautious given the fact that hatred, violence, aggression and strife are often touching on the pulse of our belief structures (Pisces).

April 7th Saturday

Moon in Sagittarius

	PDT	EDT	
Mercury sextile Venus	9:11 AM	12:11 PM	
Moon square Uranus	6:34 PM	9:34 PM	
Moon trine Sun	9:22 PM	12:22 AM	(April 8)
Moon trine Saturn	9:59 PM	12:59 AM	(April 8)
Sun sextile Neptune begins (see April 11)			
Venus square Mars begins (see April 22)			

Mood Watch: Sun and Moon both being in fire signs brings a very active and creative time. From Greek mythology, the centaur is the symbol of Sagittarius. Centaurs are a race of creatures that are half human and half horse. They are famous in children's books for being star-gazers, foretellers of the future, and they are also considered to be benevolent and wise, loyal to the very end. Throughout the course of the day, our moods are touched by the need to look ahead and to apply the wisdom and moral self-discipline to overcome the troublesome limitations of a treacherous and uncertain new century. Even when life's continuing difficulties seem insurmountable, the wisdom of the centaur reminds us to hold an optimistic outlook, no matter what. This evening's Moon square Uranus brings moods challenged by chaos. Moon trine Sun brings peace to our moods, while the Moon trine Saturn brings harmony to our disciplines and work efforts.

Mercury sextile Venus (occurring March 13 – April 12) Mercury is currently in Pisces, while Venus is in Taurus. This brings imaginative and creative communications with regard to beautiful and sensual pleasures. Mercury sextile Venus teaches us of the necessity to speak out about our love needs, and focuses discussion on the things to which we are attached and which we treasure. This is an opportunistic and beneficial time to sing your praises of love! This aspect last occurred on March 16, and it will repeat on September 17 and October 16.

April 8th Sunday

Easter / Holy Day of Thelema (Nuit)
Moon in Sagittarius / Capricorn   PDT   EDT

	PDT	EDT
Moon conjunct Jupiter	12:53 AM	3:53 AM
Moon sextile Neptune	4:09 AM	7:09 AM
Sun trine Saturn	4:57 AM	7:57 AM
Moon square Mercury	2:15 PM	5:15 PM
Moon conjunct Pluto goes v/c	6:36 PM	9:36 PM
Moon enters Capricorn	8:37 PM	11:37 PM

" Every man and every woman is a star. "   - LIBER AL vel LEGIS, 1904

Mood Watch: Overnight, Moon conjunct Jupiter brings blessed joy. Moon sextile Neptune brings tranquil morning moods. This afternoon, Moon square Mercury brings moods challenged by communications. This evening, Moon conjunct Pluto brings intense moods, and the waning Sagittarius Moon also goes void-of-course. For a couple of hours, our moods will be distracted by detours, or by the sense of feeling lost. As the Moon enters Capricorn, our moods will be much more determined, and fixed on success.

Sun trine Saturn (occurring April 2 – 11) This aspect particularly affects Aries people celebrating birthdays April 2 – 11 this year. This is a positive time for these Aries folks to get a handle on their lives, and it may be easier for them to take on the responsibilities of life with fewer complications and less difficulty in the year to come. These birthday folks may notice more acceptable forms of control, responsibility and work occurring in their lives. Now is your time (birthday people) to successfully work on putting some structure into your life; the kind of structure you've needed and wanted awaits you in the coming year. It is possible that time (Saturn) is on your side to make that move you've been thinking about. This aspect will repeat this year on December 30, when the Sun will be in Capricorn and Saturn will be in Virgo, affecting the birthday Capricorns of that time.

April 9th Monday

Holy Day of Thelema (Hadit)
Moon in Capricorn

	PDT	EDT
Moon sextile Mars	12:58 AM	3:58 AM
Sun trine Jupiter	5:08 PM	8:08 PM

" Let the rituals be rightly performed with joy & beauty ! " - LIBER AL vel LEGIS, 1904

Mood Watch: The feeling of importance is hatching – springtime is here! The waning Capricorn Moon sextile Mars brings energetic dreams where attitudes are headstrong and triumphant. The Capricorn Moon gives some folks the feeling they could create or crush a whole universe, while the courageous days of Aries lead us fearlessly onward. Capricorn Moon keeps us on the straight and narrow. A determined world of doers sets a busy, but steady, pace. This opening weekday is a good one to take charge, and to get the week rolling along progressively.

Sun trine Jupiter (occurring April 3 – 12) This aspect is bringing those Aries people celebrating a birthday from April 3 – 12 to a favorable natal solar position with relation to Jupiter. This represents a time of gifts and expansion for these birthday folks and there are good times ahead for them in the coming year. Despite Jupiter's retrograde pattern (since April 5,) this is a grace period for them and opportunity and fortune will shine for a time. This aspect will bring a better sense of what it means to expand and attain one's personal desire. Be sure to take the time right now (Aries birthday people) to enjoy and appreciate life. This is always true for everyone and particularly relevant for those who are being given the gifts of opportunity this aspect often brings. This aspect will repeat on August 2, affecting the Leo birthday people of that time.

April 10th Tuesday

Holy Day of Thelema (Ra-Hoor-Khuit)
LAST QUARTER MOON in CAPRICORN

	PDT	EDT
Mercury square Pluto	12:26 AM	3:26 AM
Moon sextile Uranus	3:59 AM	6:59 AM
Moon square Sun	11:05 AM	2:05 PM
Mercury enters Aries	4:08 PM	7:08 PM

" There is success ! " - LIBER AL vel LEGIS, 1904

Mood Watch: The day kicks off with Moon sextile Uranus, bringing moods prone to disorder or recklessness. **Last Quarter Moon in Capricorn** (Moon square Sun) is here. This Moon emphasizes issues of control – whether that means taking control or letting go of it where needed. The waning Capricorn reminds us not to give up, to persist as the mountain goat does, and to find a way to overcome the steep and rocky roads. Capricorn Moon gives moods a serious undertone of needing and wanting to take hold of our goals and create results. Saturn ruled Capricorn emphasizes time and the timeliness of important events. This may be a time to address impending deadlines. Life is so serious with Capricorn Moon in its last quarter state; it reminds us that in order to be in control we must let go of that which we can't control. Attached to success? Persistence wins overall where there is a stubborn drive to excel. How important is success to you?

Mercury square Pluto (occurring April 6 – 11) This aspect often creates obstacles in communications with other generations or age groups. It's a particularly difficult time to deal with burdensome issues and discuss them in a manner that relieves tension. Mercury square Pluto often brings harsh and sometimes fatal news. Talk revolves around the corruption of superpowers and the setbacks caused by this corruption. This may be a particularly difficult time to discuss matters involving permanent change. Mercury in Pisces square Pluto in Sagittarius often emphasizes a conflict of beliefs in our discussions, particularly with regard to the visions and outlook of another generation. This aspect will repeat on September 2, when Mercury will be in Virgo.

Mercury enters Aries (Mercury in Aries: April 10 – April 27) Mercury now enters Aries, bringing a focus of communications on selfhood, initiation, new projects, and new ways of seeing and experiencing life. We are all perpetually in the process of being initiated into some aspect of selfhood, particularly given that we are constantly learning, acquiring new skills, growing and aging. Mercury in Aries brings some lively heat to our communications and discussions. Mercury is the messenger, activating information, and Aries is the warrior and the force of nature that takes on life with fearless vigor and aggression. Communications possess a quality of command. Now through April 27, while Mercury is in Aries, talk, news and discussions will be actively focused on the challenging and demanding enterprises and battles that await us.

April 11th Wednesday

Moon in Capricorn / Aquarius

	PDT	EDT
Moon trine Venus goes v/c	2:58 AM	5:58 AM
Moon enters Aquarius	4:24 AM	7:24 AM
Moon sextile Mercury	6:07 AM	9:07 AM
Sun sextile Neptune	12:34 PM	3:34 PM
Venus enters Gemini	7:16 PM	10:16 PM
Jupiter square Uranus begins (see May 10)		

Mood Watch: Overnight, Moon trine Venus brings easily affectionate moods and, at the same time, the Capricorn Moon goes void-of-course. This is a good time to rest and not fretting over career or work. As the day begins, the Moon enters Aquarius and our moods enter into a time of scientific foresight. Moon sextile Mercury brings moods inspired by intelligence. Aquarius Moon gives us the incentive to tackle puzzling problems, and the waning Aquarius Moon often leaves us contemplative over the types of problems that could only be described as "man made". If there's some form of logic that got us into a mess, there is indeed another kind of logic that will get us out of it. The Aquarius Moon gives our moods the extra push to seek out the knowledge that is necessary to succeed.

Sun sextile Neptune (occurring April 7 – 13) This occurrence of Sun sextile Neptune creates an opportunistic time for those Aries people celebrating birthdays from April 7 – April 13. These Aries folks are experiencing an opportunity to awaken in the realm of spirituality and creativity. There is an awareness of the self that goes deep here, and these birthday people are likely to appear distracted and difficult to reach while this phenomenon of great depth is occurring. This will be your year, birthday folks, to explore personal opportunities of spiritual growth. It may be a time to get away from it all, and find a sanctuary in which to meditate and open up to some valuable answers to old questions. These folks are in a place that gives them an opportunity to better understand the work of their path, but this is probably only true if they act on their own intuitive sensibilities, without the influences of others. That shouldn't be too hard for the enterprising and self-motivated Aries natures among us. This will be your year (Aries birthday people) to enhance and strengthen your intuition and primal instincts by tapping into them while they are easily available. This aspect will repeat on December 11, when the Sun will be in Sagittarius.

Venus enters Gemini (Venus in Gemini: April 11 – May 8) Venus, the influence of love, magnetism and attraction, now enters Gemini, the personification of duality. Love desires may be split and suffer from ambivalence and schisms. Gemini people will focus more intently on personal attractions and love related matters, while Sagittarius folks may be overwhelmed by love concerns as Venus opposes their natal Sun. Virgo and Pisces people are also likely to feel affection related challenges or difficulties in their life as Venus squares their natal Sun positions. Librans and Aquarians will find things a little easier. With Venus in Gemini, there is an attraction to writing, speaking about, and recording extraordinary experiences and stories, especially about beauty and love related matters. Gossip and talk about love matters will be especially prevalent. Venus in Gemini shows us the two sides of love – the giving and the taking. As attractions appear more diverse, concerns may arise among those with a jealous nature. Love related changes are rampant – to some it's a challenge, while for others, it's a breath of fresh air.

April 12th Thursday

Moon in Aquarius

	PDT	EDT
Moon opposite Saturn	12:32 PM	3:32 PM
Moon sextile Jupiter	3:07 PM	6:07 PM
Moon conjunct Neptune	6:19 PM	9:19 PM
Moon sextile Sun	8:30 PM	11:30 PM

Mood Watch: Moon in Aquarius allows us to look at the world with a healthy respect for the knowledge we carry and the ways it will become useful. This afternoon, Moon opposite Saturn brings moods that seem particularly opposed to restrictions and oppressive authority. There may also be a high demand for serious work and concentration. Luckily, Moon sextile Jupiter inspires us with joviality and a positive spirit. By evening, Moon conjunct Neptune brings moods that will be responsive to the need for tranquility and peacefulness. Tonight, Moon sextile Sun inspires us to get in tune with the seasonal factors of this time. Aries Sun and Aquarius Moon bring brave intelligence and a cool mix of independence and humanitarianism.

April 13th Friday

Moon in Aquarius / Pisces

	PDT	EDT
Moon sextile Pluto goes v/c	6:51 AM	9:51 AM
Moon enters Pisces	8:40 AM	11:40 AM
Moon Square Venus	12:00 PM	3:00 PM
Moon conjunct Mars	6:33 PM	9:33 PM
Sun trine Pluto begins (see April 19)		

♈

Mood Watch: This morning, Moon sextile Pluto brings moods that will be easily affected by tension and stress. The Aquarius Moon goes void-of-course for a little while, causing havoc with technical equipment, and with our ability to apply basic logic. Soon enough, the Moon enters Pisces and our moods enter into a period of fluid adaptability. Moon square Venus brings moods challenged by troubles with regard to love related matters and those things to which we are attached. This evening, Moon conjunct Mars brings moods activated by complex and reactionary kinds of aggression, particularly with regard to addictions.

Why is **Friday the 13TH** considered such a bad omen? Friday the 13TH in October of the year 1307 was a really bad day in the life of Jacques DeMolay, fearless leader of the (notorious) Knights Templar. By sundown on that fateful day nearly all the Knights Templar throughout France were seized and thrown into dungeons. Thousands of men who were at one time considered nobles had their properties seized, and many suffered torture and inhumane conditions. The French King and the Pope conspired against the Templars to plunder their wealth; the Templars were then discarded as heretics and banned from the power they had held for so long. Seven years after the Friday the 13TH incident, DeMolay was executed. The fall of the Templars left such a bitter mark on the soul of Europe that Friday the 13TH has held a notorious reputation. Friday the 13TH is often still considered unlucky, however, there are some people who think of thirteen as an auspicious number, and to them this day is considered to be a lucky time. These people naturally tend to have a better experience of this day, by virtue of their more positive outlook. On a positive note, the Knights Templar remain a fascination and a fraternally honored memory to this day. Perhaps their fortunes will yet revive.

April 14th Saturday

Moon in Pisces

	PDT	EDT
Moon conjunct Uranus	12:35 PM	3:35 PM
Moon Square Jupiter	5:08 PM	8:08 PM

Mood Watch: The waning Pisces Moon is a good time for us to examine beliefs, our spiritual wellbeing, and also our intuitive and creative capabilities. The expression of art and music is a splendid way to bide your time on this springtime Saturday. Moon conjunct Uranus brings moods that may seem explosive with chaotic and exciting kinds of liberation. This evening, Moon square Jupiter may create moods challenged by broadened and explosive viewpoints. The waning Pisces Moon takes us to numerous depths emotionally; it may also be a time when we are most willing to surf fearlessly and creatively upon the surface of those emotional depths.

April 15th Sunday

Moon in Pisces / Aries

	PDT	EDT
Moon square Pluto goes v/c	8:03 AM	11:03 AM
Moon enters Aries	9:48 AM	12:48 PM
Moon sextile Venus	5:05 PM	8:05 PM

Mood Watch: This morning, Moon square Pluto brings moods that may be challenged by our hidden fears. The Moon also goes void-of-course for a short time, and our moods will seem somewhat spacey, while we seem inattentive to the things going on around us. As the Moon enters Aries, our moods enter into an assertive phase. The waning Aries Moon is a good time to purge fears and to get in touch with what motivates us individually. This evening, Moon sextile Venus brings moods inspired by kind and attractive feminine influences.

April 16th Monday

Moon in Aries

	PDT	EDT
Moon conjunct Mercury	12:09 AM	3:09 AM
Moon trine Saturn	2:35 PM	5:35 PM
Moon trine Jupiter	4:50 PM	7:50 PM
Moon sextile Neptune	8:04 PM	11:04 PM

Mood Watch: Overnight, Moon conjunct Mercury activates our nervous systems with informative dreams. The Aries Moon is working towards reaching the new mark, which is set to occur early tomorrow morning. The Moon is now in the *balsamic phase* of waning, which is often a time of internal reflection and rest. The darkly waning Aries Moon is usually a time of anticipation and expectation, as the lunar cycle has now caught up to the zodiac signs of the spring season; with that comes spring fever. This is also a time of self creation and the re-inventing of personal qualities or desires to suit the lifestyle that this spring season evokes. Moon trine Saturn emphasizes the need for full or perfect control, precision, and favorable timing. Moon trine Jupiter brings very prosperous and harmonious moods and feelings. This evening, Moon sextile Neptune brings moods inspired by spiritual tranquility and peace.

April 17th Tuesday

Moon in Aries / Taurus - NEW MOON in ARIES

	PDT	EDT	
Moon conjunct Sun	4:37 AM	7:37 AM	
Moon trine Pluto	7:28 AM	10:28 AM	
Moon in Aries goes v/c	7:28 AM	10:28 AM	
Moon enters Taurus	9:12 AM	12:12 PM	
Moon sextile Mars	11:35 PM	2:35 AM	(April 18)
Mercury trine Saturn begins (see April 21)			

Mood Watch: **New Moon in Aries** (Moon conjunct Sun) brings a classically superb time to start anew, not only because the Moon has reached the new mark and our moods are often geared in this way, but especially so because the Aries Moon invokes the powers of initiation and newness as an essential part of regenerative force. This is a time to generate and promote inspiration and happiness. Aries is the sign of the warrior. The fight to sustain love on planet Earth calls for many courageous battles, and now is an excellent time to actively initiate new projects and endeavors that will help to serve one's sense of well being. Spring is truly here and new projects abound. Moon trine Pluto brings the mood to promote harmony among generations, and those with difficult realities will feel more in tune with the sympathies of others. The Aries Moon goes void-of-course this morning and, for a couple of hours, our moods may be distracted by our own self-created struggles and by an apparent lack of patience. As the Moon enters Taurus, our moods enter into a phase of pragmatic sensibility. Much later tonight, Moon sextile Mars brings moods inspired by courage.

April 18th Wednesday

Moon in Taurus	PDT	EDT
Moon sextile Uranus	12:07 PM	3:07 PM
Moon square Saturn	1:53 PM	4:53 PM
Moon square Neptune goes v/c	7:30 PM	10:30 PM
Mercury trine Jupiter begins (see April 21)		

Mood Watch: This afternoon, Moon sextile Uranus brings moods that will inspire us to let loose and feel free. Moon square Saturn brings another dimension to our moods as many folks will be challenged by responsibility or difficult work. The Moon is newly waxing in Taurus and, while some folks are fixed on getting practical matters into order, others are more interested in being comfortably lazy and enjoying this fine spring day. This evening, Moon square Neptune brings moods that may be challenged by various conflicting of beliefs. The Moon also goes void-of-course at this point in the evening and our moods will undoubtedly be distracted by impracticality or laziness. Overall, it may be difficult to focus on work today.

April 19th Thursday

Moon in Taurus / Gemini	PDT	EDT
Sun trine Pluto	12:36 AM	3:36 AM
Moon enters Gemini	8:52 AM	11:52 AM
Saturn goes direct	2:25 PM	5:25 PM

Mood Watch: The Moon in Taurus is void-of-course this morning, bringing a tendency towards money worries. The sentiment changes quickly as the Moon enters Gemini, bringing moods that now enter into a phase of thought provoking expression. Gemini Moon keeps us curious, busy minded, and nervously at work to produce intelligent and informative perspectives.

Sun trine Pluto (occurring April 13 – 22) Positive, life altering changes are occurring, particularly in the lives of those Aries/Taurus cusp born people celebrating birthdays this year from April 13 – 22. These folks are currently undergoing the favorable trine aspect of Pluto to their natal Sun, bringing out experiences that involve transformation, and encounters with greater powers and with fate. It is always difficult to speculate just how the Pluto experience will manifest. For some of these birthday folks, the concept of receiving gifts and empowerment in the midst of fateful events may seem rocky and not particularly advantageous. Have no fear; this is a time to get in touch with your power, birthday Aries/Taurus! It is wise to remember Pluto moves slowly in our cosmos, and powerful encounters that seem deadly or harsh are actually a necessary process. Though unavoidable, matters involving fate can be positive, and the trine aspect does represent a gift being bestowed. Aries/Taurus birthday people, be grateful this is the trine aspect that brings power issues into your life in a more positive fashion with Pluto, and the work of destiny will bestow untold gifts this year. This is a time of positive transformation. Sun trine Pluto will occur again on August 19 affecting the birthday Leos/Virgos of that time.

Saturn goes direct (Saturn direct: April 19 – December 19) Saturn, which represents time, restriction, responsibility, and disciplinary acts, has been retrograde since December 5, 2006 and will go direct today until December 19 this year. Saturn retrograde often requires us backtrack on many previous, as yet unfulfilled, obligations and disciplines. The past four months of Saturn retrograde has been a time of implementing, testing and correcting various types of security measures in our lives, and many sacrifices were made in order for us to feel a sense of completion and accomplishment.

Now Saturn goes direct at the eighteen degree mark of Leo, and moves forward through Leo until September 2, when it enters Virgo. While Saturn completes its travels through Leo, the process of strengthening the will is emphasized in a timely manner. Many will be learning to discipline their senses, to end destructive habits, as well as making new lifestyle choices and changes. As Saturn begins to move forward, this may be the time for Leo, the beastly Lion, to move forward towards positive endings and new beginnings as Leo related focuses become society's priority. Saturn in Leo focuses on the power and strength of individual character and the necessity to identify and claim personal freedom and strength of will. It also focuses on Leo-like matters such as the quality of one's personal lifestyle, family, children, friendships, and entertainment. Saturn in Virgo brings a greater emphasis on practical focuses and health related disciplines (see September 2).

As Saturn resumes a forward-moving course, we can organize and stabilize our priorities and disciplines, allowing projects to get back on a productive and progressive path. Discipline is the key to perseverance. Saturn in Leo teaches us where to draw lines in our personal lives and allows us to guard and protect our families and our individual choices of lifestyle and entertainment. Saturn's lessons are there to make us stronger as individuals. As Saturn moves forward, we can focus in a more timely fashion on finding solutions to classic old problems. This is the time for many folks to get back on track with goals and disciplines, and it will be a little easier to keep a steady check on quality control. Rejoice in your lessons as the tests of today create a stronger you for the call of tomorrow. Saturn rules!

TAURUS

Key Phrase: "I HAVE"

Fixed Earth Sign

Symbol: The Bull

April 19th through May 20th

April 20th Friday

Moon in Gemini

	PDT	EDT
Moon conjunct Venus	12:28 AM	3:28 AM
Moon square Mars	2:26 AM	5:26 AM
Sun enters Taurus	4:08 AM	7:08 AM
Moon square Uranus	1:01 PM	4:01 PM
Moon sextile Mercury	1:17 PM	4:17 PM
Moon sextile Saturn	2:43 PM	5:43 PM
Moon opposite Jupiter	4:52 PM	7:52 PM
Moon trine Neptune	8:43 PM	11:43 PM
Mercury sextile Neptune begins (see April 22)		
Mars conjunct Uranus begins (see April 28)		

Mood Watch: The waxing Moon in Gemini opens us to communication and the handling of details. People will tend to communicate what has been on their minds. Gemini Moon focuses our attention on those areas of life where we have mixed feelings, and there is a tendency to mull over those things that have not settled just right in our minds. Overnight, Moon conjunct Venus brings moods that will be easily connected to attractions and affections. Moon square Mars brings moods that will seem challenged by fiery force and energies. This afternoon, Moon square Uranus brings moods intensified by undisciplined forces. Moon sextile Mercury brings moods inspired by intelligence. Moon sextile Saturn brings the potential for good feelings with regard to a sense of structure and stability. Moon opposite Jupiter brings moods that may be overwhelmed by abundance and rapid growth. Tonight, Moon trine Neptune invokes spiritual harmony.

Sun enters Taurus (Sun in Taurus: April 20 – May 21) *Happy Birthday Taurus!* The symbol of Taurus is the Bull, the most effective symbol for the birth of agricultural awareness. Taurus has an obstinate side that brings out the bull's fixed qualities of possessiveness and persistence. The key phrase for Taurus is "I have," which also translates to "I own," or "Mine!" There is a definite pride that takes place in the Taurian world of accomplishments, and Taurus people are here to learn about owning up to what is theirs. In fact, owning and sporting bulls has for many centuries been a symbol of prosperity and prestige. The horned god is a symbol of fertility, and the season of Taurus brings out the fruition of blossoming and the beauty of earth's bounty. Taurus folks have a knack for smelling money and for finding the most valuable item at every sales counter. No matter how old, battered and antiquated the item may seem, Taurus will recognize the inherent value.

Taurus is a Venus ruled sign whose attraction to beauty is second nature. As a general rule, Taurus energy promotes a strong desire to keep physically fit, and keep possessions and personal effects shining and looking good. Taurus has a very matter-of-fact way of looking at life, and likes to keep the surroundings neat and functional as well as aesthetically pleasing and socially acceptable. This is not to say all Taurus folks are orderly according to the rest of the world! They have a very sensitive and often sentimental side, and find it difficult to change and adapt swiftly when their lives seem to be in perfect order. This is perhaps the sign that finds it the most difficult to accept death since it is opposite to Scorpio, which in one sense represents death. Taurus is more interested in preserving and enhancing life. When it comes to giving up the body – or giving up anything – Taurus has a hard time justifying letting go after all the hard work of preserving. Taurus is attracted to beauty, wealth and material gain – and ah, yes – the scent of fresh dirt. It makes perfect sense that this sign would find it hardest of all to give up these accomplishments at the end of their sojourn here on planet Earth. Entropy is therefore one of Taurus's worst enemies. Sun in Taurus represents a regenerative time for many folks. These are the days of bountiful beauty, and there's a strong emphasis on pleasures and riches.

April 21st Saturday
Moon in Gemini / Cancer

	PDT	EDT
Mercury trine Saturn	12:10 AM	3:10 AM
Moon opposite Pluto goes v/c	8:53 AM	11:53 AM
Moon enters Cancer	10:51 AM	1:51 PM
Moon sextile Sun	1:10 PM	4:10 PM
Mercury trine Jupiter	3:40 PM	6:40 PM
Venus square Uranus begins (see April 26)		

Mood Watch: This morning's Gemini Moon continues to bring a busy time, tickling our nerves with exhilarating thoughts. Moon opposite Pluto brings overwhelming intensity to the mood, while at the same time, the Gemini Moon goes void-of-course for a couple of hours. Mixed feelings and distractions soon fade into a clearer picture of how we feel as the Moon enters Cancer. This afternoon, Moon sextile Sun picks up the energy and inspires us to get in touch with the season of Taurus. The waxing Cancer Moon brings deep and revealing feelings. Domestic moods dominate the average scene and warm, homey comforts bring peaceful rest.

Mercury trine Saturn (occurring April 17 – 22) Mercury is in Aries where the emphasis of information and news is placed on the strategy of attack or the plan of action. Mercury in Aries trine Saturn in Leo brings favorable communication which tells us how, and where, to draw the lines for ourselves. This is a good time to make an impression, to teach, and to communicate to others those important matters that must be clarified. This is a great time to study or practice memorization skills. Timely information and news represents a gift or blessing. News concerning the end of a long and arduous task brings relief. Mercury trine Saturn occurs again on December 25, when Mercury will be in Capricorn and Saturn will be in Virgo.

Mercury trine Jupiter (occurring April 18 – 23) This most favorable aspect brings good news of expansion and prosperity to those who are open to broadening their awareness. Ask and you shall have! Mercury in Aries trine Jupiter in Sagittarius brings direct and straightforward words which can lead to insightfulness, adventure, creativity, happiness and wellbeing. This is an excellent time to learn new skills which will improve one's livelihood and better one's outlook. This is also a great time for salespeople to make sales. Mercury brings news, while Jupiter brings wealth and prosperous change. Mercury trine Jupiter is often considered to be an advantageous time to advertise and put information out there, and to ask for a job or a loan. However, now that Jupiter is currently retrograde (since April 5,) this would be an especially good time to provide a service which may have a bearing on a potential promotion. Look openly for opportunity when sharing information, and promote yourself and your capabilities. This aspect will repeat on August 9, when Mercury will be in Leo and Jupiter will be direct in Sagittarius.

April 22nd Sunday
Earth Day

Moon in Cancer	PDT	EDT	
Moon trine Mars	8:45 AM	11:45 AM	
Moon trine Uranus	5:15 PM	8:15 PM	
Mercury sextile Neptune	9:12 PM	12:12 AM	(April 23)
Venus square Mars	10:31 PM	1:31 AM	(April 23)

" The goal of life is living in agreement with nature. "
- Zeno (335 BC – 264 BC), from Diogenes Laertius, Lives of Eminent Philosophers

Mood Watch: Cancer Moon brings out the motherly touch in our moods, leading us to tend to and care for the tender parts of our existence. Moon trine Mars activates our moods and brings energetic vibrations. Spring is a time of rejuvenation and the waxing Cancer Moon is an excellent time to spread seeds and plant the spring garden. Seeds and plants also symbolize hopes and dreams, and this is the time to access the power of your instincts and to act on your own needs for achieving some sense of rejuvenation. Home focused activities bring warm expressions of contentment. This evening, Moon trine Uranus brings positive but eccentric moods with inspired ideas, carefree attitudes, and radical instincts. The Cancer Moon urges us to share our feelings and take care of our emotional needs.

Mercury sextile Neptune (occurring April 20 – 23) Mercury in Aries sextile Neptune in Aquarius brings bold, independent messages that inform us of opportunities for spiritual growth in humanity. This is an opportunistic time to cautiously attempt communication with regard to beliefs and spiritual matters. Mercury is in Aries adding a fiery urgency to the question of how to face Neptune-related subjects such as spiritual strength, guidance, and inspiration. Address addiction problems with helpful instruction. Prayers, channeling, and spells are all very effective with Mercury sextile Neptune. This is the time to get the word out to Great Spirit, and to reinforce a sense of faith or an acceptance of the way life is going. Mercury sextile Neptune allows us to verbalize and share beliefs in a way that encourages people. This aspect will occur once again this year on December 13, when Mercury will be in Sagittarius.

Venus square Mars (occurring April 7 – May 1) Venus square Mars creates tension and obstacles between the forces of love and the forces of defense. The archetypal images of Venus and Mars are largely that of feminine and masculine counterparts, and this aspect brings stress between people in love relationships. The pain of separation or the sorrow of unrequited love may be a symptom of this time, as the rocky boat of romance is due to have some notable ups and downs. On the other hand, the difficulties of these tests may strengthen the power of love and, although it is sometimes very difficult to endure love related conflicts, it is also a necessary process to ensure the authenticity of our love experience. This aspect will repeat on August 7 and one last time on November 19.

April 23rd Monday
Moon in Cancer / Leo - FIRST QUARTER MOON in LEO

	PDT	EDT	
Moon square Mercury goes v/c	2:11 AM	5:11 AM	
Moon enters Leo	4:39 PM	7:39 PM	
Moon square Sun	11:37 PM	2:37 AM	(April 24)
Mercury trine Pluto begins (see April 26)			
Venus opposite Jupiter begins (see April 28)			
Mars square Jupiter begins (see April 30)			

Mood Watch: Overnight, Moon square Mercury brings nervousness to our dreams, and the Moon goes void-of-course for a while bringing worrisome vibrations to the sleepless folks among us. Many people awaken to a confused sort of feeling. The Cancer Moon will be void-of-course all day, bringing numerous emotional distractions and episodes. Later, as the Moon enters Leo, our moods brighten up to the commencement of an entertaining evening. **First Quarter Moon in Leo** (Moon square Sun) brings playfulness. Leo Moon raises the energy level of our moods with anticipation and optimism. Self-indulgent or self-conscious attitudes may seem prevalent, along with the need for adoration or attention. Personal appetites and desires are observed and characterized. This evening, family and friends will play key roles. Leo says "I will" – this is a time to define, reexamine, or empower the will.

April 24th Tuesday
Moon in Leo

	PDT	EDT	
Moon sextile Venus	9:27 PM	12:27 AM	(April 25)
Venus sextile Saturn begins (see April 27)			

Mood Watch: The Leo Moon reached the First Quarter mark last night, and continues to wax in the sign of Leo throughout today. Leo Moon puts us in touch with personal and integral needs and desires. Much later this evening, Moon sextile Venus finds us easily captivated by love and affection. We are drawn individually to those things which we love and adore, and what we are drawn to is part of what determines who we are — we tend to become what it is we love, what we try to emulate, or appease. Quite often the Leo Moon energy helps us to feel good about our personal needs and attractions. Today will be a good day to pursue a taste of personal pleasure.

April 25th Wednesday

♉

Moon in Leo	PDT	EDT	
Moon conjunct Saturn	3:15 AM	6:15 AM	
Moon trine Jupiter	5:13 AM	8:13 AM	
Moon opposite Neptune	10:17 AM	1:17 PM	
Moon trine Mercury	10:01 PM	1:01 AM	(April 26)
Venus trine Neptune begins (see April 30)			

Mood Watch: Overnight, Moon conjunct Saturn brings moods that awaken us to the awareness of our limitations. Moon trine Jupiter brings a sense of harmony and wellbeing. Moon opposite Neptune brings that which may be overwhelmed by opposing beliefs. Today the Moon is in Leo and our moods are energetic and openly focused on identity. The Sun and Moon are both in fire signs and archetypes abound with tales of the self, bursting with character and ego. A waxing Moon in Leo uplifts our moods with entertainment, magnetism and stimulating energy. This is a good time to be sure to do something special for yourself and to reinforce your own integral outlook on the importance of living life according to will power. Get in touch with a sense of person desire and vitality, then call it your own. Tonight's Moon trine Mercury brings moods that will be in harmony with thoughts, and our late night communications are likely to go well.

April 26th Thursday

Moon in Leo / Virgo	PDT	EDT
Moon trine Pluto goes v/c	12:03 AM	3:03 AM
Moon enters Virgo	2:25 AM	5:25 AM
Mercury trine Pluto	10:07 AM	1:07 PM
Moon trine Sun	2:55 PM	5:55 PM
Venus square Uranus	8:21 PM	11:21 PM

Mood Watch: Overnight, Moon trine Pluto brings moods in harmony with those rapid and irreversible changes in life. The Leo Moon goes void-of-course while we sleep and as it enters Virgo, our moods enter into an awareness of cleanliness. Virgo Moon brings vigilant, cautious, and observant moods. There will be a lot to take in, and a lot to assess emotionally as well. Virgo Moon helps to get us in touch with the physical world in a way we can feel good about. Moon trine Sun brings harmonious vibes, particularly if we take this time to get organized and become clear with our thoughts.

Mercury trine Pluto (occurring April 23 – 27) Mercury in Aries is trine to Pluto in Sagittarius. This aspect brings hope like a gift, and the myth of Pandora's box shows us that hope regenerates our senses and fills us with the potential for triumph over difficulties. Mercury in Aries gives a very direct and courageous quality to our methods of communicating. This would be a good time to share tales of triumph, spreading those miraculous stories that remind us of the great potential of winning against all odds. This positive aspect aids communication about struggles with fate, trouble, loss, and fatal kinds of illnesses. This is a good time to express encouraging words and reinforce the troubled people of our world with a sense of hope. This aspect repeats this year on August 17, when Mercury will be in Leo.

Venus square Uranus (occurring April 21 – 29) Venus in Gemini square Uranus in Pisces brings swift change in love matters. It may be difficult for love (Venus) to flourish in a spontaneous and carefree fashion (Uranus), and there may be obstacles or obligations placed on love and spiritual freedom. This is a difficult time for rebels and revolutionaries, as their causes may not be popular. Anger, not loving patience, may be the behavioral tendency of some folks, especially while Mars is conjunct Uranus (see April 28). Be careful not to become too affronted personally by explosive manifestations of radical love. This influence may be testing the power of your love to withstand the extremes of chaos, disorder, and sudden change. Be assured in self-love, and empower affection with personal integrity. People are changing at a rapid rate and it is essential to let love take its course where it relates to personal freedom. Focuses on love and the pursuit of sensual pleasures may seem to send some folks stir-crazy for awhile, but within a few days to a week, matters will settle down from the disruption. This aspect will repeat in January 2008, when Venus will be in Sagittarius.

April 27th Friday
Moon in Virgo

	PDT	EDT
Mercury enters Taurus	12:17 AM	3:17 AM
Moon opposite Mars	11:13 AM	2:13 PM
Venus sextile Saturn	1:08 PM	4:08 PM
Moon opposite Uranus	1:19 PM	4:19 PM
Moon square Venus	3:04 PM	7:04 PM
Moon square Jupiter	4:32 PM	7:32 PM
Sun conjunct Mercury begins (see May 2)		

Mood Watch: The Moon in Virgo gives us the incentive to face complexities and doubts with clarity and practicality. Sun in Taurus and Moon in Virgo emphasize accounting and managing the physical world. Moon opposite Mars brings moods opposed to offensive kinds of pressures. Moon opposite Uranus brings moods that will be overwhelmed by chaotic energies – this may be especially true with the Moon in Virgo. This afternoon, Moon square Venus brings complications with regard to matters of love and attraction. Moon square Jupiter brings moods that will be challenged by matters of wealth, and with our sense of wellbeing. The Virgo Moon energies and moods of today attempt to apply some dignity and some prudence, despite the lunar aspects that suggest otherwise.

Mercury enters Taurus (Mercury in Taurus: April 27 – May 11) Mercury moves into the sign of Taurus, and communications will focus on manifesting sales and generating economic growth. It is a good time to clarify matters involving valuables, and to focus on documents, contracts, speeches, and business procedures. Mercury in Taurus brings on a new wave of discussion about the natural beauties and luxuries that surround us, and there is also an equal concern for practicality. Mercury is the messenger, the speaker and the director of the subject matter at hand. Mercury is also classically known as "The Merchant," "The Trickster," and "The Thief." In the fixed earth sign of Taurus, Mercury inspires the inclination to buy, sell, trade, barter, and negotiate terms of sale. Issues of ownership and, undoubtedly, a "steal of a deal" will appear in the arena of barter. Resourceful thinking and information processing can lead to the extra buck. This is a time to accurately record practical matters and events and to communicate about finances.

Venus sextile Saturn (occurring April 24 – 29) Venus in Gemini sextile Saturn in Leo brings flirtatious and lighthearted expressions of love which are being amicably shared between lovers and friends under strict conditions. Venus emphasizes the vibrations of love, magnetism, and beauty, and while in Gemini, Venus brings thoughtful and mentally stimulating art. Saturn's influence emphasizes the awareness of time, limitations, and restrictions; while this planet is in Leo, families, friends and loved ones all play integral roles in the manner in which the rules of love-play are established and enforced. Saturn influences also make claim to our dedication to responsibility and discipline. Saturn reminds us that beauty is temporary but with proper maintenance, it can also be preserved. This is a good time to capture a glimpse of beauty that will leave a lasting mark. There is a passionate drive to protect loved ones and limit their exposure to danger. This aspect will repeat on December 12, when Venus will be in Scorpio and Saturn will be newly in the sign of Virgo (Saturn enters Virgo: Sept. 2).

April 28th Saturday
Moon in Virgo / Libra

	PDT	EDT	
Venus opposite Jupiter	5:45 AM	8:45 AM	
Moon square Pluto goes v/c	12:16 PM	3:16 PM	
Moon enters Libra	2:46 PM	5:46 PM	
Mars conjunct Uranus	9:38 PM	12:38 AM	(April 29)

Mood Watch: This morning, the Moon in Virgo brings resourceful and communicative moods. This afternoon, Moon square Pluto brings moods challenged by difficulties and those irreversible processes of life. The Virgo Moon goes void-of-course, too, bringing moods easily distracted by doubt. For a few hours during the day, it might be best to avoid getting caught up in criticisms and arguments that might end up distracting us from enjoying this fine Saturday. As the Moon enters Libra, our moods enter into a phase of deliberation and a desire to put some balance back into our relationships. Friends and lovers will need to take some time to smooth over the events of the day with encouraging words. Relax and enjoy the evening!

Venus opposite Jupiter (occurring April 23 – 30) Venus in Gemini brings a love for story telling, sharing information, and intelligence, while the retrograde Jupiter in Sagittarius creates an atmosphere of adventurous and outgoing expenditures and exploits. Venus opposite Jupiter brings on a significant awareness of the dynamics of attraction and wealth. During this aspect, we are often made aware of how the arts and leisure, the expense of our pleasure and fantasy, are opposed to or overwhelmed by, economic exploration. Custody battles are hard fought under these circumstances, and the process of overcoming personal loss requires a great deal of effort to attain the healing power of love. Money related tests and troubles in relationships are often a factor under this aspect. Artists and support groups struggle financially, and reach out for assistance in an attempt to survive or expand. Venus opposite Jupiter increases awareness of the need for sensual pleasure and of what determines the depth or character of that pleasure. If it seems as if the things you love or are striving for are completely out of reach, perhaps this phase of Venus opposite retrograde Jupiter is part of the cause.

Mars conjunct Uranus (occurring April 20 – May 3) Every couple of years the Mars/Uranus conjunction occurs. Since 2003, Mars and Uranus have been conjunct in the sign of Pisces. Activity and force of action (Mars) is in direct alignment with the explosive and chaotic energy of the rebel (Uranus). Both of these planets are charged with force, energy, and vitality, and are known for creating disruptive and unsettled energy. Masculine forces are erupting abruptly and loudly. The outlook is very fiery, although not necessarily completely destructive, as these masculine forces are tempered by the feminine element of the mutable water sign, Pisces. This may be a time of violence, accidents and upheaval in the world of religion. Activities are likely to be explosive over issues touching on the arts, drugs, our dreams, and those hypersensitive spiritual issues. Anger and frustration can be stifling at times, causing the fierce desire for freedom and the need for a definite revolution or revolt. Take caution with your own actions, and be aware of the potential for accidents and outbreaks of chaotic energy from others.

April 29th Sunday
Moon in Libra

Mood Watch: There are no exact aspects occurring today, either in the outer planetary world or in the world of our closest neighbor, Mother Moon. It's not as if the past week hasn't given us a fair slew of planetary line-ups – it sure has! We may well consider today a restful or peaceful day, despite the internal moods which are still responding to major events. While today's Moon in Libra waxes towards this week's Full Scorpio Moon, set to take place the morning after May Day (Tuesday). The moon also drifts in the silence of a rare occasion; there are no lunar aspects to complicate or dictate our mood patterns. This does not mean that the day is free of typical ups and downs, particularly while Libra Moon activity tips its scales back and forth between the facts and figures of life while we find ourselves searching for wisdom, truth, and justice. This is a good time to find joy in partnership and friendship, and to create balance wherever it is needed.

April 30th Monday
Moon in Libra

	PDT	EDT
Moon sextile Saturn	3:53 AM	6:53 AM
Moon sextile Jupiter	5:07 AM	8:07 AM
Moon trine Venus	10:28 AM	1:28 PM
Moon trine Neptune	11:14 AM	2:14 PM
Mars square Jupiter	3:22 PM	6:22 PM
Venus trine Neptune	6:35 PM	9:35 PM

Mood Watch: The lunar aspects of today are all favorable, although Moon sextile Saturn brings moods that tend to be serious. This is quickly smoothed over by Moon sextile Jupiter, which brings open and generous moods. Moon trine Venus brings moods easily prone to affection. Moon trine Neptune brings spiritually enriching moods. Throughout the day, the strongly waxing Moon in Libra inspires us to take measures towards creating harmony and balance in our lives. Balance can occur through inaction just as well as it can through action. This is a good time to try to preserve an inner sense of stability and to avoid excesses.

Mars square Jupiter (occurring April 23 – May 4) When Mars squares Jupiter, various activities are met with the obstacles of economic oppression and shortfall. ♉ This is a very difficult time to excel in business endeavors, especially in actively trading markets. This aspect warns us that there will be trouble when approaching the job market aggressively. Trying to make progress using headstrong attitudes and unwarranted self-confidence might impede progress. This aspect brings no-nonsense demands or increases in our workload. Mars in Pisces suggests the need for artistic and spiritually inspired actions and effort. Difficulties may arise from bold competitive moves that may end up looking like corporate takeovers. Jupiter is in Sagittarius, focusing on the expansion of wealth through global trade, travel, and focuses on the survival of Sagittarian enterprises such as space exploration. The square aspect of these two planets creates a challenging dynamic in the struggle to grow economically. This is particularly true since Jupiter is retrograde. Expect to work a lot harder and perhaps a lot longer in order to smooth the rough edges of the financial empire while Mars in Pisces squares Jupiter in Sagittarius.

Venus trine Neptune (occurring April 25 – May 3) Venus in Gemini is trine Neptune in Aquarius. This brings detail oriented feminine love right in harmony with ingenious kinds of spiritual expression. Artistic endeavors will shine with spiritual brilliance. This aspect brings calmness and tranquility that are vitally needed, particularly in love related matters. When coming from a place of love, it is easier to draw down a spiritual enhancement of that love with Venus trine Neptune. Enjoying beauty is a way to acquire gifts of the spirit world. This is a good time to actively engage in peaceful, pleasurable, and spiritual love. This aspect repeats on November 26, when Venus will be in Libra.

May 1st Tuesday
Beltane / May Day
Moon in Libra / Scorpio

	PDT	EDT
Moon sextile Pluto goes v/c	1:08 AM	4:08 AM
Moon enters Scorpio	3:42 AM	6:42 AM
Venus opposite Pluto begins (see May 6)		

Mood Watch: Overnight, Moon sextile Pluto brings dreams that are open to helping us work out our individual struggles. After an indecisive period, the void-of-course Libra Moon enters Scorpio and kicks off the day with the thrilling excitement of various kinds of passion. The Full Moon Eve is upon us. There will be an emphasis today on facing challenges, finding solutions, keeping active, and on winning. It's a good time to be cautious, to watch for the signs of thievery, deception, and violence. Adventurous and daring moods may lead to trouble, but Scorpio Moon also brings intuitive and psychic abilities which can assist people in navigating their way through rough waters. Creative projects and May Day frolic will inspire our passions.

Happy **May Day!** This is a traditional old world solar holiday, also known as **Beltane**. We have now reached the half-way mark – and the height – of the spring season. This holiday celebrates the dance of the Maypole and fertility, beauty, rapturous love, and the various kinds of youthful play, and frolic appropriate to spring. The famous European *Green Man* with his mask of leaves, the rampaging goat-footed god *Pan* whose flutes thrill us with passion, and the mischievous *Khidr* of Islam who transcends form – all these (and many more) spirited, fervent, male archetypes – these are the lads who delight in the chase of the fair maiden. Persephone, Goddess of Greek myth, returns from Hades. She brings back the mirth of Venusian beauty and represents the fertility and the blossoming of the nurturing, life-sustaining plant world. May Day is a celebration of the fruition and beauty fond in nature. It represents the awakening of the passion and youthfulness in all of life. This time calls to us all to take joy in the fertilization of those parts of ourselves and our lives that need to be brought to fruition.

May 2nd Wednesday

FULL MOON in SCORPIO	PDT	EDT	
Moon opposite Mercury	1:01 AM	4:01 AM	
Moon opposite Sun	3:11 AM	6:11 AM	
Moon trine Uranus	3:13 PM	6:13 PM	
Moon square Saturn	4:33 PM	7:33 PM	
Moon trine Mars	9:00 PM	12:00 AM	(May 3)
Sun conjunct Mercury	9:06 PM	12:06 AM	(May 3)
Moon square Neptune goes v/c	11:43 PM	2:43 AM	(May 3)
Mercury square Saturn begins (see May 5)			
Sun square Saturn begins (see May 9)			

Mood Watch: Overnight, Moon opposite Mercury brings moods that may be over-whelmed by too many thoughts. **Full Moon In Scorpio** (Moon opposite Sun) notoriously accentuates sexual urges and activities. A number of energies are all coming to the brink of fruition. Work off the built up energy in a safe, positive, and productive way. Scorpio emphasizes passion and doesn't waste an ounce of strength taking any part of life for granted. Now is the time to use your passion for the good of the earth and to revitalize the energy of the people around you who mean so much. Be careful not to overdo it, and always take precautions to avoid getting tricked by others around you who may not have your best interest in mind. Be aware, and live life to the fullest. Scorpio energy would like us to live like this all the time, so now it's important to acknowledge the precious sense of being *here now.* Moon trine Uranus brings moods that will be freedom loving and favorably explosive. Moon square Saturn brings moods challenged by authority. Moon trine Mars brings moods inspired by raw energy. Late tonight, Moon square Neptune brings moods that will be challenged by the complexity of various belief systems. The Moon also goes void-of-course — a good time to rest.

Sun conjunct Mercury (occurring April 27 – May 5) This is a very common aspect, which will create a much more thoughtful, communicative, and expressive year ahead for those Taurus born people celebrating birthdays from April 27 – May 5. This is your time (birthday Taurus) to record ideas, relay important messages, and pay close attention to your imaginative thoughts as they are touched by Mercury, creating the urge to speak and be heard.

May 3rd Thursday

Moon in Scorpio / Sagittarius   PDT   EDT   ♉

Moon enters Sagittarius   3:49 PM   6:49 PM

Mercury sextile Uranus begins (see May 5)

Mood Watch: This morning we awaken with the post-Full Moon void-of-course in Scorpio. To many folks this could equate to an emotional hangover. As with any hangover, it must be nursed with care, given some space to relax – and it would be senseless to try to kick ourselves into gear prematurely. It is always wise to keep an eye out for danger and avoid precarious situations while the Moon is void-of-course in Scorpio. Later on, the Moon enters Sagittarius, and our energy levels and social awareness begin to move in a much more amicable direction. The Sagittarius Moon, although waning, is still very full and this is a good time to work off excess emotional baggage by becoming physically active or by exploring. Some genuine rest might also be appealing to some folks today, while some philosophical exploration will be sure to inspire. There are no lunar aspects occurring today – a peaceful time for the brilliantly gleaming Sagittarius Moon.

May 4th Friday

Moon in Sagittarius

Mercury square Neptune begins (see May 7)

Sun sextile Uranus begins (see May 8)

Mood Watch: After the spin of a new month arriving, coupled with the fact that the Moon was just full in Scorpio, we currently find ourselves drawn to the things that lie just beyond our reach with the Moon, now waning, in Sagittarius. There are no exact aspects occurring today, but do not be fooled by the long empty hours of no planetary activity. In the unsettled silence of this time we are sitting on the brink of a long winded series of lunar aspects set to take place throughout the course of tomorrow. This is a good time to air on the side of caution, and to acknowledge the internal urge to explore and be jovial may be met with a great deal more enthusiasm than we are prepared for. This is a good time not to overextend your energies or to impulsively commit to something that will demand extra labors in the next little while. Tomorrow's demands will be plenty to handle.

May 5th Saturday

Cinco de Mayo

Moon in Sagittarius	PDT	EDT	
Moon square Uranus	2:40 AM	5:40 AM	
Moon trine Saturn	3:53 AM	6:53 AM	
Moon conjunct Jupiter	4:05 AM	7:05 AM	
Mercury sextile Uranus	8:54 AM	11:54 AM	
Moon sextile Neptune	10:48 AM	1:48 PM	
Moon square Mars	11:59 AM	2:59 PM	
Mercury square Saturn	3:56 PM	6:56 PM	
Moon opposite Venus	9:51 PM	12:51 AM	(May 6)
Moon conjunct Pluto goes v/c	11:47 PM	2:47 AM	(May 6)
Mercury sextile Mars begins (see May 8)			
Mars square Pluto begins (see May 13)			

Mood Watch: Philosophical perspectives are hard-driving with the post-full Sagittarius Moon very busily conversing with the other planets. Overnight, Moon square Uranus brings the challenge of chaos. Later Moon trine Saturn blesses us with a sense of stability and control. Moon conjunct Jupiter brings outgoing and optimistic moods. Moon sextile Neptune brings moods that are influenced strongly by our beliefs. Moon square Mars brings moods that will be challenged by force and martial pressures. Tonight, Moon opposite Venus brings overwhelming beauty, and awakens the awareness of our needs for affection. Late tonight, Moon conjunct Pluto brings intense perplexity to our moods and, as the Moon also goes void-of-course, the confusion or bewilderment of such a busy and intense day brings the strong need for rest.

Mercury sextile Uranus (occurring May 3 – 6) Sensationalism may be played up in the news during this aspect. Mercury is in Taurus focusing talk, information and news on practical matters such as the value and cost of things, while Uranus is in Pisces, blowing all practicality right out of the water and stirring up chaos and havoc in the arts and religion. Mercury sextile Uranus gives us the opportunity to freely speak our minds and to address the chaos and turmoil that exists in our lives. This aspect last occurred on January 4, when Mercury was in Capricorn.

Mercury square Saturn (occurring May 2 – 7) Mercury in Taurus square Saturn in Leo creates tension in communications. Under the influence of this aspect the battle to possess and maintain valuables and sentimental objects may be strongly evident. It is wise to use caution when attempting communications during Mercury square Saturn, especially concerning matters of time and timing – communications are handled so stubbornly in the sign of Taurus. While Mercury is square to Saturn, beware of the tendency for people to make greedy assumptions about the conclusion or outcome of important matters. This aspect will repeat on December 6 when Mercury will be in Sagittarius and Saturn will be in Virgo.

May 6th Sunday
Moon in Sagittarius / Capricorn PDT   EDT

	PDT	EDT
Jupiter trine Saturn	12:12 AM	3:12 AM
Moon enters Capricorn	2:22 AM	5:22 AM
Venus opposite Pluto	7:06 PM	10:06 PM
Sun square Neptune begins (see May 12)		

Mood Watch: Overnight, as the Moon enters Capricorn, our moods enter into a phase of determination and the need for control. This past week of strong lunar influences brings us to a serious and determined time for our moods. Some seriously seek rest and others seriously want to get on top of the busy events in their lives and to be in control of the bustling buzz of spring.

Jupiter trine Saturn (occurring February 11 – June 9) Jupiter in Sagittarius is trine Saturn in Leo. Creative adventures bring the potential for a very positive outcome. This is a good time to realize personal dreams and to empower them with devotion and discipline. The good news of experiencing harmonious economic conditions is down to its last precious month of activity. For the important recap of the story of how this long lasting and very significant aspect brings positive economic growth,

100

see **March 16**, when it first reached its peak. This aspect will repeat next year on January 21, only by then Jupiter will be in Capricorn and Saturn will be in Virgo. This January, during its next occurrence, Jupiter trine Saturn will create a much more industrious and physically noticeable economic advantage with these two social planets in earth signs.

Venus opposite Pluto (occurring May 1 – 9) Venus in Gemini now opposes the retrograde Pluto in Sagittarius. Matters concerning love, beauty, and affection may be overwhelmed by dark forces or unforeseeable twists of fate. These fateful forces may be intruding somehow on the objects or people that we love and admire. This could include just about any kind of scenario – from being shattered over the loss of a loved one, to a terminal disease, to the process of learning how to fully accept and support some kind of total transformation of a loved one. Some people find it difficult to support loved ones through severe kinds of hardship, yet now is the time to offer support to them, despite the opposing forces that appear too harsh or overwhelming. This aspect may well bring on an acute awareness of the desire that some have for power, and the need to have power over loved ones. No one, no matter how powerful, can justifiably tell us what we love, who we love, or how we are to love. Deep in our hearts lays the truth. When the going gets tough, look to your heart!

May 7th Monday

Moon in Capricorn	PDT	EDT	
Mercury square Neptune	7:29 AM	10:29 AM	
Moon trine Sun	10:13 AM	1:13 PM	
Moon sextile Uranus	12:13 PM	3:13 PM	
Moon trine Mercury	10:24 PM	1:24 AM	(May 8)

Mood Watch: The Sun is in Taurus and the Moon wanes in Capricorn. Both Taurus and Capricorn are industrious earth signs. Waning Capricorn Moon brings assurance that strict focus and persistent effort will bring results. Moon trine Sun brings beautiful harmony to the mood of the day. Moon sextile Uranus assists us to embrace the unusual and find our freedom. Lastly, Moon trine Mercury brings moods that will be easily inclined towards thoughtfulness and communications. Capricorn Moon energy generally does not allow various types of emotional clamor to come to the surface very easily. Steady goes the work.

Mercury square Neptune (occurring May 4 – 8) This aspect often brings difficulty in communications with the spirit world, and with understanding human spirituality and beliefs. As a result, talk and discussion concerning what we believe in and strive for may be greatly misunderstood. Neptune is in Aquarius, stirring up the issue of human divinity and the structure of humanity's beliefs in the confusing shifts of this dawning age. While Mercury in Taurus is squaring Neptune, pragmatic thought and divinity will be tested, and relaying information on this subject may seem very difficult. Anticipate religious or belief related arguments and disputes. Deep subjects must not be treated lightly while Mercury squares Neptune. This aspect repeats on November 24, when Mercury will be in Scorpio.

May 8th Tuesday

Moon in Capricorn / Aquarius

	PDT	EDT
Venus enters Cancer	12:29 AM	3:29 AM
Moon sextile Mars goes v/c	12:36 AM	3:36 AM
Moon enters Aquarius	10:49 AM	1:49 PM
Sun sextile Uranus	1:26 PM	4:26 PM
Mercury sextile Mars	5:40 PM	8:40 PM

Mood Watch: Overnight, Moon sextile Mars brings dreams that are inspired by action. The void-of-course Capricorn Moon makes it difficult to rise up and be very attentive to our usual routines. Annoying career related concerns and work related setbacks are bound to turn up sometime this morning. By the time the Moon enters Aquarius, our moods are much more inclined towards finding brilliant, or possibly even unorthodox solutions to our problems. Aquarius Moon inspires the need to know, and to be in-the-know.

Venus enters Cancer (Venus in Cancer: May 8 – June 5) Venus now enters the nurturing sign of Cancer, an appropriate place for the expression of love and affection. It invites those with rocky love relationships to patch things up, and to do so with more heart and less uncertainty. Venus will be in Cancer through June 5, encouraging our affections and affinities to be carefully placed and nurtured. When attractions occur, they will have a lasting impression and will seem very strong and emotionally sound. Venus in Cancer brings out a love for things such as the ocean, leisurely aquatic sports, motherly care and expression, and all varieties of nurturing. While Venus travels over their natal Sun, those folks born in the sign of Cancer will be especially aware of their love life and their needs for pleasure.

Sun sextile Uranus (occurring May 4 -10) This occurrence of Sun sextile Uranus particularly affects those Taurus folks celebrating birthdays this year from May 4 through May 10. These birthday people are being given an opportunity to blow off some chaotic steam and to reach for qualities of freedom that have been absent in their recent past. This will be your year to make radical breakthroughs, birthday Taurus people! There is no holding back, so go for it. The victory of creative change will bring a more optimistic outlook on life. This aspect last occurred on January 2, when the Sun was in Capricorn.

Mercury sextile Mars (occurring May 5 – 10) Clear communications regarding the manner in which actions are taken may make this a superb time to seek employment. Mercury in Taurus demands the practical delivery of communications and is an excellent time to carry out promises or proclamations. Mars in Pisces demands heartfelt action. Mercury sextile Mars brings out opportunities which can be received, recognized, communicated and acted upon. News or information may lead to immediate action. Commands made with conviction are quickly acted upon. It's an advantageous time to apply one's word with a full backing of action for a very favorable outcome. This aspect will repeat on July 1, when Mercury will be retrograde in Cancer and Mars will be in Taurus. Finally, Mercury sextile Mars occurs for the third time this year on August 3.

May 9th Wednesday
LAST QUARTER MOON in AQUARIUS

♉

	PDT	EDT	
Sun square Saturn	5:06 AM	8:06 AM	
Moon sextile Jupiter	7:29 PM	10:29 PM	
Moon opposite Saturn	8:20 PM	11:20 PM	
Moon square Sun	9:28 PM	12:28 AM	(May 10)

Mood Watch: Thoughtful moods keep us busily interacting on this waning Aquarius Moon day. Tonight's Moon sextile Jupiter brings moods that will be inspired by prospects, positive output, and optimism. Later, Moon opposite Saturn brings moods that may be overwhelmed by the logistics and the feasibility of handling responsibilities. **Last Quarter Moon in Aquarius** (Moon square Sun) brings humanitarian focuses to the scope of our experience. A kind word or sympathetic ear has great healing power and oftentimes promotes peace. This Moon beckons us to find solutions, however temporary, to human problems. This Moon of Aquarius connects us with the dichotomies and ironies of the human experience. This is a time when the work of genius is ever present, but often goes undetected.

Sun square Saturn (occurring May 2 – 12) This occurrence of Sun square Saturn especially affects those Taurus born people who are celebrating birthdays May 2 – 12. These folks are undergoing personal challenges of impatience, loss of control and poor timing. The challenge is therefore to overcome those obstacles that intrude on one's control of discipline and accuracy. Often, false starts occur during the phase of life when Saturn squares the natal Sun. Since Saturn has moved into Leo (July 16, 2005) the square aspect of Saturn affects the lives of Taurus and Scorpio people, and this will continue until September 2, 2007, when Saturn enters Virgo. This challenge will pass, but it will also force these people to take a good look at what really matters in life, and to appreciate it. This may be a time of sacrifice, loss or compromise. It may also be a time of complexity and insecurity for these birthday folks. Saturn represents those things in life that we are willing to work for and maintain. It is reflected in our sense of discipline and our application of effort and focus. Here we learn about our limitations, and where our strengths can be realized. Just because there is a challenge on the path does not mean that it is time to give up. This is a good time for Taurus birthday folks to conserve energies and take losses and difficulties in stride. Through the tests of this time, a stronger human being emerges to take on future tests with greater confidence and ability. Running away from responsibilities or hardships now will only make life more difficult later. The Taurus in you knows this! This aspect will repeat on November 30, when the Sun will be in Sagittarius and Saturn will be in Virgo, affecting the birthday Sagittarians of that time.

May 10th Thursday

Moon in Aquarius / Pisces	PDT	EDT	
Moon conjunct Neptune	2:28 AM	5:28 AM	
Moon sextile Pluto	2:03 PM	5:03 PM	
Moon square Mercury goes v/c	2:48 PM	5:48 PM	
Moon enters Pisces	4:33 PM	7:33 PM	
Jupiter square Uranus	8:33 PM	11:33 PM	
Moon trine Venus	10:07 PM	1:07 AM	(May 11)

Mood Watch: The waning Moon in Aquarius inspires intelligence and brings an open interest in gadgets, novelties, books, politics, and scientific experiments. Overnight, Moon conjunct Neptune brings moods that are able to merge easily with spiritual awareness. Moon square Mercury occurs later in the day, bringing mental challenges and communications may be difficult. For a short time the void-of-course Moon in Aquarius brings the potential for traffic delays and/or technical glitches. As the Moon enters Pisces, we may find our moods more flexible to adapt to a wide range of emotional experiences. Later, Moon trine Venus tops the day nicely with moods that will be blessed with fond affections.

Jupiter square Uranus (occurring April 11 – June 23) This aspect last occurred on January 22, and it is now reoccurring due to the fact that Jupiter is currently retrograde. Expansive exploits and business endeavors overseas (Jupiter in Sagittarius) are likely to be thwarted by radical conflict, usually of a spiritual or religious nature (Uranus in Pisces.) Economic moves carry a high degree of risk, and the conflict that is bound to come up as a result of the immense challenge caused by this aspect will be unpredictable and will spread quickly. This aspect will occur once again this year on October 9 when Uranus will be retrograde.

May 11th Friday

Moon in Pisces	PDT	EDT	
Mercury enters Gemini	2:18 AM	5:18 AM	
Moon square Jupiter	11:04 PM	2:04 AM	(May 12)
Moon conjunct Uranus	11:19 PM	2:19 AM	(May 12)

Mood Watch: Waning Pisces Moon is an especially good time to meditate, pray and contemplate profound subjects. Tonight, Moon square Jupiter brings moods which may be challenged by our expenditures and with matters having to do with travel. Also tonight, chaotic energies have a peculiar way of liberating our moods when Moon conjunct Uranus unites us with a brilliant sense of freedom. Here, our moods merge with mysterious kinds of chaos and disorder. Keep an eye on the tendency to be challenged by temptations, addictions, or depression. Strong characters are empowered by their strength of conviction, while weaker characters tend to give up all too easily during a waning Pisces Moon.

Mercury enters Gemini (Mercury in Gemini: May 11 – 28) Mercury is the ruling planet of two astrological signs, Gemini and Virgo. When in Gemini, Mercury is known to increase our attention to detail and to cover a wide range of topics and subjects of interest. Mercury in Gemini directs and orchestrates information – like food for the brain – in an interesting and captivating way. Mercury in Gemini, the mutable air sign, is the best time to inspire a storyteller who is often looking for ways to make the story more interesting. Talk, discussion, stories, gossip, and the news media all generate flashes designed to captivate one's interest even if only for one moment. Mercury in Gemini brings out the two sides of every story. The well developed story has merit as a description of the course of our own existence. Pay heed to the message if the storyteller happens to be telling *your* story while Mercury is in Gemini.

♉

May 12th Saturday
Moon in Pisces / Aries

	PDT	EDT
Moon sextile Sun	5:03 AM	8:03 AM
Moon conjunct Mars	4:02 PM	7:02 PM
Moon square Pluto goes v/c	4:54 PM	7:54 PM
Moon enters Aries	7:20 PM	10:20 PM
Sun square Neptune	7:57 PM	10:57 PM

Mood Watch: The waning spirit of Pisces Moon brings bubbly and fluid moods, complete with a rapid cycle of emotional ups and downs. Sometimes those ups and downs blend together in a poetic sort of way, giving us insights, signs, omens, and psychic impressions of the spiritual paths we choose to travel. Moon sextile Sun brings moods open to the practical beauty of this time. Later, Moon conjunct Mars ensures that our moods will be energized. Moon square Pluto brings moods challenged by hardship. The Pisces Moon also goes void-of-course at this point and many folks may be easily distracted by a trance of some kind. At last, as the Moon enters Aries, our moods enter into a place of greater assurance and confidence.

Sun square Neptune (occurring May 6 – 16) This occurrence of Sun square Neptune especially affects those Taurus people celebrating birthdays from May 6 – 16. Neptune, in the square position to these folk's natal Sun, brings a perception that obstacles are getting in the way of Spirit, the spiritual path, or the acknowledgment of one's beliefs. The challenge for these Taurus birthday folks is to overcome the doubts and confrontations that interfere with their beliefs. Over the next year, there will undoubtedly be some spiritual adjustments, and perhaps a change of belief is required for those encountering birthdays at this time. Taurus change? Never! Well, unless it suits them, of course. This aspect will repeat on November 11 when the Sun will be in Scorpio, affecting the lives and beliefs of some Scorpio people.

May 13th Sunday
Mother's Day
Moon in Aries

	PDT	EDT
Moon sextile Mercury	2:03 AM	5:03 AM
Moon square Venus	4:42 AM	7:42 AM
Mars square Pluto	8:16 AM	11:16 AM

" My mother had a great deal of trouble with me, but I think she enjoyed it. "   - Mark Twain (1835 – 1910)

Mood Watch: Overnight, Moon sextile Mercury brings dreams inspired by encouraging messages. Early this morning, Moon square Venus brings moods that may be challenging with regard to matters concerning loved ones. While the Moon is in Aries, many folks will be concerned with their own needs and desires. Aries

Moon is great for inspiration and ambition. There is an eagerness to get started, but with the Moon waning and the Sun in Tauru,s we are swiftly reminded to pace ourselves, to approach the day with practicality.

Mars square Pluto (occurring May 5 – 17) Mars in Pisces square Pluto in Sagittarius often brings emotionally stirring battles over the seemingly unchangeable realities of the future. Mars emphasizes all forms of action while Pluto represents the transformational powers of destiny. These two planets in the square position spell out the potential for trouble with regard to our actions. Strong disputes and war related action between generations, and among those of different cultures, are likely to occur. This aspect does imply a more likely time for an attack from groups seeking to take power, but with such attacks there will be struggles. These actions against or conflicts with higher powers are likely to backfire – it is best not to bluff those of a higher or unanticipated authority at this time as taking action in an attempt to create a transformation may be very dangerous. This may be a particularly difficult time to fight addiction, disease, and war related stress – it is also the most crucial time not to give up the fight.

May 14th Monday

Moon in Aries / Taurus	PDT	EDT
Moon trine Jupiter	12:01 AM	3:01 AM
Moon trine Saturn	1:43 AM	4:43 AM
Moon sextile Neptune	7:03 AM	10:03 AM
Moon trine Pluto goes v/c	5:25 PM	8:25 PM
Moon enters Taurus	7:49 PM	10:49 PM

Mood Watch: Overnight, Moon trine Jupiter brings a joyous start to this new day and to this new week ahead of us. Moon trine Saturn brings a sense of perfect control or perfect timing while we dream and sleep. This morning, Moon sextile Neptune brings peacefulness. Waning Moon in Aries is a time when our moods may be influenced by the efficiency with which tasks are carried out, and by how much self-assurance and self-confidence can be mustered. Waning Moon in Aries challenges individuals to take charge and to take initiative in areas of life that require immediate action. This is the time to empower personal expertise with bold confidence. Tonight, Moon trine Pluto brings strongly tolerant moods with regard to life's unchangeable transformations. The Aries Moon also goes void-of-course which, ironically, tests our patience. While we may not be so patient over that which we end up tolerating, it may also be wise to avoid heavy confrontations with others that would probably result in nasty fights. As the Moon enters Taurus, our moods will become much more practical and down-to-earth.

May 15th Tuesday

Moon in Taurus	PDT	EDT
Mars enters Aries	7:07 AM	10:07 AM
Moon sextile Venus	8:39 AM	11:39 AM

Mood Watch: This is the eve of the New Moon and, as the Taurus Moon wanes darkly, there is a quality of wisdom in our moods. The wise old soul of the Taurus Moon puts us in touch with our needs, the essentials of life, and reminds us to keep a handle on practical matters. Moon sextile Venus brings the potential for very pleasurable, affectionate, and beautiful feelings to occur. Taurus Moon invites us to enjoy simple comforts and pleasures.

♉

Mars enters Aries (Mars in Aries: May 15 – June 24) Mars, the planet of action and masculine drive and force, is at home in Aries, the sign it rules, where it initiates activities in the most forward and direct manner possible. Mars is the god of war in mythology; often Mars related experience is generated through our impulses, our anger and rage, our fear and compulsion, our need to confront and bring forth the primal force of energy and zeal that is our ability to take action – it's our spark of life. Mars now in Aries boosts the lives of Aries people and gives them both the energy and the incentive to take action in their lives, and there are undoubtedly heated matters going on in their lives as well. Mars' influence generates activity and heat which can often appear explosive under pressure. Aries people are reminded to keep a cool sense of control at all times, and to build on their crucible of energy with a direct sense of clarity and purpose. Aries folks can strike now while the iron is hot, but use caution: be aware of fires, potential accidents, and fevers. Capricorn and Cancer folks need to be especially cautious as Mars now squares to their natal Sun sign, causing the events around them to seem personally abrasive and particularly maddening at times. Libra people may be aware of extreme fiery activity in their lives with Mars opposing their natal Sun sign. The other fire signs of the zodiac may benefit too. Leo and Sagittarius people are experiencing the favorable trine of Mars to their natal Sun signs; this gives our fire sign friends a boost of energy, some hot and some all too hot. Fire signs have within them the means to naturally identify with the forces of Mars activity in their lives. However, even when one is in one's element, the relentless spirit of Mars must be carefully tempered in their busy lives, or they'll burn out. A lot goes on with Mars in Aries, so when the strain becomes too absorbing, remember to rest now and then.

May 16th Wednesday
Moon in Taurus / Gemini - NEW MOON in TAURUS

	PDT	EDT	
Moon sextile Uranus	12:37 AM	3:37 AM	
Moon square Saturn	1:40 AM	4:40 AM	
Moon square Neptune	6:50 AM	9:50 AM	
Moon conjunct Sun goes v/c	12:28 PM	3:28 PM	
Moon enters Gemini	7:35 PM	10:35 PM	
Moon sextile Mars	9:32 PM	12:32 AM	(May 17)
Mercury opposite Jupiter begins (see May 19)			

Mood Watch: Overnight, Moon sextile Uranus brings moods and dreams inspired by liberation. Moon square Saturn may bring troublesome dreams about our struggles over having control. This morning, Moon square Neptune brings moods that may challenge us with regard to spiritual beliefs. **New Moon in Taurus** (Moon conjunct Sun) emphasizes the acquisition of new possessions, or it could mean there is a need to restore, replenish, and maintain the old ones. Either way, establishing a sense of personal contentment with possessions will bring relief. We must find the value of what we need and want but, while the Taurus Moon is void-of-course all day long, the struggle to get what we want will be trying at times. Despite the minor setbacks, Taurus is an exalted place for the Moon, and the New Moon encourages us to bring newness into our physical surroundings. This is a great time to enjoy the emerging beauty found in nature. Later, the Gemini Moon brings curious and talkative moods. Active opportunities are stirred this evening, as Moon sextile Mars occurs.

May 17th Thursday

Moon in Gemini	PDT	EDT	
Moon conjunct Mercury	4:32 PM	7:32 PM	
Moon opposite Jupiter	11:24 PM	2:24 AM	(May 18)
Mercury square Uranus begins (see May 20)			

Mood Watch: The Gemini Moon newly waxes and today we will be more inclined to communicate what's been on our minds, as well as sorting out the details. Gemini Moon entices us to satiate our curiosities and to carry through on our thoughts and ideas. This is a good time to organize, improvise, negotiate, and pontificate. Moon conjunct Mercury in Gemini brings especially talkative and curious moods and this is a great time to catch up on correspondences. Later tonight, Moon opposite Jupiter brings moods that may seem overwhelmed by expenditures and the rising cost of living. Gemini Moon assists us to think matters through.

May 18th Friday

Moon in Gemini / Cancer	PDT	EDT
Moon square Uranus	1:00 AM	4:00 AM
Moon sextile Saturn	2:09 AM	5:09 AM
Moon trine Neptune	7:21 AM	10:21 AM
Moon opposite Pluto goes v/c	5:58 PM	8:58 PM
Moon enters Cancer	8:39 PM	11:39 PM
Mercury sextile Saturn begins (see May 21)		

Mood Watch: Overnight, Moon square Uranus brings chaotic and difficult moods and dreams. Moon sextile Saturn brings moods that tend to be serious. The waxing Gemini Moon assists us to pull all the busy details of life together. This is a good time to learn to flip the coin of duality by taking in both sides of the equation and enjoying alternative perspectives. As you flip the coin, learn to laugh at the comedy of spontaneous confusion that permeates a knowledge driven society full of layered ignorance and unsorted data — a great time to play around with new data and allow for new ideas. This morning, Moon trine Neptune brings moods which will be blessed with peacefulness. This evening, Moon opposite Pluto brings moods that will inspire awareness of life's more intense qualities. The Gemini Moon also goes void-of-course for a spell and our moods will probably be somewhat scattered. As the Moon enters Cancer, our moods enter into a much more keen emotional awareness of all those things we've been thinking about lately.

May 19th Saturday

Moon in Cancer	PDT	EDT	
Moon square Mars	1:28 AM	4:28 AM	
Moon conjunct Venus	6:32 PM	9:32 PM	
Mercury opposite Jupiter	10:31 PM	1:31 AM	(May 20)
Mercury trine Neptune begins (see May 23)			
Venus trine Uranus begins (see May 24)			

Mood Watch: Overnight, Moon square Mars brings challenging moods and dreams which will assist us to vent any anger or anguish we have been feeling. Domestic focuses and maternal instincts take the stage today. Cancer Moon is a rewarding time to focus on brightening the home atmosphere with warmth, love, and nourishing foods. Tonight, Moon conjunct Venus brings moods that will be drawn to beauty and pleasurable delights.

Mercury opposite Jupiter (occurring May 16 – 21) Mercury in Gemini is opposite Jupiter in Sagittarius bringing detailed observations about overwhelming visions, adventures and travels. We may find ourselves bartering for things that cannot be sold. An economic shift may bring financial or political awareness, and the incessant chatter which fills the airwaves has a further effect on the sharp movements occurring in the stock market. This aspect also focuses news on the opulent lifestyles of the rich and famous, as people find themselves unable to stop talking about their financial situation or their need for advancement, a raise, or an income. Wealth is highlighted, and there is considerable debate as to what wealth really represents. Most of the time wealth is an illusion, and people really don't know what they're talking about when they make assumptions about the apparent well being of others. As class separation continues, it is a time of acute concern in this realm.

May 20th Sunday

Moon in Cancer	PDT	EDT
Moon trine Uranus	3:57 AM	6:57 AM
Mercury square Uranus	4:27 PM	7:27 PM

Mood Watch: Overnight, Moon trine Uranus brings exciting and librating feelings and dreams. Although we often mask our true feelings, our moods are affected by the shifts of the Moon and are shared collectively by those we encounter. Waxing Cancer Moon reminds us that our inner feelings do eventually change and new feelings need to emerge. Today many folks will be in the mood to give hints about how new feelings are affecting them.

Mercury square Uranus (occurring May 17 – 22) As a general rule, this aspect creates excessive disruptions in communications. Mercury in Gemini is square to Uranus in Pisces. Communications, talks, discussions and news are troubled and challenged by unusual or explosive circumstances. It is also possible that important news of a radical nature will be obscured by sensationalism or overlooked as insignificant. Mercury in the sign of Gemini emphasizes the need to communicate about absolutely everything, while Uranus in the sign of Pisces emphasizes the need to deal with the revolutionary processes of beliefs, religion, and spiritual matters. The two focuses are creating a tension between people as they discuss their beliefs. Religious debates bring out the two sides of an issue repeatedly. Be careful what you say and how you say it; stirring up chaos can sometimes cause disruptive damage that is not really necessary, and in this case may be a contributing factor that costs some folks their jobs or something else important to them. Mercury square Uranus will repeat again on December 10, when Mercury will be in Sagittarius.

GEMINI

Key Phrase: "I THINK"

Mutable Air Sign

Symbol: The Twins

May 21st through June 21st

May 21st Monday

Victoria Day, Canada

Moon in Cancer / Leo

	PDT	EDT
Moon sextile Sun goes v/c	12:47 AM	3:47 AM
Moon enters Leo	12:58 AM	3:58 AM
Sun enters Gemini	3:13 AM	6:13 AM
Mercury sextile Saturn	3:49 AM	6:49 AM
Moon trine Mars	9:23 AM	12:23 PM

Mood Watch: Overnight, Moon sextile Sun brings inspiration to our dreams with regard to the seasonal factors occurring at this time. Simultaneously, the Cancer Moon goes void-of-course and just minutes later, it enters Leo. The waxing Leo Moon will bring joyous and playful moods today as the Sun enters Gemini. Frisky and flirtatious moods are likely to entice our spirit. Tonight, Moon trine Mars brings positive strength and might. The final round of spring is here.

Sun enters Gemini (Sun in Gemini: May 21 – June 21) The final lap of springtime now commences! Discussions, debates, writing, speeches, and investigations are all Gemini related events -- Gemini people love to think. They're often thinking of ways to change the picture and to make it brighter and more detailed. The mutable, adaptable mind must be free to roam with different concepts and ideas that haven't been fully integrated into the big picture. Gemini weaves tapestries of thought; great storytellers, Geminis are often articulate and eloquent speakers, captivating audiences with details and keen observations. Gemini is a mutable air sign; this Mercury-ruled sign works hard to get the message across. The Gemini downside is that there is an endless curiosity that can drive the Gemini personality (or the people around them) to complete restlessness or nervousness. Duality is the key factor that shapes the Gemini perspective, and there is always a need to explore the two sides of life, as well as act out the two sides or viewpoints of their personalities. They usually identify with both the male and female perspectives on life, and have a high level of refinement. Gemini *needs* to keep thinking and paying attention to the details, which makes meditation and the stilling of the mind a true challenge for them. The Gemini days are those in which we can become easily distracted, scattered, or spread too thin on our mental plane. This is a good time to stay focused, but also to have fun.

Mercury sextile Saturn (occurring May 18 – 22) Mercury in Gemini is sextile Saturn in Leo. Communications occurring at this time place great emphasis on seeing both sides of each story. Controversial issues bring the need to speak out, one way or the other, on personal perspectives. Opportunities are now available to assist us in creating more security and control over how we conduct our personal and family lives and how we communicate and incorporate personal values with regard to the family structure. For a short time, this aspect gives people an opportunity to learn vital lessons concerning boundaries, limitations, responsibilities and timely completion. This is a favorable aspect to discuss where to set up boundaries and how to implement security systems, and to teach people about handling responsibilities and disciplines. This aspect will repeat three more times this year; September 30, October 19, and November 16, when Mercury will be in Scorpio and Saturn will be newly in the sign of Virgo (Saturn enters Virgo: Sept. 2).

May 22nd Tuesday

Moon in Leo	PDT	EDT
Moon trine Jupiter	7:53 AM	10:53 AM
Moon conjunct Saturn	12:28 PM	3:28 PM
Moon sextile Mercury	5:06 PM	8:06 PM
Moon opposite Neptune	6:03 PM	9:03 PM

Mood Watch: The waxing Moon in Leo encourages us to unleash our wild and beastly tendencies. This morning, Moon trine Jupiter brings generous moods blessed with prosperous feelings. This afternoon, Moon conjunct Saturn brings moods that are connected to our disciplines and to our sense of accomplishment. Many people will be very focused and structured in their work. This evening, Moon sextile Mercury brings moods inspired by communications and news. Moon opposite Neptune brings moods that may be opposed to, or overwhelmed by, spiritualism. This Leo Moon evening will be a good time to enjoy friends and family and to seek entertainment.

May 23rd Wednesday

Shavuot
Moon in Leo / Virgo - FIRST QUARTER MOON in VIRGO

	PDT	EDT
Mercury trine Neptune	12:48 AM	3:48 AM
Moon trine Pluto goes v/c	6:10 AM	9:10 AM
Moon enters Virgo	9:27 AM	12:27 PM
Moon square Sun	2:04 PM	5:04 PM
Mercury opposite Pluto begins (see May 27)		
Sun sextile Mars begins (see June 11)		

Mood Watch: This morning, Moon trine Pluto brings harmonious moods with regard to matters of fate. The Leo moon also goes void-of-course for more than a few hours this morning bringing beastly moods. As the Moon enters Virgo, practical moods begin to surface. **First Quarter Moon in Virgo** (Moon square Sun) brings a strong investigative curiosity that occurs with the Sun in Gemini and the Moon in Virgo. Both these Mercury ruled signs are emphasizing the need to keep the flow going both on a logical and a practical level, particularly when it comes to relaying information. This is a busy time of spring when the quickening of summer will soon be upon us, and the preparation for the long days of the Sun has begun. As we anticipate our summer plans, there is a strong desire to follow through on dreams and desires with detailed clarity. Virgo Moon encourages us to assess matters properly, and to be pragmatic and specific when delegating certain tasks or jobs. First Quarter Virgo Moon is an excellent time to launch a health program and to cleanse the body of excess toxins.

Mercury trine Neptune (occurring May 19 – 25) This is a superb aspect for discussing personal philosophies and metaphysical subjects, and a good time to communicate with the spirit world. Mercury trine Neptune brings gifts of encouraging news from Spirit. Out of the upheaval will come a much needed boon. Those who are open to communication and prayer will have a spiritual channel now open to their hearts and minds, a place where peace and tranquility can be found. Mercury in Gemini is trine to Neptune in Aquarius. Thoughtful discussions bring intuitive knowledge. Communicate about spiritual needs with helpful counsel and receive gifts of renewed faith in your own beliefs. Accept that some messages are there to spiritually uplift you, despite the clamor of this busy time of the Sun in Gemini. This aspect will occur again on September 18 when Mercury will be in Libra.

May 24th Thursday
Moon in Virgo

	PDT	EDT	
Moon square Jupiter	5:53 PM	8:53 PM	
Neptune goes retrograde	6:08 PM	9:08 PM	
Moon sextile Venus	9:35 PM	12:35 AM	(May 25)
Moon opposite Uranus	9:46 PM	12:46 AM	(May 25)
Venus trine Uranus	11:42 PM	2:42 AM	(May 25)

Mood Watch: Sensible, cautious, observant, and meticulous moods make this day interesting enough with the Moon waxing in Virgo. This Moon is reminding us that health practices are important. A wholesome diet, therapeutic treatment, and a more thorough level of care taken with grooming and personal hygiene – these are all good things to apply during Virgo Moon. This is also a good time to be decisive about record keeping and accounting. This evening, Moon square Jupiter may bring some apprehension with regard to the need to prosper, and our moods may be somewhat prudent about spending. Moon sextile Venus will bring moods that will be responsive to love. Later, Moon opposite Uranus brings explosive dreams and radical feelings.

Neptune goes retrograde (Neptune retrograde: May 24 – October 31) Like clockwork, every year, the planet Neptune goes retrograde for about five months. Today Neptune goes retrograde in Aquarius, and it remains in this celestial pattern until October 29. Neptune governs the spiritual dimensions, and when in Aquarius it inspires a special interest in the spiritual development of humanity. While Neptune is retrograde, many of the spiritual issues that have come up in the last five to six months will reoccur. Neptune harmonizes spiritual vibrations and represents intuition and higher feminine wisdom. For the next five months, be aware of the frequency of escapist tendencies, and of the inclination to internalize deep-rooted spiritual matters. Being firm with your own spiritual center will allow for progressive spiritual growth. Be careful not to blindly disrupt the core of another's belief system, nor to become ensnared by someone else's blindness with regard to your own beliefs during Neptune's retrograde months.

Venus trine Uranus (occurring May 19 – 28) Venus in Cancer is trine Uranus in Pisces. Tender hearted and motherly kinds of love and attraction will make positive breakthroughs in matters of belief and believing. Venus trine Uranus brings a favorable attraction to revolutionary concepts. This is a time of freedom fighters and rebel love, and youth is easily attracted to the spirit of rebellion. Dangerous love and taking chances become common occurrences. This aspect creates an attraction to the unusual, yet it allows a harmony to exist in love related matters while chaotic occurrences are taking place. Love at first sight is explosive at this time, but not necessarily long lasting. This aspect will repeat on December 17, when Venus will be in Scorpio.

May 25th Friday
Moon in Virgo / Libra (PDT)

	PDT	EDT	
Moon square Mercury	12:39 PM	3:39 PM	
Moon square Pluto goes v/c	5:45 PM	8:45 PM	
Moon enters Libra	9:17 PM	12:17 AM	(May 26)

Mood Watch: While the Moon is in Virgo, the energy suggests there is a need to examine resources. This is a good time to do research and to stay on top of shifting, acquiring, or selling the resources that are currently available. This is also a good time to clean, and to tidy up paperwork and to search for missing objects. This afternoon, Moon square Mercury brings moods that will be challenged by communications – a good time to be careful what you say. This evening, Moon square Pluto may be a difficult time to collaborate with people of another generation or those of a different cultural background. The Moon goes void-of-course at this point in the evening – skepticism and doubt could be the cause of evening delays or minor setbacks. As the Moon enters Libra on the west coast tonight, our moods enter into the necessity for balance.

May 26th Saturday
Moon in Libra

	PDT	EDT
Moon trine Sun	7:23 AM	10:23 AM
Moon opposite Mars	2:39 PM	5:39 PM

Mood Watch: The Libra Moon waxes and places the emphasis of our moods on the joyous company of good friends, loving companions, and supporters. Libra Moon also focuses our sights on carrying out important objectives and on harmonizing teamwork. The Moon trine Sun brings a joyous and harmonious start to the day. This afternoon, Moon opposite Mars brings moods at odds with disharmonizing force. This may also be an accident prone time, as moods tend to be aggressive, and competitive attitudes may seem to dominate the atmosphere. The Libra Moon energies always hold firmly to the concept of striving for balance.

May 27th Sunday

Moon in Libra	PDT	EDT
Moon sextile Jupiter	6:00 AM	9:00 AM
Mercury opposite Pluto	8:14 AM	11:14 AM
Moon sextile Saturn	12:43 PM	3:43 PM
Moon square Venus	4:15 PM	7:15 PM
Moon trine Neptune	6:03 PM	9:03 PM

Mood Watch: Once again, the Libra Moon reminds us that this is a good time to focus on teamwork and to discuss decision making matters with others. This morning, Moon sextile Jupiter brings optimistic and hopeful moods to start the day. This afternoon, Moon sextile Saturn brings moods that are inspired by a sense of control and precision. Moon square Venus may challenge our sense of love and affection. Lastly today, Moon trine Neptune brings moods that will be in harmony with beliefs. A calm and peaceful evening is in store for many folks tonight.

Mercury opposite Pluto (occurring May 23 – 29) Mercury in Gemini opposes Pluto in Sagittarius. Dual perspectives of the intense and grotesque aspects of the news may be emphasized, causing horror, fascination, realization, and for some people, a kind of triumph as well. The news highlights power issues and the ensuing struggles for a breakthrough. This aspect will only be evident for a short time, but the long term affects for some folks may be unforgettable. Mind boggling awareness abounds now as the need to comprehend awakening powerful issues comes through in our thoughts and discussions.

May 28th Monday

Memorial Day, USA

Moon in Libra / Scorpio	PDT	EDT
Moon sextile Pluto	6:33 AM	9:33 AM
Moon trine Mercury goes v/c	9:18 AM	12:18 PM
Moon enters Scorpio	10:12 AM	1:12 PM
Mercury enters Cancer	5:57 PM	8:57 PM
Mars trine Jupiter begins (see June 4)		

Mood Watch: This Libra Moon, amicable and gentle moods are coupled with strong intent. Moon sextile Pluto opens up the day with moods receptive to the inevitable factors of life, and many folks will feel as though they can tolerate just about anything. Moon trine Mercury brings harmonious communications and, at the same time, the void-of-course Moon begins, producing a brief hour of indecisiveness. As the Moon enters Scorpio, our moods enter into a phase of passionate awareness. The waxing Scorpio Moon is rarely dull.

Mercury enters Cancer (Mercury in Cancer: May 28 – August 4) During this phase of Mercury in Cancer, Mercury will go retrograde from June 15 – July 9. This is why Mercury will remain in this sign for a longer than usual period of time. The shift in communications turns our attention from an emphasis on details and logic (Mercury in Gemini) to a focus on feelings and senses (Mercury in Cancer). This is a time when many people will appear to intuit their way through conversations. Thoughts may blend with mood as the emphasis on emotional expression takes the stage. As Mercury goes through the sign of Cancer, take special note of a tendency for people to talk more specifically about their feelings, defenses, and the need to be nurtured. Mercury in Cancer makes some people more intuitive to the thoughts of others, and this may be an easier time to interpret people's thoughts by observing their emotional body language. While Mercury is retrograde in Cancer, beware of the tendency for people to overstress the morals and dogma of home related or domestic points of interest. Through Cancer, thoughts and communications are shaped by the course of our complex world of emotions.

May 29th Tuesday

Moon in Scorpio	PDT	EDT	
Moon trine Uranus	11:16 PM	2:16 AM	(May 30)

Mood Watch: The Moon is in Scorpio and social complications tend to be dealt with in a more abrupt manner. Sometimes our moods are more inclined to handle intense kinds of circumstances in a more secretive manner. Either way, it may seem as if there is some kind of contentious force infringing on the harmony of our moods and urging us to look more intently at the fixed core of our emotional realm. Scorpio Moon brings challenging and demanding moods that often lead people to do more dramatic kinds of things. This is also a good time to work out intense feelings with creative activities that sharpen and increase our skills and allow us to work through and transform hidden emotional turmoil. Tonight's Moon trine Uranus brings moods that will be, pleasantly, surprisingly, in harmony with the forces of chaos and disorder.

May 30th Wednesday

Moon in Scorpio / Sagittarius	PDT	EDT	
Moon square Saturn	1:29 AM	4:29 AM	
Moon square Neptune	6:22 AM	9:22 AM	
Moon trine Venus goes v/c	10:13 AM	1:13 PM	
Moon enters Sagittarius	10:08 PM	1:08 AM	(May 31)

Mood Watch: The Scorpio Moon invokes desire, and the creative spark of springtime yearnings are ever present. Overnight, Moon square Saturn brings moods and dreams which may be disquieting to our sense of stability and control. This morning, Moon square Neptune brings a spiritually challenging time. Early in the day, Moon trine Venus brings the strong urge for love, and loving energy won't be hard to find. The Scorpio Moon also goes void-of-course at this point, and the heavily waxing Moon in Scorpio will remain hopelessly and dangerously void-of-course for the next twelve hours. The frolic and mischief of today is likely to disrupt all sense of pragmatism and solidity. The Pluto-ruled sign of Scorpio is an intense place of emotional transformation, and when the Moon is void-of-course in Scorpio at such a full stage, dramatically swift and remarkable changes can occur in our expressions of mood. This is a good time to be cautious, guarded, and to be aware of dangers and troubling factors that could do a lot of psychological damage, as well as physical or emotional harm. This is not a good time to count on getting a lot of work completed, or to make progress on mundane levels. Later tonight, when the Moon enters Sagittarius, insightful reverie tops this day very nicely.

May 31st Thursday
FULL MOON in SAGITTARIUS PDT   EDT

	PDT	EDT	
Moon opposite Sun	6:05 PM	9:05 PM	
Moon trine Mars	10:39 PM	1:39 AM	(June 1)
Sun opposite Jupiter begins (see June 5)			

Mood Watch: **Full Moon in Sagittarius** (Moon opposite Sun) emphasizes such focuses as sports, travel, exploration of the senses, and philosophical endeavors. There is a tendency to go out beyond the usual bounds and discover new territory. How we chose to perceive and develop our understanding of this new territory has a lot to do with what stage in our life we have come to, and what kind of philosophy best suits our own individual needs. Profound and extraordinary realizations and events often occur during the Full Sagittarius Moon. These turning points in our lives may be very obvious, or a more subtle but just as important kind of shift can occur through a simple change of attitude in our outlook on life. Later tonight, Moon trine Mars brings moods in harmony with the influence of masculine forces.

June 1st Friday
Moon in Sagittarius

	PDT	EDT
Moon conjunct Jupiter	4:20 AM	7:20 AM
Moon square Uranus	10:09 AM	1:09 PM
Moon trine Saturn	12:32 PM	3:32 PM
Moon sextile Neptune	4:55 PM	7:55 PM

Mood Watch: We begin this first day of the month with a post-full waning Sagittarius Moon. While the Sagittarius Moon already reached its big crescendo of maximal lunar fervor last night, the energy of our moods is still highly sensitive to the changes taking place at this time. This morning's Moon conjunct Jupiter brings jovial optimism and explorative moods abound. Unfortunately, Moon square Uranus brings moods that will be challenged by chaos and by radical attitudes. It may be messy at times but, this afternoon, Moon trine Saturn brings moods that will allow for precise and focused efforts to create a sense of order and stability. This evening's Moon sextile Neptune brings moods inspired by Spirit, and the tranquil peace that Spirit brings may well be a comfort to those who seek it.

June 2nd Saturday
Moon in Sagittarius / Capricorn PDT   EDT

	PDT	EDT
Moon conjunct Pluto goes v/c	4:30 AM	7:30 AM
Moon enters Capricorn	8:10 AM	11:10 AM
Moon opposite Mercury	6:28 PM	9:28 PM
Mars trine Saturn begins (see June 11)		

Mood Watch: The waning Sagittarius Moon conjunct Pluto brings extraordinary perspectives for our moods to absorb. This morning's early void-of-course Moon brings moods that are somewhat spacey, and it could be easy to wander off the beaten track and, possibly, get lost. However, soon enough, the Moon enters Capricorn and our senses snap to it, with a firm affirmation towards getting a handle on our boundaries. The waning Capricorn Moon brings clear, focused, work-oriented moods that allow us to filter out all the cloudy, uncertain kinds of perspectives impeding on our work and our progress. This evening, Moon opposite Mercury brings moods that may be overwhelmed by too much information. Be careful how you handle conversation, as some folks may tend to take matters much too seriously.

June 3rd Sunday

Moon in Capricorn	PDT	EDT
Moon square Mars	11:25 AM	2:25 PM
Moon sextile Uranus	7:04 PM	10:04 PM
Sun square Uranus begins (see June 9)		

Mood Watch: Masculine forces are at work with the Moon in an aspect to Mars, and to Uranus. It starts with Moon square Mars, and this brings moods likely to be challenged by martial force, or by crude, abrupt actions. Our moods may appear more guarded at this stage of the Moon's phase, known as *Waning Gibbous* – the waning stage of the post-full Moon. On the emotional level, Capricorn is a barren place for the Moon, often reflected in a somewhat serious tone or work obsessed manner. The Moon itself is a cold, rocky mass of matter that has no light of its own but shines by sunlight reflected from its surface. The cold, hard facts – that's the way the Capricorn Moon spirit wants it, with no refuge for emotional sensation to flourish. This is *not* to say that emotional experiences won't be occurring today; it simply means that our moods may appear limited or restricted by the necessity for practicality. It all shakes loose tonight, as Moon sextile Uranus brings moods inspired by rebellion and by the need for freedom.

June 4th Monday

Moon in Capricorn / Aquarius	PDT	EDT
Mars trine Jupiter	7:59 AM	10:59 AM
Moon opposite Venus goes v/c	2:45 PM	5:45 PM
Moon enters Aquarius	4:16 PM	7:16 PM

Mood Watch: The Full Moon events that took place late last week have been too much for some people to bear. For now, it is more convenient to ignore the anomaly of unsettled feelings and to focus more intently on the tedious and mundane tasks of everyday life. The Moon now wanes and the process of letting go of useless feelings is common with the Capricorn Moon. This is an excellent time to work on setting aside worries and fears, and to concentrate more clearly on handling basic needs with practical, purposeful, and undaunted care. As the Moon goes void-of-course, Moon opposite Venus brings moods that may be opposed to, or overwhelmed by, compelling attractions. For awhile our moods may seem to be distracted by serious matters and there may be the need to stabilize the situations that arise. As the Moon enters Aquarius, our moods enter into the need to know. Aquarius says: "I know," and in knowledge there is truth.

Mars trine Jupiter (occurring May 28 – June 7) Mars is in Aries activating a strong focus on self-reliance, competition, winning, and placing an all-around emphasis on the power of success. Jupiter is in Sagittarius, expanding our economic growth through global awareness, travel, sports, and special skills. Act on opportunities as they arise and set visions and dreams into a feasible plan that holds the potential for favorable actions to occur. The drive to create some expansion of our livelihood involves resourceful awareness. Mars activates and stirs action, while

Jupiter represents not only economy and advancement, but our sense of philosophic and visionary awareness as well – especially now that retrograde Jupiter recedes through the mid-degrees of its home sign, Sagittarius. Here, introspective reflections will help us to realize new talents and new means of livelihood, and perhaps even some prosperity, joy and well being. For some people this aspect brings gifts of inheritance; for all of us it brings opportunities for growth. Mars trine Jupiter allows us to activate a stronger grasp of our domain, and gives many folks the extra energy and spark to boost their sense of achievement and advancement.

June 5th Tuesday

Moon in Aquarius	PDT	EDT	
Venus enters Leo	11:00 AM	2:00 PM	
Sun opposite Jupiter	4:14 PM	7:14 PM	
Moon sextile Jupiter	7:24 PM	10:24 PM	
Moon trine Sun	7:41 PM	10:41 PM	
Moon sextile Mars	9:52 PM	12:52 AM	(June 6)

Mood Watch: The Aquarius Moon brings clever, innovative, and intelligent perspectives. The Sun and Moon are in air signs and this is the time to compile data and research, and to integrate it into spring projects and social endeavors. Aquarius Moon is a good time to socialize, work with large groups of people, and to learn about the things that get people excited. Experimental moods lead to amazing discoveries. This evening's Moon trine Sun brings harmonious intelligence

Venus enters Leo (Venus in Leo: June 5 – July 14) Venus in Leo brings out the more playful side of love. Venus represents the expression of love and affection; it is the influence of magnetism, beauty, and of feminine refinement. In the sign of Leo, Venus brings out desires and needs for personal attention. Magnetism is one of Leo's most endearing traits, and it is this magnetism that brings what Leos want most: loving attention. The entertainment industry will be highlighted as music, poetry, art, singing and acting are all enhanced with heartfelt expression. Leos will be more aware of their need for love. The love of looking good, having the best, and being the best is alluring to the ego. Wild lust will abound and the love of fantasies will be enhanced. Love affairs may be torrid and dramatic, while affections, when first initiated, can seem very ardent and sincere. One might be hesitant to believe that a too-good-to-be-true relationship is actually occurring. On the other hand, if it doesn't feel harmonious, it may be because the love affair is more focused on the demands and needs of just one person. Leo demands a lot of affection and, when Venus comes into play, the need for attention sometimes outweighs the need to reciprocate that attention. It is always wise not to have expectations in love matters and to be sure that the joys of exchanging love are balanced. Venus will be in Leo for a longer than usual period of time, as Venus will go retrograde from July 27 – September 8, and it will re-enter the tail-end of Leo on August 8, remaining there until October 7.

Sun opposite Jupiter (occurring May 31 – June 8) Gemini birthday people, celebrating birthdays from May 31 – June 8, are experiencing the opposition of Jupiter to their natal Sun. This brings an acute awareness of the shifts in personal economic conditions and issues, for better or worse. There is a strong personal awareness, or perhaps an obsession, at work to obtain a sense of wealth, joy, and well being. The need for peace in the shifting economy of these times is strong for these Gemini birthday folks. Use your best techniques, birthday Gemini, to abstain from impulse buying or credit card use. Governing your expenditures with wisdom instead of impetuosity will assuredly bring you around to the place you know you need to be. While it all comes at you at an overwhelming pace, remember this, Gemini – you can have (just about) anything you want – you just can't have *everything*.

June 6th Wednesday

Moon in Aquarius / Pisces	PDT	EDT	
Moon opposite Saturn	4:44 AM	7:44 AM	
Moon conjunct Neptune	8:10 AM	11:10 AM	
Moon sextile Pluto goes v/c	6:48 PM	9:48 PM	
Moon enters Pisces	10:25 PM	1:25 AM	(June 7)
Sun trine Neptune begins (see June 13)			

Mood Watch: Waning Moon in Aquarius leads our moods on a quest towards knowledge. On some level the desire for a certain kind of freedom or personal breakthrough calls out to some folks. The restlessness of spring season stirs our hearts. People we haven't seen in some time are starting to come out in droves. With the Moon and Sun both now in air signs, there will be a lot on our minds and much to talk about. This morning, Moon opposite Saturn brings moods that will be acutely affected by matters of security or authority. Moon conjunct Neptune brings moods keenly connected to our beliefs. This evening, Moon sextile Pluto brings moods intrigued by matters of fate. The Aquarius Moon goes void-of-course for a number of hours, bringing moods which will be distracted by technical glitches, eccentric behavior, and possibly, by matters of scientific thought or phenomena. Later, as the Moon enters Pisces, our moods will exhibit numerous kinds of intuitive responses.

June 7th Thursday

Moon in Pisces	PDT	EDT
Moon trine Mercury	2:29 PM	5:29 PM
Sun sextile Saturn begins (see June 11)		

Mood Watch: Today's only lunar aspect, Moon trine Mercury, brings moods which will be in harmony with various kinds of talk and discussions. The Moon wanes in Pisces and the overall spirit of the day will be more inclined towards the need to ease stress, alter the senses, and escape from the mundane. Waning Pisces Moon allows us to express our moods best through art, music, dance and creative endeavors. A positive experience emerges through the purging of old habits and destructive tendencies. This is a time when intuition and psychic impressions flow more fluently and when synchronicities and coincidences are experienced with insightful clarity.

June 8th Friday
LAST QUARTER MOON in PISCES

	PDT	EDT	
Moon square Jupiter	12:02 AM	3:02 AM	
Moon square Sun	4:44 AM	7:44 AM	
Moon conjunct Uranus	6:56 AM	9:56 AM	
Moon square Pluto goes v/c	10:53 PM	1:53 AM	(June 9)
Mars sextile Neptune begins (see June 13)			

Mood Watch: Overnight, Moon square Jupiter brings moods and dreams that are challenged by the fear of loss, and by unexpected economic shifts. The **Last Quarter Moon in Pisces** (Moon square Sun) arrives early this morning. The Pisces Moon influence brings a dreamy sort of atmosphere. A mysterious and enchanting quality of reflection is occurring, allowing the imagination to roam with consistent accuracy and touching the core of our beliefs. Waning Pisces Moon tends to keep us entranced by those areas of our life that bring depth and meaning. This is a good time to cleanse the spiritual cobwebs from our own lives. Reinforce personal fortitude with the strength to overcome addictions by using sheer willpower and belief in oneself. This morning's Moon conjunct Uranus brings moods that may be interpreted as being rather radical, and possibly, explosive. Later tonight, Moon square Pluto finds our moods challenged by the unchangeable factors of life. As the Moon goes void-of-course in Pisces, empty, trance-like moods will be common and this may be a good time for deep rest.

June 9th Saturday
Moon in Pisces / Aries

	PDT	EDT
Moon enters Aries	2:27 AM	5:27 AM
Moon trine Venus	8:52 AM	11:52 AM
Sun square Uranus	1:09 PM	4:09 PM
Moon square Mercury	7:50 PM	10:50 PM

Mood Watch: As the Moon enters Aries our moods enter into the spirit of competitiveness. The waning Aries Moon brings restlessness and forces numerous folks to rustle up some energy around special interest activities. This morning, Moon trine Venus brings harmony and beauty, and our moods will be somewhat kind and affectionate. Later on, Moon square Mercury brings moods challenged by complex communications and difficult subjects, and defensive moods become argumentative. Aries Moon encourages us to act on aggressive moods while we still have the volition and the courage to fight the battles that are calling to us.

Sun square Uranus (occurring June 3 – 12) This occurrence of Sun square Uranus particularly affects those Gemini people celebrating birthdays June 3 – 12. The square of Uranus to these Gemini folks' natal Sun brings a strong dose of unrestrained chaos some and challenging events. This may be the year for you, Gemini birthday folks, to surrender to those aspects of life that are truly out of your control, and to concentrate more rationally on those facets of life over which you do have control. Sometimes the aftermath of Uranus influence is an improvement, but with the square aspect at work, it is likely that these people will feel personally challenged. It is important to understand that some kinds of personal challenges are best left alone, while other challenges must be confronted directly without causing destructive damage, particularly to one's self. On the other hand, birthday Gemini folks, if your life has no foundation, there is no point in holding on to the illusion of stability at this juncture of your sojourn. Albeit slowly, this aspect will pass in due time. Try to be detached from chaotic events as they occur, and the outcome will seem less costly. It is vital not to give rapid change too much resistance, lest you be subject to the reversals of trying to fight chaos with logic at a time when resistance is futile. Project the picture of peace and it will be there for you at the other end. This aspect will repeat on December 7 this year, when the Sun will be in Sagittarius.

June 10th Sunday

Moon in Aries	PDT	EDT
Moon trine Jupiter	2:36 AM	5:36 AM
Moon sextile Sun	11:10 AM	2:10 PM
Moon conjunct Mars	11:25 AM	2:25 PM
Moon trine Saturn	12:43 PM	3:43 PM
Moon sextile Neptune	3:15 PM	6:15 PM

Mood Watch: As the Moon in Aries wanes, assertive moods are drawn to whatever particular battle-cry appeals to us at this time. Moon trine Jupiter brings moods and dreams that are in harmony with a true sense of wellbeing. With Moon sextile Sun, our moods are inspired by the seasonal factors of late spring. Moon conjunct Mars in the sign of Aries brings moods that tend to reflect a strong sense of conviction to act on our ambitions. Fiery, masculine energy abounds. Moon trine Saturn brings moods in tune with disciplines, responsibilities, and duties. Moon sextile Neptune tops the day nicely with moods inspired by a sense of peace and tranquility.

June 11th Monday

Moon in Aries / Taurus	PDT	EDT	
Moon trine Pluto goes v/c	12:58 AM	3:58 AM	
Sun sextile Mars	3:28 AM	6:28 AM	
Moon enters Taurus	4:30 AM	7:30 AM	
Sun sextile Saturn	12:41 PM	3:41 PM	
Moon square Venus	2:09 PM	5:09 PM	
Mars trine Saturn	3:44 PM	6:44 PM	
Moon sextile Mercury	10:36 PM	1:36 AM	(June 12)

Mood Watch: Overnight, Moon trine Pluto brings moods and dreams that will be in harmony with healing energies. The waning Aries Moon will also go void-of-course until early morning, bringing restlessness to our dreams. As the Moon enters Taurus, early this morning, our moods enter into a time of practical and material awareness. Waning Taurus Moon is a good time to review finances and to set financial matters straight. Moon square Venus brings moods that may be challenging with matters concerning beauty and various attractions. Much later, Moon sextile Mercury brings thoughtful moods.

Sun sextile Mars (occurring May 23 – June 20) Sun sextile Mars brings a surge of favorable and also challenging energy and activity into our lives, particularly enlivening the lives of those people born in Gemini who will be celebrating a birthday this year from May 23 through June 20. There are opportunities at work, which must be acted upon, in order for all of this extra energy to pay off. There may also be a lot of anguish and pressure with regard to self-image, and the heat stirred up by these feelings requires direction and assertiveness. Now is the time for Gemini birthday folks to take action, to get in shape, and to build up their energy and strength.

Sun sextile Saturn (occurring June 7 – 13) This occurrence of Sun sextile Saturn particularly affects those Gemini people celebrating birthdays between June 7 – 13, helping them focus their energy and disciplines with greater clarity throughout the year. As Saturn enters the sextile aspect to the natal Sun of these Gemini people, they will have a greater sense of making progress through discipline, and they may very well begin to see the rewards of their diligent labor in the coming year. This is only true, however, has long as they apply themselves to their work and maintain a vigilant and persistent effort to master personal discipline and training. Birthday Gemini folks of this time must remember: greater control comes with genuine effort. This aspect will repeat on October 29, when the Sun will be in Scorpio and Saturn will be in Virgo.

Mars trine Saturn (occurring June 2 – 16) Mars in Aries is trine Saturn in Leo. This is an excellent time to execute creative projects, and to confidently take action with personal goals. Our actions bring gifts with this aspect, provided there is an application of discipline and timing. This may be a time for those who are affected by this aspect to become noticed or actively acknowledged. Activities will be naturally work oriented. This may be a good time to apply diligent practice with one's favorite sport, especially those physical activities which demand precision and perfect timing. Offensive and defensive forces will tend to work harmoniously now. It is always important to pay attention to those aspects of one's life that hold the potential to receive recognition. A timely gift of will-power and the rewards of hard work harmonize to bring positive results. To fully benefit from this aspect, one must use the energy (Mars) responsibly (Saturn). This is a time of transition when endings and new beginnings are merged.

June 12th Tuesday

Moon in Taurus	PDT	EDT
Moon sextile Uranus	10:57 AM	1:57 PM
Moon square Saturn	2:07 PM	5:07 PM
Moon square Neptune goes v/c	4:18 PM	7:18 PM

Sun opposite Pluto begins (see June 18)

"By the time a man realizes that maybe his father was right, he usually has a son who thinks he's wrong." – Charles Wadsworth (1814 – 1882)

Mood Watch: The waning Taurus Moon encourages us to handle finances and banking. The physical world stands out today, as the need to do away with impractical things leads many of us to do some spring cleaning. Taurus Moon activities often bring an improved and more desirable atmosphere for us to relax and enjoy. However, there may seem to be a bit of turmoil and upheaval as Moon sextile Uranus brings lively and outgoing expressions of mood. This afternoon's Moon square Saturn brings moods that may be challenged by the inability to concentrate. Moon square Neptune brings moods challenged by beliefs and the tendency to doubt those beliefs. The Moon also goes void-of-course for the remainder of the evening, and our moods will be distracted, most likely, by complications of a material nature.

II

June 13th Wednesday

Moon in Taurus / Gemini	PDT	EDT
Sun trine Neptune	12:31 AM	3:31 AM
Moon enters Gemini	5:25 AM	8:25 AM
Mars sextile Neptune	1:36 PM	4:36 PM
Moon sextile Venus	6:18 PM	9:18 PM
Venus trine Jupiter begins (see June 19)		
Mars trine Pluto begins (see June 21)		

Mood Watch: The void-of-course Taurus Moon brings heavy sleepers through the night. The Moon wanes darkly towards the new mark, set to occur tomorrow evening. This morning as the Moon enters Gemini, our moods enter into a very thoughtful, almost pensive time. This evening, Moon sextile Venus brings moods responsive to beauty and to luxury. Gemini is ruled by the nervous system; the waning Gemini Moon is here to remind us of the need to work through nervous feelings with intelligent efforts.

Sun trine Neptune (occurring June 6 – 16) This occurrence of Sun trine Neptune particularly affects those Gemini people celebrating birthdays from June 6 – 16. These Geminis are experiencing the favorable trine aspect of Neptune to their natal Sun, bringing gifts of spiritual encounters and awareness, as well as a calming effect on life. This serves as a good time (particularly for these birthday folks) to seek visions, apply prayer and meditation, and to explore spiritual avenues and beliefs that are being presented. This aspect will occur once more on October 12, when the Sun will be in Libra.

Mars sextile Neptune (occurring June 8 – 16) Mars in Aries is sextile to Neptune in Aquarius. Personal initiative – when taken – brings the potential for a spiritual awakening in humanity. Mars sextile Neptune is a splendid time to *act* on our *beliefs*. This aspect brings the vitality of Mars' energy into a favorable position with the spirit-awakening influence of Neptune. This is a place where we can safely dump our anger and can potentially make a connection with a spiritual healing process. Those who act on their visions and the ceremonies of their particular belief systems will have an opportunity to connect with a very profound spiritual experience. This aspect makes the active work of artists, poets, and musicians into unique and very powerful statements about being in an endowed and sacred state of awareness. There is an irony at work with these two forces; Mars is active and masculine, while Neptune has a very nebulous and passive guise that affects our deeper inner sense of beliefs and spirit. When these two planets are placed in a favorable position to each other, personal spiritual breakthroughs can be made.

June 14th Thursday

Flag Day, USA

NEW MOON in GEMINI

	PDT	EDT
Moon opposite Jupiter	4:00 AM	7:00 AM
Moon square Uranus	11:56 AM	2:56 PM
Moon sextile Saturn	3:26 PM	6:26 PM
Moon trine Neptune	5:19 PM	8:19 PM
Moon sextile Mars	6:50 PM	9:50 PM
Moon conjunct Sun	8:14 PM	11:14 PM

Mood Watch: The Moon now wanes through the darkest phase in Gemini and this brings out the "old soul" of the curious child who lives in each one of us. We may find ourselves pondering simple questions or concepts that are loaded with dichotomies, ironies, and contradictions. Despite the mixed messages that cloud our moods during a darkly waning Gemini Moon, an indefatigable persistence to learn and understand keeps us busy researching and collecting information. This morning, Moon opposite Jupiter may bring the overwhelming sense that too much abundance of some kind is occurring. Moon square Uranus brings moods that may seem challenged by rebellion. Moon sextile Saturn brings moods inclined towards the need for focus and accuracy. This evening, Moon trine Neptune brings moods blessed with peacefulness and acceptance. Moon sextile Mars brings moods inspired by action. Lastly, the **New Moon in Gemini** (Moon conjunct Sun) allows for new thoughts, ideas and feelings to flow. New Moons are like clean slates. It's a time to begin a process of strengthening and celebrating your energy, and to plan new vistas for growth, particularly mental growth. Pay attention to those newer thoughts, ideas, and caprices in the wind. This would be a good time to initiate a new round of creative writing.

June 15th Friday

Moon in Gemini / Cancer

	PDT	EDT
Moon opposite Pluto goes v/c	3:00 AM	6:00 AM
Moon enters Cancer	6:46 AM	9:46 AM
Mercury goes retrograde	4:41 PM	7:41 PM

Mood Watch: Early today, Moon opposite Pluto brings overwhelming intensity to the scope of our dreams and our moods. The Gemini Moon goes void-of-course for a while, bringing temporarily scattered feelings before the Moon enters Cancer and we come face to face with our feelings. Here, the quality and scope of our emotional depths are reflected upon, and we enter into a time of emotional clarity.

Mercury goes retrograde (Mercury retrograde: June 15 – July 9) Mercury will be retrograde in the sign of Cancer for the next few weeks. Mercury retrograde in Cancer is likely to bring communication disruption to issues with regard to motherhood, nurturing or care-giving, and domestic or home-related subjects. Emotional subjects, especially mother-related, will be very difficult to articulate. This is a good time to attempt communications more than once or twice, and to be persistent as well as patient. A real test of our patience occurs while Mercury is retrograde in Cancer, causing susceptibility to worry, callousness, or rejection. At first it may be difficult to sit through everyone's excuses and misinformation, but eventually there

124

will be a logical explanation to Mercury related setbacks. For more information on Mercury retrograde, see the section in the introduction about *Mercury retrograde periods.*

Ⅱ

June 16th Saturday

Moon in Cancer	PDT	EDT
Moon conjunct Mercury	2:22 AM	5:22 AM
Moon trine Uranus	2:33 PM	5:33 PM

Mood Watch: Ever so early, Moon conjunct Mercury affects our dreams and moods with the need to connect to intelligent ideas. The newly waxing Moon in Cancer during June is an excellent time to do some gardening, particularly to plant seeds and to transplant plants and shrubs. This is also a good time to enjoy domestic settings, barbeques, and good home cooking. This afternoon's Moon trine Uranus brings free-spirited and wild moods. This young crescent Moon in Cancer has a subtle but assuring way of apprising us of the underlying truths behind our feelings, inviting us to acknowledge or express our true feelings about each situation that comes up. Although often masked, our moods are subtly affected by the shifts of the Moon and are shared collectively with those we meet.

June 17th Sunday

Father's Day

Moon in Cancer / Leo	PDT	EDT
Moon square Mars goes v/c	12:40 AM	3:40 AM
Moon enters Leo	10:26 AM	1:26 PM

"By the time a man realizes that maybe his father was right, he usually has a son who thinks he's wrong." – Charles Wadsworth (1814 – 1882)

Mood Watch: Overnight, Moon square Mars affects our moods and dreams with challenging forceful energy. The Cancer Moon also goes void-of-course for a number of hours causing many emotional distractions throughout the early part of the day. As the Moon enters Leo, our moods enter into a playful stage. This is a good time to entertain family members on Father's Day, and also to enjoy positive vibrations with friends and loved ones.

June 18th Monday

Moon in Leo	PDT	EDT	
Moon conjunct Venus	8:07 AM	11:07 AM	
Moon trine Jupiter	10:30 AM	1:30 PM	
Sun opposite Pluto	11:50 PM	2:50 AM	(June 19)

Mood Watch: Positive lunar aspects are lined up on this lovely spring day. Waxing Leo Moon brings delight to our moods as the groovin' party spirit continues to build throughout the day and into the course of this evening. The spirited harmony of Gemini Sun and Leo Moon brings a blend of spring and summer related focuses, and invites us to venture out into favorite hobbies, crafts — and gregarious kinds of fun. Leo Moon activities commonly revolve around friends or family, and sometimes both. This morning, Moon conjunct Venus brings a sense of oneness with regard to beautiful attractions. Moon trine Jupiter brings moods that will be blessed by abundance, and the spirit of happiness and wellbeing will be shared by many.

Sun opposite Pluto (occurring June 12 - 22) Sun in Gemini is opposite Pluto in Sagittarius. Geminis and early born Cancer folks having birthdays from June 12 – 22 are undergoing the effects of Pluto being in a lengthy opposition to their natal Sun sign. Birthday folks, with Pluto in opposition to your identity, this is the time to accept transition, however overwhelming the circumstances. Persist in recognizing the empowering differences that each generation embodies. Gemini folks – here's the good news: it won't be that much longer (only until January 2008) that Pluto will be in opposition to the sign of Gemini. Pluto has been teaching Gemini people about the necessity of regeneration, and the shifting of the powers that be. Gemini is aware of irreversible change and the power of new generations of thinkers who will defy much of the logic of the previous generation. These transformative visions will alter our perceptions, and expand our awareness of travel, disease, permanent loss, nuclear realities, and the cruelty in the world. These challenges appear threatening and are often perceived as a painful process of loss and destruction. Late Gemini and early born Cancer birthday folks, do not get hung up on high expectations of life or you are likely to burn out. These lessons are meant to be, so open up to the need for endurance and perseverance during this time – use wisdom as your guide. Survival counts! Use your senses and your sensibilities well, but do not resist the forces of great change. Surviving all this means the best of life is yet to come, as you will grow to appreciate life in a delightfully transformed way. This is also true for your opposites, the Sagittarians and early born Capricorns, who are feeling the conjunction of Pluto to their natal Sun.

June 19th Tuesday

Moon in Leo / Virgo	PDT	EDT
Moon conjunct Saturn	1:04 AM	4:04 AM
Moon opposite Neptune	2:23 AM	5:23 AM
Moon trine Mars	10:38 AM	1:38 PM
Moon trine Pluto	1:15 PM	4:15 PM
Moon sextile Sun goes v/c	2:23 PM	5:23 PM
Venus trine Jupiter	3:49 PM	6:49 PM
Moon enters Virgo	5:47 PM	8:47 PM

Mood Watch: Overnight, Moon conjunct Saturn in Leo brings serious kinds of moods and dreams. Moon opposite Neptune brings moods and dreams that may seem to be at odds with spirituality. As the day progresses, Moon trine Mars brings moods that will be gifted with lots of energy. Moon trine Pluto brings a harmonious time to do some trouble-shooting, and to face problems between generations amicably. This afternoon, Moon sextile Sun brings a positive openness to the qualities of this time of the season, when summer is about to begin. The Moon in Leo goes void-of-course for awhile today and there may be a tendency towards laziness, or distractions may occur due to egocentric kinds of behavior. Our moods may appear to be self-absorbed and preoccupied. As the Moon enters Virgo, our moods are rapidly affected by the need to be resourceful and precautionary. Virgo Moon encourages us to take care of practical matters and to find the time to mull matters over for awhile.

126

Venus trine Jupiter (occurring June 13 – 22) Venus in Leo trine Jupiter in Sagittarius brings entertaining and endearing affection that inspires adventurous and joyous prosperity. Under this influence, love may grow and expand. Love (Venus) is harmoniously placed with prosperity and opportunity (Jupiter.) This is a great time to give gifts of love and for many people, it offers an expansive outlook. Without love in your life and a love for what you are doing, an expanding empire will eventually lose its luster. Venus trine Jupiter reminds us that fortune can be realized with simple aesthetics and quality moments. This aspect last occurred on March 8, when Venus was in Aries.

June 20th Wednesday

Moon in Virgo	PDT	EDT
Moon sextile Mercury	2:31 PM	5:31 PM
Moon square Jupiter	7:01 PM	10:01 PM

Mood Watch: The Moon waxes in Virgo and our moods are inclined towards more meticulous types of attention being placed on our work. There will be much to communicate and converse about with the Moon and Sun now in Mercury ruled signs. This is a good time to focus on cleaning and grooming as well as organizing and rearranging. Sun in Gemini with Moon in Virgo is a splendid time for writing tasks, making speeches, record or bookkeeping and secretarial duties. Moon sextile Mercury brings communicative moods, yet we must be cautious with how our thoughts are received while Mercury is retrograde in Cancer (June 15 – July 9.) Moon square Jupiter brings moods challenged by matters of wealth and money.

CANCER

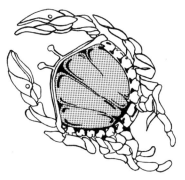

Key Phrase: "I FEEL"

Cardinal Water Sign

Symbol: The Crab

June 21st through July 22nd

June 21st Thursday

Summer Solstice

Moon in Virgo	PDT	EDT	
Moon opposite Uranus	6:10 AM	9:10 AM	
Mars trine Pluto	6:37 AM	9:37 AM	
Sun enters Cancer	11:08 AM	2:08 PM	
Moon square Pluto goes v/c	11:51 PM	2:51 AM	(June 22)

Mood Watch: In the final hours of the Gemini Sun, the Virgo Moon opposes Uranus and our moods may be overwhelmed by a sense of chaos and disorder. Virgo Moon keeps us questioning and guessing, which also leads to the need to research our resources and find answers to rising concerns. Much later tonight, long after the Sun has entered Cancer, Moon square Pluto brings moods challenged by matters of fate. The Moon also goes void-of-course creating moods and dreams that may be affected by minor feelings of doubt and skepticism.

Mars trine Pluto (occurring June 13 – 25) Mars in Aries is trine to Pluto in Sagittarius. Confident action leads to positive and powerful transformations. Actions taken now are more likely to have favorable results or to be influential with higher powers. This is a good time to resolve personal aggression directed towards the views and differences of another generation or established powers. This is also a good time for vital discoveries in the fight against diseases. Mars trine Pluto brings opportunity for favorable direct action that may well make a powerful and impressionable impact. Youthful or strong new influences will reach places of power, and a new generation will take many seats of power in political offices of the world. Mars, the god of war, and Pluto, the underworld god (or hell raiser), may actually be reaching some favorable kind of truce.

Sun enters Cancer (Sun in Cancer: June 21 – July 22) Today the Sun enters Cancer and this is the time when Summer Solstice enthusiasts are out celebrating old traditions and creating new ones, while thanking the Sun for life and light. The dominion of the sign of Cancer is expressed by cardinal water, affecting people in deep and unconscious ways. Cancer people are extremely intuitive and often very psychic or perceptive. Cancers are often thought of, like the crab, as having hard exteriors. Why so hard? You Cancer folks certainly understand; there is a great deal at stake! Cancer's key phrase is: "I feel." Cancers value and prize their deep emotional attachments and treasured memories and feelings – not just anyone gets to share in their hard earned legacy. Those who do share an experience with Cancer must honor Cancer's special needs to create goals and fulfill them with perfection. Cancers are leaders and when a Cancer is certain, there is no disputing their chosen path. Moon rules the sign of Cancer; the need to love and be loved, to nurture and be nurtured in a gentle and motherly fashion is indeed a part of the Cancer makeup. Cancers must be free to protect and defend themselves as they please and because their feelings tends to run deeper than most, they need a lot of extra armor. Cancer is a home oriented sign, and making the home a well-loved place is of great importance at this time. Barbecues, home improvements, and other home based events are the focuses of many folks during Cancer Sun days.

June 22nd Friday
Moon in Virgo / Libra - FIRST QUARTER MOON in LIBRA

	PDT	EDT
Moon enters Libra	4:45 AM	7:45 AM
Moon square Sun	6:16 AM	9:16 AM
Venus opposite Neptune begins (see June 30)		
Venus conjunct Saturn begins (see July 1)		

Mood Watch: The void-of-course Moon in Virgo continues to bring skepticism throughout the very early hours, but it isn't long before the Moon enters Libra and our moods enter into a phase of openness towards others. The **First Quarter Moon in Libra** (Moon square Sun) encourages us to harmonize with our partners and friends. This is the Moon that beckons us to create balance in our relationships, particularly with those people we consider close. It's all about making adjustments with the Moon in Libra, and these adjustments must be made for your own sake, as well as for the sake of others. Teamwork requires balance.

June 23rd Saturday

Moon in Libra	PDT	EDT
Moon square Mercury	12:23 AM	3:23 AM
Moon sextile Jupiter	6:28 AM	9:28 AM
Uranus goes retrograde	7:44 AM	10:44 AM
Moon sextile Venus	2:01 PM	5:01 PM
Saturn trine Pluto begins (see August 6)		

Mood Watch: Overnight, Moon square Mercury brings nightmarish thoughts and dreams — it's probably something of a Mercury retrograde nature. This morning, Moon sextile Jupiter brings generous and joyous moods. The Moon waxes in Libra, making this Saturday a good day for wedding bells and marital vows. It is also a good time to enjoy the company of loved ones and friends and to work towards creating peace and harmony among them. Moon sextile Venus tops this day of lunar aspects very nicely, as moods tend to be receptive and open to love.

Uranus goes retrograde (Uranus retrograde: June 23 – November 24) Uranus, the outer planet representing revolution, chaos, explosive energy, and big changes, now appears to turn back through the zodiac in the sign of Pisces. Uranus in Pisces has been stirring up a revolution in religion, music, the arts, poetry, psychic research, occultism, movie making and plays. Outer planets move slowly, and this one will take five months to backtrack only four degrees before it moves forward once again. Uranus influences chaos and volatile or abrupt energies, and inspires the need for change and breakthroughs in the pursuit of freedom. When retrograde, the influence of Uranus teaches us to handle uncertainty. Many aspects of chaos tend to be sporadically repeated until the boundaries of restriction loosen enough so we can move more freely. Uranus retrograde is a time when humanity as a whole must backtrack over their revolutionary practices in order to make breakthroughs in the long run. Uranus liberates, although for some people the retrograde process may seem to be excessively inhibiting, particularly if one's surroundings do not allow for much freedom. For rebels, contemplation and internalization brings greater inner strength. While Uranus is retrograde, be sure to set a standard for a certain degree of freedom in your life, so that you can stop and smell the flowers this summer and into the days of autumn. Don't let this valuable time of the year slide by without allowing your inner rebel to kick up his or her heels once in awhile. Freedom is a worthy thing to claim.

June 24th Sunday

Moon in Libra / Scorpio	PDT	EDT
Moon sextile Saturn	12:31 AM	3:31 AM
Moon trine Neptune	12:50 AM	3:50 AM
Moon sextile Pluto goes v/c	12:24 PM	3:24 PM
Mars enters Taurus	2:28 PM	5:28 PM
Moon enters Scorpio	5:28 PM	8:28 PM
Moon opposite Mars	5:39 PM	8:39 PM

Mood Watch: Overnight, Moon sextile Saturn brings moods and dreams that will be inspired by precision. Moon trine Neptune brings dreams filled with blessed tranquility. The Moon is in Libra this morning, creating some relatively intelligent and sensible interactions between people. Moon sextile Pluto occurs this afternoon, bringing moods open to the acceptance of fate. The Libra Moon goes void-of-course at this point, inspiring moods distracted by indecision. As the Moon enters Scorpio this evening, our moods enter into a phase of dramatic awareness. Scorpio Moon puts us in touch with our passions. Moon opposite Mars brings moods that may be opposed to, or overwhelmed by, masculine force. This evening would be a good time to be aware of the potential for accidents — or there may be violent reactions spurred in some people.

Mars enters Taurus (Mars in Taurus: June 24 – August 6) Mars represents all modes of action. In the fixed earth sign of Taurus, Mars' action is particularly worked out through the physical realm, making this a primary time to work active energy through the body, or to take affirmative action in the physical world, moving or activating it to change. This is a time when many of us will take strong actions with our financial and material welfare. The last time Mars was in Taurus (July 27, 2005 – February 18, 2006,) we were forced to take action with the physical world due to hurricane Katrina, which was followed by more hurricanes and immense fund raising efforts to resolve the mess they caused. Mars' energy enlivens Taurus related activities such as bargain hunting, buying and selling, bidding, investing, banking, decorating, and creating a practical work space. Mars in Taurus boosts the life energy of Taurus people and gives them the incentive to take action. Mars generates heat which can often appear explosive under pressure. Taurus people are reminded to keep a cool sense of control at all times and to be aware of the tendency towards temper tantrums when events get overheated. Taurus folks can strike while the iron is hot but they must use caution and be aware of fires and fevers. Aquarius and Leo folks also need to be especially cautious as Mars now squares to their natal Sun, causing actions around them to seem abrasive to them personally. Scorpios may be particularly aware of fiery activity in their lives at this time with Mars opposing their natal Sun.

June 25th Monday

Moon in Scorpio

	PDT	EDT
Moon trine Sun	12:18 AM	3:18 AM
Saturn opposite Neptune	8:55 AM	11:55 AM
Moon trine Mercury	10:34 AM	1:34 PM

Mood Watch: Overnight, Moon trine Sun brings harmonious dreams and moods. Today, Moon trine Mercury brings amicably communicative moods. We awaken to a Moon in Scorpio day, and this reminds us of the vital importance of living life without taking things for granted. Sometimes it is a brush with death, or a glance at something tragic that puts our encounters with monotony and the daily grind back into perspective. Scorpio Moon encourages us to take on great challenges with the courageous desire to overcome fear; sometimes it is through the act of acknowledging our trials and troubles that we can battle our weaknesses and triumph over our fears. Whatever will turn that around for us today, Scorpio Moon is there to allow us to face our doubts and fears through each step.

Saturn opposite Neptune (occurring February 2 – July 18) Today, the direct moving Saturn in Leo is opposite the retrograde moving Neptune in Aquarius. This aspect is occurring for a prolonged period of time, and reaches its peak for the second time this year since February 28, only then Saturn was retrograde and Neptune was direct. Today, Saturn opposite the retrograde Neptune occurs with an emphasis on the need for spiritual sensitivity and an introspective spiritual approach with regard to the setting up of our perimeters and determining our limitations. For the full scale story of this lengthy and significant aspect, see February 28 when it last reached its peak.

June 26th Tuesday

Moon in Scorpio	PDT	EDT
Moon square Venus	6:54 AM	9:54 AM
Moon trine Uranus	7:02 AM	10:02 AM
Moon square Neptune	1:08 PM	4:08 PM
Moon square Saturn goes v/c	1:24 PM	4:24 PM
Sun conjunct Mercury begins (see June 28)		

Mood Watch: This morning, Moon square Venus brings moods challenged by feminine attractions, beauty, and the like. Moon trine Uranus brings foot-loose and fancy-free moods. This afternoon, Moon square Neptune brings foot-loose and fancy-free moods may seem challenged by matters concerning religion and our beliefs. Moon square Saturn adds challenge from our responsibilities and our disciplines. As the Scorpio Moon goes void-of-course, we may get distracted by emotional dramas. The Scorpio Moon works its magic on the subconscious level, giving each one of us the space to recuperate and to release the static of emotional disruption. Sexual prowess and the passion of Eros and Psyche are ascending on the horizon. The Sun is in Cancer and the Moon is in Scorpio – these are water signs and the general theme of today focuses on passion and emotional flow. Caution and care are advisable.

June 27th Wednesday

Moon in Scorpio / Sagittarius	PDT	EDT
Moon enters Sagittarius	5:25 AM	8:25 AM

Mood Watch: Overnight the void-of-course Moon in Scorpio brings moods which may be described as withdrawn, and perhaps even distant or secretive in nature. Early this morning, the vibrantly waxing Moon enters Sagittarius, bringing strong philosophical perspectives and moods. Sagittarius Moon urges a spirit of fascination, profound wonder, and insight. Adventure, exploration and exercise are excellent ways to enjoy this summer day. Sagittarius says: "I see," and today's overall activities call for vision and creative effort to enjoy this valuable time.

June 28th Thursday

Moon in Sagittarius	PDT	EDT	
Moon conjunct Jupiter	5:10 AM	8:10 AM	
Sun conjunct Mercury	11:41 AM	2:41 PM	
Moon square Uranus	5:38 PM	8:38 PM	
Moon trine Venus	9:20 PM	12:20 AM	(June 29)
Moon sextile Neptune	11:25 PM	2:25 AM	(June 29)

Mood Watch: This morning, Moon conjunct Jupiter in Sagittarius brings abundantly joyful moods. Sagittarius Moon inspires powerful visions and rich insights into the future. It is times like this that facilitate opening the porthole to new adventure. This evening, Moon square Uranus brings moods that may be challenged by explosive or radical kinds of energies. Moon trine Venus helps to smooth chaotic energies over with loving and kind moods. Later, Moon sextile Neptune brings peaceful moods, responsive to spiritual expression.

Sun conjunct Mercury (occurring June 26 – July 2) This is a very common aspect, which will create a much more thoughtful, communicative, and expressive year ahead for those Cancer born people celebrating birthdays from June 26 – July 2. This is your time (birthday Cancers) to record ideas, relay important messages, and pay close attention to your imaginative thoughts as they are touched by Mercury, creating the urge to speak and be heard.

June 29th Friday

Moon in Sagittarius / Capricorn	PDT	EDT	
Moon trine Saturn	12:14 AM	3:14 AM	
Moon conjunct Pluto goes v/c	10:09 AM	1:09 PM	
Moon enters Capricorn	3:06 PM	6:06 PM	
Moon trine Mars	10:19 PM	1:19 AM	(June 30)
Venus trine Pluto begins (see July 8)			

Mood Watch: Overnight, Moon trine Saturn brings moods and dreams that will be inspired by a feeling of progress. Today's Moon conjunct Pluto aspect brings moods strongly affected by matters and conditions of fate. When the Sagittarius Moon goes void-of-course, our moods are easily distracted and misdirected. For a time, miscommunications may have disastrous affects while Mercury remains retrograde. As the Moon enters Capricorn, our moods enter into a phase of seriousness. Cautious but confident moods set the stage for this Full Moon Eve. Moon trine Mars brings moods that will be blessed with positive energy and fiery force.

June 30th Saturday

FULL MOON in CAPRICORN	PDT	EDT
Moon opposite Mercury	1:54 AM	4:54 AM
Moon opposite Sun	6:50 AM	9:50 AM
Venus opposite Neptune	8:32 AM	11:32 AM
Mercury sextile Mars begins (see July 1)		

Mood Watch: Overnight, Moon opposite Mercury brings very nervous kinds of dreams and moods. As the morning unfolds, the **Full Moon in Capricorn** (Moon opposite Sun) reaches its peak. This Full Moon grips our attention in significant and demanding ways. The Capricorn influence focuses our energy on accomplishing goals and on taking work and career efforts seriously. Laborious tasks and great efforts bring deeply satisfying accomplishments with this Moon; this is also a time when we tend to reflect on our achievements with an inspiration towards furthering our development.

Venus opposite Neptune (occurring June 22 – July 4) Venus in Leo is opposing Neptune in Aquarius. What we are attracted to may be opposed to what we (or others) believe in. Selfishness conflicts with philanthropy. Wild and instinctual expressions of love and beauty are at odds with universal beliefs. This aspect brings an awareness of the dichotomy between fashion's feminine archetypes versus a natural or spiritual expression of femininity. The feminine spirit needs to be free and connect with a more divine image of womanhood; however, the goddess that lives within may seem distant or hard to reach. Nonetheless, the feminine parts of the spirit (Venus) are being made acutely aware of the divine parts of the spirit (Neptune) in one way or another. The opposition of Venus to Neptune may seem like an overwhelming time to try to make a spiritual connection with large groups of people, especially through the mediums of art, music, and theater. There may be a desire to create a spiritual refuge or retreat – an attractive, sensual, and aesthetically pleasing sanctuary.

July 1st Sunday

Canada Day
Moon in Capricorn / Aquarius

	PDT	EDT	
Moon sextile Uranus goes v/c	1:46 AM	4:46 AM	
Venus conjunct Saturn	7:39 AM	10:39 AM	
Mercury sextile Mars	12:09 PM	3:09 PM	
Moon enters Aquarius	10:25 PM	1:25 AM	(July 2)

" I want to express my profound gratitude to all Canadians ... for the loyalty, encouragement and support you have given to me over these past 50 years. " -- Queen Elizabeth II – 2002, Quebec)

Mood Watch: Overnight, Moon sextile Uranus occurs and our moods, as well as our dreams, are inspired by excessive energy – then the post-full Capricorn Moon goes void-of-course. By the time the day comes into full swing, the energy suggests that there is an earthy, complacent, lazy sort of atmosphere hovering around our senses. Our moods are distracted by the duties and obligations that call to us and, while there is a tendency to be serious about matters, there is also an unconcerned sort of detachment from it all – an acceptance of the way things are. Later tonight, the Moon finally enters Aquarius and our moods enter into the necessity to seek knowledge.

Venus conjunct Saturn (occurring June 22 – July 6) Venus conjunct Saturn in Leo creates willful and serious bonding between family and friends. A favorable time to apply discipline in the arts and in love related matters, Venus conjunct Saturn represents our commitment and responsibility to the people we love and the disciplines we care about. Love matters may undergo a restriction, or possibly even closure of some kind. This aspect can go either way on relationships, since the loving attraction of Venus can be either encouraged or thwarted by the responsible, serious, and limiting discipline of Saturn's energy. Love oaths are emphasized, and

133

love commitments at this time will be taken extremely seriously as a whole. This could be the ideal time to create a security system to protect valued objects. Venus conjunct Saturn can bring an intense focus on guarding and protecting loved ones while these planets are conjunct in Leo.

Mercury sextile Mars (occurring June 30 – July 5) Mercury sextile Mars brings opportunities that can be recognized, received, communicated and acted upon. News or information may lead to the taking of immediate action. Bear in mind that Mercury is currently *retrograde* (June 15 – July 9) and communications have the potential of being misunderstood. As for now, Mercury in Cancer moves in a pattern that creates thoughtful and emotionally stirring introspection, while Mars in Taurus puts high demands on physical activities. Careful deliberation leads to effective action. Applying active communication has the potential for a very favorable outcome. This aspect last occurred with Mercury *direct* on May 8, and it will repeat for a final time this year on August 3, when Mercury will be *direct* again.

July 2nd Monday

Moon in Aquarius	PDT	EDT
Moon square Mars	8:29 AM	11:29 AM
Moon sextile Jupiter	7:30 PM	10:30 PM

Mood Watch: The Moon, still somewhat full from this past weekend, now wanes in Aquarius. Today we will be more inclined to seek knowledgeable solutions to labor intensive troubles. Once we've worked our way through the various duties, more exciting ideas and interesting thoughts will occupy our minds. The summertime Aquarius Moon is an excellent time to explore innovative outdoor activities and new or spontaneous kinds of leisurely hobbies. This morning, Moon square Mars brings moods that might be easily swayed towards aggressive tendencies, or anger. Tonight, Moon sextile Jupiter brings moods inspired by new prospects.

July 3rd Tuesday

Moon in Aquarius	PDT	EDT	
Moon conjunct Neptune	1:08 PM	4:08 PM	
Moon opposite Saturn	2:53 PM	5:53 PM	
Moon opposite Venus	5:22 PM	8:22 PM	
Moon sextile Pluto goes v/c	11:04 PM	2:04 AM	(July 4)

Mood Watch: Waning Aquarius Moon encourages us to let go of our grudges and sharp criticisms of others, and to honor humanity in a more positive way with knowledge and wisdom. It also reminds us that when we fail, we must be forgiving of ourselves in order to progress in a more positive and forward moving direction. Moon conjunct Neptune brings tranquil and harmonious moods. Moon opposite Saturn brings an overwhelming sense of responsibility. Moon opposite Venus brings moods that will make us acutely aware of our affections – both the giving of, and the desire for, all kinds of affection. Later tonight, Moon sextile Pluto brings moods that are influenced by the deeds of superpowers. The Aquarius Moon also goes void-of-course, and our moods and dreams will be distracted by all claims to the impossible. In other words, expect the most strange and unusual dreams.

July 4th Wednesday

Independence Day, USA

Moon in Aquarius / Pisces	PDT	EDT
Moon enters Pisces	3:53 AM	6:53 AM
Moon trine Mercury	10:12 AM	1:12 PM
Moon sextile Mars	4:35 PM	7:35 PM
Sun trine Uranus begins (see July 10)		

" America is a young country with an old mentality. "
– George Santayana (1863 – 1952) - US (Spanish-born) philosopher

Mood Watch: As the Moon enters Pisces early this morning, our moods enter into a time of general openness. There is a peaceful and festive kind of acceptance, although the waning Pisces Moon can sometimes bring daunting glimpses of the mysteries of the soul, complete with its innumerable ups and downs. Moon trine Mercury helps us to communicate more easily and our moods will be gifted with a sense of intelligence. However, it is wise to be mindful of emotional communication trends that may cause miscommunications while Mercury is retrograde in Cancer (June 15 – July 9). Moon sextile Mars brings moods that will be inclined towards the need to take action. Pisces Moon is a great time for music and fireworks.

July 5th Thursday

Moon in Pisces	PDT	EDT
Moon square Jupiter	12:02 AM	3:02 AM
Moon trine Sun	2:37 AM	5:37 AM
Moon conjunct Uranus	12:23 PM	3:23 PM

Mood Watch: Overnight, Moon square Jupiter brings less outgoing or generous moods, and our dreams may appear like a gambler's losing streak. All the while, Pisces Moon brings flexible moods in the areas of intuition and instinct. Moon trine Sun brings promising harmony to our moods, and our dreams will begin to take shape in a more positive way. As for the events of the day, while the Sun is in Cancer and the Moon wanes in Pisces, we are drawn towards finding cool getaways, cozy cottages, and dreamy summer retreats. Street music draws large crowds, and artistic dress and attire alter our moods. Moon conjunct Uranus brings rebellious moods that are prone to rule breaking. Beware of the tendency towards chaotic or unusual behavior.

July 6th Friday

Moon in Pisces / Aries	PDT	EDT
Moon square Pluto goes v/c	3:10 AM	6:10 AM
Moon enters Aries	7:58 AM	10:58 AM
Moon square Mercury	12:56 PM	3:56 PM

Mood Watch: Moon square Pluto starts off the earliest part of the day with moods oppressed by dramatic losses. The Pisces Moon goes void-of-course, bringing moods distracted by mysterious kinds of feelings or, for some, down-right depression. After a short time of disorientation, the Moon enters Aries and the day may officially begin with a sense of renewed action. Our moods now enter into a phase of assurance and confidence. Moon square Mercury brings challenges with regard to the need to communicate complex thoughts. Retrograde Mercury is moving down the home stretch towards the reoccurrence of its direct movement through the zodiac degrees. By next week, communications will begin to turn around in a more positive way.

July 7th Saturday
LAST QUARTER MOON in ARIES

	PDT	EDT	
Moon trine Jupiter	3:19 AM	6:19 AM	
Moon square Sun	9:55 AM	12:55 PM	
Moon sextile Neptune	8:39 PM	11:39 PM	
Moon trine Saturn	11:16 PM	2:16 AM	(July 8)

Mood Watch: Moon trine Jupiter kicks off the day with jovial and explorative moods. **Last Quarter Moon in Aries** (Moon square Sun) brings energetic moods, but we may find that barriers can occur between emotions and our sense of personal identity. Since the Moon is in Aries, this expression of mood has little trouble emerging and creating new energies. Last Quarter Moon requires us to release pent-up emotional energy, unless of course the energy creates a desired positive response – in which case, congratulations! Dropping problems with the ego is one of the keys to this waning Moon. Overcoming tension, anxiety and grudges are other ways to work out the energy of Last Quarter Moon in Aries. Tonight, Moon sextile Neptune brings inspirational tranquility. Moon trine Saturn brings moods that will seem pleasantly guarded, and in control.

July 8th Sunday
Moon in Aries / Taurus

	PDT	EDT
Moon trine Venus	5:36 AM	8:36 AM
Moon trine Pluto goes v/c	6:07 AM	9:07 AM
Moon enters Taurus	10:55 AM	1:55 PM
Moon sextile Mercury	3:10 PM	6:10 PM
Venus trine Pluto	6:10 PM	9:10 PM

Mood Watch: Moon trine Venus brings moods that will be pleasant and blessed with kindness. This morning, Moon trine Pluto brings moods enriched with the acceptance of hardships. The Moon also goes void-of-course at this point, bringing an impatient sort of morning, and our moods may be distracted by competitors and the like. As the Moon enters Taurus, our moods enter into the need to be down-to-earth and practical. Moon sextile Mercury inspires communicative moods. Waning Taurus Moon brings the need to relax.

Venus trine Pluto (occurring June 29 – July 14) Venus in Leo is trine to Pluto in Sagittarius. Venus trine Pluto is certainly exciting – with fate, power, love, and intensity at work! This aspect represents a love or fascination occurring with regard to the work of fate as well as power. Venus trine Pluto often allows a breakthrough to occur for those who are under stress while accepting the hardship of this time. This aspect can often help us to overcome the pain of separation. It is the place where love triumphs over death. In this there is great power. This aspect last occurred on March 16, when Venus was in Aries, and since Venus will go retrograde (July 27) this aspect will return on August 15 and October 3.

July 9th Monday

Moon in Taurus	PDT	EDT	
Moon conjunct Mars	4:26 AM	7:26 AM	
Moon sextile Sun	4:02 PM	7:02 PM	
Moon sextile Uranus	6:06 PM	9:06 PM	
Mercury goes direct	7:16 PM	10:16 PM	
Moon square Neptune	10:58 PM	1:58 AM	(July 10)

Mood Watch: Waning Taurus Moon is a good time to get the financial side of our lives in order, and to create a comfortable, practical and relaxing environment that will help to make life more pleasurable. The day is kicked off with force and vigor as Moon conjunct Mars brings moods affected by masculine energies. The Taurus Moon sextile Cancer Sun brings moods that will be open to beautifying the home and making it more comfortable. This evening, Moon sextile Uranus brings moods awakened by abrupt energies. Moon square Neptune causes moods that may be challenged by religious beliefs, or by our need for peace.

Mercury goes direct (Mercury direct: July 9 – October 11) Since June 15, Mercury has been retrograde in the sign of Cancer, commonly causing heated and emotional confusion in the area of communication. Now we can breathe a greatly needed sigh of relief as Mercury, the planet governing the realms of communication, becomes stationary and will soon begin to move forward. Take note that our faculties and manner of communicating will definitely improve within the next few days, and we can begin to clear up various misunderstandings that have occurred over the past few weeks. For more information on this recently completed phase of Mercury retrograde, see June 15. For more on Mercury retrograde patterns throughout this year, see the introduction on *Mercury retrograde periods.*

July 10th Tuesday

Moon in Taurus / Gemini	PDT	EDT	
Moon square Saturn	2:01 AM	5:01 AM	
Moon square Venus goes v/c	9:55 AM	12:55 PM	
Moon enters Gemini	1:11 PM	4:11 PM	
Sun trine Uranus	10:34 PM	1:34 AM	(July 11)

Mood Watch: Moon square Saturn brings moods and dreams revolving around the theme of challenging responsibilities. Moon square Venus brings difficulties that have to do with the need for affection. The waning Taurus Moon goes void-of-course for a few hours today, causing laziness, the need for luxury – and there may be a tendency for some folks to be forgetful of practical things. As the Moon enters Gemini, our moods enter into a phase of thoughtfulness.

Sun trine Uranus (occurring July 4 – 14) This occurrence of Sun trine Uranus favorably affects our Cancer friends celebrating birthdays between July 4 – 14. It puts the radical forces of Uranus in the favorable trine position to the natal Sun of these Cancer folks. This is the time for these birthday people to make the break-through. Don't hold back, Cancer folks: chaos is here to stay for awhile, and the apparent madness occurring in your lives is there for a reason. Let the experience be positive as long as this aspect brings gifts. Expect restless desires for freedom and a heartfelt need to break out of your personal prison. These challenges are a necessary part of Cancer folks' growth patterns, and the resultant changes are positive in nature, though on the surface they may seem harsh and overbearing. Freedom knocks loudly and the course of change for these people is inevitable in the next year. The trine aspect bestows gifts of triumph, and this could be a good time to let chaos be the force that brings freedom. This aspect repeats on November 7, and will affect the Scorpio birthday people of that time.

July 11th Wednesday

Moon in Gemini	PDT	EDT
Moon opposite Jupiter	7:34 AM	10:34 AM
Moon square Uranus	8:18 PM	11:18 PM

Mood Watch: This waning Gemini Moon is here to assist us in getting our thoughts and communications more evenly aligned. Gemini is a Mercury ruled sign and now that Mercury, which was retrograde June 15 – July 9, is direct, the flow of our communications can be experienced with greater ease. All of this is particularly so while the Moon is in Gemini, reminding us how to mediate, interpret, deliberate, and negotiate in all those areas of life where discernment is needed most. This evening, Moon square Uranus brings moods challenged by recklessness and wild situations or behavior. Gemini Moon brings a restless or nervous time for some people, and they must remember to feed the brain selectively and not to get distracted by disruptive and nonproductive chatter.

July 12th Thursday

Moon in Gemini / Cancer	PDT	EDT
Moon trine Neptune	1:12 AM	4:12 AM
Moon sextile Saturn	4:46 AM	7:46 AM
Moon opposite Pluto	10:40 AM	1:40 PM
Moon sextile Venus goes v/c	2:13 PM	5:13 PM
Moon enters Cancer	3:40 PM	6:40 PM
Moon conjunct Mercury	8:34 PM	11:34 PM

Mood Watch: The Gemini Moon enlivens our moods with detailed observations of the experience of life. Moon trine Neptune brings relaxing and enchanting dreams and moods. This morning, Moon sextile Saturn brings moods inspired by the usefulness of structure and stability. Moon opposite Pluto brings an acute awareness of the troubles and the transformations occurring in our lives. Moon sextile Venus brings moods inspired by love. The Gemini Moon goes void-of-course for under two hours, bringing moods that will be easily distracted by scattered thoughts and nervousness. As the Moon enters Cancer, our moods enter into a state of emotional clarity. Tonight will be a good time to enjoy domestic comforts.

July 13th Friday

Moon in Cancer	PDT	EDT	
Moon sextile Mars	2:54 PM	5:54 PM	
Moon trine Uranus	11:33 PM	2:33 AM	(July 14)

Mood Watch: With a darkly waning Cancer Moon on a New Moon eve, today's lunar aspects suggest that there will be some emotional anxiety. The New Moon eve often represents a purging process for emotional clamor; the Cancer Moon is definitely characterized as an internalization process that requires care, nurturing and reassurance. Moon sextile Mars brings moods inspired by action. Later tonight, Moon trine Uranus brings moods in harmony with chaos. This is a good time to let go of negative energy, superstition, and all those unfounded, reckless myths of old that exist both in our minds and in our collective cultures. Why else would such old wives' tales continue to haunt some folks? Why is **Friday the 13th** considered such a bad omen? For the second time this year, the 13th of the month falls on a Friday. For a recap of the story, see Friday, April 13th.

July 14th Saturday
Moon in Cancer / Leo - NEW MOON in CANCER

	PDT	EDT
Moon conjunct Sun goes v/c	5:05 AM	8:05 AM
Venus enters Virgo	11:25 AM	2:25 PM
Moon enters Leo	7:44 PM	10:44 PM

Mood Watch: **New Moon in Cancer** (Moon conjunct Sun) will reach its peak this morning at the same time the Moon goes void-of-course. At this point, a rewarding sense of overcoming those emotional curve balls gives us the impetus to run successfully to home plate unscathed. However, while the Moon is void-of-course, our moods are sure to be spacey and preoccupied with emotionality. New Moon in Cancer brings renewed hope or renewed faith for those who happen to be going through emotional challenges. It also puts us directly in touch with our feelings and allows us to make room for new feelings to emerge. This newly waxing water Moon is an opportunity for garden lovers to start new cuttings and to transplant plants and shrubs successfully. Taking the time to do a little extra pampering, or to do things that make us feel good about ourselves is a marvelous way to enjoy this New Moon in Cancer. Tonight, the moody edge of the day's activities seem to dissolve and happiness ensues as the Moon enters Leo.

Venus enters Virgo (Venus in Virgo: July 14 – August 8) Venus now enters the sign of Virgo, where love and attraction are highlighted with such Virgo-like traits as shyness, prudence, purity, and virginal beauty. Due to its retrograde motion this year, Venus will be traveling in Virgo for an extended period of time, going retrograde on July 27 and re-entering the sign of Leo on August 8. While Venus is retrograde in Virgo, the expression of love and beauty will be analyzed and reflected upon from a distance, and love related activities are more often reserved or calculated than they are acted upon. Venus in Virgo is referred to as "the fall," a less ideal position for Venus and a time when disappointment in love matters may be felt by some folks. Keep faith in your affections, despite the cooling of passions. Later on this year, Venus will re-enter Virgo on October 7.

July 15th Sunday
Moon in Leo

	PDT	EDT	
Moon trine Jupiter	2:54 PM	5:54 PM	
Moon square Mars	11:07 PM	2:07 AM	(July 16)
Mars sextile Uranus begins (see July 20)			

Mood Watch: It's a Leo Moon day, bringing forth both the expression of playfulness and the need to keep life interesting and entertaining, particularly after all the emotional purging our moods have undergone recently. Moon trine Jupiter brings moods in harmony with a sense of wellbeing and wealth. A newly waxing Leo Moon on a summer Sunday is a good time to enjoy picnics and barbeques with family and friends. Entertainment is a must! Be careful later tonight, as Moon square Mars tends to bring moods that may be challenged by aggression and forcefulness.

July 16th Monday

Moon in Leo	PDT	EDT
Moon opposite Neptune	10:30 AM	1:30 PM
Moon conjunct Saturn	3:34 PM	6:34 PM
Moon trine Pluto goes v/c	8:56 PM	11:56 PM
Mars square Neptune begins (see July 24)		

Mood Watch: Waxing Leo Moon starts off the week with creative zeal and energy. Moon opposite Neptune brings strong spiritual themes to our moods. Moon conjunct Saturn brings moods that may seem somewhat guarded, or serious; however, this will be a really good time to concentrate on getting some work done. Tonight, Moon trine Pluto brings moods in harmony with the process of healing wounds, and a lot of trouble-shooting and problem solving will occur between the generations. The Leo Moon will also go void-of-course and our moods may become distracted by various issues between family and friends. Void-of-course Leo Moon is the time to be patient with battered egos and restless children.

July 17th Tuesday

Moon in Leo / Virgo	PDT	EDT	
Moon enters Virgo	2:40 AM	5:40 AM	
Moon conjunct Venus	4:41 AM	7:41 AM	
Moon sextile Mercury	12:19 PM	3:19 PM	
Moon square Jupiter	10:45 PM	1:45 AM	(July 18)

Mood Watch: As the Moon enters Virgo, our moods enter into a phase of watchfulness and resourcefulness. This morning, Moon conjunct Venus brings a sense of oneness with those we love and with those things that we are attracted to. Moon sextile Mercury brings inspiring communications. The Virgo Moon reminds us to be sensible, smart, and precise about our facts. Later tonight, Moon square Jupiter brings challenging moods and dreams with regard to economic factors, and we may be feeling especially sensitive or hesitant about how we spend.

July 18th Wednesday

Moon in Virgo	PDT	EDT
Moon trine Mars	11:07 AM	2:07 PM
Moon opposite Uranus	2:07 PM	5:07 PM

Mood Watch: Waxing Moon in Virgo opens up communication and encourages stamina, efficiency, order, and cleanliness. Cultural pursuits and good conversations abound. Important communications will be covered today, as the Virgo Moon energy stresses the need for us to engage in valuable considerations and essential contemplations. This is a good time to get things done and to aid the body with nourishing and cleansing foods. Moon trine Mars brings moods in harmony with masculine energies and courageous activities. Chaotic or rebellious tendencies may occur; Moon opposite Uranus brings moods that may seem out of the ordinary.

July 19th Thursday

Moon in Virgo / Libra	PDT	EDT
Moon sextile Sun	5:58 AM	8:58 AM
Moon square Pluto goes v/c	6:45 AM	9:45 AM
Moon enters Libra	12:55 PM	3:55 PM

Mood Watch: Moon sextile Sun brings moods inspired by the shifts of the season. We are now completing the last couple of days with the Sun in Cancer, which means we are already a third of the way through summer. The waxing Virgo Moon will go void-of-course this morning, while Moon square Pluto brings moods which will be challenged by matters of fate. The Virgo Moon allows us to investigate and dissect our feelings with an analytical fervor that seems thorough and comprehensive. The void-of-course Virgo Moon may bring argumentative or doubtful moods. As the Moon enters Libra, our moods enter into a phase of striving for harmony and balance. Libra Moon emphasizes the need to find neutral ground and to be at peace.

July 20th Friday

Moon in Libra	PDT	EDT
Moon square Mercury	3:13 AM	6:13 AM
Moon sextile Jupiter	9:42 AM	12:42 PM
Mars sextile Uranus	3:14 PM	6:14 PM
Mars square Saturn begins (see July 31)		

Mood Watch: Overnight, our moods and dreams are met with Moon square Mercury, causing mind-boggling thoughts. As the day progresses, Moon sextile Jupiter sets the tone of the day with the potential for positive, upbeat feelings, and a sense of wellbeing and prosperity. The Libra Moon waxes and places the emphasis of our moods on the joyous company of good friends, loving companions, and supporters. Libra Moon also focuses our sights on carrying out important objectives and on harmonizing teamwork. The Libra Moon emphasizes the importance of law and justice.

Mars sextile Uranus (occurring July 15 – 23) Mars in Taurus is sextile to Uranus in Pisces. Earth shaking forces of combat are ignited in unanticipated ways as Mars governs all activities and forces of action. Mars in Taurus is symbolic of a bulldozer razing a site for an industrial development. The sextile aspect puts this bulldozer energy of Mars in Taurus into a position of opportunity and hope with regard to the explosive, unpredictable and chaotic energies of Uranus in Pisces. There is also the potential for a vast eruption of creativity. Those who are affected by this aspect are likely to be stir-crazy and in strong need of a revolution. Anger and frustration can be stifling at times, requiring freedom and a definite breakthrough. Take caution with your actions and be aware of the potential for accidents when you feel compelled to vent some heat. This aspect last occurred on February 3 when Mars was in Capricorn.

July 21st Saturday
FIRST QUARTER MOON in LIBRA

	PDT	EDT	
Moon trine Neptune	7:35 AM	10:35 AM	
Moon sextile Saturn	2:30 PM	5:30 PM	
Moon sextile Pluto	6:56 PM	9:56 PM	
Moon square Sun goes v/c	11:30 PM	2:30 AM	(July 22)

Mood Watch: The very peaceful lunar aspect – Moon trine Neptune, starts the day and brings greater harmony with regard to our beliefs. Moon sextile Saturn brings moods inspired by our disciplines and by a sense of duty. This evening, Moon sextile Pluto brings moods that will be inspired to look for solutions to the troubles generated by superpowers. **First Quarter Moon in Libra** (Moon square Sun) encourages us to harmonize with partners and friends. With the Moon in Libra, life is all about making adjustments, and these adjustments must be made for your own benefit as well as for that of others. Teamwork requires balance. Peace begins with the self and is also experienced through the loving kindness of others. Libra Moon focuses our attention on peace efforts, literary works, civil law and the justice system, and fine foods. It reminds us the experience of pleasure can have a great impact on the culturally refined and intellectually developed levels of human interaction.

LEO
Key Phrase: "I WILL"

Fixed Fire Sign

Symbol: The Majestic Lion

July 22nd through August 23rd

July 22nd Sunday
Parents' Day
Moon in Libra / Scorpio

	PDT	EDT	
Moon enters Scorpio	1:19 AM	4:19 AM	
Moon sextile Venus	6:17 AM	9:17 AM	
Moon trine Mercury	9:33 PM	12:33 AM	(July 23)
Sun enters Leo	10:01 PM	1:01 AM	(July 23)

" Parents were invented to make children happy by giving them something to ignore. "
- Ogden Nash (1902 – 1971)

Mood Watch: As the Moon enters Scorpio our moods enter into a transformations process. While the Sun is still in Cancer, the Scorpio Moon brings a surge of emotional responses. Our moods are affected by the intensity that notoriously goes along with this Moon. This may be the time to seek rest, shelter, and take cover from danger. Scorpio Moon teaches us to live passionately. It also challenges us to apply discipline to our passion, recognizing that intense emotions such as anger, jealousy, hurt, fear, hate, etc. are all catalysts for damage and destruction. For the most part, this waxing Scorpio Moon day will be positive and regenerative in spirit. This evening, Moon sextile Venus brings moods inspired by love and by feminine influences. Moon trine Mercury brings moods in harmony with communications.

Sun enters Leo (Sun in Leo: July 22 – August 23) Today the Sun enters Leo, and the stately lion saunters into town like something out of an old western. Leo, the sign ruled by the Sun, fills the season with strong, instinctive fervor and deep, fiery desire. Leo focuses on will, identity, truth, selfhood, integrity, pride, and strength. Yours is a lustful time of year, Leo, and your totem, the lion, is one of the most self-assured of the zodiac's symbols. Sun in Leo focuses our attention on Sun related frolic and play, outdoor activities for children and families, and the entire entertainment industry. This is a time for self-development and fulfillment. For many, it is a time of self-affirmation and of launching personal projects and hobbies. Sharing affections is another vital part of Sun in Leo activity. Leo says, "I Will," and it is important for a Leo to be expressive in the act of will. The Leo part within us all must remember with a true affirmation of will we can have *anything* we want – we just can't have *everything*. Choose what is true to the self! Leo emphasizes the establishment of identity. To identify with the Sun is to identify with the self and the source of one's own fire. Just as the Sun projects light and energy, the Leo personality can personify and project great intention. Leos are notoriously great actors and performers. This is the fixed fire sign, capable of maintaining whatever fire is necessary to persist in a resolute manner towards the achievement of a willed purpose. The Sun in Leo is the time for all you solar types to let your hair down, enjoy entertainment events, and bask in the Sun whenever possible. You are applauded, Leo! Bravo, bravo! Please, by all means, take another bow!

July 23rd Monday

Moon in Scorpio	PDT	EDT
Moon trine Uranus	2:18 PM	5:18 PM
Moon opposite Mars	6:44 PM	9:44 PM
Moon square Neptune	7:59 PM	10:59 PM

Mood Watch: The hot and stinging intensity of the waxing Scorpio Moon brings us to the limit of our tolerance levels. New plateaus of emotional release will bring relief, but this is a time to remain aware and guarded. Scorpio Moon energy brings the daunting reality of life's unexpected ordeals, and often results in the need for compromise or sacrifice. The Scorpio Moon intensity works like a warning system as it tests our ability to cope with harsh realities. This afternoon, Moon trine Uranus brings disruptive moods, and there will be a strong need for a sense of freedom. This evening, Moon opposite Mars brings moods that may appear to be obsessed by aggressive forces. Moon square Neptune brings moods which may seem challenged by a lack of spiritual harmony, or possibly by addictions, temptations, and a lack of resistance.

July 24th Tuesday

Moon in Scorpio / Sagittarius	PDT	EDT
Moon square Saturn goes v/c	3:31 AM	6:31 AM
Moon enters Sagittarius	1:31 PM	4:31 PM
Mars square Neptune	4:11 PM	7:11 PM
Moon trine Sun	4:52 PM	7:52 PM
Moon square Venus	7:05 PM	10:05 PM
Mercury trine Uranus begins (see July 28)		

Mood Watch: Before the day fully arrives, Moon square Saturn brings moods and dreams that will be challenged by fears concerning deadlines. The Scorpio Moon goes void-of-course before most people are awake in North America, bringing a long day of emotional interferences. Many people will be distracted by the need for some kind of therapeutic process. This afternoon, as the waxing Moon enters Sagittarius, our moods enter into an explorative phase, and a much more philosophical outlook brings positive vibrations and hope. Moon trine Sun ensures that there will be adventurous and creative moods. This evening, Moon square Venus may bring moods that are challenging with regard to matters of love and attraction.

Mars square Neptune (occurring July 16 – 29) Heated activities run into obstacles concerning the work of Great Spirit and the fulfillment of spiritual harmony. Mars is in Taurus and there may be a physical disruption that intrudes on or impedes our spiritual level of experience. Martial forces are bursting through temples, belief systems, and holy moments. Active aggression occurs around spiritual groups and religious institutions, often targeting the belief systems of others. Mariners at sea may run into challenging storms. This aspect also brings the potential for accidents and temper tantrums, especially with regard to opinions about substance abuse and sacred matters. It is important not to get so wrapped up in the spiritual side of things that physical world realities, such as fire, are overlooked. Angry outbursts are likely to affect sacred land or the personal territory of spiritual sentiment. While Mars is square to Neptune it is best to anticipate confrontations concerning moral or spiritual issues. As this aspect passes, it will be easier to put spiritual beliefs and practices back on course without much conflict or interference. Meanwhile, stay aware and ready to deal with whatever comes along.

July 25th Wednesday

Moon in Sagittarius	PDT	EDT
Moon conjunct Jupiter	9:27 AM	12:27 PM

Mood Watch: The strongly waxing Sagittarius Moon brings very active and creative events and scenarios for us to choose from and enjoy. The Sun and Moon are in fire signs, encouraging outgoing, creative, and entertaining activities. Today's only significant lunar aspect is an especially positive one; Moon conjunct Jupiter brings moods that will be strongly connected to a sense of wealth, joviality, prosperity, and wellbeing. Summer vacation trips may be successfully carried out at this time. Sagittarius Moon is a time of discovery and exploration.

July 26th Thursday

Moon in Sagittarius / Capricorn PDT   EDT   ♌

	PDT	EDT	
Moon square Uranus	1:07 AM	4:07 AM	
Moon sextile Neptune	6:33 AM	9:33 AM	
Moon trine Saturn	2:26 PM	5:26 PM	
Moon conjunct Pluto goes v/c	5:14 PM	8:14 PM	
Moon enters Capricorn	11:22 PM	2:22 AM	(July 27)

Mood Watch: Overnight, Moon square Uranus brings moods and dreams challenged by a sense of turmoil and recklessness. This morning, Moon sextile Neptune helps to turn things around as our moods will become more inspired by tranquility and peacefulness. This afternoon, Moon trine Saturn brings the perfect time when our moods are in harmony with a sense of discipline and structure. This evening, Moon conjunct Pluto brings moods which will be at one with a sense of acceptance of those things which we cannot change. The Sagittarius Moon also goes void-of-course at this point, bringing moods that will be repeatedly distracted by a deep underlying philosophical awareness. It will be best not to get so distracted as to find yourself lost or misguided somehow. Much later tonight, the Moon enters Capricorn; our moods will enter into a much more grounded and practical level of awareness – a good time to rest.

July 27th Friday

Moon in Capricorn   PDT   EDT

	PDT	EDT
Moon trine Venus	4:55 AM	7:55 AM
Venus goes retrograde	10:29 AM	1:29 PM
Sun trine Jupiter begins (see August 2)		

Mood Watch: The strongly waxing Moon in Capricorn brings moods that are more serious, and there is a greater effort to handle big jobs and responsibilities. Today's focuses will be largely work oriented. Capricorn Moon gives us the impetus to work through tedious chores that require our focus and attention. There is only one significant lunar aspect occurring today; early this morning, Moon trine Venus brings moods in harmony with beauty and affection. Perhaps this is the best lunar aspect to have while Venus goes retrograde (see below.)

Venus goes retrograde (Venus retrograde: July 27 – September 8) The retrograde phase of a planet causes more of an internal than an external process of experience. Today the planet of love and magnetism, Venus which just entered Virgo on July 14, is now going retrograde at the two degree mark of Virgo. While Venus is retrograde in Virgo, the expression of love and beauty is analyzed and reflected upon from a distance, and love related activities are more often reserved or calculated than they are acted upon. While Venus is retrograde in Leo, the internal process of our love related focuses will be commonly examining our desires for personal attention or affection. Venus brings a yearning for affection, pleasure, beauty, and for the things we love. Venus retrograde may be especially difficult for people born during the cusps of Taurus/Gemini, Aquarius/Pisces, and Scorpio/Sagittarius. It is important to maintain and respect the source from which love flows, as well as maintaining a love and respect for yourself and your personal appearance. Hang in there, lovers. Venus retrograde in Leo/Virgo will be teaching us about the importance of not trying to control our love pursuits and pleasures, but simply to learn to enjoy what comes our way. True control comes from within, and the retrograde Venus helps us to internalize our understanding of love relationships altogether.

July 28th Saturday

Moon in Capricorn

	PDT	EDT
Moon opposite Mercury	7:28 AM	10:28 AM
Moon sextile Uranus	9:03 AM	12:03 PM
Moon trine Mars goes v/c	7:24 PM	10:24 PM
Mercury trine Uranus	8:26 PM	11:26 PM

Mood Watch: This morning, Moon opposite Mercury brings moods that will be especially communicative and, at times, too communicative. Moon sextile Uranus brings moods be inspired by rebelliousness. The heavily waxing Capricorn Moon mesmerizes us with drive, ambition, and efforts to supersede expectations. Tonight, Moon trine Mars brings energetic and feisty moods. Expect to take it easy however; the Capricorn Moon also goes void-of-course for the rest of the night, as some folks may be prone to overexerting their energies. Soothing pool dips and baths and comforting kinds of spa treatments may be just the ticket to easing Full Moon tension.

Mercury trine Uranus (occurring July 24 – 30) Mercury, emphasizing the transmission of news and information, is now in the favorable trine position to Uranus, representing disruption and chaos. This aspect brings news of disorder and calamity which (through the trine aspect) represents a gift, probably one of freedom or a break in the mundane routine. There are many premature or radical breakthroughs waiting in the wings, and Mercury trine Uranus often brings news of these discoveries. Mercury is in Cancer trine to Uranus in Pisces. Talk will be generated about changes in our belief structures and in the arts throughout the world. Catch phrases, or radical concept statements and ideas, are often born under this aspect. Mercury trine Uranus also allows for brilliant concepts to shine through and be worded in a way that radically makes sense. This is a good time to record thoughts and appreciate brilliant thinking. This aspect will occur again with Mercury in Scorpio on November 21.

July 29th Sunday

Moon in Capricorn / Aquarius – FULL MOON in AQUARIUS

	PDT	EDT	
Moon enters Aquarius	6:15 AM	9:15 AM	
Moon opposite Sun	5:49 PM	8:49 PM	
Moon sextile Jupiter	11:59 PM	2:59 AM	(July 30)

Mood Watch: The void-of-course Moon in Capricorn awakens some folks to serious moods, but as the Moon enters Aquarius this morning, our moods enter into a phase of intelligence and uniqueness. Today's **Full Moon in Aquarius** (Moon opposite Sun) enlivens our senses, inspires brilliance, and we feel the need to apply clarity and definition. Today is likely to be blanketed by bizarre and unusual occurrences as the Moon reaches fullness this evening. Quite often, the Full Aquarius Moon brings social gatherings, as well as charity events. People may seem idealistic and generous in some respects, and out of control – or downright unrealistic – in other respects. This is a good time to celebrate our knowledge and intelligence and to encourage the furthering of our education. Later tonight, Moon sextile Jupiter brings optimistic moods, creating feelings of prosperity.

♌

July 30th Monday

Moon in Aquarius	PDT	EDT
Moon conjunct Neptune	7:09 PM	10:09 PM
Mercury sextile Mars begins (see August 3)		

Mood Watch: This is a good time to celebrate the love of humankind and to enjoy the company of good friends. Aquarius Moon brings the potential for technological breakthroughs and great feats of accomplishment in the world of invention. Some folks may be a bit overwhelmed by the immensely busy and electrical kind of energy this past Full Moon weekend has brought. A cool steady pace will keep the atmosphere calm, especially this evening, as Moon conjunct Neptune brings comfortable moods and some notably peaceful and tranquil energy.

July 31st Tuesday

Moon in Aquarius / Pisces	PDT	EDT
Moon square Mars	2:56 AM	5:56 AM
Moon opposite Saturn	3:29 AM	6:29 AM
Moon sextile Pluto goes v/c	4:57 AM	7:57 AM
Moon enters Pisces	10:42 AM	1:42 PM
Moon opposite Venus	3:10 PM	6:10 PM
Mars square Saturn	5:00 PM	8:00 PM

Mood Watch: Overnight, Moon square Mars brings moods and dreams challenged by aggressive kinds of energy. Moon opposite Saturn brings sleepless moods or difficult dreams that may be overwhelmed by the theme of carrying out responsibilities. Early this morning, Moon sextile Pluto brings moods inspired by intense kinds of changes. The Aquarius Moon also goes void-of-course at this point, and our moods may become distracted by complex types of problems and human foibles. By the time the Moon enters Pisces, our moods enter into a time of artistic and intuitive expression. Moon opposite Venus brings moods that may seem overwhelmed by matters of love and beauty. As the evening progresses, the post-full Pisces Moon brings spacey, dreamy, imaginative, and meditative moods.

Mars square Saturn (occurring July 20 – August 6) Mars is in Taurus and Saturn is in Leo; competition is very stiff as independent companies take a beating in actively trading markets. This aspect is known for creating confrontations between offensive and defensive forces, and is not a good time to start a new enterprise. When deploying forces in battle, this aspect often brings fiery and sometimes tragic endings. It is wise to proceed with extra caution. This may be an especially difficult time to muster the strength to finish up projects, or to end affairs amicably. Hang in there; it's less than a week until we kiss this cycle of Mars square Saturn goodbye.

August 1st Wednesday

Lammas / Lughnassad

Moon in Pisces	PDT	EDT
Moon square Jupiter	3:47 AM	6:47 AM
Moon conjunct Uranus	5:36 PM	8:36 PM

Mood Watch: The waning Pisces Moon brings a dreamy, rather psychic level of awareness. Today's first lunar aspect, Moon square Jupiter, brings prudent moods, and many people may be challenged or irritated by rising costs or added expenses. Throughout the day, moods remain somewhat contemplative, clairvoyant, artistic, and full of belief, prayer, and meditation. This evening, Moon conjunct Uranus brings a feeling of acceptance with the disorder and chaos that currently exists. Bold, free and explosively creative attitudes are commonly expressed with this lunar aspect.

Today brings us to the solar holiday of *Lammas* and we have now reached the halfway mark of summer. The word *Lammas* comes from the term loaf-mass and it traditionally represents the first harvest of corn. The Druids call this festival holiday Lughnasadh, a time dedicated to Lugh, the Celtic Sun god whose name means "shining one." Just as the first crops are cut, this time represents a sacrifice, for Lugh was killed, but he came back to life. After Summer Solstice (June 21) the Sun's light begins to die – not literally but symbolically – and rebirth occurs at Winter Solstice (December 21). Lammas takes place when the crops are thirsty and the green traces of spring have long gone. The fields become strawlike and golden. The Green Man of spring (May 1/Beltane) has been transformed, and he now appears to us as a straw figure popularly known as The Wicker Man or Jack Straw. Although the Sun's light dies away, the life of the Sun is retained in the living harvest. Let unwanted worries and fears die with the Sun King, and reaffirm the picture of self with the promise of the life contained in the harvest of seeds. Collect seeds of wisdom and contemplate in the heart of summer what part of you must die, and what part must be sustained and preserved through the impending autumn and winter, until it can be reborn at Solstice. Celebrate life in the bounty of the summer harvest.

August 2nd Thursday

Moon in Pisces / Aries	PDT	EDT
Moon trine Mercury	6:49 AM	9:49 AM
Moon square Pluto	8:02 AM	11:02 AM
Sun trine Jupiter	8:13 AM	11:13 AM
Moon sextile Mars goes v/c	8:38 AM	11:38 AM
Moon enters Aries	1:44 PM	4:44 PM

Mood Watch: The waning Pisces Moon assists us with adaptable and psychic inclinations. This morning, Moon trine Mercury brings talkative and mindful moods. Moon square Pluto brings moods which tend to focus on the challenges of hardship, particularly those that exist between generations and cultures. A little later this morning, Moon sextile Mars brings energetic but defensive moods, especially since the Pisces Moon also goes void-of-course. For over five hours, the early part of the day may bring preoccupied moods as people tend to be spacey, lazy, and inattentive to practical routines. By afternoon, the Moon enters Aries, and our moods liven up into a much more aggressive and assertive phase of expression.

Sun trine Jupiter (occurring July 27 – August 5) This aspect is bringing those Leo people celebrating a birthday from July 27 – August 5 to a favorable natal solar position with relation to Jupiter. This will be a time of gifts and expansion for these birthday folks, and there are good times ahead for them in the coming year. This aspect will bring a better sense of what it means to expand and attain one's personal desire. Be sure to take the time right now (Leo birthday people) to enjoy and appreciate life, especially now that Saturn is about to leave Leo (see September 2). Life will definitely improve for those who are being given the gifts of opportunity that this aspect often brings. This aspect last occurred on April 9, affecting the Aries birthday people of that time.

August 3rd Friday

Moon in Aries	PDT	EDT
Mercury sextile Mars	2:54 AM	5:54 AM
Moon trine Jupiter	6:31 AM	9:31 AM
Moon trine Sun	8:08 AM	11:08 AM

Mood Watch: Ambitious and, at times, pushy moods prevail with the waning Aries Moon. This morning's lunar aspect, Moon trine Jupiter, brings moods that will be largely generous and optimistic. Moon trine Sun ensures our moods will be in tune with the joys of summer. Today's a good day to get things done, but it may be wise to pace yourself; this weekend's variety of lunar aspects implies that upcoming events and attitudes will be busy and complex.

Mercury sextile Mars (occurring July 30 – August 4) Mercury in Cancer sextile Mars in Taurus brings heartfelt messages of physical triumphs and actions. This aspect last occurred on July 1, when Mercury was retrograde. Mercury sextile Mars presents opportunities which can be received, recognized, communicated and acted upon. News or information may lead to immediate action, especially now that Mercury is *direct* (since July 9). It's an advantageous time to apply one's word with a full backing of action for a very favorable outcome. This aspect also occurred on May 8, when Mercury was in Taurus and Mars was in Pisces.

August 4th Saturday

Moon in Aries / Taurus	PDT	EDT
Moon sextile Neptune	12:56 AM	3:56 AM
Moon trine Saturn	10:08 AM	1:08 PM
Mercury enters Leo	10:16 AM	1:16 PM
Moon trine Pluto goes v/c	10:32 AM	1:32 PM
Moon enters Taurus	4:17 PM	7:17 PM
Moon square Mercury	5:14 PM	8:14 PM
Moon trine Venus	6:57 PM	9:57 PM
Venus square Mars begins (see August 7)		

Mood Watch: Sun in Leo and Moon in Aries brings creative, entertaining, and ambitious moods. This is a good time to focus on the self, as Leo says: "I will," and Aries says" "I am." Personal goals and desires are good things to review or carry out. Overnight, Moon sextile Neptune brings peaceful moods and dreams. Moon trine Saturn brings the best time to concentrate and practice disciplines requiring perfect timing. Moon trine Pluto brings moods that will lean amicably towards therapeutic methods of easing pain. The Aries Moon goes void-of-course for a number of hours today – be careful not to pick a fight and beware of the tendency for people to be impatient. Later today, when Moon enters Taurus, our moods enter into a practical phase. Finding comfort – for instance, a refuge from hot summer weather – may be the type of thing that will stand out with this evening's moods. Moon square Mercury may bring argument prone communications. Moon trine Venus will help to smooth over our evening attitudes with a great emphasis on beauty, comfort, and feminine wisdom.

Mercury enters Leo (Mercury in Leo: August 4 – 19) Mercury in Leo is an excellent time to effectively write or perform screenplays and comedy. When Leo the lion speaks, it's a penetrating sound! Mercury in Leo puts the focus of information, news and discussions on entertainment, personal interests, and connection with families. This is the time when many kids are turning to – or away from – family in an effort to find answers. They seek answers they can live with, answers about determining self-identity as well as survival skills. This is a time when do-it-yourself themes and self-help information assist us to respond to our individual needs. Mercury in Leo is a time when the mind establishes, reaffirms and maintains a self-created identity. Connections with Leos will come easily as expressed thoughts become more colorful and dramatic, and communications shift toward charismatic interplay. Self-expression and soulful fortitude will be more evident in our communications while Mercury is in Leo.

August 5th Sunday

Friendship Day
LAST QUARTER MOON in TAURUS

	PDT	EDT	
Moon square Sun	2:21 PM	5:21 PM	
Moon sextile Uranus	10:39 PM	1:39 AM	(August 6)

Mood Watch: The Sun is in Leo, the place of friends, family, and summer fun. Today is **Friendship Day**, and the **Last Quarter Moon in Taurus** is an excellent time to give a gift to a friend. Go ahead – boost a good friend's morale with the gift of friendship – the results will go far. Today's Moon brings a focus on creature comforts and aesthetically pleasing or luxurious surroundings. There may also be a focus on cleaning up or selling the various artifacts we have collected in our lives. The Last Quarter Taurus Moon often brings yard sales, auctions and flea markets into full swing. Letting go of attachments to material things that have burdened us with too much maintenance or with disruptive costs may very well be the best move. Specific types of sacrifice bring relief and freedom. Giving up responsibility for a beloved object can be very liberating in the Eastern mindset. Here in the West, those who are more sentimentally attached will have to make commitments to work on their finances in order to manage and hold on to the things they love. Take care and choose well. Material possessions must not own us. Less is more! Later tonight, Moon sextile Uranus brings moods inspired by the need for freedom. Rebelliousness may be detected in our late night attitudes.

August 6th Monday

Civic Holiday, Canada

Moon in Taurus / Gemini

♌

	PDT	EDT	
Moon square Neptune	3:28 AM	6:28 AM	
Saturn trine Pluto	3:36 AM	6:36 AM	
Moon square Saturn	1:17 PM	4:17 PM	
Moon conjunct Mars goes v/c	6:51 PM	9:51 PM	
Moon enters Gemini	7:02 PM	10:02 PM	
Jupiter goes direct	7:06 PM	10:06 PM	
Moon square Venus	8:27 PM	11:27 PM	
Mars enters Gemini	11:02 PM	2:02 AM	(August 7)
Mercury trine Jupiter begins (see August 9)			

Mood Watch: Activities will continue to seem busy as another long day of lunar aspects brings summer activity into a whirlwind of expressions. Overnight, Moon square Neptune brings spiritually challenging moods and dreams. This afternoon, Moon square Saturn challenges our moods with guarded feelings, and it may appear the demands of authorities are troubling at times. This evening, Moon conjunct Mars activates our moods with energy and adrenaline that may seem refreshingly positive for some, and overly aggressive for others. At this point the Taurus Moon goes void-of-course, briefly, and then enters Gemini. Waning Gemini Moon often brings helpful or interesting information for each of us, individually, to internalize. A little later, Moon square Venus brings a time when people may step on the toes of other people's personal needs and attachments. Late tonight will be a good time to avoid conflicts with loved ones.

Saturn trine Pluto (occurring June 23 – August 28) Saturn and Pluto are both in fire signs (Leo and Sagittarius) bringing creative and exciting kinds of permanent change and re-structuralizing. When Saturn was in the challenging *opposite* aspect to Pluto back in August/September 2001, we all felt the brunt of some serious trials through the events of 9/11 and all that followed. It was not until April 26, 2003 that the Saturn opposite Pluto aspect came to an end of its cycle. Now, through the trine aspect, we are being given the long awaited rewards of our hard work and persistence during the difficult trials and transformations that the Saturn opposite Pluto tests demanded. Through the events of Saturn opposite Pluto, the security guidelines we've created for ourselves, and to which we've adhered as a result of recent events, have created a new foundation to sustain us.

Now that Saturn and Pluto are spending this summer in the favorable trine position to one other, it is up to us to determine how we will benefit and grow stronger as a result of the recent transformation process. This is a time for a more positive sense of control to be gained through the current channels of power. It is through the trine aspect that we will redefine our responsibilities and shift our goals and priorities to suit the rapidly changing ways of the 21st century. The gifts and rewards that we will acquire at this time become survival tools during the next phase of humanity's trials and transformations when Pluto enters Capricorn in 2008. New tests will commence when the opposition of Saturn and Pluto occurs again in 2009 and 2010. For now, be grateful that time is agreeably on our side while restrictive Saturn is in the favorable trine position to the harsh and unrelenting forces of Pluto.

Jupiter goes direct (Jupiter direct: August 6, 2006 – May 8, 2008) Let us celebrate as the planet Jupiter moves forward! Jupiter represents skill, fortune, luck, wealth, expansion, well being, and joviality; it's also associated with advancement, prosperity, opportunity, fulfillment, and inheritance. However, Jupiter has been retrograde in the sign of Sagittarius for the past four months, since April 5. The process of Jupiter retrograde is sometimes difficult for systems, and for the predictability of economic growth, such as business and market control Jupiter is in its native sign, Sagittarius, and as it moves *direct* throughout the remainder of the year, it will enter Capricorn on December 18. Jupiter engages one with a sense of happiness and fulfillment. Blessed are the Sagittarius people, as this ruling planet of Sagittarius – the prosperity planet – has been and will continue to be sweeping through Sagittarians' personal realm, giving them the opportunities and tools for growth needed to advance, and also bestowing a sense of joy. Next year will be Capricorn's year to identify with prosperity and happiness, as Jupiter proceeds through the sign of Capricorn.

Mars enters Gemini (Mars in Gemini: August 6 – September 28) Mars, the planet of war, energy, action, force and pressure will focus its attention through Gemini, the sign of thinking, communicating, and duality. Gemini people will experience heated thoughts, challenges with anger and fevers, and will most likely endure extended surges of energy and strength. When the energy is harnessed, action manifests as oral or written communications – and all of these expressions will have a fiery and inspired flare. As a general rule, Mars in Gemini helps to stimulate and activate dual perspectives, making it easy to see and understand both sides of a heated discussion while making it more difficult to take sides. Forces may seem scattered and restless for some people at this time. Other people will find that Mars in Gemini sharpens the perception and insight, and these people will stand out through their clear outspokenness. This is a good time to avoid being talked into fighting other people's battles – watch out for smooth talking recruiters. Mars will go retrograde on November 15, and as it traverses back through the early degrees of Cancer, it will eventually re-enter the tail end of Gemini on December 31.

August 7th Tuesday
Moon in Gemini

	PDT	EDT	
Moon sextile Mercury	4:24 AM	7:24 AM	
Moon opposite Jupiter	12:00 PM	3:00 PM	
Venus square Mars	4:37 PM	7:37 PM	
Moon sextile Sun	9:08 PM	12:08 AM	(August 8)
Sun opposite Neptune begins (see August 13)			

Mood Watch: This Gemini Moon day begins with a great deal on our minds and it also begins with opportunistic thoughts while Moon sextile Mercury occurs in the early morning. By afternoon, Moon opposite Jupiter brings deeply involved moods, especially with regard to our livelihoods, our fortunes, and our sense of wellbeing. There will be a strong desire to excel, to be adventurous, and to explore new perspectives. Later tonight, Moon sextile Sun helps to modify the strong tug of today's peak performance of Venus square Mars (see below), and an overall feeling of accomplishment is possible by appeasing our attention loving, beastly side (Sun in Leo) with communicative persistence (Moon in Gemini).

Venus square Mars (occurring August 4 – 12) Retrograde Venus in Virgo is at the Leo/Virgo cusp in a square position to Mars in Gemini at the Taurus/Gemini cusp. This square aspect often drives people to set up protective barriers, and some people will feel the need to let certain defenses remain intact long enough for tender egos and emotional battle wounds to mend. Others may feel abandoned and become angry about the barriers. Of course, there are more specific circumstances and astrological factors at work that also influence our love relationships, and this aspect does not challenge all relationships equally. This is a good time to play it cautiously in matters of love. This aspect last occurred on April 22 and will repeat one more time on November 19.

♌

August 8th Wednesday

Moon in Gemini / Cancer

	PDT	EDT		
Moon square Uranus	1:42 AM	4:42 AM		
Moon trine Neptune	6:38 AM	9:38 AM		
Moon opposite Pluto	4:35 PM	7:35 PM		
Moon sextile Saturn	5:12 PM	8:12 PM		
Venus enters Leo	6:11 PM	9:11 PM		
Moon sextile Venus goes v/c	10:28 PM	1:28 AM	(August	9)
Moon enters Cancer	10:37 PM	1:37 AM	(August	9)

Mood Watch: Moon square Uranus rips through the night with moods and dreams that have unconventional tones of expression. Despite the harsh overtones of the night, we awaken to a pleasant morning, while Moon trine Neptune brings peaceful and artistic moods. The waning Gemini Moon keeps us busily communicating and thinking through various expressions of mood. Later today, Moon opposite Pluto intensifies our moods with a strong underlying awareness of the real difficulties that exist in our lives. Later tonight, Moon sextile Saturn brings guarded but optimistic moods. Moon sextile Venus brings the potential for affectionate and gentle moods, as the Gemini Moon goes void-of-course. Swiftly, the Moon enters Cancer. The waning Cancer Moon brings intuitive and psychic impressions that are more readily accessible when we – individually - internalize and reflect upon our moods.

Venus enters Leo (Venus in Leo: August 8 – October 7) The retrograde Venus re-enters the late degrees of Leo today. Venus retrograde in Leo reminds us of the need for affection, and the tender care required to keep the human ego well intact, contented, and preserved. For more information on Venus retrograde, see July 27. The retrograde Venus is now entering Leo for the second round this year; for more information on Venus in the sign of Leo, see June 5.

August 9th Thursday

Moon in Cancer

	PDT	EDT
Mercury trine Jupiter	8:37 AM	11:37 AM
Venus conjunct Saturn begins (see August 13)		
Venus trine Pluto begins (see August 15)		

Mood Watch: There are no lunar aspects occurring on this Cancer Moon day. The whole day will have a natural flow to it, although it may appear moody in nature. As the natural placement of the Moon (Cancer) wanes, emotional processes are occurring. There is a need to let ourselves feel the mood and move through it if it's uncomfortable, or to feel the mood and bask in it – enjoy it to the fullest – if it's positive, comfortable, and nurturing. Waning Cancer Moon is the time to clean house emotionally. It's also a time when we must check our instincts and intuition to see if what we are feeling is moving along on the right track according to what's going on around us.

Mercury trine Jupiter (occurring August 6 – 10) Mercury gets the message out there, the trine aspect brings gifts and positive breakthroughs, and Jupiter brings prosperity. This most favorable aspect brings good news of expansion and prosperity to those who are open to broadening their awareness. Ask and you shall have! Mercury in Leo trine Jupiter in Sagittarius brings entertaining words which can lead to a gold mine of happiness and wellbeing. This is an excellent time to learn new skills which will improve one's livelihood and better one's outlook. This is also a great time for salespeople to make sales, and for everyone to advertise and put information out there. For some folks, Mercury trine Jupiter is an advantageous time to ask for a job or a loan, or to provide a service which may have a bearing on a potential promotion. Look openly for opportunity when sharing information, and promote yourself and your capabilities. This aspect last occurred on April 21, when Mercury was in Aries.

August 10th Friday

Moon in Cancer

	PDT	EDT
Moon trine Uranus goes v/c	5:58 AM	8:58 AM
Sun conjunct Mercury begins (see August 15)		

Mood Watch: This time of the Sun in Leo and Moon in Cancer draws us to our natural urges and instincts. The day begins strangely enough with Moon trine Uranus just as the waning Cancer Moon goes void-of-course. Our morning moods may be pleasantly rebellious, freedom loving, and explosive in temperament — but positive in spirit. The void-of-course Cancer Moon is relentless and it is very likely that many employees will call in sick even though they aren't physically sick. However, travelers may find themselves somewhat homesick. Those who must work may seem to mope their way through the day and be too preoccupied with emotional stuff to notice what's really going on around them. Traffic lines and shopping lines are expected to move slowly, mostly due to selfish complaints and basic insecurities. Indulge in a deep sigh and, if at all possible, close up shop early today and enjoy domestic comforts instead.

August 11th Saturday

Moon in Cancer / Leo

	PDT	EDT	
Moon enters Leo	3:43 AM	6:43 AM	
Moon sextile Mars	8:52 AM	11:52 AM	
Moon trine Jupiter	9:50 PM	12:50 AM	(August 12)
Mercury opposite Neptune begins (see August 14)			

Mood Watch: Bouts of light sleeping may have occurred in the wee small hours of last night's void-of-course Cancer Moon. Finally, the Moon enters Leo very early this morning and our moods shift into a dynamic level of enthusiasm and expression. Moon sextile Mars picks up the early part of the day with energetic and confident moods. This summertime Saturday with the Moon in Leo is an excellent time to enjoy barbeques, picnics, and various forms of entertainment with family and friends. This is also and important time to individually internalize our personal needs, and to do what is necessary to ensure that we are getting some fun out of our summer. Later tonight, Moon trine Jupiter tops the evening with optimistic and prosperous feelings and moods.

August 12th Sunday

NEW MOON in LEO

	PDT	EDT
Moon conjunct Mercury	9:14 AM	12:14 PM
Moon conjunct Sun	4:04 PM	7:04 PM
Moon opposite Neptune	5:32 PM	8:32 PM

Mood Watch: The first lunar aspect of today, Moon conjunct Mercury brings communicative and talkative moods in the early part of the day. Later today, the heavily waning Leo Moon reaches the new mark and a new perspective begins to unveil itself. **New Moon in Leo** (Moon conjunct Sun) is a time of personal discovery. Leo is the optimist, and the New Leo Moon brings positive new perspectives to personal goals, as well as inspiring a new outlook on the personal image. This is a good time to work on raising self-esteem. Image comes from within and is generated by the sheer magnitude of the will – it can come from no other than the self. Everyone has room to grow if they take time to apply some self-respect and discipline. This evening, Moon opposite Neptune brings a strong and compelling awareness of the art, poetry, music, and spiritual beliefs that shape and form who and what we are in spirit and at heart. Enjoy our beautiful world!

August 13th Monday

Moon in Leo / Virgo

	PDT	EDT
Moon trine Pluto	4:24 AM	7:24 AM
Moon conjunct Saturn	6:16 AM	9:16 AM
Moon conjunct Venus goes v/c	6:35 AM	9:35 AM
Moon enters Virgo	11:04 AM	2:04 PM
Sun opposite Neptune	11:26 AM	2:26 PM
Venus conjunct Saturn	12:17 PM	3:17 PM
Moon square Mars	7:25 PM	10:25 PM
Sun trine Pluto begins (see August 19)		
Mars opposite Jupiter begins (see August 23)		

Mood Watch: Early this morning, Moon trine Pluto brings a profound sense of renewed hope and optimism with regard to the difficult realities that we have faced up to this point. Moon conjunct Saturn brings serious and determined moods and, as the morning progresses, Moon conjunct Venus brings gentle and loving moods. At this point, the Leo Moon goes void-of-course and our moods tend to become preoccupied over personal matters. As the Moon enters Virgo, our moods shift over to a much more judicious and discerning quality of expression. Beware this evening, as Moon square Mars brings the potential for irritability, fights, aggressiveness, and forcefulness.

Sun opposite Neptune (occurring August 7 – 16) This occurrence of Sun opposite Neptune especially affects those Leo people celebrating birthdays from August 7

– 16. Neptune in opposition to these folks' natal Sun brings a strong awareness of Spirit, the spiritual path, and the acknowledgment of one's beliefs. The challenge facing these Leo birthday folks is to confront and overcome all disruptive personal doubts that cause them to question the practice of believing. These people will be eminently aware this year of the vast shifts in spiritual beliefs, and they may feel quite overwhelmed by the confusion and fluctuations of their own spiritual awareness. This is no surprise – it is occurring for numerous people at this time – Leos will just experience it more directly. This is the time to go to a personal sanctuary of choice and tune into Spirit.

Venus conjunct Saturn (occurring August 9 – 21) Now that Venus is retrograde since July 27, Venus conjunct Saturn in Leo is occurring for the second time this year (since July 1) creating willful and serious bonding between family and friends. Also, Venus conjunct Saturn in Leo can bring an intense focus on guarding and protecting loved ones. While Venus is retrograde, love matters are more thoroughly contemplated on an internal level. This is the last time Venus and Saturn will be conjunct in Leo until August, 2035. For more information on Venus conjunct Saturn, see July 1. Venus will be conjunct with Saturn one more time this year on October 13, only by then Saturn will have entered the sign of Virgo (Sept. 2).

August 14th Tuesday

Moon in Virgo	PDT	EDT
Moon square Jupiter	6:08 AM	9:08 AM
Mercury opposite Neptune	1:10 PM	4:10 PM
Moon opposite Uranus	8:57 PM	11:57 PM
Mercury conjunct Venus begins (see August 16)		
Mercury trine Pluto begins (see August 17)		
Sun conjunct Saturn begins (see August 21)		

Mood Watch: While the youthfully waxing Moon is in Virgo, cautious and attentive attitudes pervade the atmosphere. Moon square Jupiter starts off the day with the spirit of prudence, causing many folks to be less generous than usual and especially tight with their wallets. Virgo Moon brings a general attitude of cautious resourcefulness, and we often lean towards the more practical method of satisfying our needs. Tonight, Moon opposite Uranus brings rebellious, freedom loving moods, and it shakes up our Virgo Moon shyness with explosive energy and unconventional avenues of thought.

Mercury opposite Neptune (occurring August 11 – 16) Mercury opposite Neptune makes us acutely aware of discussions concerning religious beliefs. Beliefs go beyond the physical to the metaphysical realms, where information is accessed and spiritual fortification occurs. It is wisest to be clear on one's own beliefs, and not to put oneself in a position of having to defend or expose those beliefs before a pack of merciless critics. Spiritual growth and enlightenment are not easy things to relay in conversation, and during this aspect it may seem particularly overwhelming for some folks to try to communicate effectively, or to comprehend what others are trying to communicate about spiritual matters.

August 15th Wednesday

Moon in Virgo / Libra

	PDT	EDT	
Venus trine Pluto	6:45 AM	9:45 AM	
Sun conjunct Mercury	12:57 PM	3:57 PM	
Moon square Pluto goes v/c	2:03 PM	5:03 PM	
Moon enters Libra	9:05 PM	12:05 AM	(August 16)
Mercury conjunct Saturn begins (see August 18)			

Mood Watch: This morning, the waxing Virgo Moon builds on our curiosities. A discriminating and analytical blend of intelligence fills us with anticipation. This Moon brings a determination to perfect and change the stagnant energies around us. The Virgo Moon time places an emphasis on cleanliness and organization. As the Virgo Moon goes void-of-course today, Moon square Pluto brings challenging moods with regard to troublesome realities. The Moon will remain void-of-course for seven long hours. Beware of the tendency for our moods to be full of doubt, skepticism, or criticism. Also be aware of the tendency for some folks to feel depressed. By the time the Moon enters Libra, our moods enter into a much more balanced perspective.

Venus trine Pluto (occurring August 9 – 25) Today, Venus and Pluto are both retrograde, and this aspect is occurring for the third time this year, with one round to go. Venus trine Pluto allows a breakthrough to occur for those who have trouble accepting the work of fate. Loving energy flows more easily between generations. While Venus and Pluto are retrograde in this favorable aspect, an internal transformation may be occurring for some folks. Love triumphs over all, especially with Venus trine Pluto. This is a great time to let love cure the pain. Venus trine Pluto last occurred on July 8 and before that, on March 16. This aspect occurs for the fourth and final time this year on October 3.

Sun conjunct Mercury (occurring August 10 – 18) This is a very common aspect, which will create a more thoughtful, communicative, and expressive year ahead for those Leo born people celebrating birthdays from August 10 – 18. This is your time (Birthday Leos) to record ideas, relay important messages, and pay close attention to your imaginative thoughts as they are touched by Mercury, creating the urge to speak and be heard. Your thoughts will reveal a great deal about who you are, now and in the year to come. This may well be a time of great passage for many Leos, as Saturn is about to leave the constellation Leo and enter the realm of Virgo on September 2. Leo people's speeches will be awe inspiring, as they will be commemorating the past couple of years of their hard work and achievement while Saturn has been traveling through Leo's territory.

August 16th Thursday

Moon in Libra

	PDT	EDT	
Moon trine Mars	9:02 AM	12:02 PM	
Moon sextile Jupiter	5:07 PM	8:07 PM	
Mercury conjunct Venus	10:28 PM	1:28 AM	(August 17)
Sun conjunct Venus begins (see August 17)			

Mood Watch: Last night, the Moon entered Libra bringing friendship, partnership, and congenial interactions with others. In the early part of the day, Moon trine

Mars brings energetic and optimistic moods that will inspire us to take action. This evening, Moon sextile Jupiter brings explorative and jovial moods, and this is an excellent time to bestow gifts on loved ones, especially while Mercury is conjunct with Venus later this evening.

Mercury conjunct Venus (occurring August 14 – 18) When these two planets are conjunct, the energy suggests the need to communicate love. Today's conjunction of Mercury and Venus takes place in the courageous realm of Leo. This is often a time when intimate and loving thoughts are shared with assertive playfulness. With this aspect, loving gestures are usually very sincere and genuine, despite the fact that Venus is currently retrograde (since July 27). For some folks, there may be a tendency for love-related communication to seem somewhat reserved, or overly internalized, although the need to communicate love is definitely there. It would be best to communicate love without getting too hung up on emotional issues, and there will be a lot of talk about our commitment to love. Hold no expectations in the expression of love, and take no offense if your own attempts to express your love are poorly interpreted.

August 17th Friday
Moon in Libra

	PDT	EDT		
Mercury trine Pluto	10:24 AM	1:24 PM		
Moon trine Neptune	2:05 PM	5:05 PM		
Sun conjunct Venus	8:42 PM	11:42 PM		
Moon sextile Venus	10:43 PM	1:43 AM	(August	18)
Moon sextile Sun	11:00 PM	2:00 AM	(August	18)

Mood Watch: Waxing Libra Moon brings the potential for positive progress to be made among friends and between marital partners. This is a good time to review decisions that have to be made and to work towards making adjustments and compromises with others. This afternoon, Moon trine Neptune brings peaceful and harmoniously spiritual moods. Tonight, Moon sextile Venus brings the potential for positive vibes between loved ones, but a definite effort to create those positive vibes will have to be made. Later tonight, Moon sextile Sun brings peaceful summer reverie and pleasant dreams.

Mercury trine Pluto (occurring August 14 – 19) Mercury in Leo trine Pluto in Sagittarius brings the message of hope. Mercury in Leo gives a very colorful and theatrical flare to our methods of communication. Mercury trine Pluto brings greater definition to the meaning of fate, and allows us to more easily communicate about the power struggles that are occurring collectively around the world. Mercury is the communications tower that transmits information. Pluto's disruptive energy is focusing our attention on such issues as contagious diseases, senseless crime, misunderstandings between cultures, facing up to addiction, and many other painful realities. This is a good time to express encouraging words and reinforce the troubled people of our world with a sense of hope. This aspect last occurred on April 26, when Mercury was in Aries.

Sun conjunct Venus (occurring August 16 – 21) The Sun and Venus are conjunct in Leo. This occurrence of Sun conjunct Venus particularly affects the love lives of those Leo people celebrating birthdays from August 16 – 21. These birthday folks are being filled with the need to have or express love, and this is the year for them to address the love matters in their lives. There is an attraction which draws us to beauty, romance, and love when Venus connects with the natal solar degrees. The issue of love is unavoidable, and these birthday folks' love needs will become very evident. It is through the attraction magnet of Venus that the personality (Sun sign) is assured of that with which they choose to identify, be affected by, or attracted to. Sometimes sheer magnetism is unavoidable, as the Sun and Venus in Leo often brings entertaining love-play, animal attraction, and flirtatiousness. Under such circumstances, an event or relationship cannot be chosen – it just happens. This can encompass not only love matters, but also other areas such as the arts, aesthetics or appreciation of beauty. This will be a year of love, birthday Leo people.

August 18th Saturday

Moon in Libra / Scorpio	PDT	EDT
Moon sextile Pluto	1:58 AM	4:58 AM
Moon sextile Mercury	5:07 AM	8:07 AM
Moon sextile Saturn goes v/c	5:22 AM	8:22 AM
Mercury conjunct Saturn	6:45 AM	9:45 AM
Moon enters Scorpio	9:14 AM	12:14 PM

Mood Watch: Overnight, the waxing Libra Moon sextile Pluto brings deeply thera-peutic dreams and moods. This morning, Moon sextile Mercury brings thoughtful moods. Moon sextile Saturn brings guarded and serious moods. The Libra Moon goes void-of-course at this early stage of the morning, and for just under four hours, our moods tend to be spacey and preoccupied, probably with regard to concerns about teamwork or partnership. This morning may be an indecisive time for many of us, but by the time the Moon enters Scorpio, our moods will shift over to a much more perceptive quality of expression. The hot and stinging intensity of the waxing Scorpio Moon brings us to the limit of our tolerance levels. New plateaus of emotional release will bring relief, but this is a time to remain aware and guarded. Scorpio Moon energy brings the daunting reality of life's unexpected ordeals, and often results in the need for compromise or sacrifice. The Scorpio Moon intensity works like a warning system as it tests our ability to cope with harsh realities. No worries — sometimes Scorpio Moons are just plain creative and energizing fun.

Mercury conjunct Saturn (occurring August 15 – 20) Mercury conjunct Saturn will bring talk about putting an end to the useless or unwanted components of our lives. When occurring in Leo, this conjunction implies that strong rules or guidelines will be laid down with regard to personal needs or limitations, and also family related restrictions and disciplines will be communicated. There is a dis-cerning quality at work with Mercury conjunct Saturn, making this aspect a very good one for speakers and writers to inspire, initiate and capture vital thoughts. News concerning the end of a cycle is likely to occur. Examples include retirement announcements, job loss, and possibly even the news of a notable death. Overall, Mercury conjunct Saturn tends to bring out a strong tone of seriousness in com-munications. There is a restriction, a discipline, a carefully considered emphasis of thoughts placed on our communications. There is a serious intent to get the word across in no uncertain terms. Governments and corporations may make new and restrictive proclamations for order. There is the strong implication at work that we must be seriously responsible for what we say, particularly around authority and in official public statements. "Anything you say can and will be used against you..."

August 19th Sunday

Moon in Scorpio

	PDT	EDT
Mercury enters Virgo	6:02 AM	9:02 AM
Sun trine Pluto	11:15 AM	2:15 PM
Moon trine Uranus	8:40 PM	11:40 PM

Mood Watch: Perceptive moods will carry us gregariously through this fine summer Sunday. Scorpio Moon focuses our energies on the need for a positive and uplifting outlook. Physical exertion will help to defuse intense emotions. This will be a good time to be objective and not to judge matters too hastily. Moon trine Uranus brings crazy, fun-loving, and unusual kinds of moods and focuses. Sun in Leo and Moon in Scorpio is the time to conquer adversity, improve self-image, and to work on personal power, inner strength, and confidence.

Mercury enters Virgo (Mercury in Virgo: August 19 – September 5) Virgo is a most advantageous place for Mercury – the place where it both rules and is exalted. Mercury in Virgo brings clarity to our plan for the coming events of autumn. It also puts the focus of talk on such issues as computers, budgets, systems analysis, harvesting, accounting, filing, and organizing. Mercury in Virgo brings out the skeptical and analytical side of every argument and topic of discussion, keeping us on our toes. Overall, this is a great time for communicating, research, and strategic planning.

Sun trine Pluto (occurring August 13 – 22) Positive, life-altering changes are occurring in the lives of Leo people celebrating birthdays this year from August 13 – 22. They are currently undergoing the favorable trine aspect of Pluto to their natal Sun, bringing out experiences that involve transformation and encounters with greater powers and fate. It is always difficult to speculate just how the Pluto experience will manifest itself. Have no fear; this is a time to get in touch with your power, birthday Leos! Pluto moves slowly in our cosmos, and powerful encounters that seem deadly or harsh are actually a necessary part of the process. Matters involving fate can be positive, and the trine aspect does represent a gift being bestowed – however unlikely it may seem. Be grateful this trine brings power issues into your life in a more positive fashion, leading to positive transformation. Finding out how to benefit from this power is a big part of discovering Pluto's gifts. This aspect last occurred on April 19, affecting the Aries/Taurus cusp born birthday folks of that time.

August 20th Monday

Moon in Scorpio / Sagittarius - FIRST QUARTER MOON in SCORPIO

♌

	PDT	EDT	
Moon square Neptune	2:36 AM	5:36 AM	
Moon square Venus	8:21 AM	11:21 AM	
Moon square Sun	4:55 PM	7:55 PM	
Moon square Saturn goes v/c	6:35 PM	9:35 PM	
Moon enters Sagittarius	9:45 PM	12:45 AM	(August 21)

Mercury square Mars begins (see August 25)
Venus opposite Neptune begins (see August 25 and September 21)

Mood Watch: Overnight, Moon square Neptune brings spiritually challenging moods and dreams. As the day begins, Moon square Venus brings challenging interactions between loved ones. The **First Quarter Moon in Scorpio** (Moon square Sun) arrives later today and, simultaneously, it goes void-of-course. The waxing quarter Moon of Scorpio brings out our moods in a precise and very concentrated manner. Today may play itself out like a spy novel. All forms of professionalism, expertise, and intellectualism are activated under the Scorpio Moon influence. The waxing Scorpio Moon often brings out strong sexual appetites and desires. This is a good time to tap into your creative and imaginative side. Awareness and staying on the ball are very important since con games, crime, violence, accidents, or theft may be somewhat prevalent during the void-Moon period. Being alert and using simple precautions will greatly help us to avoid or survive pain and trouble. Later tonight, the Moon enters Sagittarius, and by tomorrow, our moods will become much more optimistic and outgoing.

August 21st Tuesday

Moon in Sagittarius

	PDT	EDT
Moon square Mercury	5:21 AM	8:21 AM
Moon opposite Mars	4:15 PM	7:15 PM
Sun conjunct Saturn	4:29 PM	7:29 PM
Moon conjunct Jupiter	6:08 PM	9:08 PM

Mercury square Jupiter begins (see August 24)

Mood Watch: Moon square Mercury makes it difficult for many folks to communicate easily, or to understand complex concepts so early in the morning. Despite this, optimistic moods fill the air with the waxing Moon in Sagittarius. The late Leo Sun coupled with the young Sagittarius Moon brings no hesitation at all when it comes to satisfying our late summer needs and exploring beyond the usual bounds. The Sun and Moon are in fire signs and many folks will be drawn towards the need to be creative and to fulfill their desires. This is a great time to play in the sun, or to initiate a trip. Later today, Moon opposite Mars may bring pushy, impatient, or overly defensive moods. By this evening, Moon conjunct Jupiter impresses our moods with rich and prosperous feelings of wellbeing and happiness.

Sun conjunct Saturn (occurring August 14 – 25) This occurrence of Sun conjunct Saturn in the late degrees of Leo especially affects those Leo and early born Virgo people celebrating birthdays from August 14 – 25. These birthday people are experiencing a perfect time to focus on change. Saturn is also reminding you birthday folks to take charge of your life more responsibly, and to recognize the importance of your limitations. Maybe its time for an overhaul, Leo/Virgo – at least until certain areas of your life become more comfortable again. Saturn is urging you to connect with a sound dose of responsibility that fits your lifestyle and energy level. This may be the time to tune into the body and give it what it needs, and to deal succinctly with health matters. This year, it may be best for these birthday Leos/Virgos to incorporate a healthy exercise and diet routine that is fun and effective. Don't be so hard on yourself either, Leo/Virgo; try to remember to reward yourself throughout this year with each measure of your progress – it's good for the soul. Make up for lost time, and apply some self-love and nurturing to your renewed self-discipline. Hang in there and keep up the work, birthday folks, and don't be so glum; the tedious work in which you are now immersed will bring you genuine rewards later on. You'll see.

August 22nd Wednesday

Moon in Sagittarius	PDT	EDT
Moon square Uranus	8:08 AM	11:08 AM
Moon sextile Neptune	1:54 PM	4:54 PM
Moon trine Venus	4:50 PM	7:50 PM

Mood Watch: Sagittarius Moon in summer invites us to be outdoors, to be adventurous, explorative, and creative, and to make new discoveries. This morning, Moon square Uranus complicates our moods with explosive conflicts and radical activities. Later this afternoon, Moon sextile Neptune settles our moods with a calm, cool acceptance of the way things are. Sagittarius Moon brings very active and creative events and scenarios for us to choose from and to enjoy. The day only gets better as Moon trine Venus invites harmonious and loving feelings and moods to improve our outlook on life.

VIRGO

Key Phrase: " I ANALYZE "

Mutable Earth Sign

Symbol: The Virgin

August 22nd through

September 22nd PDT / 23rd EDT

August 23rd Thursday

Moon in Sagittarius / Capricorn	PDT	EDT
Moon conjunct Pluto	1:24 AM	4:24 AM
Sun enters Virgo	5:09 AM	8:09 AM
Moon trine Saturn goes v/c	5:55 AM	8:55 AM
Moon enters Capricorn	8:21 AM	11:21 AM
Moon trine Sun	8:37 AM	11:37 AM
Mars opposite Jupiter	9:04 AM	12:04 PM

Mood Watch: Overnight, during the final hours of Moon in Sagittarius, Moon conjunct Pluto puts our moods and dreams in tune with important world events which are busily shaping our lives and our lifestyles forever. Not long after the Sun enters Virgo, Moon trine Saturn brings moods to inspire us to take control of the day — but the Sagittarius Moon goes void-of-course and, despite industrious moods, we may find ourselves getting easily lost or off-track at times during this morning. By the time the Moon enters Capricorn, richly practical and earthy attitudes will allow us to feel and act more responsibly. Moon trine Sun brings down-to-earth harmony and a realistic picture of the final month of the summer season which we have just entered. Serious moods prevail while we get down to practical matters.

Sun enters Virgo (Sun in Virgo: August 23 – September 23) We now enter the final round of summer, and a more down-to-earth perspective on life calls out to us. *Happy Birthday Virgo!* May rich encounters with the earth bring out fond childhood memories! This is harvest time, and not only do the orchards full of ripe fruit and the fields of bountiful corn and wheat call out to be harvested, but we are also called to gather the other resources needed to get us through the winter. Preparing for the autumn season is a vast and costly endeavor for many people. Virgo concentrates the power of the mind on practicality, commerce, school, and our physical resources. Fastidiousness keeps the Virgo spirit preoccupied with maintaining cleanliness and order on a fairly constant basis. This does not always manifest on the physical level, as some Virgos remain locked in their minds, striving to build thoughts into scholarly mountains of truth. Other Virgos are content to take refuge in gardening, cleaning, pruning and grooming the imperfections of their troubled world. They may also be found fussing over makeup, health products, flossing and brushing, and making sure the details of their fashion statement are in keeping with the proper social expectations. Virgo's key phrase is "I analyze," and the pragmatic spirit of Virgo examines all avenues of life. It is just like Virgo to pick everything apart, detail by detail, and yet Virgo strives to get as much of an overview of the whole picture as possible. Virgo questions, Virgo doubts, and Virgo says, "Prove it." The Mercury ruled mutable sign of earth is keen, sharp-witted, and not so quick to believe any sort of random information, unless it's painstakingly researched by some reputable sources or published in a weighty book. Virgo will question the source every time. Virgo people have swift and practical minds, and are often known for supporting traditional values and for following the scientific edicts that reflect the laws of nature and the universe with exacting clarity. Without using the wisdom of Virgo to assess and pull together as much of the big picture as possible, the efficiency of the harvest would not provide enough nourishment to sustain our needs through autumn and winter. Virgos are famous for their ability to count, calculate and measure everything that must be accounted for – Virgo's job is immense. This is why the archetypal Virgos make such good accountants. Stretching out every last dollar and every last grain of food is the gift behind Virgo's prudence. It is the frugal one who is chosen to watch over the bounty of this season. Be sure to take this time to enjoy the final month of the summer season as the bounty of the harvest rests at your feet.

Mars opposite Jupiter (occurring August 13 – 29) Heated activities and those areas of life where we wage battles (Mars) are at odds with our economic welfare and outlook (Jupiter). Mars in Gemini opposes Jupiter in Sagittarius. Initiatives, when activated, will quickly come up against high levels of curiosity coupled with overwhelming market demands. This aspect brings an abrupt awareness of economic oppression or shortcomings. Fortunes may be mishandled due to unanticipated or accidental circumstances. While Mars is opposed to Jupiter, active forces are diametrically opposed to expansive fortitude, and sometimes our anger is spurred due to a lack of flow or growth in our economic resources. This is a very busy and often overwhelming time to attempt to excel in business endeavors, especially in actively trading markets. While Mars is opposing Jupiter it is wise to remember that when you're roused to anger, you must take heed not to "bite the hand that feeds you."

August 24th Friday

Moon in Capricorn	PDT	EDT
Moon trine Mercury	1:36 AM	4:36 AM
Moon sextile Uranus goes v/c	4:42 PM	7:42 PM
Mercury square Jupiter	6:04 PM	9:04 PM

Mood Watch: Overnight, Moon trine Mercury brings positive thoughts that are reflected in our moods and our dreams. The waxing Capricorn Moon takes us through the day with serious and determined moods that are often focused on the accomplishment of goals and big tasks. The demands of the boss will be upbeat, but demanding. Later today, Moon sextile Uranus brings moods inspired by original thinking and unusual inventions. The Capricorn Moon goes void-of-course at this point in the early evening and, for a short while, many forms of production or service will come to a slowly grinding halt. Tonight, the void-of-course Capricorn Moon may bring a strong work ethic; however, a distinct lack of incentive disrupts our Capricorn Moon sensibilities, and it will be tricky to find much enthusiasm among those who are out there working, as it will be difficult to get any decent service from them. Perhaps it is best not to take it all too seriously.

Mercury square Jupiter (occurring August 21 – 26) This aspect may bring discussions or complaints which revolve around the difficulties of getting funds or capital to grow. Mercury is in Virgo squaring to Jupiter in Sagittarius, and this may be a difficult time to make breakthroughs with even the most prudent types of investments, or it may be a difficult time to get extensions for business contracts. This aspect sometimes creates a difficult relationship between the communications industry and the sponsors of expansive production. The block in this energy flow occurs between the powers of Mercury represented as the salesman, informant, or negotiator, and the powers of Jupiter represented as the sources that allow wealth to flow (i.e., the manufacturer, banker, fund raiser, etc.) This is the place where value is realized and assessed, and the potential for growth is emphasized, but a whole lot of effort will be required to work through the obstacles. Mercury square Jupiter last occurred on April 4, when Mercury was in Pisces.

August 25th Saturday

Moon in Capricorn / Aquarius

	PDT	EDT
Mercury square Mars	9:00 AM	12:00 PM
Venus opposite Neptune	2:49 PM	5:49 PM
Moon enters Aquarius	3:36 PM	6:36 PM
Mercury opposite Uranus begins (see August 28)		
Mars square Uranus begins (see September 3)		

Mood Watch: Yesterday's void-of-course Capricorn Moon carries on throughout today bringing industrious but lethargic moods. After repeated attempts to get our sense of timing just right, our efforts pay off, as the Moon enters Aquarius later in the day. Moon in Aquarius brings gregarious, people loving, philanthropic moods. Suddenly, brilliance becomes more important than industriousness, and the overall scope of our mood leans toward the unconventional needs of humankind. Our desire for freedom and equality is tested at different stages of our human experience. The mortal self is limited, but what he or she leaves behind is a reflection of the immortal soul which does not die. What we leave behind is not always seen; it is sometimes heard, or spoken. Our contributions to others may be received and perceived in many gifted ways.

Mercury square Mars (occurring August 20 – 27) Mercury in Virgo is square Mars in Gemini. Skeptical thinking creates complications, and indecisiveness occurs around some activities. Under the influence of this aspect, it is not a good time to lose one's temper. Be especially careful to watch what you say, preferably thinking before you speak; words can be easily taken the wrong way. This aspect stimulates arguments and mental blocks concerning the actions of others. Mercury square Mars makes it difficult for some to justify their actions or explain why they take a certain stand in life. Refrain from making risky comments, and be careful not to misinterpret information as being hostile or personal. Remember, during this complex time of Mercury square Mars, not to shoot the messenger.

Venus opposite Neptune (occurring August 20 – September 27) Venus and Neptune are currently both retrograde, and Venus opposite Neptune will be occurring for longer than usual due to the fact that Venus will go direct on September 8. In less than a fortnight, Venus will catch up to the Neptune opposition and this aspect will repeat on September 21. For more information on Venus opposite Neptune, see June 30 when this aspect last occurred.

August 26th Sunday

Moon in Aquarius

	PDT	EDT
Moon sextile Jupiter	10:09 AM	1:09 PM
Moon trine Mars	1:12 PM	4:12 PM

Mood Watch: The spirit of this strongly waxing Aquarius Moon reminds us to learn from our mistakes and to add to our knowledge from our experiences of life. Early in the day, Moon sextile Jupiter brings positive, upbeat vibes and expressions of wellbeing. This afternoon, Moon trine Mars brings harmonious assertions and pleasantly energetic moods. Strength and skill may unite under today's lunar aspects, and great and small feats of humankind will generate hope. Be a contributor in some vast or tiny way, and oddly, eventually, your mark will resonate through time, like that piece of wisdom someone once told you years ago that still sticks with you.

August 27th Monday

Moon in Aquarius / Pisces

	PDT	EDT
Moon opposite Venus	1:51 AM	4:51 AM
Moon conjunct Neptune	3:01 AM	6:01 AM
Moon sextile Pluto	1:23 PM	4:23 PM
Moon opposite Saturn goes v/c	6:25 PM	9:25 PM
Moon enters Pisces	7:35 PM	10:35 PM

Mood Watch: Overnight, Moon opposite Venus brings dramatic moods and dreams about our needs for affection and beauty. A little later, Moon conjunct Neptune brings the feeling or experience of powerful spiritual connections. The heavily waxing Aquarius Moon brings the spirits of brotherhood, and especially sisterhood, to our early morning dreamstate. This afternoon, Moon sextile Pluto brings positive moods geared towards the necessity to find ways to change our apparent destiny. Powerful feelings bring the potential for great change. This evening, Moon opposite Saturn focuses our moods on serious and important duties that cannot be put off. The Aquarius Moon also goes void-of-course at this point and, for just over an hour, we may notice that our moods are put off by idealistic attitudes. Many folks may feel burned out by technology and the like. As the Moon enters Pisces, our moods are deepened by the call of the jackals. The Full Pisces Moon brings depth, mystery, and intrigue.

August 28th Tuesday

FULL MOON in PISCES – Total Lunar Eclipse

	PDT	EDT
Moon opposite Sun	3:36 AM	6:36 AM
Mercury opposite Uranus	12:40 PM	3:40 PM
Moon square Jupiter	1:27 PM	4:27 PM
Moon square Mars	6:20 PM	9:20 PM
Sun square Jupiter begins (see September 3)		

Mood Watch: Brace yourself and pace yourself – this lunar ecliptic Full Moon in Pisces will be a busy time emotionally for everyone. **Full Moon in Pisces** (Moon opposite Sun) happens in the early hours of the morning. This Moon brings out the psychic in everyone. Sensitivity runs very high on a Full Pisces Moon, and people express themselves in very artistic or perhaps nonsensical ways. Dance, music, art, and enchantment set the stage for Full Pisces Moon activity. Imaginations will run wild today and anything is possible. This afternoon's Moon square Jupiter brings less adventurous or less generous than usual moods among folks, and it may be difficult to get a smile out of some people. This evening, Moon square Mars brings the potential for violent or turbulent moods and, while Mars is in Gemini, beware of the potential for cruelty in language. Pisces says: "I believe," and while the Moon is full in Pisces, it is vitally important to carry our beliefs wisely, as destructive tendencies may bring us down if we're not careful. This will also be a time to watch out for low self-esteem or substance abuse.

Total Eclipse of the Moon in Pisces – This lunar eclipse may have negative effects on the ocean and on our travels by sea. Violation or corruption may affect the condition of coastlines and rivers. The dark side of the Pisces Moon eclipse is also evident in depressing or melancholic feelings; be watchful for the true signs of despair. Immorality and ugly hate crimes are possible, particularly with themes of religious intolerance, and there will probably be more news of destruction somewhere in the world. Eclipses in Pisces bring out the dark side of our beliefs and are a time of vulnerable confidences and deep sensitivity. The sanctity of human life gets pondered, and our souls are baffled by the unfathomable crimes of the heartless. Take heart and be cautious as well as vigilant. Our susceptibilities are running high; beware of those subjects and areas of life that may bring out people's weakness, or their vulnerability.

Mercury opposite Uranus (occurring August 25 – 30) Mercury in Virgo opposes Uranus in Pisces. Explosive events under discussion are testing our ability to trust or be convinced. Many will approve openly but will still maintain a healthy dose of skepticism. Ideas may seem bigger than life, and talk seems to focus on concepts which have not been fully grasped, but appear to be presented with assured confidence. Shocking or liberating statements tend to come out with this aspect. There is an acute awareness of the need to speak out for freedom, and the dialogue may appear sharp; radical and sometimes vulgar language may erupt. Outrageous claims and verbal presumptions made at this time may bring fiery or irrational flare-ups in discussion groups and chat rooms. This is a really good time to watch your mouth.

August 29th Wednesday
Moon in Pisces / Aries

	PDT	EDT	
Moon conjunct Uranus	12:17 AM	3:17 AM	
Moon opposite Mercury	1:54 AM	4:54 AM	
Moon square Pluto goes v/c	3:23 PM	6:23 PM	
Moon enters Aries	9:26 PM	12:26 AM	(August 30)
Mars trine Neptune begins (see September 8)			

Mood Watch: The lingering affects of yesterday's Ecliptic Full Moon in Pisces is still present. Moon conjunct Uranus pervades our moods and our dreams with turbulent emotions. Moon opposite Mercury brings complex nervous responses and complex thoughts with regard to what we are feeling or sensing. This afternoon, Moon square Pluto brings dramatic complexity to our moods, which very often end up affecting everyone. This is no time to take chances with fate, as the odds of an acceptable outcome are not always good. Don't leave depressed or suicidal people alone at this time! The Pisces Moon will go void-of-course at this point and remain this way for six hours. Spacey moods are inevitable and there may be a tendency towards substance abuse, or there may be struggles with temptations. By the time the Moon enters Aries, a much more defensive and self-confident tone of mood leads the way. Many people will begin to lean towards a more independent means of working out the estranged feelings left by this recent Full Moon event.

August 30th Thursday

Moon in Aries	PDT	EDT	
Moon trine Jupiter	3:07 PM	6:07 PM	
Moon sextile Mars	9:45 PM	12:45 AM	(August 31)
Mercury square Pluto begins (see September 2)			

Mood Watch: The Aries Moon brings out self-awareness and self-assertiveness, and focuses our attention on pushing forward with force and vigor, with strength and intent. A waning Aries Moon reminds us to be cautious of other people's equal needs to assert themselves. This is not a time to get into a pushing match, though such behavior may be rather common. Some folks may seem somewhat defensive after a tiresome lunar eclipse, and others may seem to be loaded with extra energy looking for an outlet. This afternoon, Moon trine Jupiter brings optimism, joy, and generosity to our moods. Later tonight, Moon sextile Mars brings positive strength and courage to our moods.

August 31st Friday

Moon in Aries / Taurus	PDT	EDT	
Moon trine Venus	2:51 AM	5:51 AM	
Moon sextile Neptune	6:27 AM	9:27 AM	
Moon trine Pluto	4:33 PM	7:33 PM	
Moon trine Saturn goes v/c	10:20 PM	1:20 AM	(September 1)
Moon enters Taurus	10:37 PM	1:37 AM	(September 1)

Mood Watch: Overnight, Moon trine Venus brings gentle, beautiful, and harmonious moods and vibrations. Moon sextile Neptune brings the potential for many folks to rise with calm and relaxed moods. However, the waning Aries Moon brings ambitious moods that are running strong while the Moon is still quite full. Aries Moon often inspires us to focus on something new or to delve into our work with a new spirit of determination. This afternoon, Moon trine Pluto brings positive vibes to heal old wounds. Later tonight, as the Aries Moon goes void-of-course, Moon trine Saturn brings a harmonious time to focus on a closure or ending of some type. It is not long before the Moon enters Taurus and our moods are likely to quickly accept a very practical focus on life at this late hour — such as the need for rest and relaxation.

September 1st Saturday

Moon in Taurus	PDT	EDT
Moon trine Sun	1:29 PM	4:29 PM
Venus sextile Mars begins (see September 3)		

Mood Watch: Today's waning Taurus Moon stirs a heartfelt awareness of what we have, what we have lost, and what we hope to gain. Moon trine Sun brings a good time to harmonize energies and to get in sync with the season. When the Moon is in Taurus it is said to be "exalted," an ideal aspect to get in tune with the earth and our bodies. Taurus Moon reminds us to take thorough care of our worldly possessions, before the damaging elements of time and neglect take care of them first. Sun in Virgo and Moon in Taurus demand prudent and practical measures towards gaining satisfaction. Today will be a good day to tackle physical tasks and to move with ease.

September 2nd Sunday

♍

Moon in Taurus	PDT	EDT	
Moon sextile Uranus	2:44 AM	5:44 AM	
Moon square Venus	3:21 AM	6:21 AM	
Saturn enters Virgo	6:50 AM	9:50 AM	
Moon square Neptune	7:54 AM	10:54 AM	
Moon trine Mercury goes v/c	5:48 PM	8:48 PM	
Mercury square Pluto	10:05 PM	1:05 AM	(September 3)
Jupiter square Uranus begins (see October 9)			

Mood Watch: A Moon sextile Uranus night brings turbulent but liberating moods and dreams. Moon square Venus brings a time of complexity and it may be difficult to get in tune with personal affections. Moon square Neptune doesn't help the morning mood, as spiritual conflicts may be to blame. It's no wonder that no one is relaxing very easily with so many blatant shifts occurring. The waning Taurus Moon brings an emphasis on practical needs and comforts, and also on pushing away all the useless clutter. Moon in Taurus and Sun in Virgo reminds us that accounting for what we have is important, and money related matters are also significant right now. This evening, Moon trine Mercury will have us talking and relaying all sorts of messages.

Saturn enters Virgo (Saturn in Virgo: September 2, 2007 – October 29, 2009) Saturn in Virgo demands prudent and carefully analyzed measures with regard to setting up perimeters and implementing rules. Approximately every 2 to 2.5 years, depending on the retrograde periods, Saturn enters a new zodiac sign. The expression of Saturn in Virgo focuses our disciplines in Virgo related activities such as accounting, secretarial duties, analytical science, writing, researching, statistics, gardening, inspecting, craftsmanship, private investigating, teaching, alternative health care, purging and cleansing practices, esthetics, massage therapy, dental hygiene, and all those careers connected with health, particularly alternative and preventative care and hygiene. Saturn's travels through Virgo may place disciplinary actions or restrictions on such Virgo-like things as computers, many forms of commonly used technical communications devices, hypochondriac, melancholic or obsessive behavior patterns, as well as skepticism and pedantic approaches to life which are ostentatiously oriented towards formal rules. What? Placing restrictions on formal rules? Saturn in Virgo can go that far!

SATURN'S RECENT HISTORY IN LEO:

During the time of Saturn in Leo: July 16, 2005 – September 2, 2007, it has been important to recognize and to empower the structure of personal will and the creative drive. Focuses like family, pleasure pursuits, entertainment, and the apparent nature of our animal instincts have all been subject to Saturnian kinds of restriction. Leo people will not deny that the past couple of years have been a time of hard work for them, but also a time when their disciplines have allowed them to claim a greater sense of control over their lives. While there has been no way for Leos to avoid taking on responsibilities and to face personal limitations, by now a more dignified and confident level of discipline and achievement can be claimed by Leo people. Take it easy, Leo folks and congratulations – this particular Saturn influence is now completed! Now the master of discipline and focus, Saturn, wends its way through the sign of Virgo. In the next couple of years to come, discerning, calculating, and meticulous efforts will be the backbone of structure while Saturn is in Virgo.

WHAT SATURN REPRESENTS:

Saturn's influence represents the times in our lives when we take authority and responsibility for something. It represents commitment. Saturn makes us realize that sometimes we are driven to make choices we do not want to make, and sometimes we are forced to participate in a system with which we don't agree. In our quest to perform our true will and to accomplish important goals, we are beset by obstacles, challenged by difficulty, and overwhelmed by the unpredictable factors of a vastly changing world. Saturn is the planet which gives us the edge to proceed with clarity and focus. It is also our protection mechanism, our lock-and-key to the issues in our lives on which we choose to work, determining when and how these matters are to be unlocked, handled, and completed. Saturn represents those areas in life where we earnestly work to focus and concentrate our energies; it is where we manage and maintain some control.

Ahhh, Saturn. So much to do about Saturn. This is the planet that puts us in touch with reality, and challenges us to apply discipline and a sense of limitation if we are to stay on course enough to survive. Saturn is the great teacher and the grim reaper all in one. Saturn is where the line is drawn in every chapter of the story of our lives. Beginnings and endings occur when Saturnian experiences penetrate our lives. There is a hard edge to creating new disciplines as well as giving up old ones. Saturn reflects time constantly and doesn't skip a beat. Time waits for no one, not even Virgos, so this is your time, Virgo folks, to get your sense of timing in gear and to do what you do best.

HOW SATURN IN VIRGO AFFECTS VIRGOS:

Saturn in Virgo imposes greater responsibility and work on our Virgo friends for the next couple of years while Saturn is transiting the Sun sign of Virgo people. This may be the time for Virgos to connect with their work and to use their talents to achieve goals that are important to them. Virgos will need to make it through and succinctly handle many completion processes, and they may pass some significant milestones in the next couple of years to come. There will be a strong inclination to put an end to trifling details, and Virgo people will be busily focused on some of the things they do best, like: working in a timely manner, completing goals, organizing, and handling important responsibilities. Virgo the Virgin, the shy, analytical, skeptical and doubtful practitioner, will be put to the working test of setting up perimeters and territorial lines in an ever changing environment. Virgos must create their own guidelines and set their own standards of what kind of work they will do and how much it will be worth to them. This is a very important time for Virgos, a time of work and career related establishment or closure, and it is an important time in their family life, too.

HOW SATURN IN VIRGO WORKS IN OUR SOCIETY:

Discipline and the act of setting limits will now be emphasized in such Virgo

related things as health, the control and study of mental diseases, and the world of ♍
computers and communications technology. Virgo represents the development of
structure through communications, and the preservation of the power and unique
qualities of cultural and artistic pursuits.

While Saturn is in Virgo, many work contracts will be based on people's accounting skills, their capabilities for financial analysis, as well as their communication
skills. Important issues will be raised over the trillions of dollars which have slipped
through North American hands since the century began, and there will be massive
efforts to calculate and account for the numerous deficits which have set back North
American commerce. One might expect that with Saturn in Virgo, disciplinary
measures and carefully planned budgets will mean serious business for competitive companies. Saturn in Virgo may play a strong role in society's influence on
what takes place in the world of health. Virgo represents our health, our health
practices, and our health related disciplines. Over the next two years, more strict
disciplines may be applied with regard to how we care for and gauge our health.
Saturn is the teacher that instills guidelines and allows us to create new structure
and a new foundation upon which to stand at a time when we are dealing with the
crumbling remains of dysfunctional situations or behavior which might threaten
our wellbeing. In Virgo, the influences of Saturn cover a great deal of emphasis on
daily maintenance, cleanliness, communications, and of course, practical forms of
discipline.

THE DOWN SIDE OF SATURN IN VIRGO:

Saturn's travels through Virgo may well place disciplinary limitations or boundaries
on some of the negative Virgo-like things such as querulous, fussy, servile, petty,
prudish, modest, or fault finding behavior. Hypochondriacs are likely to discover
that their compulsive complaints will fall on deaf ears. Melancholic behavior may
swing with the timeliness of a pendulum while the dark dross of earth dredges
up saturnine trials and hardship. Obsessive-compulsive behavior is likely to be
blatantly obvious and not so easy to hide, as the demand for practical effort and
discipline does not allow for comfortable wallowing. THE UP SIDE OF SATURN
IN VIRGO:

Saturnian structure and concentration of effort will be reflected in a positive way
through such Virgo-like things as humor, articulation, sincerity, careful analysis,
dependability, accuracy, resourcefulness, scrupulousness, prudence, carefulness,
and scholarly precision. Good-humored efforts will have a serious message, and on
the positive side, there will be a more entertaining or witty, creative, and intelligent
approach to work. More serious efforts in accounting and health care will bring
a greater respect for the quality of our lives. Pure intent, as well as altruistic and
indefatigable efforts will be the cutting edge tools for Virgo's accomplishments
while Saturn travels through Virgo.

SATURN'S SQUARING AND OPPOSING AFFECTS ON THE MUTABLE
SIGNS OF THE ZODIAC:

Now the mutable signs of the zodiac go into a disciplinary mode as Saturn goes
through the mutable sign of Virgo. Sagittarians and Geminis will experience

Saturn's squaring affect to their natal Sun signs over the next two years. Sagittarius and Gemini people must learn to pace themselves and to be aware that Saturn squaring their natal Sun will bring career and work related tests, challenges, and difficulties. These people may have a great deal of doubt about their ability to identify with the work they are doing. Sagittarius and Gemini people will need to be more focused on cleaning up unfinished business, solving repetitive problems, and they will be undergoing tedious kinds of work. This is the time to face personal limitations and find a way to work with them or around them. It's an opportunity for these folks to gain a real sense of accomplishment and mastery over the inevitable challenges that life brings.

Saturn in Virgo will be opposing the mutable sign of Pisces, creating a more acute awareness of personal responsibilities on the part of our Pisces friends. The work levels and disciplines in Pisceans' lives will be trying and overwhelming at times, and occasional bouts of exhaustion will inconvenience Pisces. This is not a time for Pisceans to set themselves up with heavy commitments or work loads in the months ahead; the test of the days ahead will prove to be demanding enough. Pisces people must learn to pace themselves in the next couple years.

SATURN'S TRINE AFFECTS ON THE EARTH SIGNS OF THE ZODIAC:

Saturn in the earth sign of Virgo will be trine to the other earth signs of the zodiac, Capricorn and Taurus. This will activate and stimulate Capricorn and Taurus people's abilities to identify with the need for order and structure in their lives. They will experience a greater sense of ease in applying their work and creating more structure or discipline where they need it.

SATURN'S SEXTILE AFFECTS ON THE WATER SIGNS – SCORPIO AND CANCER:

Scorpio and Cancer people are likely to experience more career or work opportunities, and get a better grasp on their personal disciplines, as Saturn goes through a sextile to their natal Sun signs. These people must act on their disciplines in order to find these opportunities and get results.

SATURN'S PERSONAL AFFECTS:

Saturn represents ability (responsibility), Sun represents identity (willingness). When Saturn transits a person's Sun sign, the tests they endure affect how they identify with the manner in which disciplines, responsibilities, and structures work in their lives – but it does *not* necessarily test their actual abilities. In order to find out how a person's actual abilities are being tested, the current transits of Saturn may be compared to the position of a person's natal Saturn in the birth chart. If a person's natal Saturn is afflicted in the chart, anything from health to career may be affected. Afflictions may be overcome, and that is the purpose of facing them and working through them. In the transits of Saturn to people's Sun signs, the main thing that stands out is their need to identify with what they are doing, usually in terms of career, work or responsibilities. Sagittarius and Gemini people may encounter trouble identifying with their work in the next couple years due to the square of Saturn to their natal Sun signs, but this doesn't necessarily mean that they won't accomplish goals and create structure in their lives; it just simply means that they will probably struggle with their own personal seal of approval with regard to their work – there may also be an inability for them to identify with their work, or they may have a difficult time accepting constructive forms of criticism as to how they are personally handling their work. ♍

Saturn is there to remind us of the work required to deal with the harsh realities of life. When the work is done, our efforts are often rewarded with a sense of real accomplishment, as long as we act responsibly on the things in life that really matter to us and that are actually posing a threat or needing attention. Virgo says: "I analyze." While Saturn travels through Virgo, structure and discipline when applied to analysis and forethought, brings magnanimous results. Here, there is no room for Virgo's ability to question or to cast doubt. Here, it is skill, persistence, and indefatigable management that will support grand feats of accomplishment for Virgo.

Mercury square Pluto (August 30 – September 4) Mercury in Virgo is square to Pluto in Sagittarius. Scrutiny and doubt make it difficult to communicate with those of another generation. This is a particularly difficult time to deal with burdensome issues and discuss them in a manner that relieves tension. Mercury square Pluto often brings harsh and sometimes fatal news. Talk revolves around the corruption of superpowers and the setbacks caused by this corruption. This may be a particularly difficult time to discuss matters involving permanent change. This aspect last occurred on April 10, when Mercury was in Pisces.

September 3rd Monday

Labor Day, USA / Labour Day, Canada
Moon in Taurus / Gemini - LAST QUARTER MOON in GEMINI

	PDT	EDT
Moon enters Gemini	12:31 AM	3:31 AM
Moon square Saturn	12:40 AM	3:40 AM
Mars square Uranus	1:10 PM	4:10 PM
Venus sextile Mars	4:37 PM	7:37 PM
Sun square Jupiter	5:05 PM	8:05 PM
Moon opposite Jupiter	7:24 PM	10:24 PM
Moon square Sun	7:33 PM	10:33 PM

Sun opposite Uranus begins (see September 9)
Sun square Mars begins (see September 17)

Mood Watch: There are many astrological labors in store for us on this holiday Monday. Just after the Moon enters Gemini, Moon square Saturn slips into our inner consciousness, bringing unseen adjustments to the new shift in our awareness; ahh yes, Saturn has entered an earth sign (see yesterday). Today's Gemini Moon will certainly allow us to comb trough a myriad of details in order to keep up with the peak performances of today's planetary aspects. Moon opposite Jupiter brings a bit of a roller coaster ride on the collective wheel of fortune, which in turn brings a lot of excitement with regard to our expenditures and our sense of wellbeing. **Last Quarter Moon in Gemini** (Moon square Sun) brings out talkative moods and informative interactions. People will have a lot on their minds today. Intellectual pursuits are emphasized – a great time to enjoy games and puzzles. It is also the time to release any unwanted or frustrating mixed thoughts by talking them through with others. Sun in Virgo and Moon in Gemini is a good time to discuss business details and strategies, as varied viewpoints and perspectives will arise today. Both Virgo and Gemini are ruled by Mercury, the famous messenger of the gods.

Mars square Uranus (occurring August 25 – September 8) Mars square Uranus is sometimes tyrannical, and is never an aspect to be underestimated. Masculine fortitude and the enigmatic force of chaos are in a volatile and difficult phase of expression when Mars is square to Uranus. This aspect was suspiciously present when the December 26, 2004 tsunami tidal wave disaster of the century swept the Indian Ocean. Today, Mars is in the sign of Gemini and while it squares to Uranus; the resulting tensions may cause a schism in the forces of offensive and defensive action. While Uranus is in Pisces, chaos abounds in the sacred territory of our beliefs. Mars, the god of war, is often the cause of heated discussions and disputes while it is in Gemini. The events of Mars square Uranus do not always predictably yield natural disasters, but unfortunately they are often the catalyst for difficult human trials. This aspect is like a pressure cooker; it may seem dormant at first, but if not carefully handled, the aftermath can be a real mess! It is wise to completely avoid extremely risky undertakings that may rock the boat of fiery activity during Mars square Uranus. This is no time to step into the eye of the storm!

Venus sextile Mars (occurring September 1 – 10) Retrograde Venus in Leo is now sextile Mars in Gemini. Venus in Leo allows us to use personal magnetism and performance skills to draw towards ourselves the affection we desire. Since Venus is retrograde in Leo, this may be a time of contemplating internal love, or self-love. Venus will go direct on September 8. Mars in Gemini is reminding us to put some action into that love while also maintaining logic, intelligence, and communication. This aspect is favorable, bringing opportunities to situations that involve love and beauty. Venus emphasizes the vibrations of love, magnetism, beauty and sensuality. The Mars influence emphasizes the awareness and application of action, movement, involvement, might, strength and energy. It is here that feminine (Venus) and masculine (Mars) forces have an opportunity (the sextile aspect) to support each other. People may become strong messengers, making their intentions known (Mars in Gemini), while applying their devotion and affections to family, personal hobbies, and self-love (Venus in Leo). This aspect last occurred on February 13 and will occur once again this year on October 16.

Sun square Jupiter (occurring August 28 – September 7) This aspect particularly affects those Virgo people celebrating birthdays from August 28 – September 7. Sun square Jupiter creates difficulties with and obstacles to the personal joy and prosperous welfare of these birthday folks. For these people, getting ahead financially or just staying on top of current trends or financial shifts may be personally challenging right now. To stay on top of financial matters, persistence and determination are essential. Some Virgo folks are not likely to fare well with this challenge since Saturn has newly entered Virgo (see yesterday, Sept. 2). Although some Virgos are not living as prosperously as they may desire at this time, they do have the ability to come through this and be much better for it. Hang in there, Virgos, your hard work will pay off eventually. Obstacles create challenges, but do not necessarily dictate an end to efforts to improve our welfare. It is the Virgo personality (Sun) that is being challenged (square aspect) in matters of advancement (Jupiter), requiring Virgos to make do with less than they were anticipating. This may be a time to redefine and redirect personal goals, especially now that Saturn is in Virgo. Virgo birthday folks must reexamine what truly brings prosperity for them in their lives. This aspect last occurred on March 9, affecting the birthday Pisces folks of that time.

September 4th Tuesday

Moon in Gemini	PDT	EDT	
Moon square Uranus	5:23 AM	8:23 AM	
Moon sextile Venus	5:24 AM	8:24 AM	
Moon conjunct Mars	6:07 AM	9:07 AM	
Moon trine Neptune	10:48 AM	1:48 PM	
Moon opposite Pluto	9:40 PM	12:40 AM	(September 5)

Mood Watch: Moon square Uranus brings explosive morning moods and there may be a strong feeling of disarray. Fortunately, much of this feeling is smoothed over by the calming and gentle affects of Moon sextile Venus. Moon conjunct Mars activates our moods with a feeling of get-up-and-go. Moon trine Neptune brings good spiritual vibrations. Here, in the days of Virgo, the waning Gemini Moon keeps us busily planning, communicating, and calculating. This is a good time to get organized. Later tonight, Moon opposite Pluto brings a stormy nightcap, and our moods may be weighed down by deep concerns. Gemini Moon guides us to think matters through intelligently.

September 5th Wednesday

Moon in Gemini / Cancer	PDT	EDT
Moon square Mercury goes v/c	4:02 AM	7:02 AM
Moon enters Cancer	4:09 AM	7:09 AM
Moon sextile Saturn	4:48 AM	7:48 AM
Mercury enters Libra	5:03 AM	8:03 AM

Mood Watch: Early this morning, the waning Gemini Moon goes void-of-course, and Moon square Mercury brings complexity and nervousness. Swiftly, the Moon enters Cancer and the process of nervous thinking is washed over with a lot of expressive feeling instead. The waning Cancer Moon is a good time to enjoy domestic comforts and nurturing care. Moon sextile Saturn gives us the incentive to apply ourselves and to get a handle on matters. Many folks will be defining their perimeters and firming up their goals.

Mercury enters Libra (Mercury in Libra: September 5 – 27) Mercury in Libra aligns us with diplomacy, tact, and the need to connect with friends and loved ones. Libra is the autumn sign that emphasizes balance and adjustment. Today through September 27, Mercury in Libra will bring a focus on harmonizing and adjusting to the changing season. This is a good time for people to communicate by gathering important information, as our decision making process kicks into high gear. Due to the retrograde pattern of Mercury this autumn (Oct. 11 – Nov. 1) Mercury will re-enter the tail end of Libra on October 25.

September 6th Thursday

Moon in Cancer	PDT	EDT
Moon sextile Sun	4:04 AM	7:04 AM
Moon trine Uranus goes v/c	10:05 AM	1:05 PM

Mood Watch: Moon sextile Sun puts us in touch with the season. While the Sun is in Virgo and the Moon wanes in Cancer, our moods are cautious, defensive, sensitive and, at times, highly emotional. Just as Moon trine Uranus occurs, the Cancer Moon goes void-of-course this morning. This brings a positive command for freedom and there may be a liberating need to blow off work, and to face up to emotional demands. Many of us are really beginning to sense the importance of this time, and the necessity to focus our efforts towards the preparation of autumn season, set to begin in a couple of weeks. However, most people will be in denial of their obligations as the void-of-course Cancer Moon does not quit throughout the whole day and night. An emotional day of ups and downs often impedes on our sense of progress.

September 7th Friday

Moon in Cancer / Leo	PDT	EDT
Pluto goes direct	7:56 AM	10:56 AM
Moon enters Leo	10:00 AM	1:00 PM
Moon sextile Mercury	5:13 PM	8:13 PM

Mood Watch: The waning void-of-course Cancer Moon brings spacey and, at times, emotionally stirring moods throughout the morning. As the Moon enters Leo, our moods begin to drop some of our emotional attachments, and the need to enjoy the summer calls out to many people. This evening, Moon sextile Mercury brings a potentially opportunistic time to communicate with friends and family. Waning Leo Moon is a good time to enjoy hobbies and entertainment.

Pluto goes direct (Pluto direct: September 7, 2007 – April 1, 2008) After the long – but common – retrograde period of Pluto (March-September 2007), the planet of transformation now moves into a smooth, direct pattern for the rest of the year. Since March 31 of this year, Pluto has been going back through the late degrees of Sagittarius. Now that it is direct, we can better acknowledge the evolution of humankind's condition in order to survive the challenges that are occurring on planet Earth. This transformation is about consciousness, without which we would not be. This is not a time to take life for granted; rather, it is a time to participate in making life better by consciously transforming fear into determination and despair into belief in oneself. Pluto in Sagittarius (since 1995) is changing both our global community and our awareness of it, transforming our point of view.

September 8th Saturday

Moon in Leo	PDT	EDT	
Moon trine Jupiter	7:17 AM	10:17 AM	
Venus goes direct	9:15 AM	12:15 PM	
Moon conjunct Venus	4:48 PM	7:48 PM	
Mars trine Neptune	9:06 PM	12:06 AM	(September 9)
Moon opposite Neptune	11:06 PM	2:06 AM	(September 9)
Moon sextile Mars	11:11 PM	2:11 AM	(September 9)

Mood Watch: A day of positive aspects helps to turn around the affects of the significant events and astrological shifts which have been occurring so far this month. ♍ The waning Leo Moon keeps us active and inclined towards introspective desires and needs. Moon trine Jupiter starts off the day beautifully with optimistic and contented moods. Moon conjunct Venus puts us in touch with those things we are attracted to. Later tonight, Moon opposite Neptune awakens our spiritual nature and impresses upon us the need to apply our faith. Lastly, Moon sextile Mars brings strong impulses and urges, and our dreams may be very martial.

Venus goes direct (Venus direct: September 8, 2007 – March 5, 2009) Since July 27, Venus has been retrograde through the signs of Virgo and Leo. This has probably been creating many difficulties and challenges in the love lives of those Sagittarius, Gemini, Scorpio, and Taurus folks who have been experiencing the square aspect of the retrograde Venus to their natal sun signs. Pisces and Aquarius people have been experiencing a particularly strong awareness of their love lives, or lack thereof, as Venus has opposed their natal sun signs during this retrograde period. It is not only our love lives or our affections and attractions that are affected by Venus; beauty, art, and aesthetics are impacted as well. Today Venus in the sign of Leo goes direct, bringing a forward moving sense of harmony in our relationships. Now that Venus is direct, expressions of affection and love matters can be begin to move forward with much more clarity and certainty.

Mars trine Neptune (occurring August 29 – September 14) Mars in Gemini is trine to Neptune in Aquarius. Carefully considered action, when it is taken, can bring gifts which will aid in the empowerment of our intuitive, imaginative, and artistic endeavors. While Mars is in Gemini, the written or spoken word definitely qualifies as an "action." Through our actions, a faith in humanity is renewed. This will be an energetic time of obtaining spiritual gifts and helpful guidelines from the spirit world. Mars guarantees that significant activities will occur, and with Neptune in the trine position, these activities will be favorably stirred up with spiritual and psychic awareness, all gifts from Neptune. This serves as a good time to initiate creative and imaginative spiritual practices and ceremonies and to empower the personal outlook and spiritual well being.

September 9th Sunday

Grandparents' Day

Moon in Leo / Virgo	PDT	EDT
Moon trine Pluto goes v/c	11:08 AM	2:08 PM
Sun opposite Uranus	11:47 AM	2:47 PM
Moon enters Virgo	6:11 PM	9:11 PM
Moon conjunct Saturn	7:59 PM	10:59 PM
Mars opposite Pluto begins (see September 21)		

" The reason grandparents and grandchildren get along so well is that they have a common enemy. " – Sam Levenson (1911 – 1980)

Mood Watch: This morning's waning Leo Moon goes void-of-course while Moon trine Pluto brings harmonious and therapeutic strength to our moods. A series of individual dramas play out like a subtle catharsis inside each one of us. The Leo Moon remains void-of-course throughout the day, which may cause our moods to be somewhat preoccupied, and a number of folks will be entirely self-absorbed. As the Moon enters Virgo, our moods will become more communicative but with a great deal more discernment. Ideally, this is the time to clean, purge, purify, relax, and rest. Sweet summer smells are delicious and inviting as the harvest ripens. Tonight, the Moon is conjunct with Saturn in the sign of Virgo for the first time this century; serious, down-to-earth, practical and realistic moods will bring a new and confident sense of control.

Sun opposite Uranus (occurring September 3 – 12) This occurrence of Sun opposite Uranus particularly affects Virgos celebrating birthdays September 3 – 12. The opposition of Uranus creates an acute awareness of the revolutionary forces in one's life. There will undoubtedly be a lot of chaos occurring, and the challenge (in part) may be to accept the rebel within you, and to persevere through the drastic and edgy discord. This is the time to go with the flow of unusual and unpredictable occurrences. It's also a good time to learn the Tao of chaos, and to understand that this awakening force is enlivening a sense of freedom. The only alternatives are to break through, or to break down if one resists. Survival counts; use your senses and your sensibilities well but do not resist the forces of great change. In the year to come, Uranus in opposition to Virgo will both challenge and strengthen our Virgo (birthday) friends to live a life of freedom. This may be particularly challenging given the fact that Virgos must now face the traverses of Saturn through their natal sun sign (see Saturn enters Virgo: September 2). It may seem overwhelming; however, as long these birthday Virgos avoid staying attached to the way things once were, all will be well. All of this might be likened to a Virgo trying to describe, in the most technical terms, just how a dramatic tornado works while simultaneously experiencing it. Uranus opposite the Virgo Sun teaches Virgo the value in allowing for a greater range of possibilities. This will be an exciting and, at times, exhausting year ahead for these Virgo folks.

September 10th Monday
Moon in Virgo

	PDT	EDT
Moon square Jupiter	4:47 PM	7:47 PM

Mercury sextile Jupiter begins (see September 13)

" Doubt is not a pleasant condition, but certainty is absurd. " – Voltaire (1694 – 1778)

Mood Watch: Introspection becomes more grounded as we reach the balsamic phase (darkest stage) of the Moon's waning process. Today we can expect to see our moods become more cautious, yet we are instinctually willing to communicate our doubts. The general mood of the day might be summed up in one word: apprehension. The uncertainty of this time brings a strong desire for purification. Today's only lunar aspect, Moon square Jupiter, brings financial doubts and people may tend to be shy with their expenditures. Tomorrow's New Virgo Moon brings a Solar Eclipse. Apply some caution tonight; beware of frequent displays of natural stupidity.

September 11th Tuesday
NEW MOON in VIRGO – Partial Solar Eclipse

♍

	PDT	EDT	
Moon opposite Uranus	2:19 AM	5:19 AM	
Moon conjunct Sun	5:45 AM	8:45 AM	
Moon square Mars	11:32 AM	2:32 PM	
Moon square Pluto goes v/c	9:15 PM	12:15 AM	(September 12)

" I show you doubt, to prove that faith exists " – Robert Browning (1812 – 1889)

Mood Watch: Overnight, our moods are explosive with Moon opposite Uranus kicking off this challenging day with a rebellious bang. It is always darkest before the light and, in this case, darkness has been appearing in more ways than one. This morning, the darkly waning Moon reaches the new mark. The **New Moon in Virgo** (Moon conjunct Sun) emphasizes our need to get the most basic and practical components of our lives in order. This includes our organizational skills, our common sense and, especially, our health. As the Virgo Moon reaches the new mark, it gives us a chance to breathe a sigh of relief. Now we can reassess our moods and begin to get a clearer understanding about how to proceed practically and reasonably. New Moon invites us to start all over again. This Moon asks us to apply a new form of skepticism, and try on new ways of analyzing and approaching our communications. How about a new way of accounting? Or a new set of health practices? School season sets the stage for children to adapt to something new, as they acquire and contemplate new information and learning tools. This Moon prepares us for the changes that occur around us in the physical world. This is the time to enjoy the harvest and the dwindling days of summer and to prepare for the new season ahead, remembering however, to apply caution when making changes. Moon square Mars will challenge our patience levels and it may be difficult to get amicably motivated during midday. Tonight, Moon square Pluto brings moods challenged by feelings of hardship or oppression. The Virgo Moon will also go void-of-course and this could bring the darkest phase of our doubts. Believe in the light.

A **Solar Eclipse in the sign of Virgo** brings an emphasis on controversy and conspiracy. Eclipses in the earth signs of the zodiac often highlight agricultural problems and the need to conserve resources, particularly with the Sun and Moon in Virgo. Once again the celestial script reads like a classic Greek tragedy, implying that we must beware of the death of great men, the potential for drought or crop failure, the suffering of writers, poets, and mercurial thinkers and, most importantly, we must be conscious of the general scarcity of supplies. Dark Virgo Moons classically bring the potential for melancholic behavior and, during the Solar Eclipse in Virgo, we must be doubly careful not to be swept into a dark cloud of depression.

September 12th Wednesday
Ramadan begins (ends October 11)

Moon in Virgo / Libra	PDT	EDT
Moon enters Libra	4:32 AM	7:32 AM

Mood Watch: After a dark ecliptic time, and the overnight remains of the void-of-course Virgo Moon end this morning with a new feeling of relief. A newly waxing Libra Moon allows us to approach the day with an open and informed mind. We will need to support each other today and to work together as a team. The dark phase of the Moon is past, and even though many folks will continue to feel the raw challenges of dark emotional shifts, the aftermath of this emotional cleansing will be more balanced and acceptable with the Moon in Libra. Now our moods have entered into the need for balance and it will become quickly apparent what we must do. This is the perfect time to commence in the art of making decisions – make wise ones.

September 13th Thursday

Rosh Hashanah

Moon in Libra	PDT	EDT
Mercury sextile Jupiter	3:44 AM	6:44 AM
Moon sextile Jupiter	4:25 AM	7:25 AM
Moon conjunct Mercury	4:30 AM	7:30 AM
Moon sextile Venus	2:39 PM	5:39 PM
Moon trine Neptune	8:07 PM	11:07 PM
Sun square Pluto begins (see September 19)		

Mood Watch: Moon sextile Jupiter brings optimism and hope on this Libra Moon morning. Moon conjunct Mercury engages us in mindful and resourceful planning. Later today, Moon sextile Venus brings beauty to our hearts, and our moods will be responsive to gentle and loving gestures. This evening, Moon trine Neptune brings peace and tranquility. This is a good time to make up for lost time with others.

Mercury sextile Jupiter (occurring September 10 – 14) Mercury in Libra is sextile Jupiter in Sagittarius. Mercury influences news and talk, while Jupiter influences commerce, wealth, and prosperous advancement. This would be an excellent time to inquire about opportunities, to discuss travel, and to assist others during their travels. This is also a good time to help people to improve their skills and apply them. Putting our minds to work on diplomatic, patient, and harmonious communications, particularly while Mercury is in Libra, is the sort of thing that gets noticed by employers and business partners. Opportunity is out there for both the employer and the employee. This is a good time to share information and promote your capabilities. Mercury sextile Jupiter brings joyful, philosophical, and mind expanding conversations. This aspect last occurred on January 22, when Mercury was in Aquarius.

September 14th Friday

Moon in Libra / Scorpio	PDT	EDT
Moon trine Mars	2:01 AM	5:01 AM
Moon sextile Pluto goes v/c	9:11 AM	12:11 PM
Moon enters Scorpio	4:38 PM	7:38 PM
Moon sextile Saturn	7:47 PM	10:47 PM
Mercury sextile Venus begins (see September 17)		
Mercury trine Neptune begins (see September 18)		

Mood Watch: Moon trine Mars kicks off the pre-dawn hours with moods and dreams that may revolve around the theme of strength and courage. Moon sextile

Pluto brings moods which will be relatively gung-ho about facing life's problems, but since the Libra Moon also goes void-of-course at this point, we may become indecisive or uncertain about how to proceed. For a fair portion of the day, the void-of-course Moon in Libra brings the constant need for adjustments and re-adjustments. By the time the Moon enters Scorpio, our moods will be less inclined to attempt to make adjustments and more inclined to observe our passions. Scorpio Moon often guides us through challenges and teaches us about stabilizing our emotional core in the midst of handling intensity or stress. Moon in Scorpio, a fixed water sign, reminds us that the psyche requires house cleaning now and then. When this occurs, we need to face our fears and to confront worry or paranoia with brave certainty. Moon sextile Saturn brings serious moods that will allow us to be clear about our limitations, and this will indicate where not to cross the lines.

September 15th Saturday

Moon in Scorpio
Mood Watch: Instinctive urges and intuitive observations are running strongly now. Scorpio Moon reminds us that life is a struggle in the process of coming and going, from a state of the impermanent to the permanent, and back again. We are reminded on some level of the importance and significance of certain events in our life, and how those events have shaped us through the year. Sometimes change happens faster than we are able to process. Scorpio Moon is a vital and swift processor of emotional expression. It is through this procedure that we are able to work through an extraordinary build up of awareness and pressure. Scorpio Moon helps us to find creative ways to accept those unfathomable mysteries of life's twists of fate, which deeply affects us all from time to time.

September 16th Sunday

Moon in Scorpio	PDT	EDT
Moon trine Uranus	1:57 AM	4:57 AM
Moon square Venus	4:32 AM	7:32 AM
Moon square Neptune	8:42 AM	11:42 AM
Moon sextile Sun goes v/c	4:42 PM	7:42 PM

Mood Watch: Moon trine Uranus brings dreams and moods that will be liberating and very exciting. Moon square Venus often brings difficulties with regard to loved ones. Our spiritual side will also be disrupted a bit as Moon square Neptune brings a lot less tolerance of the beliefs of others and quite a bit of spiritual doubt. Feminine wisdom seems to be absent this morning, but the waxing Scorpio Moon will allow us to work through our quandaries with concentrated strength. As Moon sextile Sun brings seasonal inspiration, the Scorpio Moon goes void-of-course for the remainder of the evening. This is likely to call up situations that require our undivided attention — this will be exciting, challenging, and (at times) tiring for many people. The weaker and more vulnerable facets of our moods tend to surface on a void-of-course Scorpio Moon, and there may be a tendency for people to become overly emotional and lash out unexpectedly, either against themselves or others. A Scorpio Moon experience reminds us of where the extreme edge is hidden in emotional responses.

September 17th Monday

Moon in Scorpio / Sagittarius	PDT	EDT
Moon enters Sagittarius	5:22 AM	8:22 AM
Moon square Saturn	9:08 AM	12:08 PM
Sun square Mars	1:50 PM	4:50 PM
Mercury sextile Venus	2:29 PM	5:29 PM

Mood Watch: A potentially restless night with the Moon void-of-course in Scorpio may bring sleepy heads this morning. As the Moon enters Sagittarius, our moods become a little more optimistic and explorative. Moon square Saturn is bound to bring a few rubs with regard to our attempts to get to work. There may be some kind of run-in with authority figures and it may be wisest to work a little harder, and to cautiously control different situations that come up today.

Sun square Mars (occurring September 3 – 23) This occurrence of Sun square Mars particularly affects Virgo people with birthdays September 3 – 23. It creates the illusion that obstacles are constantly getting in the way of the actions (and the will) of these birthday people. This may be a time when harnessing energy seems like a chore and personal levels of strength or stamina may be challenged. This may also be an accident prone time in the lives of these birthday folks, and the year ahead may bring difficulty relating to warlike events – this also includes their individual battles with themselves. Consequently, this will be a time for these birthday people to learn how to pace themselves, and to work through the obstacles in order to activate personal visions and goals. Virgo folks – lighten up on your expectations of yourselves for awhile, and don't let such setbacks get in the way of enjoying life. Relax! In time, it will be easier – once again – to get your personal goals and your willpower into a state of action.

Mercury sextile Venus (occurring September 14 – 19) Mercury in Libra is sextile Venus in Leo. Friends and partners will enjoy loving communications. This is an opportunistic and beneficial time to sing your praises of love! Mercury sextile Venus teaches us of the necessity to speak out about our love needs, and focuses discussion on the things to which we are attached and which we treasure. This aspect last occurred on April 7 and before that on March 16, and it will repeat one more time on October 16.

September 18th Tuesday

Moon in Sagittarius	PDT	EDT
Moon conjunct Jupiter	6:35 AM	9:35 AM
Moon square Uranus	2:05 PM	5:05 PM
Moon trine Venus	6:27 PM	9:27 PM
Mercury trine Neptune	7:01 PM	10:01 PM
Moon sextile Neptune	8:45 PM	11:45 PM
Moon sextile Mercury	8:58 PM	11:58 PM
Mercury trine Mars begins (see September 26)		

Mood Watch: Cheerful moods greet us today as Moon conjunct Jupiter puts us in touch with our visions, hopes and dreams. Moon in Sagittarius is a great time to dream, to enliven the imagination with new discoveries, and to explore the creative side of our beings. This afternoon, Moon square Uranus brings chaos, the kind of chaos which requires extra clean up work, and our moods may be shaky at times. This evening, Moon trine Venus brings harmonious attractions and loving energy. Moon sextile Neptune brings spiritual hope and reassuring beliefs, followed by Moon sextile Mercury, putting us in the mood for communication. It's all good.

Mercury trine Neptune (occurring September 14 – 21) This is a superb aspect for discussing personal philosophies and metaphysical subjects, and a good time to communicate with the spirit world. This aspect brings gifts from Spirit. Mercury in Libra is trine to Neptune in Aquarius. Diplomacy in speech brings intuitive and uplifting knowledge. This is the time to communicate about spiritual needs and breakthroughs. Receive gifts of renewed faith in your beliefs. This aspect last occurred on May 23, when Mercury was in Gemini.

September 19th Wednesday
Moon in Sagittarius / Capricorn - FIRST QUARTER MOON in SAGITTARUS

	PDT	EDT	
Moon opposite Mars	8:05 AM	11:05 AM	
Sun square Pluto	9:00 AM	12:00 PM	
Moon conjunct Pluto	9:45 AM	12:45 PM	
Moon square Sun goes v/c	9:49 AM	12:49 PM	
Moon enters Capricorn	4:53 PM	7:53 PM	
Moon trine Saturn	9:05 PM	12:05 AM	(September 20)

Mood Watch: It may seem as if everything happens in the early part of the day, starting with Moon opposite Mars, which kicks off this late summer day with extreme force. Moon conjunct Pluto brings a deep awareness of the forces of fate. **First Quarter Moon in Sagittarius** (Moon square Sun) allows our moods to be adaptable and responsive to the situations that arise. Likely interests include sports events, adventure, vision quests, and philosophical perspectives. While the Virgo Sun reminds us to budget our resources for the changing season ahead, the Sagittarius Moon reminds us to reach out there while the brilliant beauty of summer is still occurring. Adventure and hope abound. Sagittarius says: *"I see"* – make use of the vision and take the time to *see beyond*. The Moon will go void-of-course for a number of hours today. Be careful not to go so far as to get lost! As the Moon enters Capricorn our moods become more grounded and practical. Moon trine Saturn brings harmonious ambitions; it's a great time to empower our goals.

Sun square Pluto (occurring September 13 – 22) This occurrence of Sun square Pluto particularly affects those Virgo and early born Libra cusp people celebrating birthdays from September 13 – 22. For them, Pluto squaring their natal Sun brings disruptive changes and many challenges to overcome, such as the pain of loss and the severity of transformation. These tests often involve illness, irreparable damage, and dramatic life changes. Trying to hold onto the regrets and the pain of the past will only bring greater destruction later. This is the time to persevere through the obstacles of hardship. The hardships that are taking place now will resurface again in time, and that necessitates finding methods of release and of attitude adjustment in order to survive the anxiety and stress. Take it one day at a time and do not let fear and worry rule you. Know that you are not alone in facing these challenges. Move steadily through the required transformation, as stagnation and fear will only bring extended suffering. This aspect last occurred on March 19, when the Sun was in Pisces, affecting the Pisces/Aries birthday people of that time.

September 20th Thursday

Moon in Capricorn

	PDT	EDT	
Moon sextile Uranus	11:55 PM	2:55 AM	(September 21)
Mercury sextile Pluto begins (see September 24)			

Mood Watch: The Capricorn Moon brings clear and decisive interactions between people. The Sun is still in Virgo, and with the Moon waxing in Capricorn, this is a very earthy time. It's a good time to get some business done and to focus on money related matters. Moon sextile Uranus brings moods responsive to recklessness and rebelliousness. Strong ambitions are at work today and it may be necessary to be careful not to get stepped on by anyone, particularly while in the process of trying to get your own work done. Capricorn Moon, notoriously, brings serious demands. Time is a wastin' – show 'em who's boss!

September 21st Friday

Moon in Capricorn

	PDT	EDT	
Mars opposite Pluto	1:41 AM	4:41 AM	
Moon square Mercury	12:54 PM	3:54 PM	
Venus opposite Neptune	1:04 PM	4:04 PM	
Moon trine Sun goes v/c	11:16 PM	2:16 AM	(September 22)

Mood Watch: The Capricorn Moon gives our moods a cool and calm composure in which to focus our energies, and also helps us to control our various levels of progress with greater concentration. Capricorn Moon and Virgo Sun bring a nose-to-the-grindstone sensibility to our moods, and a serious, determined, down-to-earth effort to get things accomplished will bring a lot of progress today. However, as the Moon squares with Mercury, beware of the possibility for arguments and complex communications. Later tonight, Moon trine Sun turns everything around and good vibes fill the air once more. The Moon in Capricorn goes void-of-course, and this is an excellent time to drop obsessive work patterns and to get some rest.

Mars opposite Pluto (occurring September 9 – 27) This aspect brings on very abrupt and often alienating change. Fiery force and action are at odds with the estranged and mysterious workings of greater powers. Mars, the planet governing all modes of action, aggression, fire, and force, is opposite to Pluto, the planet of the generations, power structures, and the work of fate. For some this means more action with regard to war and destruction. There may be a strong battle in the war against life threatening diseases. This aspect creates an acute awareness of the demands and actions of generations and cultures. Mars is in Gemini stirring up dual perspectives on actions being taken, while Pluto is in Sagittarius creating an illuminating picture of how the infrastructure of struggling powers can undergo such extensive change. There is certainly a conflict of perspectives in the big picture of life, and the conflicts may be unreasonable and challenging. This aspect last occurred on April 8, 2006.

Venus opposite Neptune (occurring August 20 – September 27) This aspect occurs for a longer than usual period and, since Venus went direct on September 8, it has been catching up to the opposition to Neptune which is now occurring for the third time this year. This aspect last occurred on August 25, when the two planets were both retrograde, and before that on June 30, when only Neptune was retrograde. For more information on Venus opposite Neptune, see June 30, when this aspect first occurred this year.

♎

September 22nd Saturday
Yom Kippur
Moon in Capricorn / Aquarius

	PDT	EDT
Moon enters Aquarius	1:19 AM	4:19 AM

Mood Watch: Overnight, the void-of-course Capricorn Moon enters Aquarius and our moods enter into the need for ingenuity. The waxing Aquarius Moon reminds us to take comfort in what we know for certain, but it also puts us in touch with the need to know more and the drive to discover more. While we may feel confident with our source of knowledge and experience, we are driven to test this knowledge with an observant and curious mind, and often the Aquarius Moon leads us to unusual discoveries about ourselves and the world around us. Essential human rights issues or debates are taking place all the time, and it is often the Aquarius Moon influence that gives us the chance to collectively share special human interests and promote humanitarian causes. Enjoy this day wisely – it's the last full day of summer!

LIBRA

Key Phrase: "I BALANCE"

Cardinal Air Sign

Symbol: The Scales

September 23rd through October 23rd

September 23rd Sunday
Autumnal Equinox
Moon in Aquarius

	PDT	EDT	
Moon sextile Jupiter	12:53 AM	3:53 AM	
Sun enters Libra	2:52 AM	5:52 AM	
Moon conjunct Neptune	12:10 PM	3:10 PM	
Moon opposite Venus	1:53 PM	4:53 PM	
Moon trine Mercury	11:24 PM	2:24 AM	(September 24)
Moon sextile Pluto	11:46 PM	2:46 AM	(September 24)
Venus trine Pluto begins (see October 3)			

Mood Watch: Overnight, Moon sextile Jupiter brings the potential for positive dreams and moods. Before most people are fully awake in North America, the

Sun enters Libra, and the Moon continues to wax in Aquarius, bringing active humanitarian exploits and pursuits. This afternoon, Moon conjunct Neptune brings us closer to a sense of spiritual oneness with the universe, and the common bonds that connect us are felt beyond the physical realms. Moon opposite Venus brings obsessive tendencies with regard to the need for love and attention. Later tonight, Moon trine Mercury brings a helpful time to rest the mind, but for those who are awake, this may seem like an excellent time to think matters through more easily. This is followed swiftly by Moon sextile Pluto, which brings a strong emphasis on the need to overcome hardship.

Sun enters Libra (Sun in Libra: September 23 – October 23) *Happy Birthday, Libra people!* It's autumn. A mild chill tints the air and the Sun's brilliant light begins its departure from the northern hemisphere. Today, daytime and nighttime are equally long: it's the magical time of the Autumnal Equinox, calling on us to create a support system and network of helpful friends to prepare for the darker and colder days ahead. This often means securing a mate as well as balancing and reconciling relationships. Love is the reason behind Libra's hard drive for perfection and harmony. The key phrase for Libra is, "I balance," and Librans engage in a perpetual state of adjustment in order to meet their need for balance. Libra strives towards perfecting equilibrium in order to create a socially acceptable, harmonious environment. This is not to say that making decisions comes easily to Librans – it is only to say that it is a very important process to them. Quite often, the decisions people make during the Libra time of year keep them busy throughout the entire autumn season. Be careful not to take on too many responsibilities this season if you've already got your hands full. Balancing your schedule is as important as sticking to it. Work hard to keep your life and relationships stable. May this new autumn season be a pleasurable and fruitful but, most of all, balanced.

September 24th Monday
Moon in Aquarius / Pisces

	PDT	EDT
Moon trine Mars goes v/c	2:15 AM	5:15 AM
Mercury sextile Pluto	3:56 AM	6:56 AM
Moon enters Pisces	5:56 AM	8:56 AM
Moon opposite Saturn	10:31 AM	1:31 PM

Mood Watch: Just as the Aquarius Moon goes void-of-course, Moon trine Mars brings brave and daring activities in the course of our dreams and moods. It may be difficult to get the morning started off just right, but swiftly enough, the Moon enters Pisces and our moods will become more mystical and more emotionally vibrant. The waxing Pisces Moon brings out our artistic side. Moon opposite Saturn awakens our need to take control of that which is important to us.

Mercury sextile Pluto (occurring September 20 – 26) This aspect brings an opportunity for us to get the message across to people in strong positions of power and authority. Mercury is currently in Libra focusing discussions on matters of law and diplomacy. Will the scales of justice be tipped once again? Pluto in Sagittarius is forcing us to see beyond the norm by creating a long term transformation of our views on the quality and understanding of life. Mass media may well be entranced by news concerning world superpowers and/or challenging power issues, particularly with regard to changes in the law. This is an opportunistic time to reach out to those of another generation and make an attempt to communicate something vital. This aspect occurs six times this year; it last took place on March 16, when Mercury was in Aquarius. The first time it occurred was on January 31 and then again on February 28. While Mercury is in Libra, it will go retrograde (Oct. 11 – Nov. 1), causing this aspect to repeat two more times; October 26 and November 8.

September 25th Tuesday
Moon in Pisces

	PDT	EDT
Moon square Jupiter	4:25 AM	7:25 AM
Moon conjunct Uranus	8:46 AM	11:46 AM

Mood Watch: The Pisces Moon highlights the need for a strong spiritual exchange among people. This can be done with music, chanting, spellbinding fragrances, enchanting elixirs, and with artistry and charismatic charm. This morning, Moon square Jupiter may cause people to put the brakes on their expenditures, and our attitudes may not be so positive and upbeat. Also this morning, Moon conjunct Uranus brings explosive moods. Rebellious tendencies are likely to lead to an out-and-out revolt if our desires for freedom are not appeased. A restless energy comes with the pending Full Aries Moon, set to take place tomorrow afternoon. Pace yourself!

September 26th Wednesday
Moon in Pisces / Aries - FULL MOON in ARIES

	PDT	EDT
Moon square Pluto	1:34 AM	4:34 AM
Moon square Mars goes v/c	5:32 AM	8:32 AM
Moon enters Aries	7:24 AM	10:24 AM
Mercury trine Mars	10:54 AM	1:54 PM
Moon opposite Sun	12:46 PM	3:46 PM
Mercury sextile Saturn begins (see September 30)		
Mars sextile Saturn begins (see October 8)		

Mood Watch: Overnight, Moon square Pluto brings troublesome moods and dreams. This morning, Moon square Mars brings offensive and maddening challenges to our moods while the nearly Full Moon goes void-of-course. For a couple of hours, disoriented moods make for a time of uncertainty. As the Moon enters Aries, our moods enter into a new cycle. The **Full Moon in Aries** (Moon opposite Sun) reaches its peak this afternoon and initiates rich vibrant feelings. In everyone is a warrior spirit, inspiring the confidence and fortitude to persevere through the endless tests of life, especially the challenging tests of selfhood. For some this is a restless and impatient time, and in many circles of life there will be a strong competitive spirit. Strength and vitality are blessings that Aries Moon energy allows us to tap into, helping us handle the mounting tasks of autumn in preparation for the pending storms of the season -- a good time to take initiative with autumn projects. While the spirit of Aries Moon may seem relentless to some, taking action to complete personal goals is the most natural way to channel this hard driving energy of Aries Moon. Happy Full Moon, and be careful not to burn yourself out today.

Mercury trine Mars (occurring September 18 – October 2) Mercury in Libra is trine to Mars in Gemini. Diplomacy and tact when applied during communications brings intelligent and thoughtful responses from others. This aspect brings news, thoughts, and communications into a most favorable position when it comes to taking action. Mercury trine Mars activates the world of communications with an energetic punch that often persuades people to take immediate and appropriate action. This aspect will repeat two more times: on October 17, when Mercury will be retrograde in Scorpio, and again on November 19, when Mercury is direct in Scorpio and Mars will be retrograde in Cancer.

September 27th Thursday

Moon in Aries	PDT	EDT
Moon trine Jupiter	5:24 AM	8:24 AM
Mercury enters Scorpio	10:19 AM	1:19 PM
Moon sextile Neptune	2:41 PM	5:41 PM
Moon trine Venus	8:04 PM	11:04 PM

Mood Watch: The Aries Moon reached the Full Moon mark yesterday and although it now wanes, the energy and vitality of the Aries Moon is still filling us with lots of energy, as well as ambition to complete important tasks. Moon trine Jupiter brings good luck, happiness, and positive vibes to start off the day. This afternoon, Moon sextile Neptune brings a calmness that allows us to pace ourselves comfortably, and our moods will be pleasant for the most part. This evening, Moon trine Venus puts us in the mood for love and for all those things that bring us comfort. Tonight will be a good time to pursue pleasure and good company.

Mercury enters Scorpio (Mercury in Scorpio: September 27 – October 23) Mercury now enters Scorpio and it will go retrograde next month (October 11 – November 1), bringing a prolonged period of Mercury's travels through Scorpio. It is worthy to note that Mercury also hangs out in the sign of Libra for sometime, too. On October 23, the retrograde Mercury will re-enter the late degrees of Libra and will remain there for a few weeks. Finally, the forward moving Mercury will re-enter Scorpio on November 11 until December 1. Mercury in Scorpio is often a time when communications are veiled in secrecy, and talk revolves around matters of intensity and sensitivity. Passionate issues are communicated with creativity and intuition. This is also a time to be aware that a sharp tongue may easily cause a violent or challenging reaction. It is through this medium of Mercury in the sign of Scorpio that the expression of communications is seemingly fearless, obstinate, reckless, and passionate. From indecent babble to the subtle perfection of clear articulation, discussions frequently deliver a powerful punch. Not only our words but also our appearance, mannerisms and attitudes all send out the message of who we are. The mask we choose for the grand masquerade of autumn's darkening days teaches us much about ourselves. For more information on Mercury retrograde through the sign of Scorpio, see the section in the introduction about *Mercury retrograde periods.*

September 28th Friday

Moon in Aries / Taurus

	PDT	EDT
Moon trine Pluto	1:36 AM	4:36 AM
Moon sextile Mars goes v/c	7:00 AM	10:00 AM
Moon enters Taurus	7:18 AM	10:18 AM
Moon opposite Mercury	8:51 AM	11:51 AM
Moon trine Saturn	12:22 PM	3:22 PM
Mars enters Cancer	4:56 PM	7:56 PM

♎

Mood Watch: Overnight, Moon trine Pluto brings strong, powerful, and therapeutic dreams and moods. The Aries Moon goes void-of-course this morning just as Moon sextile Mars begins to motivate us. It isn't long before the Moon enters Taurus and sets the tone of the day. The Moon wanes in Taurus, and people are taking the time to assess their own values and needs. Tiredness and laziness are natural or common symptoms of this post full Moon time. Whenever possible, the luxury of relaxation is especially prized. Moon opposite Mercury will keep our minds busy, and the need to communicate will be essential for many folks during this morning. This afternoon, Moon trine Saturn brings the best time for disciplines to be implemented. A strong sense of accomplishment comes with an effort to get things done today.

Mars enters Cancer (Mars in Cancer: September 28 – December 31) The fiery drive of force, Mars, now focuses the spirit of action on Cancerian activities such as nurturing and mothering. Mars in Cancer also emphasizes a focus on the home, household improvement or remodeling – possibly even a move to a new home or on making the adjustments following a big move. Cancer represents large bodies of water such as the oceans and great lakes, and while Mars is in Cancer, marine activities are emphasized. Military ships will be preparing for battle tests and strategic training. Aquatic sports may become highly popular. Mars in Cancer represents the defenses of the emotions and the tender aspects of our being that we strive so hard to protect. Mars is a natural protector and defender but is also quite capable of offensive attack. Cancer people especially need to be aware of the potential for emotional flare ups, particularly with regard to the home. While Mars is in Cancer, Cancer born people are stirred up with a lot of heat and activity in their lives. Too much worry or fear is likely to lead to some serious anger and defensiveness. Be aware of the potential for heat, fire, and fevers, Cancer folks. Use this energy in your life to keep the flow moving, and to create to your heart's content!

September 29th Saturday

Moon in Taurus

	PDT	EDT	
Moon sextile Uranus	8:47 AM	11:47 AM	
Moon square Neptune	2:33 PM	5:33 PM	
Moon square Venus goes v/c	10:11 PM	1:11 AM	(September 30)

Mood Watch: October is approaching quickly, and today's Moon in Taurus is likely to preoccupy us with the need to get practical affairs in order. Moon sextile Uranus brings hectic but liberating moods and our energy levels will be high this morning. This afternoon, Moon square Neptune may cast some shadows of doubt, and many people may be questioning the burdening imposition of some beliefs. Later tonight,

Moon square Venus tests our affections and our ability to feel and express love. The Taurus Moon also goes void-of-course – an excellent time to rest.

September 30th Sunday

Moon in Taurus / Gemini	PDT	EDT	
Moon enters Gemini	7:35 AM	10:35 AM	
Moon square Saturn	1:11 PM	4:11 PM	
Moon trine Sun	8:02 PM	11:02 PM	
Mercury sextile Saturn	11:17 PM	2:17 AM	(October 1)

Mood Watch: The void-of-course Taurus Moon brings lazy early morning moods, but by the time the Moon enters Gemini, our moods begin to become more thoughtful and curious. This afternoon, Moon square Saturn brings complex kinds of limitations to the scope of our moods, and there may be a tendency for people to try to get out of doing their share of the work. This evening, the Gemini Moon trine Sun brings harmonious and communicative moods.

Mercury sextile Saturn (occurring September 26 – October 3) Mercury in Scorpio is sextile Saturn in Virgo. Mercury in Scorpio demands direct and accurate communications over vital and important subject matters. Meanwhile, Saturn, in Virgo since September 2, demands prudent and carefully analyzed measures with regard to setting up perimeters and implementing rules. This tends to be a time when struggles and difficulties are discussed, and people draw collective conclusions on how best to handle their problems or responsibilities. This is an opportunistic aspect for communicating work skills. Make use of it while the opportunity is here. This aspect last occurred on May 21 when Mercury was in Gemini and Saturn was in Leo. Mercury sextile Saturn will repeat on October 19, when Mercury will be retrograde in Scorpio, and this aspect occurs for the fourth and final time this year on November 16, when Mercury will be direct.

October 1st Monday

Moon in Gemini	PDT	EDT
Moon opposite Jupiter	7:17 AM	10:17 AM
Moon square Uranus	9:53 AM	12:53 PM
Moon trine Neptune	3:59 PM	6:59 PM

Mood Watch: The Sun in Libra and Moon in Gemini energy focuses our attention on matters of law, justice and the application of information; this will bring out a number of issues that require a second look. Don't let mixed feelings lead to confusion; stay clear with your facts and figures. Moon opposite Jupiter brings the compulsory need to gain, profit, and get ahead of all the financial commotion. Moon trine Neptune brings very pleasant spiritual vibrations. Peace.

October 2nd Tuesday

Moon in Gemini / Cancer	PDT	EDT
Moon sextile Venus	2:32 AM	5:32 AM
Moon opposite Pluto goes v/c	3:53 AM	6:53 AM
Moon enters Cancer	9:58 AM	12:58 PM
Moon conjunct Mars	12:56 PM	3:56 PM
Moon sextile Saturn	4:18 PM	7:18 PM
Moon trine Mercury	6:39 PM	9:39 PM

Mood Watch: Overnight, Moon sextile Venus brings pleasant dreams and moods. Moon opposite Pluto may be responsible for a few intense nightmares, particularly as our moods become scattered with the commencement of the void-of-course Gemini Moon. Moods may be spacey for a time this morning, but by the time the Moon enters Cancer, there is a feeling that our emotions have come full swing, and that an emotional cleansing process, which is about to begin, will bring a greater feeling of satisfaction. Moon conjunct Mars puts us in touch with our anger issues. Moon sextile Saturn gives us the incentive to set our limitations and to reiterate on the rules and regulations. The evening is topped nicely with Moon trine Mercury, bringing an excellent time to talk, relay thoughts, and communicate with greater ease.

Ω

October 3ʳᵈ Wednesday
LAST QUARTER MOON in CANCER

	PDT	EDT
Moon square Sun	3:07 AM	6:07 AM
Venus trine Pluto	6:17 AM	9:17 AM
Moon trine Uranus goes v/c	1:42 PM	4:42 PM

Mood Watch: The **Last Quarter Moon in Cancer** (Moon square Sun) often reminds us emotional healing takes time, and the emotional concerns now surfacing will require some extra nurturing and understanding. There will be emotional purging, and the complexity of handling emotional burdens. Some folks will be setting up emotional barriers for protection, and some folks will simply do the service of caring and preparing a nurturing environment. Cancer Moon also connects us with maternal focuses and the ways in which the mother image influences us. This afternoon, Moon trine Uranus brings positive outbursts of wild abandon, and various expressions of freedom will be there to surprise us. Patience is a must! The void-of-course Cancer Moon will be an excellent time for comfort, love and reassurance.

Venus trine Pluto (occurring September 23 – October 7) Venus in Leo is trine to Pluto in Sagittarius. This aspect is occurring for the fourth and final time this year, as the retrograde patterns of these two planets have been creating an active trine dance between them. Both Venus and Pluto are direct, and now the final round of trines commences. This aspect puts matters of love and fate in favorable conditions, and allows for positive breakthroughs in life's unchangeable process. For more information on Venus trine Pluto see August 15, July 8, and March 16.

October 4ᵗʰ Thursday
Moon in Cancer / Leo

	PDT	EDT
Moon enters Leo	3:28 PM	6:28 PM
Sun sextile Jupiter begins (see October 8)		

Mood Watch: The Moon in Cancer is void-of-course for the entire morning and for much of the day. Classically, a long void-of-course Moon period brings a less than productive time and, while in Cancer, it contributes to a great deal of moodiness and leads to tedious and often senseless delays and setbacks. People may tend to worry a lot more than usual. As the Moon enters Leo, our moods will enter into a phase of focusing on personal needs, often including family and friends. Some evening entertainment may be just the thing.

October 5ᵗʰ Friday

Moon in Leo	PDT	EDT
Moon square Mercury	3:54 AM	6:54 AM
Moon sextile Sun	2:14 PM	5:14 PM
Moon trine Jupiter	7:25 PM	10:25 PM
Venus conjunct Saturn begins (see October 13)		

Mood Watch: In the very early hours, Moon square Mercury brings a tendency towards nervousness, and our moods will be unsettled by the stirring of the mind. Like a dream, the mood fades and becomes impossible to describe. The Moon in Leo encourages our moods in more playful and uplifting ways. Moods are based on the need for affection and attention today. People like to seek out their personal choice of entertainment and often express the need to be acknowledged or noticed. Waning Leo Moon serves as a time of introspection. Moon sextile Sun invites us to enjoy the bounties of autumn season. This evening, Moon trine Jupiter brings generous, happy, and joyous feelings. The Great Pumpkin is starting to outgrow all the other pumpkins!

October 6ᵗʰ Saturday

Moon in Leo	PDT	EDT	
Moon opposite Neptune	3:48 AM	6:48 AM	
Moon trine Pluto	5:23 PM	8:23 PM	
Moon conjunct Venus goes v/c	10:29 PM	1:29 AM	(October 7)
Sun trine Neptune begins (see October 12)			

Mood Watch: Overnight, Moon opposite Neptune brings remarkable and impressionable subliminal images to our moods and our dreams. Waning Leo Moon is a good time to encourage the people around us by acknowledging them with compliments and praise for their recent accomplishments. A small compliment can go a long way to reassure people their efforts are not in vain. Credit where credit is due, but by all means, give credit! Moon trine Pluto encourages our moods to look at the bright side of those unforeseeable matters of fate. Later tonight, Moon conjunct Venus in Leo brings fun loving affection to our moods. As the Leo Moon goes void-of-course, this is no time to question a thing of beauty – enjoy it now while it's here!

October 7ᵗʰ Sunday

Moon in Leo / Virgo	PDT	EDT	
Moon enters Virgo	12:04 AM	3:04 AM	
Moon sextile Mars	7:14 AM	10:14 AM	
Moon conjunct Saturn	8:08 AM	11:08 AM	
Moon sextile Mercury	3:46 PM	6:46 PM	
Venus enters Virgo	11:54 PM	2:54 AM	(October 8)

Mood Watch: Long before dawn, the waning Moon enters Virgo. Today's moods will give us something to think about, but we must be careful not to get too caught up in tendencies to judge, doubt, or scrutinize. This is an excellent time to clean up our physical world, focus on our health, and enjoy the delights of natural foods. This morning, Moon sextile Mars inspires us to get involved with life, and many folks will start to become more motivated. Moon conjunct Saturn brings a clear objective to the scope of our moods, and it will be very obvious to many people just what sort of work they will have to do today. Moon sextile Mercury brings communicative moods and, of course, the Virgo Moon is one of the pioneers of communicative moods – so you can bet that our conversations will be interesting, practical, and constructive.

Venus enters Virgo (Venus in Virgo: October 7 – November 8) For the second time this year (since July 14) Venus enters Virgo. Venus represents our attraction to people and objects, as well as our capacity to love and find pleasure. The expression of love and magnetism will now come out in practical and fruitful ways, as we participate in the harvest of summer's bounty. Virgo people will become more aware of the loving side of their nature, and gentle, subtle expressions of love surface. Affections tend to be shy, prudent, modest, and somewhat reserved. Since Virgo symbolizes the virgin, this may be a time when attraction to virginal purity and newness in love is highlighted. Venus in Virgo is referred to as "the fall," a less ideal position for Venus and a time when disappointment in love matters may be felt by some folks. Keep faith in your affections, despite the cooling of passions.

October 8th Monday

Columbus Day, USA / Thanksgiving Day, Canada
Moon in Virgo

	PDT	EDT	
Moon square Jupiter	6:04 AM	9:04 AM	
Moon opposite Uranus	6:32 AM	9:32 AM	
Mars sextile Saturn	8:45 PM	11:45 PM	
Sun sextile Jupiter	9:05 PM	12:05 AM	(October 9)
Venus sextile Mars begins (see October 16)			
Jupiter sextile Neptune begins (see October 29)			

Mood Watch: The Virgo Moon square Jupiter starts off the day with prudent, reserved, and less than generous moods. This is swiftly followed by Moon opposite Uranus which is bound to bring discordant sounds, disruptive energies, and explosive distractions. The general course of havoc, destruction, and mayhem tells us it's a holiday! The waning Virgo Moon gives us the impetus to take hold of matters, to forge order out of chaos, and to make the most of what we've got. The pursuit of simple pleasures will make this day special.

Mars sextile Saturn (occurring September 26 – October 16) Mars in Cancer is sextile Saturn in Virgo. This is an active time for establishing cleanliness in the home. During this aspect, actions create opportunities, provided that there is an application of discipline and timing. Those who are affected by this aspect may feel noticed now. Mars sextile Saturn affects our actions with good timing. Diligently practice your favorite sport, especially those physical activities that demand precision and perfect timing. Offensive and defensive forces tend to work harmoniously with this aspect. Movement and the application of energy (Mars), plus responsibility and awareness of limitation (Saturn), allow the timely qualities of completion and new beginnings to occur. Mars sextile Saturn may be a good time to start a new enterprise, and is an especially opportunistic time to practice control or discipline. This would be the time to end a bad habit or to work to accomplish a goal. This aspect will repeat on December 8, when Mars will be retrograde.

Sun sextile Jupiter (occurring October 4 – 11) This aspect brings those Libra people celebrating birthdays from October 4 – 11 into a favorable natal Sun position to Jupiter. It's a time of opportunity and expansion for these birthday folks if they act on their desires and work towards their goals. Skills learned throughout this year will support their overall plans for career advancement and fortune building. This aspect last occurred on February 3, bringing a similar affect to the birthday Aquarians of that time.

October 9ᵗʰ Tuesday

Moon in Virgo / Libra

	PDT	EDT
Moon square Pluto goes v/c	4:09 AM	7:09 AM
Moon enters Libra	10:59 AM	1:59 PM
Jupiter square Uranus	11:25 AM	2:25 PM
Moon square Mars	8:22 PM	11:22 PM

Mood Watch: Early this morning, Moon square Pluto brings troubling moods and dreams. Waning Virgo Moon is a good time to clean and disinfect the dirty corners of the home and work space, particularly while it is void-of-course throughout much of the morning. As the Moon enters Libra, a great deal more logic infuses our moods, and we are now entering the final stages of the waning Moon. The dark Libra Moon emphasizes the need for balance in relationships and in the way we choose to conduct our lives. This is the time to reconcile our differences and give some room for change and growth in our relationships. However, it may be best to be especially cautious tonight, as Moon square Mars brings an abrupt energy, and unbalanced temperaments will seem like a bullying martial force.

Jupiter square Uranus (occurring September 2 – October 24) For the third and final time this year, Jupiter in Sagittarius is square to Uranus in Pisces. Uranus is currently retrograde and the rebel is at work making a change in the way we recognize our own prosperity. The hopes on which we hang our happiness may require a few out of the ordinary moves of our own in order to keep up with the unpredictable shifts of economic growth. For more information on Jupiter square Uranus, see January 22 and May 10, when this aspect last occurred.

October 10ᵗʰ Wednesday

NEW MOON in LIBRA

	PDT	EDT
Moon sextile Jupiter	6:36 PM	9:36 PM
Moon conjunct Sun	10:02 PM	1:02 AM (October 11)

Mood Watch: Libra Moon assists us to be objective and fair-minded. This evening, Moon sextile Jupiter sets our sights on the need to establish prosperous growth in our lives. **New Moon in Libra** (Moon conjunct Sun) reaches its conjunction with the Sun later tonight. This is a time of reaffirming and harmonizing our relationships with friends, partners and loved ones. However, be forewarned, Mercury is about to go retrograde (see tomorrow) and we may find that – already – our communication skills are declining. Despite communication challenges, this is a time of new friendship as the shift to autumn activities creates a new working environment for many people. New rules, when diplomatically agreed upon, set the standard for how to create a more harmonious environment in the autumn days to come.

October 11th Thursday

Moon in Libra / Scorpio

	PDT	EDT	
Moon trine Neptune	1:46 AM	4:46 AM	
Moon sextile Pluto goes v/c	4:24 PM	7:24 PM	
Mercury goes retrograde	9:01 PM	12:01 AM	(October 12)
Moon enters Scorpio	11:14 PM	2:14 AM	(October 12)

Mood Watch: Overnight Moon trine Neptune brings very tranquil and spiritual dreams and moods. Today's Libra Moon is newly waxing, and the perception of autumn will certainly begin to become much more noticeable. Later in the day, Moon sextile Pluto gives us the incentive to face troublesome conditions. The Libra Moon goes void-of-course at this point; the act of weighing and measuring, judging and deliberating, as well as the attempt to balance out the situations that arise, will probably become more of an ordeal than a practical process. Much later tonight, after Mercury goes retrograde, the Moon enters Scorpio and our moods will become much more secretive and hidden.

Mercury goes retrograde (Mercury retrograde: October 11 – November 1) Hold on to your thinking caps – today Mercury goes retrograde at the eight degree mark of Scorpio and will continue to be retrograde until November 1, when it goes direct at the twenty-three degree mark of Libra. Mercury retrograde in Scorpio (October 11 – 23) is likely to cause costly misunderstandings, particularly over dramatic or passionate subjects such as, birth, death, sex, secrecy, or jealousy. Mercury retrograde in Libra (October 23 – November 1) will likely cause numerous miscommunications between friends and among partners. By late October, negotiations among friends may be confusing and frustrating, and it may be difficult to make decisions. Try to give speakers a decent chance before jumping all over their words, but expect to hear a sufficient dose of harsh criticisms from other people. Interruptions and tensions are likely to occur during discussions. A key to getting through the Mercury retrograde period is to be attentive to important details, some of which may prove to be life saving details while Mercury is in Scorpio. For more on Mercury retrograde, see the section in the introduction about *Mercury retrograde periods.*

October 12th Friday

Moon in Scorpio

	PDT	EDT
Moon sextile Venus	6:14 AM	9:14 AM
Moon sextile Saturn	8:44 AM	11:44 AM
Moon trine Mars	10:44 AM	1:44 PM
Moon conjunct Mercury	5:32 PM	8:32 PM
Sun trine Neptune	6:41 PM	9:41 PM

Mood Watch: Moon sextile Venus brings the potential for loving vibrations, and early this morning, the Scorpio Moon encourages us to get in touch with our desires and our passions. Moon sextile Saturn reminds us life is short, and it will seem very significant for us to concentrate on completing important tasks and duties. Moon trine Mars activates our moods with strength, courage, and inspirational masculine energies. This evening, Moon conjunct Mercury brings pensive thoughts, and this invites us to take some time to explain various matters very carefully, especially now that Mercury is newly retrograde (see yesterday).

195

Sun trine Neptune (occurring October 6 – 15) This occurrence of Sun trine Neptune particularly affects those Libra people celebrating birthdays between October 6 – 15. These Librans are experiencing the favorable trine aspect of Neptune to their natal Sun. This brings gifts of spiritual encounters and awareness, as well as a calming effect on one's life. It also serves as a good time (particularly for these birthday folks) to seek visions, apply prayer and meditation, and to explore spiritual avenues and beliefs that are being presented. This aspect last occurred on June 13, when the Sun was in Gemini.

October 13ᵗʰ Saturday

Moon in Scorpio	PDT	EDT	
Moon trine Uranus	6:33 AM	9:33 AM	
Moon square Neptune goes v/c	2:24 PM	5:24 PM	
Venus conjunct Saturn	9:29 PM	12:29 AM	(October 14)
Mercury trine Mars begins (see October 17)			

Mood Watch: Scorpio Moon allows us to handle some of our more daunting emotional troubles with a bolder sense of courage. This is the time let our moods and feelings take their course through the transformation process of adjusting to autumn's changes. This morning, Moon trine Uranus brings positive, brilliant, freedom-loving moods. Later today, Moon square Neptune brings confused moods and challenges our sense of peace. The Scorpio Moon goes void-of-course at this point and our moods might get ugly – or they may become fascinating, thrilling, dangerous, and compelling all at once. Any number of proverbial dark strangers may cross our evening path. Scorpio focuses on birth, sex, death, and transformation and, although these events are the facts of life, they aren't always easy to experience directly.

Venus conjunct Saturn (occurring October 5 – 17) For the first time in close to three decades, Venus is conjunct with Saturn in the sign of Virgo. A favorable time to apply discipline in the arts and in love related matters, Venus conjunct Saturn represents our commitment and responsibility to the people we love and the disciplines we care about. This is a time when love related disciplines and serious love matters are handled with an eagerness to communicate and reciprocate, particularly with regard to those areas of our love lives that require definition, commitment, and perseverance. Venus and Saturn conjunct in the sign of Virgo also implies that there is a prudence or shyness towards love commitments, while at the same time there is also a great deal of analytical importance and seriousness applied to the art of love and the state of attraction. There will be a great deal of emphasis placed on the pure nature of love while Venus and Saturn are conjunct in Virgo. Venus conjunct Saturn last occurred on August 13 and before that on July 1, when Venus and Saturn were both in Leo.

October 14ᵗʰ Sunday

Moon in Scorpio / Sagittarius	PDT	EDT	
Moon enters Sagittarius	11:59 AM	2:59 PM	
Moon square Saturn	10:00 PM	1:00 AM	(October 15)
Moon square Venus	11:42 PM	2:42 AM	(October 15)

Mood Watch: The weaker and more vulnerable facets of our moods tend to surface on a void-of-course Scorpio Moon, and there may be a tendency for people to become overly emotional and lash out unexpectedly, either towards themselves or others. People are often suspicious of each other, and the emphasis is placed on the need to deal with secrets, emotional traumas, and the necessity for healing. This afternoon as the Moon enters Sagittarius, a more philosophical approach to our outlook on life settles into the evening mood. For a time, positive and optimistic moods will emerge. Later tonight, Moon square Saturn brings the possibility of sad moods with regard to good-byes and difficult endings. Moon square Venus brings challenges between loved ones. Don't make the possible mistake of interpreting tonight's love spats as a complete ultimatum.

October 15th Monday

Moon in Sagittarius	PDT	EDT	
Moon square Uranus	6:59 PM	9:59 PM	
Moon conjunct Jupiter	9:33 PM	12:33 AM	(October 16)
Mercury sextile Venus begins (see October 16)			

Mood Watch: Fascination and adventure call to us with Sun in Scorpio and Moon in Sagittarius. The waxing Sagittarius Moon brings adaptable, creative, versatile, and enterprising moods. This evening, Moon square Uranus could be very challenging, as unexpected outbursts and radical surprises may create chaotic moods. Sagittarius Moon gives us the flexibility to adapt to a number of moods as they come and go. A more philosophical approach to life gives us the feeling that we can handle whatever comes along. Sagittarius points the way with insightfulness. Also tonight, Moon conjunct Jupiter brings delightful and joyous feelings and uplifting moods.

October 16th Tuesday

Moon in Sagittarius	PDT	EDT
Moon sextile Neptune	2:50 AM	5:50 AM
Moon sextile Sun	10:06 AM	1:06 PM
Venus sextile Mars	10:38 AM	1:38 PM
Moon conjunct Pluto goes v/c	5:34 PM	8:34 PM
Mercury sextile Venus	8:19 PM	11:19 PM
Sun sextile Pluto begins (see October 20)		

Mood Watch: Moon sextile Neptune brings enchantment to our dreams and moods. The waxing Sagittarius Moon sextile Sun brings an optimistic and philosophical picture of the season, and an interest in travel and adventure may capture our moods. This evening, Moon conjunct Pluto puts us in touch with world events, and our moods may be surprised by the peculiar ways in which destiny evolves. Also this evening, the Sagittarius Moon goes void-of-course, and people may have a tendency to drift off, become distant, get lost, and be forgetful. If something important is going on tonight, pay attention! Mercury retrograde (Oct. 11 – Nov. 1) is no time to be lazy with regard to information. Tonight, check and double check all travel schedules, and expect delays.

Venus sextile Mars (occurring October 8 – 19) Venus in Virgo focuses on our affections with an emphasis on applying love articulately, and with simplicity, forethought, and grace. Mars in Cancer accents the need to take action, particularly under emotionally stirring circumstances. The Mars influence emphasizes the awareness and application of action, movement, involvement, might, strength and energy. It is here that feminine (Venus) and masculine (Mars) forces have an opportunity (the sextile aspect) to support each other. At this time, many vital love matters are being stirred and are bringing numerous opportunities. This aspect also occurred last month on September 3, and earlier this year on February 13.

Mercury sextile Venus (occurring October 15 – 19) Retrograde Mercury in Scorpio is sextile Venus in Virgo. Emotionally stirring communication mix-ups are best aided with careful and loving attention to practical needs. This aspect brings an opportunity for us to communicate love in a very helpful and beneficial way. Mercury sextile Venus teaches us of the necessity to speak out about our love needs, and focuses discussion on the things to which we are attached and which we treasure. This aspect last occurred on September 17, also appearing on April 7, and before that on March 16.

October 17ᵗʰ Wednesday

Moon in Sagittarius / Capricorn

	PDT	EDT
Moon enters Capricorn	12:04 AM	3:04 AM
Mercury trine Mars	1:38 AM	4:38 AM
Moon trine Saturn	10:18 AM	1:18 PM
Moon sextile Mercury	1:39 PM	4:39 PM
Moon opposite Mars	2:44 PM	5:44 PM
Moon trine Venus	4:08 PM	7:08 PM
Mercury sextile Saturn begins (see October 19)		

Mood Watch: Overnight, the waxing Moon enters Capricorn and our moods will definitely get into the swing of taking care of responsibilities. Moon trine Saturn brings confidence, control, and accuracy to our step, and our moods will be harmoniously productive. This is a great time to take care of business. This afternoon, Moon sextile Mercury brings a good time to reiterate plans, schedules, and messages and to handle communications very thoroughly. A little later, Moon opposite Mars brings a surge of emotional heat which, for some, may lead to anger. As a general rule, activities will be especially busy. Lastly, Moon trine Venus brings the perfect lunar aspect for enjoying beauty, pleasure, and love.

Mercury trine Mars (occurring October 13 – 21) Mercury has been retrograde since October 11, causing this aspect to occur for the second time this year since September 26. Mercury in Scorpio trine Mars in Cancer brings essential information which will be received favorably, but with Mars in Cancer, active responses are generally defensive in nature and strong emotional turmoil may be prevalent. Mercury retrograde in Scorpio tends to hinder the conditions of this generally very favorable aspect, as communications tend to be challenging, emotionally charged, and easily misinterpreted. Expect the potential for dramatic interludes when it comes to making demands for action. This aspect will repeat for a final time on November 19, when Mercury in Scorpio will be direct and Mars in Cancer will be retrograde.

October 18th Thursday

Moon in Capricorn

	PDT	EDT
Moon sextile Uranus	5:59 AM	8:59 AM
Venus opposite Uranus begins (see October 25)		

Ω

Mood Watch: In many parts of North America, the waxing Capricorn Moon keeps people industriously working to prepare for the stormiest phase of the autumn season. Even where the atmosphere is calm, there is a strong drive to take life seriously and to carry out our duties with thoroughness. This morning, Moon sextile Uranus brings unusual feelings, and at first, our moods will be carefree and potentially reckless. This will be a time of making breakthroughs in the midst of some very busy and chaotic moods. All the while, Capricorn Moon keeps us focused, diligent, and unaffected by the chaos.

October 19th Friday

Moon in Capricorn / Aquarius - FIRST QUARTER MOON in CAPRICORN

	PDT	EDT
Moon square Sun goes v/c	1:34 AM	4:34 AM
Mercury sextile Saturn	6:55 AM	9:55 AM
Moon enters Aquarius	9:53 AM	12:53 PM
Moon square Mercury	6:57 PM	9:57 PM

Mood Watch: **First Quarter Moon in Capricorn** (Moon square Sun) brings a strong emphasis on the need for serious labor. Some staunch determination is required. There is a steadily mounting concern to achieve a notable level of accomplishment or completion of projects. The need to hunt for a steady job, a marketing edge, or a secure investment keeps us vigilant and focused. As soon as this First Quarter Moon phenomenon occurs, it begins to fade as the Moon goes void-of-course. Lazy moods may catch us off guard first thing this morning. As the Moon enters Aquarius, our moods will become more technically oriented, and the brave new world will begin to show us new things – usually new things which never cease to be amazing.

Mercury sextile Saturn (occurring October 17 – 22) Mercury in Scorpio is sextile Saturn in Virgo. This tends to be a time when struggles and difficulties are discussed, and people draw collective conclusions on how to best handle their problems or responsibilities. This is a tricky time for communications while Mercury is retrograde (October 11 – November 1) so this opportunistic aspect may require unusually long debates and attempts at deliberation before agreements can be settled. Opportunities being discussed at this time are likely to be better handled next month (November 16) when this aspect returns for the final time this year. By then, Mercury will be direct and communications, as well as negotiations, are likely to run much more smoothly. This aspect first occurred on May 21 when Mercury was in Gemini and Saturn was in Leo, and it last occurred on September 30.

199

October 20ᵗʰ Saturday

Moon in Aquarius	PDT	EDT	
Sun sextile Pluto	6:40 AM	9:40 AM	
Moon sextile Jupiter	6:02 PM	9:02 PM	
Moon conjunct Neptune	9:09 PM	12:09 AM	(October 21)

Mood Watch: The waxing Aquarius Moon during Sun in Libra brings sociable and gregarious moods, and this time highlights philanthropic events. This evening, Moon sextile Jupiter brings jovial moods with a good potential here for people to be generous and open minded, making this an excellent time for fund raisers and charity balls. Later this evening, Moon conjunct Neptune calms the evening spirit with accepting and peaceful moods.

Sun sextile Pluto (occurring October 16 – 22) Sun in Libra is sextile Pluto in Sagittarius, bringing opportunities that appear both vast and demanding to Librans celebrating birthdays October 16 – 22. These birthday people will be experiencing the sextile aspect of their natal sun to Pluto, giving them opportunities to take charge and to step into positions of power and, to accept and embrace fate and permanent change in their lives. This is also an opportunity to embody what has been learned from the personal trials of the past. Go thee forth and conquer, master Librans! Persist with diligence to resolve the conflicts of your life with self-respect and assurance. Your time to triumph is always available when your will to achieve is balanced by knowledge and hard work. This holds true for all signs of the zodiac. This aspect last occurred on February 17, when the Sun was in Aquarius.

October 21ˢᵗ Sunday

Moon in Aquarius / Pisces	PDT	EDT
Moon sextile Pluto	10:29 AM	1:29 PM
Moon trine Sun goes v/c	12:37 PM	3:37 PM
Moon enters Pisces	4:03 PM	7:03 PM
Moon trine Mercury	8:24 PM	11:24 PM
Venus square Jupiter begins (see October 29)		

Mood Watch: This morning's waxing Moon in Aquarius brings brilliant, intelligent, and knowledgeable efforts to support our unrelenting curiosities. There is an intense humanitarian drive to save lives as Moon sextile Pluto brings the potential for greater intensity in our moods. Moon trine Sun harmonizes our moods and brings positive vibrations. The Aquarius Moon then goes void-of-course for several hours. Intelligence is out there, but it may be hard find after all, hydrogen and stupidity are the two most common things in the universe! Pay no mind to the mindless void-of-course Moon in that air sign, or the fact that Mercury is retrograde (Oct. 11 – Nov. 1). Pay no mind to the technical equipment that isn't working. Even though artificial intelligence is no match for natural stupidity, this doesn't mean we have to fowl things up by pretending we can correct one or the other. Just let it be. As the Moon enters Pisces, our moods shift, and a much more peaceful quality of mood assists us to drop our cares and woes. Moon trine Mercury brings a good time to discuss things and to clarify misinterpreted facts.

October 22nd Monday

Moon in Pisces

	PDT	EDT	
Moon opposite Saturn	1:48 AM	4:48 AM	
Moon trine Mars	7:20 AM	10:20 AM	
Moon opposite Venus	1:51 PM	4:51 PM	
Moon conjunct Uranus	6:00 PM	9:00 PM	
Moon square Jupiter	10:34 PM	1:34 AM	(October 23)
Sun conjunct Mercury begins (see October 23)			

Mood Watch: Moon opposite Saturn brings an awareness of deadlines, and our dreams and moods will be looking down the timeline of our lives. Moon trine Mars activates our morning moods with vibrant emotional and physical energy. Moon opposite Venus brings a tricky time to attempt to please others, and affections may be spread thin. This evening, Moon conjunct Uranus brings impulsive and unexpected moods changes. Later tonight, Moon square Jupiter may cause many late-nighters to question their happiness, or to doubt their sense of financial wellbe-ing. While the strongly waxing Pisces Moon of autumn may cause many folks to question their beliefs, the urge to find hope and faith will keep them vigilantly searching.

SCORPIO

Key Phrase: " I CREATE " or

"I DESIRE"

Fixed Water Sign

Symbol(s): The Scorpion,

The Eagle, and The Phoenix

October 23rd through

November 22nd

October 23rd Tuesday

Moon in Pisces / Aries

	PDT	EDT
Sun enters Scorpio	12:16 PM	3:16 PM
Moon square Pluto goes v/c	1:18 PM	4:18 PM
Sun conjunct Mercury	4:56 PM	7:56 PM
Moon enters Aries	6:25 PM	9:25 PM
Mercury enters Libra	8:38 PM	11:38 PM

Mood Watch: The Pisces Moon starts off this day with strong psychic inclinations. Our secret hunches reveal multiple truths as the Sun crosses the line from Libra to Scorpio. Moon square Pluto brings the potential for doubt and uncertainty, particu-larly as the Moon goes void-of-course, causing frequent delays due to emotional turmoil. This evening as the Moon enters Aries, our moods will become ambitious, and many folks will be eager to change the stagnant energies around them.

Sun enters Scorpio (Sun in Scorpio: October 23 – November 22) *Happy Birthday, Scorpio!* This time of year, like the Scorpio personality, brings in an air of mystery and mysticism. This is a time when people are more attentive to their hidden agendas and their needs to connect with their own passion. Scorpio, the sign which is ruled by the underworld god Pluto, focuses our attention on the most important events of life: birth, sex, death and regeneration (or transformation). Everyone has his or her own perspective on how to make breakthroughs when confronting difficult transitions in life. For our Scorpio friends, it is that difficulty and challenge of transformation that inspires and allures their senses. Scorpio is not known for being docile or passive, is not hindered by rules, and will often test the laws of physics and nature to the very limit – and further still. The realm of Scorpio deals with the powers of hidden meaning, the need for secrecy, and the deep, psychologically ensnaring struggles with the self-destructive nature of humans and beasts. The totem of the sign of Scorpio is the desert dweller, the scorpion. Its sting can kill; indeed, if it is not careful, this creature can sting and kill itself. If the matter at hand is deeply passionate, the Scorpio will do anything to protect or defend it. The complex Scorpio nature has other totems: the eagle and the phoenix. Scorpio perceives on many levels and can relate to the eagle's ability to observe from very far away, seeing the larger and more objective picture of life, while also noting all the details essential to life itself (much like that small field mouse dinner targeted from several hundred yards above). The phoenix totem represents the ability to rise above the burning rays of the Sun as a transformed and enlightened being. The spirit of Scorpio teaches us how to move through, and be transformed by, the times of emotional pain, drama, and strife that inevitably come with life itself. Pushing with integrity through the perilous difficulties and dangers of life is a requisite personality trait of the sign of Scorpio. Scorpios also have a massive amount of creative talent, and more evolved Scorpio personalities are often masters of their trade, noted for their craftsmanship and skill. The Scorpio days are the days to work on developing perception, survival instincts and, most of all, a connection with the divinity of passion.

Sun conjunct Mercury (occurring October 22 – 26) This is a very common aspect, which will create a much more thoughtful, communicative, and expressive year ahead for those late born Libras and early born Scorpio people celebrating birthdays October 22 – 26. This is your time (Birthday Libra/Scorpios) to record ideas, relay important messages, and pay close attention to your imaginative thoughts as they are touched by Mercury, creating the urge to speak and be heard. Your thoughts will reveal a great deal about who you are, now and in the year to come.

Mercury enters Libra (Mercury in Libra: October 23 – November 11) Mercury has been retrograde since October 11 and as a result, it's now entering Libra for the second time this year. For a recap on the story of Mercury in Libra, see September 5. For more information on Mercury retrograde through the sign of Libra, see the last paragraph in the introduction on *Mercury Retrograde Periods: 2007.*

October 24th Wednesday

Moon in Aries

	PDT	EDT	
Moon square Mars	9:39 AM	12:39 PM	
Moon trine Jupiter	11:45 PM	2:45 AM	(October 25)
Mercury sextile Pluto begins (see October 26 and November 8)			

Mood Watch: The first full day of the Sun in Scorpio has arrived, and now that we have reached the eve of the Full Moon, a definite build up of energy can be widely felt. While the Moon is in Aries, the start of the day is bound to be turbulent with Moon square Mars – this is a recipe for accidents, fights, headaches, and many people will find that they are being especially defensive as well as impatient. Later tonight, Moon trine Jupiter brings much more pleasant moods, and our dreams are bound to lead us into a pot of gold.

October 25th Thursday

Moon in Aries / Taurus - FULL MOON in TAURUS

	PDT	EDT	
Moon sextile Neptune	1:14 AM	4:14 AM	
Venus opposite Uranus	2:09 AM	5:09 AM	
Moon trine Pluto	1:17 PM	4:17 PM	
Moon opposite Mercury goes v/c	2:47 PM	5:47 PM	
Moon enters Taurus	6:08 PM	9:08 PM	
Moon opposite Sun	9:53 PM	12:53 AM	(October 26)
Sun sextile Saturn begins (see October 29)			

Mood Watch: Calm and peaceful moods assist us in our rest during the predawn lunar aspect of Moon sextile Neptune. This afternoon, Moon trine Pluto brings the strong incentive to tackle problems and find solutions. Moon opposite Mercury brings an intense need to communicate, to reiterate on complex messages, and to set the record straight wherever Mercury retrograde (Oct. 11 – Nov. 1) has brought havoc. The Aries Moon also goes void-of-course at this point, and people may be completely impatient or overly impulsive. As the Moon enters Taurus, our moods become more grounded. **Full Moon in Taurus** (Moon opposite Sun) reminds us to take the time to enjoy and create beauty around us and to indulge a little in some luxurious pleasures or leisure time. To not have the things that are needed to live a practical existence is to be acutely aware of those needs. For most, this usually translates into a lack of money or a lack of stable surroundings. The standards we set for ourselves will often determine our sense of stability. Start by believing that the thing you need is something you deserve to have. Ask Mother Moon to bring you ownership, and she will teach you how to sow for the harvest of your needs, as well as your desires. The Taurus Moon is exalted; this is the time to tap into your sensibilities and to go after those things you need and want in life.

Venus opposite Uranus (occurring October 18 – 28) Venus in Virgo opposes Uranus in Pisces. Prudent love is tested by radical beliefs. Conflict may surface as love relationships are tested by fundamental differences of belief or by drug related problems. On the up side, exciting and unusual kinds of pleasure bring radical new awareness. On the down side, this type of love is explosive in nature, creating radical obsessions – some healthy and some not. Although they are often short-lived, this aspect allows for unusual, exciting, and torrid love affairs. This is a good time for artists to make breakthroughs and for eccentric expressions of affection. Issues of freedom are likely to be raised in love related disputes. Strong psychic connections will occur more rapidly, invoking hypersensitivity that could easily get out of hand. No matter how you look at it, issues of love are surely being activated with a broadening sense of awareness.

October 26th Friday

Moon in Taurus	PDT	EDT
Moon trine Saturn	3:33 AM	6:33 AM
Moon sextile Mars	9:43 AM	12:43 PM
Mercury sextile Pluto	10:53 AM	1:53 PM
Moon sextile Uranus	5:46 PM	8:46 PM
Moon trine Venus	8:33 PM	11:33 PM

Mood Watch: The post-full Taurus Moon ties us into the need to appeal to our senses, and also to the need for our sense of security. Moon trine Saturn allows us to see clearly down the time-line of our lives, and gives us a good picture of what it will take to reach our goals. Moon sextile Mars gives us the strength and the motivation to tackle big jobs. This evening, Moon sextile Uranus inspires our moods to break routines and to take on spontaneous kinds of actions. After a hard day's work, the Taurus Moon is a great time to seek relaxation. Tonight, Moon trine Venus tops our evening moods with pleasurable pursuits and loving kindness.

Mercury sextile Pluto (occurring October 24 – November 10) Due to Mercury's current retrograde process in Libra (October 11 – November 1), this aspect returns to us, once again, since September 24. Mercury is currently in Libra focusing discussions on matters of law and diplomacy. Mercury sextile Pluto focuses our attention on power issues, and there may be a tendency for communications to be challenging and even confusing, and difficult subjects may seem to be easily misinterpreted. For more information on Mercury sextile Pluto, see January 31, when this aspect first occurred. This aspect also occurred on March 16, February 28, September 24, and it will take place for a final time this year on November 8.

October 27th Saturday

Moon in Taurus / Gemini	PDT	EDT
Moon square Neptune goes v/c	12:17 AM	3:17 AM
Moon enters Gemini	5:12 PM	8:12 PM
Sun trine Mars begins (see November 4)		

Mood Watch: Long before many North Americans have seen the light of day, Moon square Neptune may haunt our dreams with deceptive misconceptions. The Taurus Moon goes void-of-course throughout the entire day and stubbornness refuses to yield. This will be a tough day to make a sale, and it may be best to remember you can't please everyone. As the Moon enters Gemini, we may find our moods will be easily triggered by the things we think and say. Remember that Mercury is retrograde (Oct. 11 – Nov. 1) – positive thoughts will bring positive moods, and it is wise to keep thoughts and communications as simple as possible.

October 28th Sunday

Moon in Gemini

	PDT	EDT	
Moon square Saturn	3:02 AM	6:02 AM	
Moon square Uranus	5:18 PM	8:18 PM	
Moon square Venus	11:41 PM	2:41 AM	(October 29)
Moon opposite Jupiter	11:49 PM	2:49 AM	(October 29)

Mood Watch: Today's waning Gemini Moon will keep us fussing over the details of life. Mercury is the ruler of Gemini; it is currently retrograde (since October 11) and this may cause many folks to be in a perpetual state of correcting, reiterating, and modifying. Gemini Moon brings determined efforts to think through matters and find logical answers to unsolved puzzles. Moon square Saturn brings difficult struggles with regard to the never ending cycle of beginnings and endings, and our predawn dreams and moods may be poignantly serious. This evening, Moon square Uranus may bring troublesome chaos or rebelliousness to our moods. Later tonight, Moon square Venus may cause unpleasant moods due to a lack of kindness or love wherever it is needed. Also later tonight, Moon opposite Jupiter brings a tendency to overindulge, and there may be a lot of defensiveness over expenditures. Today's advice is as follows: Don't let irresponsibility and recklessness ruin relationships, particularly with regard to our loved ones' livelihoods and their own search for happiness.

October 29th Monday

Moon in Gemini / Cancer

	PDT	EDT	
Moon trine Neptune	12:06 AM	3:06 AM	
Venus square Jupiter	2:09 AM	5:09 AM	
Moon trine Mercury	8:34 AM	11:34 AM	
Moon opposite Pluto goes v/c	12:52 PM	3:52 PM	
Moon enters Cancer	5:51 PM	8:51 PM	
Sun sextile Saturn	8:43 PM	11:43 PM	
Jupiter sextile Neptune	9:00 PM	12:00 AM	(October 30)

Mood Watch: Moon trine Neptune brings positive subliminal images to our dreams. The Gemini Moon awakens us to mindful and curious moods. Moon trine Mercury gives us the benefit of optimistic moods to make an effort to simplify various details and communicate them clearly. By the end of the week, communications will start to improve, but for now we'll need all the help we can get, and this morning is a good time to set the record straight. By afternoon the spirit of the day will be embraced by a great deal of strife, and there will be an overpowering effort to handle large scale problems and concerns. The void-of-course Moon period that follows may bring a great deal of confusion and a lot of mindless chatter throughout the day. This evening as the Moon enters Cancer, our moods will enter into a much more withdrawn and, perhaps, defensive mode. The need to purge emotional clutter will be evident.

Venus square Jupiter (occurring October 21 – November 1) Venus in Virgo is square to Jupiter in Sagittarius. A love for purity, precision, and perfection may be interrupted or challenged by the need to handle such costly economic pursuits as travel and exploration. Love relationships complicated by difficult money issues may be prevalent. Don't let money matters spoil the beauty of loving affection, but expect the strong possibility that this might well be the case with others. The art world may suffer a bit while economic shifts are occurring. This aspect reminds us that something more than love's blindness is required in order for us to fully realize our riches and the value of what we care about most. Venus square Jupiter last occurred on February 9, when Venus was in Pisces.

Sun sextile Saturn (occurring October 25 – November 1) This occurrence of Sun sextile Saturn particularly affects those Scorpio people celebrating birthdays October 25 – November 1, helping them focus their energy and discipline with greater clarity throughout this year. As Saturn traverses the sextile aspect to the natal Sun of these Scorpio people, there is a sense of making progress through discipline, and they may very well begin to see the rewards of their diligent labor in the coming year. This is only true as long as they apply themselves to their work, and maintain a vigilant and persistent effort to master personal discipline and training. For the birthday Scorpio folks of this time, greater control comes with genuine effort. This aspect last occurred on June 11, presenting better opportunities and allowing more control in the lives of Gemini birthday people.

Jupiter sextile Neptune (occurring October 8 – November 9) Jupiter directs our senses to prosperity and brings expansion and new realms of fulfillment and discovery. Neptune brings the unknown and life's great mysteries into a place in the human spirit where they can be felt and experienced. Jupiter in Sagittarius sextile Neptune in Aquarius provides us with opportunities for new awareness and confidence, and the spirit may be newly empowered with divine intuition.

Jupiter represents wealth and commerce, while Neptune represents spiritual movements, addictive substances, the sea, and all those things dredged up from the sea, such as petroleum – North America's most widely consumed addiction. The fishing industry and the Navy may appear to prosper during this time of Jupiter sextile Neptune. There is also a chance for prosperity to flourish (Jupiter) in the arts and in the world of music (Neptune). This sextile of Jupiter and Neptune gives us the illusion that gas prices couldn't possibly go any higher and that (maybe) a shortage doesn't really exist. These are the dwindling glory days of a gas guzzling culture. While we are currently finding insightful ways to believe in our economy, and to try to explore further to meet our growing expenditures (Jupiter in Sagittarius), we cannot continue to build our fortunes and our dependencies on petroleum products alone. The North American economy may well step over the boundaries of oil consumption at this time by plunging (on a minor scale) into the national reserve, just as it did when Jupiter was *trine* Neptune in early 2005.

Jupiter sextile Neptune gives us the awareness of the chance for abundance, but we must not be fooled by a false sense of permanent abundance. The spirit of humankind will eventually be challenged by its dependencies. Checks and a large line of credit do not mean there's money in the bank, but while we have the means to avoid the truth, we tend to assume that it will always be there for us. Are we really prospering (Jupiter) or have we come to depend on a Neptunian illusion? For some folks, this aspect brings the ability to perceive beyond the unknown, and that's good because it allows us to see beyond our current situation and to search for solutions to the big energy crisis scenarios of the future. Jupiter's workings appeal to our nature as consumers. When the planet of expansion (Jupiter) is sextile to the planet of spirituality (Neptune) discoveries may occur, showing us how to stretch out our spiritual experience of life, and to empower our beliefs with something that brings us pure joy and fulfillment. ♏

As long as one is working with a meditative process or is focusing on a spiritual quest of some nature, this aspect gives the believer the opportunity to expand to great heights and empower his or her imagination and personal realms of intuition. Jupiter sextile Neptune allows us to expand our beliefs and to take on a more uplifting viewpoint of life. This aspect brings a better understanding of the play of Spirit in our daily lives.

October 30th Tuesday
Moon in Cancer

	PDT	EDT
Moon sextile Saturn	4:32 AM	7:32 AM
Moon trine Sun	5:05 AM	8:05 AM
Moon conjunct Mars	12:12 PM	3:12 PM
Moon trine Uranus	7:22 PM	10:22 PM

Mood Watch: The Sun and Moon are both in water signs, and this often brings wet and stormy October weather. Emotional storms and purging will also be prominent in many places throughout North America. The Cancer Moon brings out the need for domestic comforts and nurturing. This is an excellent time to spread seeds in the garden, as well as seeds of hope in the heart. Moon sextile Saturn kicks off the day with a firm sense of resolve to redefine those areas of our lives that are out of bounds. Moon trine Sun blesses our morning moods with a feeling of acceptance of the way the season is shaping up. This afternoon, Moon conjunct Mars in Cancer may bring strong offensive and defensive reactions to emotionally heated kinds of situations. This evening, Moon trine Uranus allows us to blow off a good portion of the day's steam in a positive and liberating fashion.

October 31st Wednesday
All Hallows (Halloween) / Samhain / Witches' New Year
Moon in Cancer / Leo

	PDT	EDT	
Moon sextile Venus	6:20 AM	9:20 AM	
Moon square Mercury goes v/c	10:14 AM	1:14 PM	
Neptune goes direct	1:06 PM	4:06 PM	
Moon enters Leo	9:49 PM	12:49 AM	(November 1)
Venus square Pluto begins (see November 5)			

Mood Watch: While the Sun is in Scorpio, waning Cancer Moon is the best time to nurture emotional ills. In those places where it's applicable, we'll need to apply some motherly care while bundling up for the harsh mid-autumn weather. This morning, Moon sextile Venus brings the potential for pleasant and amicable moods. Moon square Mercury makes it especially difficult to relay information and to explain complex matters. This, of course, is not helped by the fact that Mercury is retrograde and about to make a stand-still as it prepares to go direct (see tomorrow). You know the drill – take extra care to ensure messages are reciprocated with optimal clarity. The Cancer Moon will also go void-of-course at this young stage of the day; from here on we can expect some rainy emotional weather.

Just as clouds release rain, our moods can release pent-up emotional responses. Moodiness is inevitable. Much later tonight, the clouds blow over with the sunny disposition of the Leo Moon. The Leo Moon will lead us to our instinctual patterns, and many folks will feel the need for warmth, affection, and reassurance. *Happy Halloween! Happy Witches' New Year!* The slumber of the plant and animal world will deepen, and the crops and seeds of the fields will take their rest with the promise of returning as new growth in the spring. This is the time to honor the dead and invite the beloved spirits of our ancestors to join in our celebrations. Some believe from sunset until dawn, the spirits of our deceased loved ones are able to roam the earth and converse with the living. This is a particularly important time to speak aloud the names of those who have passed away (especially within the past year) and to honor them with the food, drink and song they enjoyed during their lifetime; following old traditions will awaken the memories of these loved ones. Don't forget to set an extra plate of food and drink aside at mealtime in their honor.

Neptune goes direct (Neptune direct: October 31, 2007 – May 25, 2008) Neptune resumes a direct-moving course after five months (since May 24) of being retrograde. This will regenerate our spiritual and intuitive work and facilitate our development. Neptune is in Aquarius, influencing the flow of the Aquarian age and the evolutionary processes of belief systems. Neptune is the master of illusion, while Aquarius demands scientific proof. As Neptune proceeds further into Aquarius, we will learn to achieve a higher and freer sense of spiritual awareness – a sense that something divine is occurring, even though it cannot be explained in mortal terms. What many of us are finally coming to acknowledge is the notion that we are spiritual beings having a human experience, not human beings having a spiritual experience. A good meditation, when sincerely applied, helps to discharge our emotional baggage. Neptune's calming and forgiving nature will help us to let go of malicious and non-productive thoughts, and will melt away cold-heartedness. Frequently invoke the spiritually uplifting meditations that work for you. This practice will lead you to a positive and regenerative place in your own spiritual evolution. Neptune moving direct allows us to move freely forward, using divine wisdom and our spiritual aspirations as guides.

November 1st Thursday

All Saints Day / Day of the Dead (Mexico)
LAST QUARTER MOON in LEO PDT   EDT

	PDT	EDT
Moon square Sun	2:19 PM	5:19 PM
Mercury goes direct	4:00 PM	7:00 PM
Sun trine Uranus begins (see November 7)		

Mood Watch: The *Day of the Dead* is celebrated in Mexico and by enthusiasts of the Mayan and Aztec cultures. Colorful altars with decorative skulls, photos of the dead, and symbols of death all adorn the streets. Dramatic and colorful events will occur, and our moods will undergo playful and charismatic expressions. The **Last Quarter Moon in Leo** (Moon square Sun) preoccupies our moods with an emphasis on family and friends, and many folks will be oriented towards personal pursuits. People may also be more inclined to deal with, or let go of, personal grudges and points of contention with others. Leo Moon reminds us to call upon the core of our strength and energy, to stand up for ourselves and to express our true individual characters and needs. When the Moon wanes in Leo, it also urges us to take special care of ourselves and the children in our lives. Personal pet projects are sometimes considered "children" as well. Leo Moon encourages us to look for inner light and inspiration, and to seek the child within.

Mercury goes direct (Mercury direct: November 1, 2007 – January 27, 2008) Since October 11, Mercury has been retrograde in the sign of Scorpio, commonly causing emotional mix-ups and confusion in communications. It has also been retrograde in the sign of Libra, causing communication mix-ups with regard to relationships and decision making. Now we can breathe a greatly needed sigh of relief as Mercury, the planet governing the realms of communication, becomes stationary at the twenty-three degree mark of Libra, and will soon begin to move forward. Take note that our faculties and manner of communicating will definitely improve within the next few days, although perhaps not today. As it moves forward we can begin to clear up the various misunderstandings that have occurred over the past few weeks. For more information on this recently completed phase of Mercury retrograde, see October 11. For more on Mercury retrograde patterns throughout this year, see the introduction on *Mercury retrograde periods*.

November 2nd Friday

Moon in Leo	PDT	EDT
Moon opposite Neptune	9:17 AM	12:17 PM
Moon trine Jupiter	10:36 AM	1:36 PM
Moon sextile Mercury	5:15 PM	8:15 PM

Mood Watch: The waning Moon in Leo will preoccupy our moods with the need to focus on personal character development, self-esteem, and self-confidence. Moon opposite Neptune brings the potential for overindulgent moods, and we may be more easily susceptible to life's little deceptions. This will be masked – or overridden – by the joyous extravagance of Moon trine Jupiter, which is bound to bring very generous and gregarious moods. Leo Moon emphasizes friends, children, and family; where these companions are not present, focus is often placed on personal development and creativity. This evening, Moon sextile Mercury brings greater potential for the tethers of this recent Mercury retrograde period (Oct. 11 – Nov. 1) to wear off, and we will begin to relay messages with much clearer intent. Tonight will be a good time to think.

November 3rd Saturday

Moon in Leo / Virgo	PDT	EDT
Moon trine Pluto goes v/c	12:15 AM	3:15 AM
Moon enters Virgo	5:46 AM	8:46 AM
Moon conjunct Saturn	6:47 PM	9:47 PM

Mood Watch: While many sleep, Moon trine Pluto brings an excellent time to purge emotional pains – those kinds of pains which are forced to contend with matters of fate. The void-of-course Leo Moon is an excellent time to rest, although some early morning risers may have a bit of an identity crisis when they look in the mirror;

but this will soon be altered by the coy demeanor of the Virgo Moon. Our moods will be inclined towards thoroughness and caution. Waning Virgo Moon keeps us on the straight and narrow path, and reminds us to clean up our surroundings, create a practical working environment, and to carefully review the misfit details of the recent Mercury retrograde period (Oct. 11 – Nov. 1) which has finally passed. Tonight, Moon conjunct Saturn brings serious, calculating, and logistically-minded moods. We might need this; it's Daylight Saving Time Eve!

Daylight Saving Time ends tomorrow: Don't forget to turn all clocks and time pieces *back* one hour this evening before hitting the sack.

November 4th Sunday
DAYLIGHT SAVING TIME ENDS – Turn clocks back one hour at 2:00 a.m.

Moon in Virgo	PST	EST
Sun trine Mars	3:20 AM	6:20 AM
Moon sextile Mars	3:25 AM	6:25 AM
Moon sextile Sun	3:25 AM	6:25 AM
Moon opposite Uranus	9:52 AM	12:52 PM
Moon square Jupiter	8:45 PM	11:45 PM

Mood Watch: When we need it most, the waning Virgo Moon brings practical and resourceful moods laced with a bit of scrutiny and discernment. We have gained an hour, an added boon on this contemplative Sunday. A lovely trine of the Sun to Mars brings simultaneous sextile action, as the Moon sextile Mars occurs at the same time that the Moon is also sextile to the Sun. A harmonious umbrella of strength, inspiration, impulsiveness, and competitive energy sets the stage for a very active morning. By mid-day, Moon opposite Uranus brings contradictory explosive moods that will be shaken up by radical or disruptive expressions of thought. Fears of economic decline will prod our moods as the Virgo Moon square Jupiter brings prudence.

Sun trine Mars (occurring October 27 – November 7) This occurrence of Sun trine Mars particularly affects those Scorpio people celebrating birthdays from October 27 through November 4. There will be loads of energy to work with, and a strong need to activate the personality and accomplish goals. Creative work abounds. There are special gifts of triumph for those Scorpio folks who activate their dreams and desires, allowing them to easily utilize existing energy. This is a time to exercise the will and the internal sense of primal might, to stir up personal agendas into a state of action. Heated matters will come to the surface in an advantageous manner. Through the act of making things happen, personal achievement will shine forth like a long needed blessing in the year to come for these birthday folks. Keep it active, Scorpio.

November 5th Monday

♏

Moon in Virgo / Libra

	PST	EST	
Moon conjunct Venus	9:05 AM	12:05 PM	
Moon square Pluto goes v/c	10:12 AM	1:12 PM	
Moon enters Libra	3:48 PM	6:48 PM	
Venus square Pluto	10:01 PM	1:01 AM	(November 6)
Sun square Neptune begins (see November 11)			

Mood Watch: The waning Virgo Moon is an excellent time to take the oppressive chaotic energy around us and tackle it with grounded and determined efforts to create a practical and functional sanctuary – a place where clarity and precision are unscathed by distracting complications. Moon conjunct Venus brings gentleness, kindness, and love to our moods. A strong feminine touch will be somehow emphasized in the early part of the day. The love we will feel is there for a reason, yet swiftly, Moon square Pluto disrupts our moods with reminders of the harsh realities of life. The Virgo Moon goes void-of-course, and the rest of the day may be clouded with a great deal of doubt, or a lack of trust, which is likely to cause moods that will be somewhat withdrawn or, at times, critical. This Virgo Moon urges us to mind our health, and not to overtax our bodies with strong substances. Moon in Libra will bring deliberating efforts to find balance.

Venus square Pluto (occurring October 31 – November 8) Venus is in Virgo squaring to Pluto in Sagittarius. Love is sometimes confronted with sheer madness. Often, with this aspect, something valuable and pure is being corrupted or trampled on by another generation's way of thinking and behaving. Venus square Pluto can involve such difficulties as loss or death of a loved one, and it challenges our attachments to many things in life that we hold dear. If something of this nature is occurring to you, it is best to recognize that love will triumph in every dimension despite the pain that life inevitably brings. Denying these processes of life (rejection, death, disease and loss) is to prolong pain and delay the necessary transformations we must make. As with any hardship, acceptance comes with time. Let the obstacles of love's pain become building blocks towards a better outlook; stronger love will supersede the current trials of the heart. This aspect last occurred on February 19, when Venus was in Pisces.

November 6th Tuesday

Moon in Libra

	PST	EST
Moon square Mars	3:52 PM	6:52 PM

Mood Watch: The waning Libra Moon brings a time to seek balance, with the idea of finding some peace. Where there is not peace, there is usually a pretty strong battle cry waiting to happen. Some say there is no peace without justice, and this may be the sort of Libra Moon day that holds that theme to be true. Today, the only significant lunar aspect reveals all; Moon square Mars suggests our moods will be challenged by invasive forcefulness. Hot feelings are likely to flare up on some level. To some, this means war! Beware of accident prone behavior, too. The Libra Moon impresses upon us the necessity to work together as a team, to work on our angry feelings diplomatically, and to empower our relationships with commitment and effort.

211

November 7th Wednesday

Moon in Libra	PST	EST	
Moon trine Neptune	6:35 AM	9:35 AM	
Sun trine Uranus	8:50 AM	11:50 AM	
Moon sextile Jupiter	10:01 AM	1:01 PM	
Moon conjunct Mercury	9:25 PM	12:25 AM	(November 8)
Moon sextile Pluto goes v/c	10:47 PM	1:47 AM	(November 8)

Mood Watch: Today's waning Moon in Libra emphasizes the need to harmonize friendships and relationships. There is also a strong emphasis placed on such Libra-like things as law, justice, and the necessity to understand their presence or absence. This is a good time to focus on refinement: to correct the mistakes of the past, to empower the experience of the moment, and to work towards improving the future. Libra is the cardinal air sign that endows our thoughts and knowledge with the spirit of wisdom – in the days of Scorpio this brings a sense of renewal, or rebirth. Moon trine Neptune starts the day with a very spiritual and pleasant sort of tranquility. Moon sextile Jupiter brings the potential for positive, outgoing and adventurous feelings. Tonight, Moon conjunct Mercury brings mental clarity and acuity. Much later tonight, Moon sextile Pluto brings good possibilities for therapeutic breakthroughs and, as the Moon goes void-of-course, a good night's rest will be the best medicine to combat our existing troubled feelings.

Sun trine Uranus (occurring November 1 – 10) This occurrence of Sun trine Uranus favorably affects our Scorpio friends celebrating birthdays between November 1 – 10. It puts the radical forces of Uranus in the favorable trine position to their natal Sun. It is time for these people to make a breakthrough. Don't hold back, birthday Scorpios; chaos is here to stay for awhile. Let the experience be positive as long as this aspect brings gifts. Expect restless desires for freedom and the need to break out of the personal prison. Freedom knocks loudly, and the course of change is inevitable in the coming year. Change is necessary for growth. These influential changes are positive in nature, though on the surface they may seem harsh. This represents a favorable state of chaos. Birthday people, the madness that has been occurring in your life is there for a reason. You will find a clearer picture in the long run by keeping up the good fight to preserve your inspiration, intelligence, and Scorpio passion. The trine aspect gives gifts of triumph, and this may be a good time to let chaos be the force that brings freedom. This aspect last occurred on July 10, affecting the birthday Cancer folks of that time.

November 8th Thursday

Moon in Libra / Scorpio	PST	EST
Moon enters Scorpio	4:19 AM	7:19 AM
Venus enters Libra	1:06 PM	4:06 PM
Mercury sextile Pluto	2:28 PM	5:28 PM
Moon sextile Saturn	6:42 PM	9:42 PM

Mood Watch: Today's events may be laced with strong doses of emotion. A waning Scorpio Moon calls to us to let go of destructive tendencies, challenges us to cease hurting ourselves and others, and invites us to transform our lower impulses into higher aspirations. Under supportive circumstances, this is a good time to let go of the pain you've been concealing. Tonight marks the eve of the New Moon in Scorpio, and this is always a good time to apply caution and to beware of the possibility of violent outbreaks and possessive or melodramatic behavior. This is also a time to be careful not to get overworked or overstressed. Whether through purging, healing, or grieving, Sun and Moon in Scorpio are likely to bring stormy and torrential weather both to our emotions and throughout the northern hemisphere. Excitement abounds. This evening, Moon sextile Saturn reminds us to keep a firm sight on our boundary lines. ♏

Venus enters Libra (Venus in Libra: November 8 – December 5) Venus will be in Libra today through December 5, stimulating our Libra friends with a strong sense of affection. Venus is at home in Libra and brings out a love of libraries and scholarly works, and a greater attraction to large bodies of information. Venus in Libra also emphasizes the love of such Libran things as diplomacy, law and order, friends and loved ones, culinary delights – and it particularly brings out the desire to instill balance and harmony wherever possible.

Mercury sextile Pluto (occurring October 24 – November 10) For the sixth and final time this year, Mercury sextile Pluto occurs. Now that Mercury has been direct in Libra since November 1, this aspect brings greater ease and opportunity to the world of power issues and difficult subjects. This will be a time for those who are in positions of power to rectify media related blunders. For more information on Mercury sextile Pluto, check the other dates of its occurrence this year: January 31, February 28, March 16, September 24, and October 26.

November 9ᵗʰ Friday
NEW MOON in SCORPIO – HECATE'S MOON

	PST	EST
Moon trine Mars	5:04 AM	8:04 AM
Moon trine Uranus	10:25 AM	1:25 PM
Moon conjunct Sun	3:04 PM	6:04 PM
Moon square Neptune goes v/c	7:20 PM	10:20 PM
Jupiter conjunct Pluto begins (see December 11)		

Mood Watch: This morning, Moon trine Mars puts us in touch with our strength, and this is a positive time to get things rolling. Moon trine Uranus brings wild and liberating moods, and various expressions of brilliance will intrigue us. **New Moon in Scorpio** (Moon conjunct Sun) marks the regenerative point of the New Moon – and the sign of Scorpio just happens to represent the phenomenon of regenerative force and transformation. The New Moon in Scorpio focuses on a rebirthing process for our emotional body, and this is the time when we are sure to address the proverbial skeletons in our emotional closet. New Moon in Scorpio encourages us to regenerate our hopes while transforming our fears into a courageous and renewed outlook for ourselves. This is the time to take bold steps to defeat undesirable emotional patterns and fear mechanisms. New Scorpio Moon casts new light on our ability to overcome pain and suffering. Tonight, Moon square Neptune is likely to bring very susceptible or vulnerable types of moods, and this is a good time to avoid being around potentially abusive people or scenarios. This is especially true, as this Scorpio Moon will be void-of-course – tonight and tomorrow.

This New Moon is **Hecate's Moon**, and this begins a time of wild and stormy weather, both in the emotional sense and the virtual sense. Hecate is the Witches' goddess of the underworld who leads us through death towards a cycle of rebirth. She guides lost souls to their final destiny and can be called on at this time to guide those who have passed on, especially those who have met their ends under challenging circumstances such as violent death or suicide. Hecate cures the ills that accompany death. The Hecate Moon occurs on the New Moon closest to October 31, which in this case is the New Moon in Scorpio.

November 10ᵗʰ Saturday

Moon in Scorpio / Sagittarius

	PST	EST	
Moon enters Sagittarius	5:00 PM	8:00 PM	
Moon sextile Venus	10:09 PM	1:09 AM	(November 11)

Mood Watch: The rebirth of the Moon's light has already occurred, but today's Scorpio Moon will remain void-of-course throughout the entire day. Through this Scorpio Moon time, there will be a few more rebirthing and regenerative processes to undergo before we can safely call ourselves emotionally purged. People may tend to lash out at each other, but most of it is just reflexes from irritable tendencies. If we are observant and respectful enough, we can avoid getting on anyone's bad side. This evening, as the Moon enters Sagittarius, our moods will become more insightful and outgoing. Later tonight, Moon sextile Venus brings loving and gentle moods to help smooth over the rough edges of the day's events.

November 11ᵗʰ Sunday

Veteran's Day, USA / Remembrance Day, Canada
Moon in Sagittarius

	PST	EST	
Mercury enters Scorpio	12:42 AM	3:42 AM	
Moon square Saturn	7:38 AM	10:38 AM	
Sun square Neptune	5:43 PM	8:43 PM	
Moon square Uranus	10:49 PM	1:49 AM	(November 12)

Mood Watch: Moon square Saturn brings a challenging time for our moods, and many folks may feel as though they're having a lot of trouble keeping things under control this morning. Much later tonight, Moon square Uranus brings harshly chaotic energy to our moods and dreams. Nevertheless, the youthfully waxing Sagittarius Moon brings optimism and resilience to the challenges of our moods, and it also invites us to explore various philosophical perspectives.

Mercury enters Scorpio (Mercury in Scorpio: November 11 – December 1) For the second time this year, Mercury enters Scorpio. It originally entered Scorpio on September 27, back before Mercury went through its final retrograde process this year (October 11 – November 1). Now that Mercury moves smoothly forward throughout the course of its travels in Scorpio, communications will no longer be greatly challenged by secrets backfiring, or by complexity related to dramatic kinds of issues.

Sun square Neptune (occurring November 5 – 14) This occurrence of Sun square Neptune especially affects Scorpio people who are celebrating birthdays November 5 – 14. Neptune in the square position to these birthday folks' natal Sun brings a sense that there are obstacles getting in the way of Spirit or the acknowledgement of spiritual beliefs. The challenge for these Scorpio birthday folks is to overcome the interfering doubts and confrontations. This especially applies to overcoming those extremely dangerous and destructive addictive tendencies. Remember, Scorpio, spiritual lessons do not have to be life threatening! Over the next year, there will undoubtedly be some spiritual adjustments, and perhaps a change of belief is required. This aspect last occurred on May 12, affecting the Taurus birthday people.

November 12ᵗʰ Monday

Moon in Sagittarius	PST	EST	
Moon sextile Neptune	7:43 AM	10:43 AM	
Moon conjunct Jupiter	1:10 PM	4:10 PM	
Moon conjunct Pluto goes v/c	11:54 PM	2:54 AM	(November 13)

Mood Watch: Sagittarius Moon keeps us open to all the visionary possibilities unfolding at this stage of autumn. Sun in Scorpio and Moon in Sagittarius focus our energies on the necessity to work under challenging conditions, and to overcome darkness with creativity and vision. The darkening days of autumn require resolute strength and warmth of spirit. The Sagittarius Moon newly waxes, bringing hope, an expanding outlook, and encouragement to move forward. This morning, Moon sextile Neptune brings calm, accepting moods, and our moods will be notably less apprehensive than they have been in recent days. Moon conjunct Jupiter brings open, enterprising, and explorative moods. Much later tonight, Moon conjunct Pluto brings deep, sometimes troubling moods that will be accented by the Moon going void-of-course. Rest will be essential, and wherever rest is not possible, there may be a tendency for folks to become lost or easily sidetracked.

November 13ᵗʰ Tuesday

Moon in Sagittarius / Capricorn	PST	EST
Moon enters Capricorn	5:02 AM	8:02 AM
Moon sextile Mercury	11:13 AM	2:13 PM
Moon square Venus	3:59 PM	6:59 PM
Moon trine Saturn	7:42 PM	10:42 PM
Mercury sextile Saturn begins (see November 16)		

Mood Watch: At first the void-of-course Sagittarius Moon may seem to disorient us, but early enough, the Moon enters Capricorn and a firm sense of resolve to get back on track will begin to emerge. Capricorn is the achiever; therefore, not only do we wish to get grounded, but now we are aspiring to climb to some higher ground. Capricorn Moon brings focus and determination, but we must know when to quit, as the days of Scorpio may be taxing for some folks. Moon sextile Mercury brings clear and succinct communications to keep business running along smoothly. Moon square Venus may be a difficult time for us to find the kind of affections we need. Later tonight, Moon trine Saturn brings a beneficial time to concentrate on making life more stable and secure.

November 14th Wednesday

Moon in Capricorn	PST	EST
Moon opposite Mars	5:33 AM	8:33 AM
Moon sextile Uranus	10:10 AM	1:10 PM
Venus square Mars begins (see November 19)		

Mood Watch: Capricorn Moon reminds us that the important things in life are worth taking seriously, and those are the things that we must try to stabilize in the midst of disruption. This morning, Moon opposite Mars brings alarming kinds of offensive and defensive energies, and our moods may be put off by various kinds of forcefulness. Moon sextile Uranus brings the possibility of rebellious or strongly independent moods. Some folks may feel the only way to get any work done is to break free from others. For those who have little choice, teamwork will require some extra concentration and a serious effort to keep people in line.

November 15th Thursday

Moon in Capricorn / Aquarius	PST	EST
Mars goes retrograde	12:26 AM	3:26 AM
Moon sextile Sun goes v/c	1:20 AM	4:20 AM
Moon enters Aquarius	3:31 PM	6:31 PM
Mercury trine Mars begins (see November 19)		

Mood Watch: Moon sextile Sun brings a positive outlook in our dreams. The Capricorn Moon goes void-of-course before we're awake, and the general course of the day will be trying at times. Void-of-course Capricorn Moon brings mostly sedate and placid moods, but there will be an underlying pressure and drive to complete duties and tasks, even though it might not be realistic to do so. As the Moon enters Aquarius, a much more brilliant outlook on the day's affairs will uplift our moods considerably. The waxing Aquarius Moon inspires, fortifies, and uplifts our knowledge, and there is usually a greater emphasis on the necessity for humanitarianism.

Mars goes retrograde (Mars retrograde: November 15, 2007 – January 29, 2008) Now the god of war, Mars, goes retrograde in Cancer, and it will eventually re-enter the tail end of Gemini on December 31. Those who have overextended themselves may be due for a recreational healing period. Mars retrograde is also likely to stir up heated energy in the lives of Cancer people as Mars is crossing over their natal Sun. Mars retrograde in Cancer will undoubtedly cause difficulties and numerous energy shifts in the lives of Aries and Libra people as Mars squares to their Sun signs for an extended period of time. Capricorn people are likely to feel overwhelmed with hot emotional energy – or even a fever – while Mars is retrograde in opposition to their natal Sun. As this energy moves backward instead of forward, it will take another two months before all these folks are likely to get their activity modes and energy levels in smooth running order. While Mars is retrograde in Cancer, this is really the time to learn to kick back intermittently and relax. Don't get impatient over projects that are slow to take off or allow hot emotions to get out of hand. For some people this may be a time of having to let go of emotional baggage that has caused them to be angry for too long. As Mars travels retrograde through Cancer, the red planet's sometimes violent, forceful, or reactionary energy may be seen in tendencies towards worry, defensiveness, and fear. Beware of the tendency to act on dangerous impulses, as Mars retrograde is not a good time to take risks – they may lead to disruptive and sometimes fateful accidents.

♏

November 16th Friday

Moon in Aquarius

	PST	EST
Moon square Mercury	4:44 AM	7:44 AM
Moon trine Venus	7:33 AM	10:33 AM
Mercury sextile Saturn	3:23 PM	6:23 PM

Mood Watch: Moon square Mercury starts off the day with nervous energy. Later in the morning, this energy is helped along by Moon trine Venus, which assists us by bringing gentle and kind patience. Progressive, open-minded, and truthful attitudes will keep us inspired as the Moon waxes in Aquarius.

Mercury sextile Saturn (occurring November 13 – 18) Mercury in Scorpio is sextile to Saturn in Virgo. Opportunities are now available to assist us in communicating vital information in a more organized and pragmatic fashion. This aspect gives people an opportunity to learn vital lessons concerning boundaries, limitations, responsibilities and timely completion. This is a favorable aspect to discuss where to set up boundaries and how to implement security systems, and to teach people about handling responsibilities and disciplines. This aspect is occurring for the fourth time this year and it first occurred on May 21, when Mercury was in Gemini and Saturn was in Leo. Since Saturn entered Virgo on September 2, this aspect is now repeating due to Mercury being retrograde (October 11 – November 1). It last occurred on October 19, when Mercury was retrograde in Scorpio, and before that on September 30, when Mercury was direct in Scorpio.

November 17th Saturday

Moon in Aquarius / Pisces - FIRST QUARTER MOON in AQUARIUS

	PST	EST	
Moon conjunct Neptune	3:49 AM	6:49 AM	
Moon sextile Jupiter	10:40 AM	1:40 PM	
Moon square Sun	2:34 PM	5:34 PM	
Moon sextile Pluto goes v/c	6:52 PM	9:52 PM	
Moon enters Pisces	11:16 PM	2:16 AM	(November 18)
Mercury trine Uranus begins (see November 21)			

Mood Watch: Moon conjunct Neptune brings restfulness. At midday, Moon sextile Jupiter inspires our moods to reach out for those things in life we are hoping to find. **First Quarter Moon in Aquarius** (Moon square Sun) puts the spotlight on eccentric and unusual breakthroughs. This is usually a superb time to work on innovative ideas and projects. Aquarius Moon emphasizes and highlights such things as science, research, charities, and humanitarian issues. Tonight, Moon sextile Pluto brings the potential for some therapeutic breakthroughs, but the Moon also goes void-of-course, which may cause our moods to be spacey or technically inept. Later, as the Moon enters Pisces, our moods will become dreamy.

November 18th Sunday

Moon in Pisces	PST	EST	
Moon opposite Saturn	1:01 PM	4:01 PM	
Moon trine Mercury	6:22 PM	9:22 PM	
Moon trine Mars	9:10 PM	12:10 AM	(November 19)

Mood Watch: Pisces Moon gets us into the imaginative joys and pleasures of the arts. A waxing Pisces Moon arouses our intuition, dreams, and beliefs. It may be best to bundle up as Sun in Scorpio and Moon in Pisces invite deeply penetrating wet weather, and patterns of wicked weather may sweep the country. This afternoon, Moon opposite Saturn makes us particularly sensitive to our limitations and our boundaries, and our moods will be especially work oriented. This evening, Moon trine Mercury brings an excellent time for us to communicate amicably and effectively. Later, Moon trine Mars activates our moods with positive masculine energies.

November 19th Monday

Moon in Pisces	PST	EST	
Moon conjunct Uranus	1:26 AM	4:26 AM	
Moon square Jupiter	4:30 PM	7:30 PM	
Venus square Mars	6:20 PM	9:20 PM	
Mercury trine Mars	6:54 PM	9:54 PM	
Moon trine Sun	11:21 PM	2:21 AM	(November 20)
Moon square Pluto goes v/c	11:27 PM	2:27 AM	(November 20)

Mood Watch: Overnight, whether it's in our dream-state, or during the waking moments, Moon conjunct Uranus brings a jolt of awakening, and some folks may be stirred by chaotic feelings. Pisces Moon takes us into the imaginative joys of the intangible – our fantasies. Spacey, yet pleasantly reverent Monday morning moods will proceed calmly throughout the day. The question is: which side is calm – the inside or the outside? Moon in Pisces and Sun in Scorpio ensure an emotionally stirring and somewhat dramatic time. The drama is there somewhere on the surface, or deep down underneath. Creative and psychic inclinations abound. Moon square Jupiter is a tricky time to do business, as people will tend to be considerably less generous or willing to spend. Later tonight, Moon trine Sun puts us in touch with the natural flow of our emotional patterns. Moon square Pluto brings a strain wherever emotional purging becomes necessary. The void-of-course Pisces Moon brings a good time to call it a night, and to attempt to get some rest – or better – sleep!

Venus square Mars (occurring November 14 – 22) Venus in Libra is square to retrograde Mars in Cancer. Love relationships are bound to sail through rocky waters. For the third time this year, since April 22 and August 7, Venus square Mars challenges and tests love in action. Remember that although letting off steam is good, it is also wise to be aware of the potential for violent or hurtful reactions, and actions taken now may be regretted later. Use common sense and realize that dealing with obstacles now is a good way of preventing them from becoming issues later. On the other hand, it might be best not to probe the tenderness of love related subjects if you're not willing to take the pain. It is certainly a good time to be patient with loved ones, no matter how hard the boat rocks.

Mercury trine Mars (occurring November 15 – 21) Due to Mercury's retrograde period last month (October 11 – November 1) Mercury trine Mars is now occurring for the third time this year. This aspect last reached its peak on October 17, and before that, on September 26. Thoughts, words and speech inspire activity, and the messages coming across often give us the incentive to get in on the action. Mercury trine Mars brings news and communications into a most favorable position when it comes to taking action. The trine aspect acts like a gift, and this is a superb time to communicate and to receive positive and uplifting information, which will inspire others to take affirmative action where needed. That said, it is important to note that Mars is currently retrograde in Cancer, creating a tendency towards worry or defensiveness. Overall, Mercury trine Mars is a very positive aspect for empowering communications with clear intent.

November 20ᵗʰ Tuesday

Moon in Pisces / Aries	PST	EST	
Moon enters Aries	3:25 AM	6:25 AM	
Moon square Mars	11:38 PM	2:38 AM	(November 21)
Mercury square Neptune begins (see November 24)			
Venus trine Neptune begins (see November 26)			

Mood Watch: Long before the day gets started, the void-of-course Pisces Moon enters Aries and a shift occurs in our mood patterns. In those areas of life where our relationships have been tested, the Aries Moon brings a certain degree of independence, and some people's patience levels may be tested further still. The Aries Moon invites us to take charge with leadership and self-reliance. A competitive, confident, and enterprising level of productivity will pick up our moods. Be careful not to let touchy matters between loved ones go unattended for too long, as much later tonight, Moon square Mars brings the potential for challenging and offensive outbursts. Sun in Scorpio with waxing Moon in Aries is not a time to be caught defenseless!

November 21ˢᵗ Wednesday

Moon in Aries	PST	EST
Moon opposite Venus	2:13 AM	5:13 AM
Mercury trine Uranus	9:59 AM	12:59 PM
Moon sextile Neptune	11:18 AM	2:18 PM
Moon trine Jupiter	6:45 PM	9:45 PM

Mood Watch: Overnight, Moon opposite Venus brings strongly compelling desires for love, and the need for harmony and peace in our relationships will be quite strong, too. By midday, Moon sextile Neptune brings the potential for a somewhat calm and meditative quality of mood. This evening, Moon trine Jupiter brings joy and a sense of wellbeing.

Mercury trine Uranus (occurring November 17 – 23) Mercury in Scorpio is trine to Uranus in Pisces. This combination stirs up an intelligent, compelling and awakening thought process, one that is usually well defined. This is a good time to record your thoughts and delight in brilliant thinking and information. Much of it may seem like propaganda or information with a radical twist. Catch phrases, radical concept statements and ideas are often born under this aspect. Sensationalism or matters of censorship may be emphasized. Mercury in Scorpio dredges up important topics such as birth, sex, death, and the regenerative force realized through overcoming illness. Uranus is in the sign of Pisces, creating radical change in areas of addiction, the arts, music, psychology, and religion. This aspect last occurred on July 28, when Mercury was in Cancer.

SAGITTARIUS

Key Phrase: "I SEE" or

" I PERCEIVE "

Mutable Fire Sign

Symbol: The Centaur

November 22st through

December 21st

November 22nd Thursday

Thanksgiving Day, USA

Moon in Aries / Taurus	PST	EST	
Moon trine Pluto goes v/c	12:41 AM	3:41 AM	
Moon enters Taurus	4:20 AM	7:20 AM	
Sun enters Sagittarius	8:51 AM	11:51 AM	
Moon trine Saturn	4:52 PM	7:52 PM	
Moon sextile Mars	11:18 PM	2:18 AM	(November 23)

"At a dinner party one should eat wisely but not too well, and talk well but not too wisely."   - W. Somerset Maugham

Mood Watch: Overnight Moon trine Pluto brings a cathartic, but positive therapeutic breakthrough in our dreams and moods – then the Aries Moon goes void-of-course. As the Moon enters Taurus, our moods enter into a time of enjoying what we have. Today's strongly waxing Taurus Moon brings inspiration to create aesthetically pleasing surroundings; hence, this is a perfect time to get into holiday dining and entertaining. The Moon is exalted in the sign of Taurus, impressing upon us the need to get a handle on the physical world. If there's ever a time our moods are struck by the daunting tasks of the impending holidays, this is it. Even those who refuse to get caught up in this particular ritual will find the demands of the physical world still require consideration. Moon trine Saturn will give us what it takes to work in harmony and to time things just right. Later, Moon sextile Mars brings an extra jolt of energy to our moods.

Sun enters Sagittarius (Sun in Sagittarius: November 22 – December 21) Sun in Sagittarius brings the final lap of autumn and the shortest days of the solar year. *Happy Birthday, Sagittarians!* The Sagittarius expression, "I See," opens our eyes to new discoveries during this time. This mutable fire sign achieves visionary awareness and reaches into the world of possibilities. Jupiter is the ruling planet of

220

Sagittarius and inspires Sagittarians to excel, expand, and prosper despite all odds. As the holidays begin, the pressure to pull together social events and purchase gifts – while also monitoring expenses – can be a monumental task for everyone. The concept of prosperity undoubtedly will be tested during this season, and it is therefore very important to get back to the basics and direct your awareness to inner wealth and wellbeing. Simple pleasures can bring prosperous joy. Sagittarius emphasizes travel, sports, and philosophy – all those things which require adaptable enthusiasm.

November 23rd Friday

Moon in Taurus

	PST	EST
Moon sextile Uranus	3:39 AM	6:39 AM
Moon opposite Mercury	8:20 AM	11:20 AM
Moon square Neptune goes v/c	10:54 AM	1:54 PM

Mood Watch: Moon sextile Uranus rustles up chaotic but liberating dreams and moods. The heavily waxing Taurus Moon places the emphasis of our moods on such things as practicality, pleasure, and comfort. Moon opposite Mercury brings a surge of morning thoughts and discussion, and it will be necessary to comprehend a lot of things at once. Moon square Neptune brings disquieting moods at times, and many folks may have an insatiable urge to find a peaceful sanctuary away from the complexities of midday clamor. The Moon also goes void-of-course at this point, and Friday traffic will be troublesome in many places. This is a good time to keep track of valuables; items tend to become easily misplaced under these lunar circumstances.

November 24th Saturday

Moon in Taurus / Gemini - FULL MOON in GEMINI

	PST	EST
Uranus goes direct	2:14 AM	5:14 AM
Moon enters Gemini	3:30 AM	6:30 AM
Moon opposite Sun	6:31 AM	9:31 AM
Mercury square Neptune	9:50 AM	12:50 PM
Moon square Saturn	4:05 PM	7:05 PM
Sun square Saturn begins (see November 30)		

Mood Watch: Throughout the night, the void-of-course Taurus Moon brings heavy snoring amidst the dreaming. Before long, the Moon enters Gemini and the height of the Full Moon energy is already upon us. Like a thief, the Gemini Moon steals the show. **Full Moon in Gemini** (Moon opposite Sun) often brings moods that may seem overwhelmed by mutable thoughts just when we are trying to make decisions. This Gemini Moon, in all of its glorious fullness, brings amazing talk, speeches, mind games, and intellectual pursuits. People may tend to babble senselessly, and very few are able to keep their minds on what they're doing, thinking, or feeling for very long. Ideally, this is a good time astrologically to pace oneself and relax the mind at various intervals. It may also be a time when our minds are relentlessly active and difficult to calm or ease. Full Moon in Gemini goes straight to charging our nervous systems, and we quickly discover that quieting down or easing an overworked nervous system takes some extra time after it has been running at top speed. This afternoon, Moon square Saturn may highlight our nervous tendencies further still, as a serious and demanding drive to get things done leads many folks into working overtime in order to get a handle on their responsibilities.

Uranus goes direct (Uranus direct: November 24, 2007 – June 26, 2008) Since June 23 Uranus, known for stirring up calamity, has been retrograde. Now the planet of chaos and rebellion moves steadily forward through the mid-course degrees of Pisces, awakening the spiritual needs of humanity, perhaps even inspiring break-throughs in human rights, or promoting creativity in art and music. The work of radical and revolutionary forces resumes course as Uranus moves direct until late June 2008. We all feel the need to break out of oppressing conditions of life. As Uranus moves forward, the volatile quality of its work demands the utmost intelligence and knowledge as each level of urgency is unveiled. Uranus is the ruler of Aquarius and teaches us to seek higher levels of intelligence through unusual, brilliant, and open minded measures. The next time the urge for unabashed rebellion makes you kick up your heels, remember to kindle the light of love for humankind's wisdom. This is, after all, the Age of Aquarius.

Mercury square Neptune (occurring November 20 – 26) This aspect often brings a struggle to communicate about the spirit world and human spirituality. Efforts to explain our beliefs may be especially challenging. Neptune is in Aquarius, stirring up issues around human divinity and humanity's beliefs in this confusing and changing period of the dawning age. While Mercury in Scorpio is squaring Neptune, dramatic kinds of thought will be challenged, particularly with respect to issues that concern divine experience (birth, sex, death); relaying this information may seem all the more difficult with this aspect. Anticipate religion related arguments and disputes. Deep subjects must not be treated lightly while Mercury squares Neptune. This aspect last occurred on May 7, when Mercury was in Taurus.

November 25th Sunday

Moon in Gemini	PST	EST	
Moon square Uranus	2:46 AM	5:46 AM	
Moon trine Venus	8:52 AM	11:52 AM	
Moon trine Neptune	10:09 AM	1:09 PM	
Moon opposite Jupiter	6:52 PM	9:52 PM	
Moon opposite Pluto goes v/c	11:39 PM	2:39 AM	(November 26)

Mood Watch: The post-full Gemini Moon is still very full today, and this will be a time of making lots of connections and of covering loads of details. Overnight, Moon square Uranus brings chaotic and explosive dreams that may be difficult to take. This morning, Moon trine Venus brings pleasant moods – a good lunar aspect to help smooth over the sleepless dreaming. Moon trine Neptune calms our moods with peacefulness. This evening, Moon opposite Jupiter boosts our excitement levels, and our moods will be drawn to matters of wealth and wellbeing. Later tonight, Moon opposite Pluto brings the potential for dramatically rocky moods, and the Moon also goes void-of-course at this point, causing confusion and a lot of uncertainty.

November 26th Monday

Moon in Gemini / Cancer

	PST	EST	
Venus trine Neptune	1:56 AM	4:56 AM	
Moon enters Cancer	3:08 AM	6:08 AM	
Moon sextile Saturn	4:22 PM	7:22 PM	
Moon conjunct Mars	9:54 PM	12:54 AM	(November 27)

Mood Watch: The void-of-course Gemini Moon may be annoying for some folks, especially for those who find they can't turn off their noisy brains during the night. Soon enough, the Moon enters Cancer and our moods will be eased by the motherly, nurturing touch. Throughout today, the waning Cancer Moon, still quite bright, impresses upon us the need to attend caringly to those parts of ourselves that need nurturing love. Classically, this post-full Cancer Moon will bring moodiness. Moon sextile Saturn brings the potential for serious and work-oriented moods. Much Later, Moon conjunct Mars impresses our moods with the need to take action on some level, and to get in touch with our true will.

Venus trine Neptune (occurring November 20 – 28) Venus in Libra trine Neptune in Aquarius enhances spiritual love. This aspect brings well balanced and generous kinds of love into harmony with a very ingenious kind of spiritual expression. It delivers a calmness and tranquility that are vitally needed, and there is a greater potential to create a spiritually enhanced atmosphere. Wherever there is spiritual turmoil, Venus trine Neptune helps to ease our woes with a support network of feminine kindness. Visiting or meditating upon sacred places and favorite sanctuaries brings visions and inner wisdom. Peaceful, pleasurable, and spiritual love is possible with this aspect, which last occurred on April 30, when Venus was in Gemini.

November 27th Tuesday

Moon in Cancer

	PST	EST
Moon trine Uranus	3:27 AM	6:27 AM
Moon square Venus	2:13 PM	5:13 PM
Moon trine Mercury goes v/c	8:23 PM	11:23 PM
Venus sextile Jupiter begins (see December 2)		

Mood Watch: Rich intuitive feelings run their course as the Cancer Moon wanes through the darkening days of Sagittarius. In the predawn hours, Moon trine Uranus brings liberating feelings to our dreams. Moon square Venus tests our ability to feel loved, especially at a time when the Cancer Moon inspires us to cook, nurture, and care for those we love. This evening, Moon trine Mercury brings an excellent time to talk matters through and find harmony when communicating. The Cancer Moon will also go void-of-course, and this may be the time to avoid indigestion by not worrying or eating too much. Waning Cancer Moon is a time of purging and moving through emotional concerns that have piled up in our lives. This is a good time to reassure ourselves and to nurture ourselves with loving motherly care.

November 28th Wednesday

Moon in Cancer / Leo

	PST	EST
Moon enters Leo	5:24 AM	8:24 AM
Moon trine Sun	4:38 PM	7:38 PM

Mood Watch: Fortunately, the majority of this month's void-of-course Moon periods have taken place during the time when most North Americans are asleep. Today's void-of-course Cancer Moon visits our predawn dreams, and our moods of emotional inadequacy are affected on those subconscious levels. As the Moon enters Leo, a much more integral emotional spark begins to burn within us. The waning Leo Moon encourages us to work things out with our family. The Sun and Moon are both in fire signs, inviting us to be creative, positive, and active. Moon in Leo emphasizes such things as personal strength, will, integrity, stamina and, of course, it emphasizes how we present and conduct ourselves. Moon trine Sun brings sunny and cheerful moods.

November 29th Thursday

Moon in Leo

	PST	EST
Moon opposite Neptune	4:13 PM	7:13 PM

Mood Watch: Fiery and entertaining showmanship will fill the atmosphere today. Waning Leo Moon is a good time to work on letting go of personal fears and on showing bravery and courage. This may be especially necessary, as Moon opposite Neptune brings spiritually challenging moods, and our moods are often overwhelmed by a conflict of beliefs and a lack of peace. The Leo Moon will help to give us the courage to fight our own individual battles. Be strong!

November 30th Friday

Moon in Leo / Virgo

	PST	EST
Moon sextile Venus	12:27 AM	3:27 AM
Moon trine Jupiter	3:58 AM	6:58 AM
Moon trine Pluto	7:59 AM	10:59 AM
Moon square Mercury goes v/c	9:26 AM	12:26 PM
Moon enters Virgo	11:45 AM	2:45 PM
Sun square Saturn	12:24 PM	3:24 PM
Venus sextile Pluto begins (see December 3)		

Mood Watch: Overnight, Moon sextile Venus touches our dreams with beauty and affection. Moon trine Jupiter also touches our dreams with a sense of wealth and wellbeing. The Moon wanes in Leo and our predawn moods will most likely be preoccupied with personal issues. This morning, Moon trine Pluto brings dramatic and yet very positive moods. Awhile later, Moon square Mercury may bring conflicts in communications, and this will be a good time to avoid becoming ensnared by challenging comments. The Leo Moon will go void-of-course for a couple of hours and, for awhile, it may be best to stay away from people's beastly sides until the moody morning passes over. Soon enough, the Moon enters Virgo, and today's activities will emphasize cleaning, organizing, and healthy foods.

Sun square Saturn (occurring November 24 – December 3) Sun in Sagittarius is square Saturn in Virgo. This occurrence of Sun square Saturn especially affects those Sagittarius people who are celebrating birthdays from November 24 – December 3. These folks are undergoing personal challenges of impatience, loss of control, and poor timing. The challenge is to overcome obstacles that intrude on one's discipline and accuracy. Often, false starts occur during the phase of life when Saturn squares the natal Sun. This may be a time of sacrifice, loss or compromise, and may also be a time of complexity and insecurity for these birthday folks. Saturn represents those things in life that we are willing to work for and maintain. Just because there's a challenge on the path does not mean it's time to give up. Saturn represents our sense of discipline and our application of effort and focus, and helps us learn about our limitations and where our strengths can be realized. This is a good time for Sagittarius birthday folks to conserve energies and take losses and difficulties in stride. Through the tests of this time a stronger human being emerges to take on future tests with greater confidence and ability. Running away from responsibilities or hardships now will only make life more difficult later. This aspect last occurred on May 9, when the Sun was in Taurus and Saturn was in Leo.

December 1st Saturday
LAST QUARTER MOON in VIRGO

	PST	EST
Moon conjunct Saturn	3:28 AM	6:28 AM
Mercury enters Sagittarius	4:22 AM	7:22 AM
Moon square Sun	4:45 AM	7:45 AM
Moon sextile Mars	7:53 AM	10:53 AM
Moon opposite Uranus	4:05 PM	7:05 PM
Sun square Uranus begins (see December 7)		

Mood Watch: The waning Moon is in the Mercury-ruled sign of Virgo; this brings tendencies to doubt, scrutinize, dispute, and analyze. Overnight, Moon conjunct Saturn brings a serious tone to our dreams. **Last Quarter Moon in Virgo** (Moon square Sun) gears our moods towards the need for pragmatic and realistic strategies to our approach to life. Virgo Moon disposes us to create protective defenses, which may cause skeptical, analytical, or even cynical interactions with others. Let the doubts and fears of your life be flushed away in order to achieve the benefits of health and wellbeing. Waning Virgo Moon emphasizes the need to dispel all doubts and to improve health matters that require some attention. This morning, Moon sextile Mars gives us the incentive to actively take on efforts to get organized, but act fast; this afternoon, Moon opposite Uranus brings wild and untamed moods, a good time to let loose. Sounds like a party.

Mercury enters Sagittarius (Mercury in Sagittarius: December 1 – 20) Mercury, the planet of communication, information, and news, will be traveling through the sign of Sagittarius. New perspectives are bound to come up. News is always more philosophical and visionary when Mercury is in this sign. Word travels fast and further than expected. Sagittarius is the challenging "detrimental" place for Mercury, and this is a time when Mercury's greatest weapon – words – are best communicated with carefully considered diplomacy. People will be increasingly curious to know what is happening in the world and to be more aware of global perspectives. Mercury in Sagittarius offers an opportunity to share your vision of a better world with others, and also brings adventure to the world of communications.

December 2nd Sunday

Moon in Virgo / Libra	PST	EST	
Venus sextile Jupiter	12:15 AM	3:15 AM	
Moon square Jupiter	2:52 PM	5:52 PM	
Moon square Pluto goes v/c	6:13 PM	9:13 PM	
Moon enters Libra	10:02 PM	1:02 AM	(December 3)
Mercury square Saturn begins (see December 6)			
Mars sextile Saturn begins (see December 8)			

Mood Watch: Moon square Jupiter brings restlessness over questions of fulfillment and happiness, or over the security of personal wealth and wellbeing. Moon square Pluto brings moods which may revolve around an intense awareness of the inevitable factors of life. Throughout the evening, the void-of-course Virgo Moon may bring a challenging time for carrying out special diets and avoiding temptations or addictions. All kinds of rationalizations will come into play. As the Moon enters Libra, our moods will settle into a much more conscientious sense of rationale; greater balance will come as North America takes its rest.

Venus sextile Jupiter (occurring November 27 – December 4) Venus is in Libra, its natural home, where harmony is emphasized in love relations. Jupiter is in Sagittarius, its natural home also, bringing a powerful sense of adventure and a joyful outreach to discover love's capabilities. A devotion to relationships (Venus in Libra) leads us to prosperous opportunities in philosophy, world travel, treasure hunting, extreme sports, and international business (Jupiter in Sagittarius.) It is here that love and beauty are potentially found in the experience of going beyond the limits. This is an excellent time to shower loved ones with gifts and compliments. This is the time to allow expansion to occur in love matters, and to take the next step towards enlivening and enhancing life. A greater opportunity for increasing skills or augmenting your livelihood is available, especially if your focus remains on doing what you love most. This aspect last occurred on January 12, when Venus was in Aquarius.

December 3rd Monday

Moon in Libra	PST	EST	
Moon sextile Mercury	4:17 AM	7:17 AM	
Venus sextile Pluto	2:35 PM	5:35 PM	
Moon square Mars	5:59 PM	8:59 PM	
Moon sextile Sun	9:25 PM	12:25 AM	(December 4)

Mood Watch: Moon in Libra focuses our attention on the need to make decisions, and to create some balance in our lives wherever it is needed, particularly with regard to our loved ones and friends. Moon sextile Mercury brings active minds and thoughtful early morning moods – a good time to think matters over, and to focus on solving complex puzzles. This evening, Moon square Mars challenges our strengths and it may be especially difficult to take initiative to do things. This is also a good time to beware of the potential for accidents to occur. Tonight, Moon sextile Sun brings hopeful moods. Some say, "Let it snow."

Venus sextile Pluto (occurring November 30 – December 5) Venus is in Libra focusing on the need for harmony, and for the empowerment of friendship and balance in love matters. There was a time when Pluto, the god of the underworld, seized Persephone who was a symbol of youth, fertility and Venusian beauty. Many have viewed this myth as a power play on the part of the underworld king. Others view it as the well understood destiny of Beauty and the Beast. Venus sextile Pluto may bring exceptional breakthroughs in relationships. Sometimes the death of a power figure occurs, and the love of that figure is empowered by the impact of their fate. This may be the place where we discover the true power of love. Sometimes this aspect helps us to recognize the devotion of our loved ones, to see the acceptance of the difficulty and hardship that comes with their devotion. This is a good time to recognize and acknowledge the efforts of loved ones. Through this, greater devotion will shine. This aspect may allow someone to find true love by virtue of some unexpected twist of fate. It is here that the beauty and the beast surprise us when, through some form of trial or sacrifice, harmony and strength in love can be found. This aspect last occurred on January 26, when Venus was in Aquarius.

December 4th Tuesday

Moon in Libra

	PST	EST
Moon trine Neptune	1:24 PM	4:24 PM

Mood Watch: The waning Libra Moon focuses our energies on the need to make important decisions that will affect the course of this month. However, big astrological changes are gearing up *(Jupiter conjunct Pluto - Dec. 11 and Jupiter enters Capricorn on Dec. 18)* so it might be best to make decisions that will allow for some flexibility in our plans. This is the time to let emotional pressure be released, and to handle situations with friends and loved ones carefully and congenially. Big economic shifts will undoubtedly affect our social endeavors this month. Today however, our moods will seem mostly carefree, as Moon trine Neptune will assist to keep us calm. For the most part, the overall mood of the day will be blessed with passive resignation.

December 5th Wednesday

Hanukkah

Moon in Libra / Scorpio

	PST	EST
Moon sextile Jupiter	4:23 AM	7:23 AM
Venus enters Scorpio	5:30 AM	8:30 AM
Moon sextile Pluto goes v/c	6:49 AM	9:49 AM
Moon enters Scorpio	10:32 AM	1:32 PM
Moon conjunct Venus	11:05 AM	2:05 PM

Mood Watch: Moon sextile Jupiter brings the potential for joyous early morning moods, as the Libra Moon guides us to make adjustments and to be more tolerant than usual with our friends and loved ones. A little later in the morning, the Moon is sextile to Pluto and then it goes void-of-course for a few hours; decisions may seem impossible to make, and it may be wisest to hold off on making them, or even discussing them at any length, until the Moon enters Scorpio. Not long after the Moon does enter Scorpio, Moon conjunct Venus will bring deeply affectionate and sometimes very intense loving moods. Waning Scorpio Moon reminds us of the need to preserve and empower our energy, our emotional wellbeing, and our stamina.

Venus enters Scorpio (Venus in Scorpio: December 5 – 30) The planet Venus, which influences matters of love, beauty, art, and attraction, now moves through Scorpio, bringing out deep and passionate levels of love's expression. While Venus is in Scorpio, we may feel preoccupied with birth, sex, death and rebirth, and transformation. Magnetism runs strong with Venus in Scorpio, and love affairs are often torrid and well hidden. Sometimes the dark side of our love and our hidden fears surface while Venus is in Scorpio; this forces us to come clean about these feelings, and to take strong measures to ensure the power of our love. Venus is in detriment in the sign of Scorpio. This may be a time to work out anxiety, fear, mourning, and emotional stress relating to love. Sex is a common outlet under this type of stress. Love with passion is an empowering thing, but it is wise to ensure the experience does not hinder the wellbeing of those who are close to you. The intensity of Scorpio love can sometimes overwhelm loved ones. Love shines best when it is mutually expressed.

December 6ᵗʰ Thursday

Moon in Scorpio	PST	EST
Moon sextile Saturn	3:35 AM	6:35 AM
Moon trine Mars	5:20 AM	8:20 AM
Mercury square Saturn	1:17 PM	4:17 PM
Moon trine Uranus	4:37 PM	7:37 PM
Mercury square Uranus begins (see December 10)		
Sun conjunct Mercury begins (see December 17)		

Mood Watch: Moon sextile Saturn brings serious intent to our dreams and our early morning attitudes. A spirit of determination leads us actively into the morning, particularly while Moon trine Mars brings positive and energetic moods. The waning Scorpio Moon brings out our survival instincts, and tunes us into the perceptivity necessary to move through intense situations and emotional concerns. Later, Moon trine Uranus brings the excitement of positive, brilliant, and innovative moods. For some, the shaking loose of emotional turmoil can be very liberating.

Mercury square Saturn (occurring December 2 – 8) Mercury in Sagittarius is square Saturn in Virgo. This may be a difficult time to acquire or to communicate travel information accurately for timely efficiency during travels. It may be a challenging time to communicate instructions or to inform someone of the end of something. It may also be challenging to sell someone on a product, or to successfully request a raise or promotion. Whatever the desired effect may be, it is wise to use caution when attempting communications during Mercury square Saturn. Saturn is in Virgo creating limitations and structural changes in matters of accounting and with regard to health related concerns and limitations. This aspect makes it difficult to put a message out there and be taken seriously. Some people may become very tongue tied and feel quite off track. This aspect last occurred on May 5, when Mercury was in Taurus and Saturn was in Leo.

December 7th Friday

Moon in Scorpio / Sagittarius

	PST	EST	
Sun square Uranus	12:35 AM	3:35 AM	
Moon square Neptune goes v/c	2:18 AM	5:18 AM	
Moon enters Sagittarius	11:12 PM	2:12 AM	(December 8)
Venus trine Mars begins (see December 11)			
Sun sextile Neptune begins (see December 11)			

Mood Watch: The Moon wanes in Scorpio during the days of Sagittarius, the shortest days of the year. Courageous, dynamic, and mysterious emotions urge us to move through this dark and often intense time. Moon square Neptune may bring spiritually disruptive dreams as the Moon goes void-of-course. Today will be a day to apply caution to everything we do. Beware of the potential for theft and crime, and for basic dangers or precarious situations. The dramas of the void-of-course Scorpio Moon may bring the need to seek shelter and protection, and to ride out the emotional storms in the best way possible. Much later, as the Moon enters Sagittarius, visionary wonder captures our moods. Half of the commonly observed planets out there are now occupying Sagittarius; this brings a very philosophical time of vision and exploration.

Sun square Uranus (occurring December 1 – 10) This occurrence of Sun square Uranus particularly affects those Sagittarius people celebrating birthdays December 1 - 10. The square of Uranus to these Sagittarius folks' natal Sun brings about challenging events and a strong dose of unrestrained chaos. This may be the year for you Sagittarius birthday folks to surrender to those aspects of life that are truly out of your control, and to concentrate more rationally on those facets of life over which you do have control. Sometimes the aftermath of Uranus influence is an improvement, but with the square aspect at work, it is likely that these people will feel personally challenged. It is important to understand that some kinds of personal challenges are best left alone, while others must be confronted directly without causing destructive damage, particularly to the self. On the other hand, birthday Sagittarius folks, if your life has no foundation, there is no point in holding on to the illusion of stability at this juncture of your sojourn. This aspect will pass, and it is vital not to give this rapid change too much resistance, lest you be bound to the reversals of trying to fight chaos with logic at a time when resistance is futile. Matters will settle down in due time; try to be detached from chaotic events as they occur, and the outcome will seem less costly. If you need it, project the picture of peace and it will be there for you at the other end. This aspect last occurred on June 9, when the Sun was in Gemini.

December 8th Saturday

Moon in Sagittarius

	PST	EST	
Moon square Saturn	4:10 PM	7:10 PM	
Mars sextile Saturn	8:00 PM	11:00 PM	
Moon conjunct Mercury	11:41 PM	2:41 AM	(December 9)

Mood Watch: In the days of Sagittarius, during the darkest time of the balsamic Sagittarian Moon, we go through deep reflection. Like the mythic Sagittarian symbol, the Centaur – we watch, we ponder, we intuit and foresee – and when instinct calls we act swiftly. In early evening, Moon square Saturn may be a difficult time to effectively concentrate on work related chores and duties, and people may tend to take their responsibilities too seriously, or not seriously enough. Later tonight, Moon conjunct Mercury brings a pensive time, and our moods will be clearly succinct and quite in tune with the course of our thinking.

Mars sextile Saturn (occurring December 2 – 19) The retrograde Mars in Cancer is sextile Saturn in Virgo. This is an active time for establishing cleanliness in the home. While Mars is currently retrograde in Cancer, there may be quite a bit of internal turmoil occurring with regard to domestic matters. During this aspect, actions create opportunities, provided there is an application of discipline and timing. For the second time this year since October 8, Mars sextile Saturn brings opportunities for perfect timing to occur. This is a good time to remain optimistic and not to let fear or worry rule the conditions of our lives.

December 9th Sunday
NEW MOON in SAGITTARIUS PST   EST

	PST	EST
Moon square Uranus	4:56 AM	7:56 AM
Moon conjunct Sun	9:42 AM	12:42 PM
Moon sextile Neptune	2:29 PM	5:29 PM
Venus sextile Saturn begins (see December 12)		

Mood Watch: Early this morning, Moon square Uranus shakes up our moods with radical energies and disruptive chaos. **New Moon in Sagittarius** (Moon conjunct Sun) inspires us to look at life in a whole new way. An optimistic outlook is strong. New Moon in Sagittarius encourages us to start new exercise programs, look into new philosophies, and to explore new territory in our lives. Sagittarius says, "I see," so vision and insight are the primary incentives to exploring new ground. Today is a good day to look ahead optimistically and to get in touch with a new vision for the new season ahead. Later today, Moon sextile Neptune brings spiritual gaiety and artful expressions to our moods.

December 10th Monday
Moon in Sagittarius / Capricorn PST   EST

	PST	EST
Moon conjunct Jupiter	7:10 AM	10:10 AM
Moon conjunct Pluto goes v/c	7:37 AM	10:37 AM
Moon enters Capricorn	10:52 AM	1:52 PM
Mercury square Uranus	4:26 PM	7:26 PM

Mood Watch: For another dozen years or so, this morning is the last time Jupiter will be conjunct with the Moon in Sagittarius. As this occurs, it may be likened to the launching of a rocket into space; our hearts and dreams will be filled with excitement and adventure. This morning, Moon conjunct Pluto occurs just as the Moon goes void-of-course. For a few hours through the early part of the day, our moods may seem to be transformed into moods that are spacey, misdirected, restless, or lost – but it is also a good time to reflect on the spirit of our visions and the upraising of our morale. As the Moon enters Capricorn, industrious moods set us on a firm path to accomplish some work.

Mercury square Uranus (occurring December 6 – 12) Mercury in Sagittarius is square to Uranus in Pisces. This creates explosive mental states and causes some people to speak abrasively or to promote overly radical ideas. Tact and diplomacy are likely to go right out the door when religion is discussed. Communications and philosophical debates may come up against unusual or explosive viewpoints. Spiritual harmony is always best achieved when we exercise discretion. This really is a time to watch what you say: communications have the potential to shake matters up considerably. Mercury square Uranus last occurred on May 20, when Mercury was in Gemini.

December 11th Tuesday

Moon in Capricorn	PST	EST
Moon sextile Venus	12:09 AM	3:09 AM
Moon opposite Mars	1:59 AM	4:59 AM
Moon trine Saturn	3:31 AM	6:31 AM
Jupiter conjunct Pluto	11:37 AM	2:37 PM
Venus trine Mars	3:17 PM	6:17 PM
Moon sextile Uranus goes v/c	3:58 PM	6:58 PM
Sun sextile Neptune	7:49 PM	10:49 PM
Mercury sextile Neptune begins (see December 13)		

Mood Watch: Overnight, Moon sextile Venus brings the potential for pleasant dreams and moods. This is eventually superseded by the energy of Moon opposite Mars, which often brings bloody battles to the forefront of our dream world. Moon trine Saturn brings a sense of purpose and optimistic willpower to our dreams. Early morning risers will be clear and focused. The newly waxing Capricorn Moon brings serious and determined moods. Later on, Moon sextile Uranus shakes up our moods with ambition, and unusual ideas may lead to crazy mischief, especially as the Moon goes void-of-course. Throughout the evening, a void-of-course Capricorn Moon brings dull, lazy, and sometimes unsympathetic moods. The best medicine for tonight's thankless and fruitless labors could be pure and simple humor – but beware of overly serious tendencies. Jupiter conjunct Pluto is a turning point for us (see below).

Jupiter conjunct Pluto (occurring November 9 – December 27) Jupiter represents expansion, prosperity, social advancement, opportunities towards growth, to name a few, while Pluto represents transformation, power, fate, and is represented as the underworld god; Hades, in the Greek mythology. This conjunction of these two highly influential planets will affect absolutely everyone, and it is likely to bring an economic shift that for some may seem especially alarming, as the course of great economic change will be inevitable. For some folks, this dynamic shift will be the beginning of a whole new economic transformation. Strong power plays are at work on the international market at this time. This conjunction will bring unforgettable dealings in large corporations and many people may be consciously choosing to override the economic mistakes of the previous generations by radically investing in futuristic markets. At first, it may seem as if we've all been sold on a future vision, but hidden behind the scenes there is a strong incentive for big profiteers to stay ahead of international markets. The age of the corporate take over will come fast and furiously as many reluctant spectators will suddenly find themselves quickly jumping on the bandwagon of new enterprises.

Sagittarius opens us up to the big picture and large scale markets are now on the brink of making large scale conversions in their manufacturing efforts. These big economic changes will affect a great deal of the world's economy. There are likely to be struggles regarding inheritances, or with the expiry of long term patents. Jupiter and Pluto are at the 28 degree mark in Sagittarius, which means that they are conjunct in Sagittarius at the Sagittarius/Capricorn cusp. This brings a dynamic schism to this very politically dominated wheel of economic change. The shift from Sagittarius to Capricorn takes us from the fiery and creative world of visionary exploration, to the earthy and domineering demands of corporate industry. Underneath, this near Capricorn conjunction demands a down-to-earth commitment to make our economic dreams a hard core reality. There are bound to be sacrifices made, as a more resourceful and dominant set of focuses will be the gist of how the pending (December 18,) Jupiter-in-Capricorn economy will work. Avoid heavy gambling, risky expenditures, and expect a few rounds of difficult transformation with regard to economics over this amazing period of the Jupiter – Pluto conjunction.

Venus trine Mars (occurring December 7 – 13) Venus in Scorpio is trine to retrograde Mars in Cancer. Dramatic, passionate, and bold expressions of affection will bring very strong feelings between loved ones. Venus trine Mars brings love in action. When Venus and Mars are well harmonized by this ideal aspect, there is a greater opportunity for peace and healing in relationships, and often gifts are exchanged. These are gifts which help people to understand how masculine and feminine expressions are harmonized. It starts with the effort to make things better, concentrating on the positive, not the negative, and continues with the persistence to bring out the best in your partner – no matter how stubborn at first (s)he may seem. Harmony is possible despite the emotionally pressuring forcefulness of current activities with Mars retrograde in Cancer. Proceed with care.

Sun sextile Neptune (occurring December 7 – 13) This occurrence of Sun sextile Neptune creates a very opportunistic time for Sagittarius people celebrating their birthdays December 7 – 13. These Sagittarius folks are experiencing an opportunity for an awakening in the realm of spirituality and creativity. There is an awareness of the self that goes deep here, and these birthday people are likely to be spacey and difficult to reach while this phenomenon of great depth is occurring. It may be a time for these birthday folks to get away from it all and find a sanctuary in which to meditate and open up to some valuable answers with regard to age old questions. These folks will have an opportunity to better understand the work of their path, but this is probably only true if they act on their own intuitive sensibilities without the influences of others. This will be your year (Sagittarius birthday people) to enhance and strengthen your intuition and primal instincts while they are easily available. This aspect last occurred on April 11 when the Sun was in Aries.

December 12th Wednesday

Moon in Capricorn / Aquarius

	PST	EST	
Venus sextile Saturn	11:34 AM	2:34 PM	
Moon enters Aquarius	9:02 PM	12:02 AM	(December 13)
Venus trine Uranus begins (see December 17)			

Mood Watch: The void-of-course Moon in Capricorn brings strong determined moods daunted by slow progress, mounting work tasks, and labor intensive setbacks. This may well try our patience and our strength. The youthfully waxing Capricorn Moon encourages us to simplify our moods by grounding out our energies and staying focused. This might be difficult to accomplish as this long void-of-course Moon day may be responsible for bringing delays, forgetfulness, and apathetic moods. Void-of-course Capricorn Moon may bring such things as obstacles, weather setbacks, confusion, laziness, and insensitive moods. Much later tonight, Moon in Aquarius picks up our moods with greater clarity, while there is an emphasis on knowledgeable, informative, and innovative thinking.

Venus sextile Saturn (occurring December 9 – 14) Venus is in Scorpio sextile to Saturn in Virgo. Venus in Scorpio invites an attraction to sharing secrets, daring love play, and passionate encounters. Venus sextile Saturn brings the opportunity for us to gain some control of our love relationships, and to better understand our boundaries and limitations. Saturn is newly in the sign of Virgo (since September 2) bringing a prudent and meticulously planned approach to applying disciplines and setting limits. It is through this aspect that love relationships are given an opportunity for stronger levels of commitment and responsibility. This is the time to protect loved ones with guidance, and to teach them about discipline. Perfect timing brings pleasure. Venus sextile Saturn teaches us how to hold on to and maintain the things we love – those places, people, and things that matter to us. True love has a binding and lasting affect, and this aspect often shows us the ways in which love stands the test of time. This aspect last occurred on April 27, when Venus was in Gemini and Saturn was in Leo.

December 13ᵗʰ Thursday

Moon in Aquarius	PST	EST
Moon square Venus	3:53 PM	6:53 PM
Mercury sextile Neptune	7:03 PM	10:03 PM

Mood Watch: Aquarius Moon breathes new hope into the holiday efforts to bring goodwill to humankind. The spirit of the season picks up as the newly waxing Aquarius Moon opens our minds and brings a progressive awareness to our attitudes. Sun in Sagittarius and waxing Moon in Aquarius generally bring insightful, brilliant, and inspired incentives and moods. Later in the day, Moon square Venus is bound to bring a few challenging spats between loved ones, and this may be a good time to avoid making idealistic promises that could possibly go unfulfilled.

Mercury sextile Neptune (occurring December 11 – 15) Mercury in Sagittarius sextile Neptune in Aquarius reassures us that communicating our philosophies and our beliefs also empowers our belief in humanity. This is an opportunistic time to cautiously attempt communication with regard to beliefs and spiritual matters. Mercury is in Sagittarius placing a philosophical emphasis of talk on such Neptune-related subjects as spiritual growth, guidance, and inspiration. Take this opportunity to transmute thoughts and beliefs into a workable understanding and to share it with others in a way that encourages them. Prayers, channeling, and spells are all very effective with Mercury sextile Neptune. This is the time to get the word out to Great Spirit, and to reinforce a sense of faith. This aspect last occurred on April 22, when Mercury was in Aries.

December 14ᵗʰ Friday

Moon in Aquarius	PST	EST
Moon conjunct Neptune	10:23 AM	1:23 PM
Moon sextile Mercury	12:29 PM	3:29 PM
Moon sextile Sun	3:37 PM	6:37 PM
Sun conjunct Pluto begins (see December 20)		

Mood Watch: Progressive, open-minded, and truthful attitudes will keep us inspired as the Moon waxes in Aquarius. Moon conjunct Neptune brings peace, tranquility and artistry to our midday moods. This afternoon, Moon sextile Mercury brings the potential for some intelligent brainstorming between people, and this will be a very good time to run your ideas by others. Moon sextile Sun brings congenial late autumn moods and interactions. Aquarius Moon awakens our understanding of the human condition. Today's activities will be blessed as we apply our knowledge, tolerance, patience, and ingenuity to each situation.

December 15ᵗʰ Saturday

Moon in Aquarius / Pisces	PST	EST
Moon sextile Pluto	2:34 AM	5:34 AM
Moon sextile Jupiter goes v/c	3:52 AM	6:52 AM
Moon enters Pisces	5:16 AM	8:16 AM
Moon trine Mars	4:19 PM	7:19 PM
Moon opposite Saturn	8:51 PM	11:51 PM
Mercury conjunct Pluto begins (see December 19)		
Sun conjunct Jupiter begins (see December 22)		

Mood Watch: Overnight, Moon sextile Pluto brings powerfully cryptic dreams, while Moon sextile Jupiter adds joy, light and color to the flavor of those dynamic dreams. The Moon in Aquarius goes void-of-course for awhile but, before most North Americans are fully awake, the waxing Moon enters Pisces. The waxing Moon in Pisces brings strong psychic inclinations among people. Pisces anatomically is represented by the feet, and symbolically represents what we stand for, or believe in, since Pisces says: "I Believe." The final days of autumn often focus on religious holidays and on spiritual beliefs and practices. Many of us may find ourselves drawn that way today. Moon trine Mars brings positive masculine energy to the course of our affairs, and the early evening will be a time of busily active movers and shakers. Later this evening, Moon opposite Saturn impresses our moods with the need to get a handle on those areas of life that have become unruly. As a result, many folks will choose to work late on the various projects that have been calling out to them.

December 16ᵗʰ Sunday

Moon in Pisces	PST	EST
Moon trine Venus	4:44 AM	7:44 AM
Moon conjunct Uranus	8:25 AM	11:25 AM
Mercury conjunct Jupiter begins (see December 20)		

Mood Watch: Early this morning, Moon trine Venus brings very pleasant and loving moods. The Moon conjunct Uranus brings a focus on unconventional or unusual beliefs erupting in our midst. Uranus is a strong and dynamic force that has been in Pisces since March, 2003 and will remain there until March, 2011. A great shake up in our belief structures will radically change what we stand for. The waxing Pisces Moon encourages us to find a calming spiritual path that will help us to strengthen our beliefs and to find peace within.

December 17ᵗʰ Monday
Moon in Pisces / Aries - FIRST QUARTER MOON in PISCES

	PST	EST	
Moon square Mercury	2:04 AM	5:04 AM	
Moon square Sun	2:19 AM	5:19 AM	
Sun conjunct Mercury	7:28 AM	10:28 AM	
Moon square Pluto	8:29 AM	11:29 AM	
Moon square Jupiter goes v/c	10:28 AM	1:28 PM	
Moon enters Aries	10:54 AM	1:54 PM	
Moon square Mars	7:57 PM	10:57 PM	
Venus trine Uranus	10:44 PM	1:44 AM	(December 18)
Venus square Neptune begins (see December 22)			

Mood Watch: Overnight, Moon square Mercury adds nervousness to the course of our dreams. **First Quarter Moon in Pisces** (Moon square Sun) brings a dreamy sort of consciousness that often leads to strong psychic awareness. While the first quarter Moon is in Pisces, music, art, and poetry will fill us with inspiration, intuition, and hope. This morning, Moon square Pluto brings dramatic types of trouble to the underlying spirit of our moods. A couple of hours later, Moon square Jupiter will bring withdrawn moods as the Pisces Moon goes void-of-course. It isn't long before the Moon enters Aries, and a new cycle of feelings and moods will begin to emerge. Aries Moon brings courageous and sometimes impulsive expressions of mood. Tonight, Moon square Mars may bring irritable, conflicting moods; this would be a good time to beware of fights.

Sun conjunct Mercury (occurring December 6 – 22) This is a very common aspect, which will create a much more thoughtful, communicative, and expressive year ahead for those Sagittarius and early Capricorn born people celebrating birthdays December 6 – 22. This is your time (birthday Sagittarians and cusp born Capricorns) to record ideas, relay important messages, and pay close attention to your imaginative thoughts as they are touched by Mercury, creating the urge to speak and be heard. Your thoughts will reveal a great deal about who you are, now and in the year to come.

Venus trine Uranus (occurring December 12 – 20) Venus in Scorpio is trine Uranus in Pisces. Passionate love and attraction will allow people to make breakthroughs in relationships and in artistic disciplines. Venus trine Uranus brings a favorable attraction to revolutionary concepts. Harmony can exist in love related matters even while chaotic occurrences are taking place. This is a time of freedom fighters, rebel love, and attraction to the unusual. Youth is attracted to and more highly susceptible to rebellion during this aspect. Dangerous love and taking chances become common occurrences. Love at first sight is explosive at this time, but not necessarily long lasting. This aspect last occurred on May 24, when Venus was in Cancer.

235

December 18th Tuesday

Moon in Aries

	PST	EST
Jupiter enters Capricorn	12:13 PM	3:13 PM
Moon sextile Neptune	8:51 PM	11:51 PM

Mood Watch: Waxing Moon in Aries activates our moods with ambitious gusto. The momentum and positive force of the energy around us picks up greatly as the final days of Sagittarius occur. Sun in Sagittarius and Moon in Aries bring creative zeal and enthusiasm to the ways in which we express ourselves. Tonight, Moon sextile Neptune brings the opportunity for us to ease some of our feelings; it's a good time to seek relaxation and enjoy spiritual practices and meditation.

Jupiter enters Capricorn (Jupiter in Capricorn: December 18, 2007 – January 5, 2009) An industrial era of economic advancement and prosperity begins today with the planet of luck and fortune, Jupiter, newly entering the constellation Capricorn. Since November 23, 2006, Jupiter has been traveling through the sign it rules, Sagittarius, focusing the magic of great wealth and expense on such Sagittarius-like things as world travel, international trade treaties, space exploration, philosophy, extreme sports, treasure hunting, and colonization. Jupiter in Sagittarius has brought adventurous enthusiasm to world affairs and in international business endeavors. This has been a time of new discoveries and, for some, new ways of making a profit or of going out on a limb, so to speak. Sagittarius says: "I see," and it is through our visions and our ability to look to the future in unprecedented ways that a sense of advancement is achieved.

Out of the insights, produced over the past year of Jupiter in Sagittarius, comes the use and construction of those visions which have been formulated, as Jupiter now passes from Sagittarius ("I See") to Capricorn ("I Use").

Jupiter in Capricorn is likely to bring high demands on such Capricorn-like focuses as construction, building, banking, corporate growth, architectural feats, estate management, and administrative expertise. Jupiter's influence brings enthusiasm, stimulates economy and focuses on prosperity. Jupiter's prosperity may be experienced through the hardworking drive of Capricorn with an emphasis on massive material production, and this often results in the necessity to find and create competent caretakers and management strategies. The key to success with Jupiter in Capricorn comes with the proper management of goods and services.

Capricorn is conservative by nature, and requires the flow of prosperity to be useful, attainable, applicable, substantive, and controllable. The wise or conservative investment is one that will stand the test of time, and since Capricorn is ruled by Saturn – the timekeeper – the joy found in Jupiter's prosperous returns through the sign of Capricorn must have a time-honored quality of value and must represent a milestone achievement. The old Capricorn adage, "I use," implies that favors will be hard won, wages will be compromised, and bargains won't come cheap. The demands and expectations of Capricorns are often high, and their stealth propensity to achieve material growth through unrelenting persistence gives this sign its not-so-jovial reputation of being cold, calculating, profiteering and exclusive. Despite the downside of this corporate attitude, efficient and well organized frontiers of economic growth are bound to persist in this pending year of Jupiter in Capricorn. Economic shifts are likely to have some weight to them, and this would be an especially useful year to take note of exactly who is prospering – and why. Jupiter expansively provides, while Saturn divides, manages, and controls. Jupiter gloats over wealth, skill, and abundance; Saturn guards, protects, owns up to, and is responsible for all those things which are attained. Jupiter's social appeal represents prosperous growth, valuable talents, fascination, joy, joviality, and the spreading of happiness. When Jupiter traverses through the Saturn-ruled domain of Capricorn, the act of prospering is taken very seriously, planned methodically, presented convincingly, and packaged commercially. Here, there are no hidden mysteries to the ways and means of attainment, and it is usually measured through the cardinal earth sign's mastery of the earth plane – through material substance and valued possessions, as opposed to the unpredictable risks of unbridled talents and highly prized creative skills.

It is the Capricorn people who will be able to enjoy some abundant opportunities and joyous personal experiences while Jupiter crosses over their natal Sun throughout the year to come. They will also have a strong influence on the wave of the economic future. The other earth signs of the zodiac, Taurus and Virgo, will enjoy the fruits of Jupiter being trine to their natal Sun signs in the next year. This will bring the potential for travel or financial boons of some kind for Taurus and Virgo people. Cancer folks would be wise to use their sensibilities and take precautions with their expenditures while Jupiter opposes their natal Sun over the next year. They may also find that the effort to handle massive volumes of business, or a large inheritance, may be overwhelming at times in the next year. Aries and Libra people may discover that it will be especially difficult to keep up with expenses and opportunities in their lives while Jupiter squares to their natal Sun signs. They would be wise to proceed cautiously in business. Scorpio and Pisces people's natal Sun signs will be in the sextile position to Jupiter this year, and this will bring the potential for business or career opportunities in those areas of life where these people have already been working hard, or where they have made some genuine effort to succeed over time.

On December 11, Jupiter reached an exact conjunction with the power-monger, Pluto, bringing some seriously disruptive changes to our economic powers and our overall perception of what it means to maintain and experience wealth and opportunity. This is a time of great change, as the slow moving planet Pluto will also be entering Capricorn in January 2008. This time of Pluto conjunct Jupiter at the Sagittarius/Capricorn cusp will give strong clues about the evolution of our ideas of prosperity and it will be one of the eye opening trendsetters of our economic future for the next decade or so to come.

December 19th Wednesday

Moon in Aries / Taurus	PST	EST
Saturn goes retrograde	6:10 AM	9:10 AM
Moon trine Sun	9:24 AM	12:24 PM
Mercury conjunct Pluto	10:51 AM	1:51 PM
Moon trine Pluto	11:29 AM	2:29 PM
Moon trine Mercury goes v/c	11:34 AM	2:34 PM
Moon enters Taurus	1:39 PM	4:39 PM
Moon trine Jupiter	2:04 PM	5:04 PM
Moon sextile Mars	8:57 PM	11:57 PM

Mercury opposite Mars begins (see December 22)

Mood Watch: This morning's waxing Moon in Aries continues to bring vibrant, energetic, outgoing, and sometimes pushy moods and attitudes. The Aries Moon also brings confident, bold and courageous moods, creating an atmosphere conducive to getting a great number of things done during the morning. Moon trine Sun brings a positive outlook on life. Moon trine Pluto will be an excellent time to work on making therapeutic breakthroughs. Moon trine Mercury also brings an excellent time communicate with others. Then, by midday, the Moon goes void-of-course for a couple of hours, and people will seem preoccupied with their own needs. There may also be a tendency for folks to seem selfish or less patient. Soon enough however, the Moon enters Taurus. Today's Taurus Moon reminds us to get a handle on the practical side of our existence. This often requires tackling financial matters or taking charge of material tasks that have built up since the week began. Those who have already handled these things can take the time to bask in the pleasures of their hard earned fruits. Moon trine Jupiter harmonizes our moods with joyous adventure. The waxing Taurus Moon draws our attention to down-to-earth pleasures and comforts. Later, Moon sextile Mars gives us a final boost of energy, and this will be a good time to finish up late night projects.

Saturn goes retrograde (Saturn retrograde: December 19, 2007 – May 2, 2008) Saturn represents discipline, responsibility, and the tenacity required to get the job done. Sacrifices may be necessary in order to complete important projects, and discipline and perseverance are essential. While Saturn is retrograde in Virgo, staying on top of health matters as well as accounting and bookkeeping will be big priorities. For some folks, this will be a time of completion, of ending the treadmill of old cycles, and of learning to let others take responsibility for themselves. During this time there will be a lot of work to do, retracing steps in the areas of life that need restructuring. When Saturn is retrograde, it is difficult to begin new endeavors that require structure and the investment of time or commitment. We may be haunted by incomplete projects, and unsolved problems of the past could dominate the stage. Being careful of what we commit to at this time may prevent the need to drop other unfulfilled commitments midstream. If we haven't already dropped a few responsibilities, we may have to do so soon. Learn how to delegate your tasks fairly to those who can handle them. Keep a steady check on quality control while Saturn is retrograde.

Mercury conjunct Pluto (occurring December 15 – 21) Mercury conjunct Pluto raises issues of power. The areas of our lives that have required challenge, struggle, sacrifice and transformation now bring us to a place where we can talk about them. This is a time when people instinctively know their own fate, and the course they must travel in the year to come. Mercury conjunct Pluto in Sagittarius allows us to voice our hardships, and to contemplate and philosophize about the powerful occurrences that challenge and change our lives. There will be a great deal of intensity in our conversations at this time, especially with regard to the fate of the world and our ongoing efforts to end hardship and suffering.

December 20th Thursday

Moon in Taurus	PST	EST	
Moon trine Saturn	3:42 AM	6:42 AM	
Mercury enters Capricorn	6:44 AM	9:44 AM	
Mercury conjunct Jupiter	1:55 PM	4:55 PM	
Moon sextile Uranus	2:15 PM	5:15 PM	
Sun conjunct Pluto	4:18 PM	7:18 PM	
Moon opposite Venus	7:42 PM	10:42 PM	
Moon square Neptune goes v/c	10:07 PM	1:07 AM	(December 21)
Sun opposite Mars begins (see December 24)			

Mood Watch: Overnight, Moon trine Saturn brings Superman-type dreams that remind us we can do anything, as long as we are determined enough. Today's strongly waxing Taurus Moon brings inspiration to create aesthetically pleasing surroundings; hence, this is an excellent time to get into holiday decorating and to treasure hunt for gifts. The Moon is exalted in the sign of Taurus, impressing upon us the need to get a handle on the physical world. This afternoon, Moon sextile Uranus brings free-spirited and liberating attitudes and moods. This evening, Moon opposite Venus will draw relationships and love related situations into focus, and it may be especially difficult to try to please everyone, especially our loved ones. Later tonight, Moon square Neptune brings spiritual challenges, and the Taurus Moon also goes void-of-course, bringing lazy and stubborn late evening moods.

Mercury enters Capricorn (Mercury in Capricorn: Dec. 20, 2007 – Jan. 8, 2008) While Mercury travels through Capricorn, communications tend to be more serious and to the point, although not necessarily less complex. In negotiations, there is an emphasis on enterprise. Mercury affects our role as negotiators, and while this versatile planet goes through Capricorn, our realms of communications have a determined and persistent quality of expression, like a demanding voice waiting to be heard and received with hospitality. This fits with the solar days of Capricorn, when the harsh realities of winter demand clarity of purpose in our communications. Communication is one of the tools of survival, and this is an important time to use those skills wisely and sensibly. Mercury in Capricorn also focuses talk on issues such as commercial and corporate progress, market control, the attainment of goods and resources, and the necessity for discipline.

Mercury conjunct Jupiter (occurring December 16 – 22) Mercury and Jupiter are conjunct at the zero degree mark of Capricorn. News and discussions (Mercury) revolve around our joys, our prosperity, and our wealth (Jupiter) – particularly with regard to fulfilling our desires and abiding by our deep passions in life. This aspect creates expansive talk which spreads quickly with news about the economic state of affairs. Thoughts and information (Mercury) with regard to a prosperous and visionary breakthrough (Jupiter) will be highlighted. This may be the time to share our thoughts and our visions with others. It's a great time to boost the moral of others by complimenting them on their skills. This could be a prosperous aspect for communicating the need for a job or financial loan. Late born Sagittarians and early born Capricorns having birthdays at this time are about to be showered with a wealth of information and opportunities which are worthy of their time and effort.

Sun conjunct Pluto (occurring December 14 – 23) For the last time in our lifetime, the Sun is conjunct with Pluto in the sign of Sagittarius, as next year's exact conjunct of the Sun with Pluto takes place at the Capricorn cusp. Pluto, a.k.a. God of the Underworld, is on the brink of entry into the Saturn ruled sign, entering Capricorn late next month. While it is retrograde next year, Pluto will re-enter the late degrees of Sagittarius in mid-June, 2008. Pluto will remain in Sagittarius for a final salute until late November, 2008 when it enters Capricorn and takes a firm stand there until March 2023. Pluto represents transformation, in particular, those ways in which the generations of humankind affect change and make their mark. Pluto in Sagittarius (1995 – 2008) has been the eye opener of global awareness. This occurrence of Sun conjunct Pluto strongly affects Sagittarians and cusp born Capricorns – most specifically, those who are celebrating birthdays December 14 – 23. These Sagittarius/Capricorn birthday folks will experience challenges of mind-altering proportions. Sun conjunct Pluto affects the core of the personality and diminishes those parts of the self which are weak and no longer viable. Pluto's energy melds with the personality to bring out the strongest points of one's character, the very best that one can muster. Pluto removes all impurities by transforming the old self through unpredictable trials. Take this opportunity to make some personal breakthroughs, birthday folks, and find your power! Learn to harness your power willingly and responsibly while great transformation is occurring in your life. Give in but don't give up.

CAPRICORN

Key Phrase: " I USE "
Cardinal Earth Sign
Symbol: The Goat
December 21st, 2007 through
January 20th, 2008

December 21st Friday

Winter Solstice
Moon in Taurus / Gemini

	PST	EST	
Moon enters Gemini	2:15 PM	5:15 PM	
Sun enters Capricorn	10:09 PM	1:09 AM	(December 22)
Mars opposite Jupiter begins (see December 26)			

Mood Watch: This morning we awaken to a void-of-course Taurus Moon. Stubborn attitudes and tenacious efforts will force a great deal of work out of us, but since the Moon is void-of-course, it is likely that our work will be done in haste, and some of it will probably have to be done all over again. By the time the Moon enters Gemini, our moods will enter into a much more thoughtful and communicative state of being. There isn't anything we haven't accomplished today that can't be successfully discussed and talked over this evening. Gemini Moon reminds us that communications and the relaying of our thoughts is often beneficial to our peace of mind.

Sun enters Capricorn (Sun in Capricorn: December 21, 2007 – January 20, 2008) Spark up the lights – it's **Winter Solstice**! Today the Sun King returns from the ashes of the longest night. This is the time of Saturn-ruled Capricorn. Sun in Capricorn is the time to step into success. Jack Frost is nipping at our heels, but the Sun King returns! The lengthening days of the Sun are finally here and a new season and cycle begins.

The symbol of Capricorn is the mountain goat. The Capricorn goat consciousness is revealed to us through the high and lofty heights the goat commands. No mountain is too high for the true archetypal Capricorn, and the focus of this season is always placed on accomplishing the highest of goals and achievements. The working pace for the New Year is established here. Capricorn energy emphasizes corporate growth, the creation and maintenance of institutions, construction and development, and the use and control of industrial services and equipment. Capricorn urges us to succeed. Many outstanding Capricorns are devoted to their careers and lifestyles with unyielding tenacity. Capricorn days of the Sun are splendid times to focus on goals and to discipline one's nature to make daily tasks add up to something worth accomplishing. Although tedious and often predictable, the Capricorn nature makes sure the job is done – and done well.

December 22ⁿᵈ Saturday

Moon in Gemini

	PST	EST	
Venus square Neptune	2:23 AM	5:23 AM	
Moon square Saturn	3:56 AM	6:56 AM	
Mercury opposite Mars	10:30 AM	1:30 PM	
Moon square Uranus	2:25 PM	5:25 PM	
Sun conjunct Jupiter	9:57 PM	12:57 AM	(December 23)
Moon trine Neptune	10:14 PM	1:14 AM	(December 23)
Mercury trine Saturn begins (see December 25)			

Mood Watch: Moon square Saturn brings the potential for nightmarish dreams, and the sleepless among us will probably be struggling with personal limitations. The radiant power of the waxing Gemini Moon brings dual perspectives and lively conversations. Pensive and curious moods abound. Moon square Uranus is bound to bring afternoon chaos, and it may be difficult to break out of inhibiting situations. Later this evening, Moon trine Neptune settles our moods with calm, pleasant, and spiritually uplifting vibrations. This Full Moon Eve is an auspicious time to enjoy holiday gatherings, and to communicate while the Moon is in Gemini.

Venus square Neptune (occurring December 17 – 24) This may be a difficult time to be drawn to or to meditate on spiritual matters or activities. Art with a spiritual approach may appear more phony than ethereal. Feminine expression may be set back by antiquated beliefs. Love matters could be rocky due to a conflict of beliefs. Venus is in Scorpio, which intensifies the art of attraction, while Neptune is in Aquarius, formulating a new spiritual outlook for humankind. Venus influences beauty, attraction, and magnetism. Neptune is the higher spiritual vibration of the feminine spirit, the higher octave of Venus herself – the imperfect yet alluring mortal versus the perfect and irresistible goddess. When these two planets are in conflict, it is a time when women are being sent mixed messages about how to live up to a higher standard of the self. The influences of this aspect are not as harsh for those who understand that true attraction and beauty are found in the core of feminine wisdom, and that magnetic attraction goes beyond temporal beauty. This aspect last occurred on April 4, when Venus was in Taurus.

Mercury opposite Mars (occurring December 19 – 24) This aspect often causes people to lose their tempers while communicating. It also creates an acute awareness of the need to let the mind spout off with regard to heated subjects. This is a time to be especially careful to watch what you say, preferably before you speak. This requires thinking before acting, for often this aspect brings heated arguments and debates over the actions or outspoken thoughts of others. Mercury opposite Mars makes it difficult for some to justify their actions, or explain why they take a certain stand in life. Communications may be misunderstood if one is too caught up in the action of what is going on. It is best to apply reason and not to take aggressive language personally, particularly if it isn't necessarily pointed at you. In other words, watch out for signs of hypersensitivity and do not to fall victim to other people's inability to handle their own anger or aggression. Many may misinterpret communications as being hostile, or perhaps war related news takes an overwhelming tone at this time. Undemonstrative and serious minded talk (Mercury in Capricorn) about the overwhelming causes and results of war (opposition to Mars) makes us especially aware of the emotional repression surrounding our actions (retrograde Mars in Cancer). The callous, listless, seemingly unfeeling tone in much of the talk going around makes some folks truly angry. For some, it's good to get their troubles off their minds and out on the table. For others, it's best not to go there. Everyone has their own way.

Sun conjunct Jupiter (occurring December 15 – 26) This occurrence of Sun conjunct Jupiter particularly affects Sagittarius and Capricorn people who are celebrating birthdays December 15 – 26. These fortunate folks are brought into a favorable position of their natal Sun to Jupiter. This represents a time of gifts and expansion for these people, and there will be good times ahead. Financial or career advancement as well as skill building, exploration, inheritance, employment opportunities, and perhaps just plain happiness, become bonuses for these folks during this time and in the year to come. Be sure to count your blessings, birthday people. You may find that there are a great many more blessings for you this year than you might have expected.

December 23rd Sunday
Moon in Gemini / Cancer - FULL MOON in CANCER

♑

	PST	EST	
Moon opposite Pluto goes v/c	12:27 PM	3:27 PM	
Moon enters Cancer	2:19 PM	5:19 PM	
Moon opposite Jupiter	4:14 PM	7:14 PM	
Moon opposite Sun	5:17 PM	8:17 PM	
Moon conjunct Mars	7:00 PM	10:00 PM	
Moon opposite Mercury	11:54 PM	2:54 AM	(December 24)

Mood Watch: Throughout morning, the Gemini Moon brings an almost urgent focus on the need to communicate numerous details and to prepare for a number of plans. The busy chatter of the morning swiftly gives way to the all-encompassing afternoon disruption brought on by Moon opposite Pluto. The Gemini Moon goes void-of-course for a couple of hours and, as the Moon enters Cancer, we are put in touch with our deep emotional currents. Moon opposite Jupiter is likely to lead to over-extravagance, and a tendency to overindulge will be rampant. The **Full Moon in Cancer** (Moon opposite Sun) emphasizes Mom and maternal energy, and people may be moody or especially preoccupied with their feelings. Nurturing activities and emotional support are the best ways to approach the Full Cancer Moon. Be careful not to overeat. This evening, Moon conjunct Mars puts some folks in touch with their strength. They may need to use up some extra energy and angry emotions are sometimes brought to the surface. As the Moon opposes Mercury, unresolved issues will be carefully thought through.

December 24th Monday
Christmas Eve
Moon in Cancer

	PST	EST
Moon sextile Saturn	4:12 AM	7:12 AM
Sun opposite Mars	11:48 AM	2:48 PM
Moon trine Uranus	3:04 PM	6:04 PM
Sun trine Saturn begins (see December 30)		

Mood Watch: A distinct sense of how to structure our day will come over us as Moon sextile Saturn sets the tone for an amicably exciting Christmas Eve day. The Cancer Moon puts us in the mood for holiday settings and domestic cheer. The post-full Cancer Moon is likely to place a great deal of emphasis on the power of Mom and on maternal kinds of nurturing and comfort. The mood at dusk might go just as expected; Moon trine Uranus will bring wild abandonment of our restrictive duties, and rebelliousness and chaotic mayhem will run their course. The mood of this time has all the right elements for a Christmas Eve worth remembering.

Sun opposite Mars (occurring December 20 – 26) This aspect creates extra awareness of accidents, attacks, outbursts of energy, and possibly anger issues, especially for the Sagittarius/Capricorn cusp born folks celebrating birthdays December 20 – 26. Something strong and full of heat opposes these birthday folks in a way that may cause defensiveness and sensitivity towards bold activities. Mars strikes to warn our late born Sagittarius and early born Capricorn friends that they must be on guard and act swiftly against life's offensive blows. Being defensive is natural, and actions may require a careful approach or the heat may backfire. Sagittarius/

Capricorn cusp people, for sometime to come, you may be sensitive to the necessity to take action in your life. Use this energy to make positive change occur in your apparently busy and active year ahead.

December 25th Tuesday

Christmas

Moon in Cancer / Leo

	PST	EST
Moon trine Venus goes v/c	5:18 AM	8:18 AM
Mercury trine Saturn	3:11 PM	6:11 PM
Moon enters Leo	3:53 PM	6:53 PM

"Tradition is a guide and not a jailer." – W. Somerset Maugham

Mood Watch: This may well be the Christmas to keep a handkerchief on hand. Early morning brings positive, loving, beautiful vibes, but the Moon also goes void-of-course, and for a number of hours into this Christmas day, our moods will undoubtedly be emotional. The waning void-of-course Cancer Moon may bring gushing, joyous, and endearing moods, and it may also bring very melancholic, worrisome, and emotionally daunting moods. Domestic situations will require some patience in order to make it through the rough spots. This evening our moods will improve as the Moon in Leo places the emphasis of our attention on family, friends, entertainment, personal hobbies and interests. Reassuring and creative interactions will top this day quite nicely.

Mercury trine Saturn (occurring December 22 – 27) Mercury is in Capricorn where essential priorities and important goals are discussed and communicated. Mercury in Capricorn trine Saturn in Virgo brings practical and clear discussions with regard to where, and how, to draw the lines for ourselves. This is a good time to make an impression, to teach and to communicate to others those important matters requiring clarification. It's also a great time to study or practice memorization skills. Timely information and news bring gifts or blessings. News concerning the end of a long and arduous task brings relief. This aspect last occurred on April 21 this year, when Mercury was in Aries and Saturn was in Leo.

December 26th Wednesday

Boxing Day

Moon in Leo

	PST	EST
Mars opposite Jupiter	11:54 AM	2:54 PM

Mars opposite Pluto begins (occurs: Jan. 2, 2008 / ends: Jan. 9, 2008 – Active force is at odds with the greater powers, causing abrupt and sometimes alienating change)

Mood Watch: There are no significant lunar aspects occurring on this Leo Moon day. This could be a day to enjoy some lazy lolling about! The waning Leo Moon of winter is a good time to slow down the pace and to enjoy introspective reflections. Personal needs will stand out and this is the time to tend to those needs. It is also a time to enjoy friends, and our interests will be focused on the theater, entertainment, and similar activities that make for some good fun.

Mars opposite Jupiter (occurring December 21, 2007 – January 3, 2008) Retrograde Mars in Cancer is currently opposing Jupiter which is newly in the sign of Capricorn (since December 18). Sharp economic shifts are common this time of year, especially on Boxing Day. For more information on Mars opposite Jupiter, see August 23, when this aspect first occurred.

December 27ᵗʰ Thursday

Moon in Leo / Virgo	PST	EST	
Moon opposite Neptune	2:54 AM	5:54 AM	
Moon square Venus	2:34 PM	5:34 PM	
Moon trine Pluto goes v/c	6:55 PM	9:55 PM	
Moon enters Virgo	8:45 PM	11:45 PM	
Moon sextile Mars	11:04 PM	2:04 AM	(December 28)
Mercury sextile Uranus begins (see December 29)			

Mood Watch: Overnight, Moon opposite Neptune brings intensely spiritual journeys in the course of our dreams. The waning Leo Moon is a good time to get in touch with things that warm the heart and uplift the spirit. Later today, Moon square Venus may bring some rocky weather between loved ones. This evening, Moon trine Pluto brings a good time to confront hardship with a lot less difficulty, and yet, the Leo Moon also goes void-of-course. Therapeutic focuses will help to ease any personal troubles. After an early evening of delays, traffic, and wandering spirits, the Moon enters Virgo and our moods will be much more communicative and mindful of the occurrences of the day. Later tonight, Moon sextile Mars brings the potential for a notable burst of energy to our moods and dreams.

December 28ᵗʰ Friday

Moon in Virgo	PST	EST	
Moon trine Jupiter	12:45 AM	3:45 AM	
Moon trine Sun	8:52 AM	11:52 AM	
Moon conjunct Saturn	12:27 PM	3:27 PM	
Moon trine Mercury	10:32 PM	1:32 AM	(December 29)

Mood Watch: Prudent resourcefulness comes in handy during waning Virgo Moon. Sun in Capricorn with Moon in Virgo is a good time to get organized and to purge the world around us of all its physical clutter. This is the time to communicate and to clean up. Overnight, Moon trine Jupiter brings joyous moods and dreams; it also puts us in touch with our sense of wealth and wellbeing. Moon trine Sun brings cheerful morning moods. This afternoon, Moon conjunct Saturn assists us to take control, get in touch with our disciplines, and to get a handle on our responsibilities. Later tonight, Moon trine Mercury brings positive thoughts.

December 29ᵗʰ Saturday

Moon in Virgo	PST	EST
Moon opposite Uranus	1:16 AM	4:16 AM
Mercury sextile Uranus	8:11 PM	11:11 PM
Jupiter trine Saturn begins (occurs on: Jan. 21, 2008 / ends: Feb. 1, 2008 – for an explanation: see March 16, 2007 when this aspect last occurred)		

Mood Watch: Overnight, Moon opposite Uranus brings crazy, chaotic dreams. As we awake, the waning Virgo Moon gets us questioning, prodding, and rethinking our strategies. Today there will be a lot on our minds and many things to do. The

Sun and Moon in earth signs is a great time to take care of our duties, and to clean up and organize the physical world around us.

Mercury sextile Uranus (occurring December 27, 2007 – January 1, 2008) Mercury in Capricorn is sextile to Uranus in Pisces. Serious investigations may lead to sensational conclusions. This aspect is now occurring for the third time this year, and it first occurred while Mercury was in Capricorn, just as it is now. For more information on Mercury sextile Uranus, see January 3, when this aspect first occurred.

December 30th Sunday
Moon in Virgo / Libra - LAST QUARTER MOON in LIBRA

	PST	EST	
Moon square Pluto	3:51 AM	6:51 AM	
Moon sextile Venus goes v/c	5:09 AM	8:09 AM	
Sun trine Saturn	5:24 AM	8:24 AM	
Moon enters Libra	5:38 AM	8:38 AM	
Moon square Mars	6:25 AM	9:25 AM	
Venus enters Sagittarius	10:03 AM	1:03 PM	
Moon square Jupiter	11:01 AM	2:01 PM	
Moon square Sun	11:52 PM	2:52 AM	(December 31)

Mood Watch: Moon square Pluto may bring nightmarish concerns to the forefront of our moods very early this morning. Moon sextile Venus brings the potential for us to receive some pleasant vibrations. For a short time the Moon goes void-of-course in Virgo and, briefly, our moods will be somewhat skeptical. Soon enough though, the Moon enters Libra, which focuses our energies on the need to bring some balance into our lives. Moon square Mars will probably test our strength and willpower, as there may be some conflicting morning moods. Moon square Jupiter will undoubtedly test us with regard to happiness, money related matters, and travel expenses. We may seem less than generous or less outgoing. **Last Quarter Moon in Libra** (Moon square Sun) reminds us of the need to continue working on the imbalances in our relationships. Libra's adage is simple: "I balance." This is the time to let the emotional pressure be released, and to handle matters with friends and loved ones carefully and congenially. The Last Quarter Moon aspect confirms the need to make amends with others and unite peacefully. If some aspect of your connection to a friend or loved one disrupts your sense of peace, reach within for the answers. A balanced response will soon follow.

Sun trine Saturn (occurring December 24, 2007 – January 3, 2008) This occurrence of Sun trine Saturn particularly affects those Capricorns celebrating birthdays December 24 – Jan 3. This is a positive time for these folks to get a handle on their lives, and it may be easier for them to take on the responsibilities of life with fewer complications and less difficulty in the year to come. Despite the fact that Saturn is now retrograde, since December 19, this will be your time (birthday people) to successfully work on putting some structure into your life; the kind of structure you've needed and wanted awaits you in the coming year. It is possible that time (Saturn) is on your side to make that move you've been thinking about. This aspect last occurred on April 8, when the Sun was in Aries, affecting the Aries birthday people of that time.

Venus enters Sagittarius (Venus in Sagittarius: Dec. 30, 2007 – Jan. 24, 2008) Now the planet of love and the expression of affection is enhanced by the inspired character of Sagittarius. Venus in Sagittarius brings out a love of the arts, travel, philosophy, cultural exploration and sports achievements. With this comes a positive and optimistic spirit of camaraderie among people in general, and the effort to take affections beyond the usual bounds is certainly present. Philosophical theories justify love matters. Venus in Sagittarius will help to boost the love life and affections of our Sagittarius friends. This is your time, Sagittarius people, to reaffirm your visions of how to enhance the beauty and the love that you are enjoying in your lives.

December 31ˢᵗ Monday

Moon in Libra	PST	EST
Mars enters Gemini	8:01 AM	11:01 AM

Mood Watch: The last day of the year is brought to us with a waning Libra Moon, which focuses our energies and moods on such Libra-like things as friendship, elegance, splendor, symmetry, justice, cooperation, peace, leisure and luxury. The skillful use of words will ring in the New Year with a firm sense of the need for balance in our lives. Books, good music, beloved company, sparkling lights, and gourmet fare are just some of the necessary tools for creating the perfect ambiance. *HAPPY NEW YEAR!*

Mars enters Gemini (Mars in Gemini: December 31, 2007 – March 4, 2008) Retrograde Mars now moves back into the late degrees of Gemini and will remain in Gemini until early March 2008. For more information on Mars in Gemini, see August 6, when Mars first entered Gemini this year.

Ephemeris 2007 Noon GMT
Longitudes based on Greenwich Mean Time (GMT) at Noon

JANUARY 2007

Date	☉	☽	☿	♀	♂	♃	♄	♅	♆	♇
1	10♑41	14♊23	07♑19	26♑41	18♐47	08♐18	24♌26R	11♓33	18♒08	27♐03
2	11 42	28 10	08 54	27 57	19 31	08 30	24 23	11 35	18 10	27 05
3	12 43	11♋43	10 30	29 12	20 14	08 42	24 20	11 37	18 12	27 07
4	13 44	24 59	12 06	00♒27	20 58	08 55	24 17	11 40	18 14	27 09
5	14 46	07♌56	13 43	01 42	21 42	09 07	24 14	11 42	18 16	27 12
6	15 47	20 34	15 20	02 57	22 26	09 19	24 10	11 44	18 18	27 14
7	16 48	02♍54	16 57	04 12	23 09	09 31	24 07	11 46	18 20	27 16
8	17 49	15 00	18 35	05 28	23 53	09 43	24 04	11 49	18 22	27 18
9	18 50	26 55	20 13	06 43	24 37	09 54	24 00	11 51	18 24	27 20
10	19 51	08♎44	21 52	07 58	25 20	10 06	23 57	11 53	18 26	27 22
11	20 52	20 32	23 31	09 13	26 04	10 18	23 53	11 56	18 28	27 24
12	21 54	02♏25	25 10	10 28	26 48	10 29	23 49	11 58	18 30	27 26
13	22 55	14 29	26 50	11 43	27 31	10 41	23 46	12 01	18 32	27 28
14	23 56	26 47	28 31	12 58	28 15	10 53	23 42	12 03	18 34	27 30
15	24 57	09♐24	00♒11	14 13	28 59	11 04	23 38	12 06	18 37	27 32
16	25 58	22 22	01 53	15 28	29 43	11 15	23 34	12 08	18 39	27 34
17	26 59	05♑42	03 34	16 43	00♑27	11 27	23 30	12 11	18 41	27 36
18	28 00	19 23	05 16	17 58	01 11	11 38	23 26	12 14	18 43	27 38
19	29 01	03♒22	06 58	19 13	01 56	11 49	23 22	12 16	18 45	27 40
20	00♒03	17 34	08 41	20 28	02 40	12 00	23 17	12 19	18 47	27 42
21	01 04	01♓55	10 23	21 43	03 25	12 11	23 13	12 22	18 50	27 44
22	02 05	16 19	12 06	22 58	04 09	12 22	23 09	12 25	18 52	27 46
23	03 06	00♈41	13 49	24 13	04 54	12 32	23 04	12 28	18 54	27 48
24	04 07	14 58	15 31	25 28	05 38	12 43	23 00	12 30	18 56	27 50
25	05 08	29 08	17 13	26 42	06 22	12 54	22 55	12 33	18 58	27 52
26	06 09	13♉10	18 55	27 57	07 06	13 04	22 51	12 36	19 01	27 54
27	07 10	27 02	20 36	29 12	07 50	13 14	22 46	12 39	19 03	27 56
28	08 11	10♊45	22 16	00♓27	08 35	13 25	22 42	12 42	19 05	27 57
29	09 12	24 16	23 55	01 42	09 19	13 35	22 37	12 45	19 07	27 59
30	10 13	07♋36	25 32	02 56	10 04	13 45	22 32	12 48	19 10	28 01
31	11 14	20 43	27 07	04 11	10 48	13 55	22 28	12 51	19 12	28 03

FEBRUARY 2007

Date	☉	☽	☿	♀	♂	♃	♄	♅	♆	♇
1	12♒14	03♌36	28♒40	05♓26	11♑33	14♐05	22♌23R	12♓54	19♒14	28♐05
2	13 15	16 16	00♓10	06 40	12 18	14 15	22 18	12 57	19 16	28 06
3	14 16	28 41	01 36	07 55	13 03	14 24	22 13	13 00	19 19	28 08
4	15 17	10♍54	02 58	09 09	13 48	14 34	22 09	13 03	19 21	28 10
5	16 18	22 56	04 16	10 24	14 33	14 43	22 04	13 07	19 23	28 11
6	17 19	04♎49	05 27	11 38	15 17	14 53	21 59	13 10	19 25	28 13
7	18 19	16 38	06 33	12 53	16 02	15 02	21 54	13 13	19 28	28 14
8	19 20	28 27	07 31	14 07	16 47	15 11	21 49	13 16	19 30	28 16
9	20 21	10♏19	08 21	15 22	17 32	15 20	21 44	13 19	19 32	28 18
10	21 22	22 21	09 03	16 36	18 17	15 29	21 39	13 23	19 35	28 19
11	22 22	04♐38	09 36	17 50	19 01	15 38	21 35	13 26	19 37	28 21
12	23 23	17 12	09 58	19 05	19 46	15 46	21 30	13 29	19 39	28 22
13	24 24	00♑10	10 11	20 19	20 31	15 55	21 25	13 32	19 41	28 24
14	25 24	13 32	10♓13R	21 33	21 16	16 03	21 20	13 36	19 44	28 25
15	26 25	27 20	10 04	22 47	22 01	16 11	21 15	13 39	19 46	28 26
16	27 26	11♒31	09 45	24 01	22 46	16 19	21 10	13 42	19 48	28 28
17	28 26	26 02	09 16	25 16	23 32	16 27	21 05	13 46	19 51	28 29
18	29 27	10♓46	08 38	26 30	24 17	16 35	21 01	13 49	19 53	28 30
19	00♓27	25 37	07 52	27 44	25 03	16 43	20 56	13 52	19 55	28 32

FEBRUARY 2007 (Cont'd)

Date	☉	☽	☿	♀	♂	♃	♄	♅	♆	♇
20	01♓28	10♈26	06♓58R	28♓58	25♑48	16♐51	20♌51R	13♓56	19♒57	28♐33
21	02 28	25 07	05 59	00♈12	26 34	16 58	20 46	13 59	20 00	28 34
22	03 29	09♉35	04 56	01 26	27 19	17 05	20 42	14 03	20 02	28 35
23	04 29	23 46	03 51	02 39	28 04	17 13	20 37	14 06	20 04	28 37
24	05 30	07♊39	02 44	03 53	28 49	17 20	20 32	14 09	20 06	28 38
25	06 30	21 14	01 39	05 07	29 34	17 26	20 28	14 13	20 08	28 39
26	07 30	04♋30	00 37	06 21	00♒20	17 33	20 23	14 16	20 11	28 40
27	08 31	17 31	29♒38R	07 34	01 05	17 40	20 19	14 20	20 13	28 41
28	09 31	00♌16	28 44	08 48	01 50	17 46	20 14	14 23	20 15	28 42

MARCH 2007

Date	☉	☽	☿	♀	♂	♃	♄	♅	♆	♇
1	10♓31	12♌48	27♒55R	10♈01	02♒35	17♐52	20♌10R	14♓27	20♒17	28♐43
2	11 31	25 09	27 13	11 15	03 21	17 59	20 05	14 30	20 19	28 44
3	12 31	07♍19	26 38	12 28	04 06	18 05	20 01	14 33	20 22	28 45
4	13 32	19 21	26 10	13 42	04 52	18 10	19 57	14 37	20 24	28 46
5	14 32	01♎17	25 48	14 55	05 38	18 16	19 53	14 40	20 26	28 47
6	15 32	13 08	25 34	16 08	06 24	18 22	19 48	14 44	20 28	28 48
7	16 32	24 57	25 26	17 21	07 10	18 27	19 44	14 47	20 30	28 48
8	17 32	06♏46	25♒25D	18 35	07 56	18 32	19 40	14 51	20 32	28 49
9	18 32	18 40	25 30	19 48	08 41	18 37	19 36	14 54	20 34	28 50
10	19 32	00♐42	25 41	21 01	09 27	18 42	19 32	14 57	20 36	28 51
11	20 32	12 56	25 57	22 14	10 13	18 47	19 29	15 01	20 38	28 51
12	21 32	25 27	26 19	23 27	10 58	18 51	19 25	15 04	20 40	28 52
13	22 32	08♑18	26 46	24 39	11 44	18 56	19 21	15 08	20 42	28 53
14	23 31	21 34	27 18	25 52	12 29	19 00	19 18	15 11	20 44	28 53
15	24 31	05♒16	27 53	27 05	13 15	19 04	19 14	15 15	20 46	28 54
16	25 31	19 25	28 34	28 17	14 00	19 08	19 11	15 18	20 48	28 54
17	26 31	03♓59	29 17	29 30	14 46	19 11	19 07	15 21	20 50	28 55
18	27 31	18 52	00♓05	00♉43	15 32	19 15	19 04	15 25	20 52	28 55
19	28 30	03♈59	00 56	01 55	16 18	19 18	19 01	15 28	20 54	28 56
20	29 30	19 09	01 50	03 07	17 05	19 21	18 58	15 31	20 56	28 56
21	00♈30	04♉13	02 47	04 20	17 51	19 24	18 55	15 35	20 58	28 56
22	01 29	19 02	03 46	05 32	18 37	19 27	18 52	15 38	21 00	28 57
23	02 29	03♊31	04 49	06 44	19 23	19 30	18 49	15 42	21 02	28 57
24	03 28	17 35	05 54	07 56	20 09	19 32	18 46	15 45	21 03	28 57
25	04 28	01♋14	07 01	09 08	20 55	19 34	18 43	15 48	21 05	28 57
26	05 27	14 27	08 10	10 20	21 41	19 36	18 41	15 51	21 07	28 58
27	06 27	27 19	09 22	11 32	22 27	19 38	18 38	15 55	21 09	28 58
28	07 26	09♌53	10 36	12 44	23 12	19 40	18 36	15 58	21 10	28 58
29	08 25	22 11	11 51	13 55	23 58	19 41	18 34	16 01	21 12	28 58
30	09 25	04♍18	13 09	15 07	24 44	19 43	18 31	16 04	21 14	28 58
31	10 24	16 17	14 29	16 18	25 30	19 44	18 29	16 08	21 15	28 58

APRIL 2007

Date	☉	☽	☿	♀	♂	♃	♄	♅	♆	♇
1	11♈23	28♍10	15♓50	17♉30	26♒16	19♐45	18♌27R	16♓11	21♒17	28♐58R
2	12 22	10♎00	17 13	18 41	27 02	19 46	18 25	16 14	21 19	28 58
3	13 21	21 49	18 37	19 52	27 48	19 46	18 24	16 17	21 20	28 58
4	14 20	03♏39	20 04	21 03	28 34	19 47	18 22	16 20	21 22	28 58
5	15 20	15 33	21 32	22 14	29 21	19 47	18 20	16 23	21 23	28 58
6	16 19	27 31	23 01	23 25	00♓07	19♐47R	18 19	16 27	21 25	28 58
7	17 18	09♐37	24 33	24 36	00 53	19 47	18 18	16 30	21 26	28 57
8	18 17	21 54	26 05	25 47	01 40	19 46	18 16	16 33	21 28	28 57
9	19 16	04♑24	27 40	26 57	02 26	19 46	18 15	16 36	21 29	28 57
10	20 14	17 12	29 15	28 08	03 11	19 45	18 14	16 39	21 31	28 57
11	21 13	00♒21	00♈53	29 18	03 57	19 44	18 13	16 42	21 32	28 56
12	22 12	13 53	02 32	00♊29	04 43	19 43	18 12	16 45	21 33	28 56

APRIL 2007 (Cont'd)

Date	☉	☽	☿	♀	♂	♃	♄	♅	♆	♇
13	23♈11	27♒50	04♈12	01♊39	05♓29	19♐42R	18♌12R	16♓48	21♒35	28♐56R
14	24 10	12♓14	05 54	02 49	06 15	19 40	18 11	16 51	21 36	28 55
15	25 09	27 01	07 38	03 59	07 01	19 38	18 10	16 53	21 37	28 55
16	26 07	12♈06	09 23	05 09	07 47	19 37	18 10	16 56	21 38	28 54
17	27 06	27 20	11 10	06 19	08 33	19 34	18 10	16 59	21 40	28 54
18	28 05	12♉34	12 58	07 28	09 19	19 32	18 09	17 02	21 41	28 53
19	29 04	27 37	14 48	08 38	10 05	19 30	18 09	17 05	21 42	28 53
20	00♉02	12♊20	16 40	09 47	10 51	19 27	18♌09D	17 07	21 43	28 52
21	01 01	26 36	18 33	10 57	11 37	19 24	18 09	17 10	21 44	28 51
22	01 59	10♋24	20 28	12 06	12 24	19 22	18 10	17 13	21 45	28 51
23	02 58	23 42	22 24	13 15	13 09	19 18	18 10	17 15	21 46	28 50
24	03 56	06♌35	24 22	14 24	13 55	19 15	18 11	17 18	21 47	28 49
25	04 55	19 06	26 21	15 33	14 41	19 12	18 11	17 21	21 48	28 49
26	05 53	01♍19	28 22	16 41	15 27	19 08	18 12	17 23	21 49	28 48
27	06 52	13 19	00♉25	17 50	16 12	19 04	18 12	17 26	21 50	28 47
28	07 50	25 12	02 29	18 58	16 58	19 00	18 13	17 28	21 51	28 46
29	08 48	07♎01	04 34	20 06	17 44	18 56	18 14	17 31	21 52	28 46
30	09 46	18 49	06 40	21 14	18 29	18 52	18 15	17 33	21 53	28 45

MAY 2007

Date	☉	☽	☿	♀	♂	♃	♄	♅	♆	♇
1	10♉45	00♏39	08♉48	22♊22	19♓15	18♐47R	18♌17	17♓35	21♒53	28♐44R
2	11 43	12 34	10 56	23 30	20 01	18 43	18 18	17 38	21 54	28 43
3	12 41	24 34	13 05	24 37	20 47	18 38	18 19	17 40	21 55	28 42
4	13 39	06♐41	15 15	25 45	21 33	18 33	18 21	17 42	21 56	28 41
5	14 37	18 57	17 25	26 52	22 19	18 28	18 22	17 45	21 56	28 40
6	15 35	01♑23	19 35	27 59	23 05	18 23	18 24	17 47	21 57	28 39
7	16 34	14 00	21 44	29 06	23 51	18 17	18 26	17 49	21 57	28 38
8	17 32	26 51	23 54	00♋12	24 37	18 12	18 28	17 51	21 58	28 37
9	18 30	09♒59	26 02	01 19	25 23	18 06	18 30	17 53	21 59	28 36
10	19 28	23 25	28 09	02 25	26 09	18 01	18 32	17 55	21 59	28 35
11	20 26	07♓13	00♊15	03 31	26 54	17 55	18 34	17 57	22 00	28 34
12	21 24	21 23	02 19	04 37	27 39	17 49	18 37	17 59	22 00	28 32
13	22 22	05♈54	04 21	05 43	28 25	17 42	18 39	18 01	22 00	28 31
14	23 20	20 44	06 21	06 49	29 10	17 36	18 41	18 03	22 01	28 30
15	24 17	05♉47	08 19	07 54	29 56	17 30	18 44	18 05	22 01	28 29
16	25 15	20 53	10 14	08 59	00♈41	17 23	18 47	18 07	22 01	28 28
17	26 13	05♊52	12 06	10 04	01 27	17 17	18 50	18 08	22 02	28 26
18	27 11	20 36	13 56	11 09	02 12	17 10	18 53	18 10	22 02	28 25
19	28 09	04♋57	15 43	12 13	02 58	17 03	18 56	18 12	22 02	28 24
20	29 07	18 50	17 26	13 17	03 44	16 56	18 59	18 13	22 02	28 23
21	00♊04	02♌14	19 07	14 21	04 29	16 50	19 02	18 15	22 02	28 21
22	01 02	15 10	20 44	15 25	05 15	16 42	19 05	18 17	22 02	28 20
23	02 00	27 43	22 19	16 28	06 00	16 35	19 09	18 18	22 03	28 19
24	02 57	09♍57	23 49	17 32	06 45	16 28	19 12	18 20	22 03	28 17
25	03 55	21 57	25 17	18 34	07 30	16 21	19 16	18 21	22 03	28 16
26	04 53	03♎49	26 41	19 37	08 15	16 14	19 19	18 22	22 03	28 14
27	05 50	15 37	28 02	20 39	09 00	16 06	19 23	18 24	22 02	28 13
28	06 48	27 26	29 20	21 41	09 45	15 59	19 27	18 25	22 02	28 12
29	07 45	09♏20	00♋34	22 43	10 30	15 51	19 31	18 26	22♒02R	28 10
30	08 43	21 21	01 44	23 44	11 15	15 44	19 35	18 27	22 02	28 09
31	09 40	03♐31	02 51	24 45	11 59	15 36	19 39	18 28	22 02	28 07

JUNE 2007

Date	☉	☽	☿	♀	♂	♃	♄	♅	♆	♇
1	10♊38	15♐50	03♋54	25♋46	12♈45	15♐29R	19♌43	18♓30	22♒02R	28♐06R
2	11 35	28 21	04 54	26 46	13 30	15 21	19 47	18 31	22 01	28 04
3	12 33	11♑02	05 50	27 46	14 15	15 14	19 51	18 32	22 01	28 03

250

JUNE 2007 (Cont'd)

Date	☉	☽	☿	♀	♂	♃	♄	♅	♆	♇
4	13♊30	23♑54	06♋42	28♋46	15♈00	15♐06R	19♌56	18♓33	22♒01R	28♐01R
5	14 28	06♒58	07 29	29 45	15 45	14 58	20 00	18 33	22 00	28 00
6	15 25	20 14	08 13	00♌44	16 30	14 51	20 05	18 34	22 00	27 58
7	16 23	03♓44	08 53	01 42	17 14	14 43	20 10	18 35	22 00	27 57
8	17 20	17 29	09 29	02 40	17 59	14 35	20 14	18 36	21 59	27 55
9	18 17	01♈31	10 00	03 38	18 43	14 28	20 19	18 37	21 59	27 54
10	19 15	15 48	10 27	04 35	19 28	14 20	20 24	18 37	21 58	27 52
11	20 12	00♉19	10 50	05 32	20 12	14 13	20 29	18 38	21 58	27 51
12	21 10	15 00	11 08	06 28	20 56	14 05	20 34	18 38	21 57	27 49
13	22 07	29 45	11 22	07 23	21 40	13 57	20 39	18 39	21 57	27 48
14	23 04	14♊27	11 31	08 19	22 24	13 50	20 44	18 39	21 56	27 46
15	24 02	28 57	11 35	09 13	23 08	13 42	20 50	18 40	21 55	27 44
16	24 59	13♋09	11♋35R	10 07	23 52	13 35	20 55	18 40	21 55	27 43
17	25 56	26 57	11 30	11 01	24 36	13 28	21 00	18 41	21 54	27 41
18	26 54	10♌19	11 21	11 54	25 21	13 20	21 06	18 41	21 53	27 40
19	27 51	23 16	11 08	12 46	26 05	13 13	21 11	18 41	21 52	27 38
20	28 48	05♍51	10 51	13 38	26 49	13 06	21 17	18 41	21 52	27 37
21	29 45	18 06	10 30	14 29	27 33	12 59	21 22	18 41	21 51	27 35
22	00♋43	00♎08	10 06	15 20	28 17	12 52	21 28	18 41	21 50	27 34
23	01 40	12 02	09 38	16 09	29 00	12 45	21 34	18 41	21 49	27 32
24	02 37	23 52	09 08	16 58	29 43	12 38	21 40	18 41	21 48	27 30
25	03 34	05♏43	08 36	17 46	00♉27	12 31	21 46	18 41	21 47	27 29
26	04 32	17 41	08 02	18 34	01 10	12 25	21 52	18♓41R	21 46	27 27
27	05 29	29 48	07 27	19 21	01 53	12 18	21 58	18 41	21 45	27 26
28	06 26	12♐07	06 51	20 06	02 36	12 12	22 04	18 41	21 44	27 24
29	07 23	24 40	06 16	20 51	03 19	12 06	22 10	18 41	21 43	27 23
30	08 20	07♑26	05 41	21 35	04 02	11 59	22 16	18 40	21 42	27 21

JULY 2007

Date	☉	☽	☿	♀	♂	♃	♄	♅	♆	♇
1	09♋18	20♑26	05♋07R	22♌18	04♉45	11♐53R	22♌22	18♓40R	21♒41R	27♐20R
2	10 15	03♒39	04 36	23 00	05 28	11 47	22 28	18 40	21 40	27 18
3	11 12	17 04	04 07	23 41	06 11	11 41	22 35	18 39	21 39	27 17
4	12 09	00♓39	03 41	24 21	06 54	11 36	22 41	18 39	21 38	27 15
5	13 06	14 23	03 18	25 00	07 37	11 30	22 48	18 38	21 37	27 14
6	14 04	28 17	02 59	25 38	08 20	11 25	22 54	18 38	21 35	27 12
7	15 01	12♈20	02 44	26 14	09 03	11 19	23 01	18 37	21 34	27 11
8	15 58	26 30	02 34	26 50	09 45	11 14	23 07	18 36	21 33	27 09
9	16 55	10♉47	02 29	27 24	10 28	11 09	23 14	18 35	21 32	27 08
10	17 52	25 07	02♋28D	27 56	11 10	11 04	23 20	18 35	21 30	27 06
11	18 50	09♊28	02 33	28 28	11 51	11 00	23 27	18 34	21 29	27 05
12	19 47	23 43	02 43	28 58	12 33	10 55	23 34	18 33	21 28	27 03
13	20 44	07♋49	02 58	29 26	13 15	10 51	23 41	18 32	21 27	27 02
14	21 41	21 39	03 19	29 53	13 57	10 46	23 48	18 31	21 25	27 01
15	22 39	05♌12	03 45	00♍18	14 39	10 42	23 55	18 30	21 24	26 59
16	23 36	18 23	04 16	00 42	15 20	10 38	24 01	18 29	21 22	26 58
17	24 33	01♍14	04 52	01 04	16 02	10 34	24 08	18 28	21 21	26 57
18	25 30	13 46	05 34	01 24	16 44	10 31	24 15	18 27	21 20	26 55
19	26 28	26 01	06 22	01 43	17 26	10 27	24 22	18 26	21 18	26 54
20	27 25	08♎04	07 14	01 59	18 07	10 24	24 30	18 25	21 17	26 53
21	28 22	19 58	08 12	02 14	18 48	10 21	24 37	18 23	21 15	26 51
22	29 19	01♏50	09 14	02 27	19 30	10 18	24 44	18 22	21 14	26 50
23	00♌17	13 43	10 22	02 37	20 10	10 15	24 51	18 21	21 12	26 49
24	01 14	25 43	11 35	02 45	20 51	10 13	24 58	18 19	21 11	26 48
25	02 11	07♐54	12 52	02 52	21 32	10 10	25 05	18 18	21 09	26 46
26	03 09	20 19	14 14	02 56	22 12	10 08	25 13	18 17	21 08	26 45
27	04 06	03♑01	15 41	02 57	22 52	10 06	25 20	18 15	21 06	26 44

JULY 2007 (Cont'd)

Date	☉	☽	☿	♀	♂	♃	♄	♅	♆	♇
28	05♌03	16♑01	17♋12	02♍57R	23♉32	10♐04R	25♌27	18♓14R	21♒05R	26♐43R
29	06 01	29 19	18 47	02 54	24 12	10 03	25 34	18 12	21 03	26 42
30	06 58	12♒53	20 27	02 48	24 52	10 01	25 42	18 10	21 02	26 41
31	07 55	26 42	22 10	02 40	25 32	10 00	25 49	18 09	21 00	26 40

AUGUST 2007

Date	☉	☽	☿	♀	♂	♃	♄	♅	♆	♇
1	08♌53	10♓43	23♋57	02♍30R	26♉12	09♐59R	25♌57	18♓07R	20♒58R	26♐39R
2	09 50	24 51	25 47	02 18	26 53	09 58	26 04	18 05	20 57	26 38
3	10 47	09♈04	27 40	02 03	27 32	09 57	26 11	18 04	20 55	26 37
4	11 45	23 19	29 35	01 46	28 12	09 57	26 19	18 02	20 54	26 36
5	12 42	07♉33	01♌33	01 26	28 52	09 56	26 26	18 00	20 52	26 35
6	13 40	21 45	03 32	01 04	29 31	09 56	26 34	17 58	20 50	26 34
7	14 37	05♊51	05 33	00 41	00♊10	09♐56D	26 41	17 56	20 49	26 33
8	15 35	19 50	07 36	00 15	00 49	09 56	26 49	17 55	20 47	26 32
9	16 32	03♋40	09 39	29♌47	01 28	09 56	26 56	17 53	20 45	26 31
10	17 30	17 19	11 42	29 17	02 06	09 57	27 04	17 51	20 44	26 30
11	18 27	00♌43	13 46	28 46	02 44	09 58	27 12	17 49	20 42	26 29
12	19 25	13 53	15 49	28 13	03 23	09 59	27 19	17 47	20 41	26 29
13	20 23	26 48	17 53	27 39	04 01	10 00	27 27	17 45	20 39	26 28
14	21 20	09♍26	19 55	27 04	04 39	10 01	27 34	17 43	20 37	26 27
15	22 18	21 50	21 57	26 28	05 17	10 02	27 42	17 41	20 36	26 26
16	23 16	04♎00	23 59	25 52	05 55	10 04	27 50	17 38	20 34	26 26
17	24 13	16 01	25 59	25 14	06 33	10 06	27 57	17 36	20 32	26 25
18	25 11	27 55	27 58	24 37	07 11	10 08	28 05	17 34	20 31	26 24
19	26 09	09♏46	29 56	24 00	07 48	10 10	28 12	17 32	20 29	26 23
20	27 06	21 39	01♍52	23 23	08 26	10 12	28 20	17 30	20 28	26 23
21	28 04	03♐39	03 48	22 46	09 03	10 15	28 28	17 28	20 26	26 23
22	29 02	15 49	05 42	22 11	09 40	10 18	28 35	17 25	20 24	26 22
23	00♍00	28 15	07 35	21 36	10 16	10 21	28 43	17 23	20 23	26 22
24	00 58	11♑00	09 26	21 02	10 52	10 24	28 51	17 21	20 21	26 21
25	01 55	24 06	11 16	20 30	11 28	10 27	28 58	17 19	20 19	26 21
26	02 53	07♒35	13 05	19 59	12 04	10 30	29 06	17 16R	20 18	26 20
27	03 51	21 26	14 52	19 30	12 40	10 34	29 13	17 14	20 16	26 20
28	04 49	05♓36	16 38	19 03	13 15	10 38	29 21	17 12	20 15	26 20
29	05 47	20 02	18 23	18 38	13 51	10 42	29 29	17 09	20 13	26 19
30	06 45	04♈38	20 06	18 15	14 26	10 46	29 36	17 07	20 12	26 19
31	07 43	19 17	21 48	17 55	15 02	10 50	29 44	17 05	20 10	26 19

SEPTEMBER 2007

Date	☉	☽	☿	♀	♂	♃	♄	♅	♆	♇
1	08♍41	03♉54	23♍29	17♌36R	15♊37	10♐55	29♌51	17♓02R	20♒09R	26♐19R
2	09 39	18 23	25 09	17 20	16 12	10 59	29 59	17 00	20 07	26 18
3	10 37	02♊40	26 47	17 07	16 47	11 04	00♍07	16 58	20 05	26 18
4	11 35	16 43	28 24	16 55	17 21	11 09	00 14	16 55	20 04	26 18
5	12 33	00♋30	00♎00	16 47	17 55	11 14	00 22	16 53	20 02	26 18
6	13 31	14 01	01 35	16 40	18 29	11 19	00 29	16 50	20 01	26 18
7	14 30	27 17	03 09	16 36	19 03	11 25	00 37	16 48	20 00	26♐18D
8	15 28	10♌18	04 41	16 35	19 36	11 30	00 44	16 46	19 58	26 18
9	16 26	23 05	06 12	16♌35D	20 09	11 36	00 52	16 43	19 57	26 18
10	17 25	05♍39	07 42	16 39	20 41	11 42	00 59	16 41	19 55	26 18
11	18 23	18 02	09 11	16 44	21 14	11 48	01 06	16 38	19 54	26 18
12	19 21	00♎15	10 38	16 52	21 46	11 54	01 14	16 36	19 53	26 19
13	20 20	12 18	12 05	17 01	22 18	12 00	01 21	16 34	19 51	26 19
14	21 18	24 15	13 30	17 13	22 50	12 07	01 29	16 31	19 50	26 19
15	22 17	06♏07	14 54	17 27	23 22	12 13	01 36	16 29	19 48	26 19
16	23 15	17 58	16 16	17 43	23 53	12 20	01 43	16 26	19 47	26 19
17	24 14	29 50	17 38	18 01	24 25	12 27	01 50	16 24	19 46	26 20

SEPTEMBER 2007 (Cont'd)

Date	☉	☽	☿	♀	♂	♃	♄	♅	♆	♇
18	25♍12	11♐48	18♎58	18♌21	24♊56	12♐34	01♍58	16♓22R	19♒45R	26♐20
19	26 11	23 55	20 16	18 43	25 26	12 41	02 05	16 19	19 43	26 20
20	27 09	06♑18	21 33	19 06	25 57	12 49	02 12	16 17	19 42	26 21
21	28 08	18 59	22 49	19 31	26 27	12 56	02 19	16 15	19 41	26 21
22	29 07	02♒02	24 03	19 58	26 56	13 04	02 26	16 12	19 40	26 22
23	00♎05	15 32	25 15	20 26	27 25	13 12	02 33	16 10	19 39	26 22
24	01 04	29 28	26 26	20 56	27 54	13 20	02 40	16 08	19 38	26 23
25	02 03	13♓49	27♎35	21 27	28 22	13 28	02 47	16 05	19 36	26 23
26	03 01	28 32	28 41	22 00	28 50	13 36	02 54	16 03	19 35	26 24
27	04 00	13♈30	29 46	22 35	29 18	13 44	03 01	16 01	19 34	26 24
28	04 59	28 34	00♏49	23 10	29 46	13 52	03 08	15 59	19 33	26 25
29	05 58	13♉36	01 48	23 47	00♋13	14 01	03 15	15 57	19 32	26 26
30	06 57	28 26	02 46	24 25	00 41	14 10	03 22	15 54	19 31	26 26

OCTOBER 2007

Date	☉	☽	☿	♀	♂	♃	♄	♅	♆	♇
1	07♎56	12♊58	03♏40	25♌04	01♋08	14♐18	03♍29	15♓52R	19♒30R	26♐27
2	08 55	27 08	04 32	25 45	01 35	14 27	03 35	15 50	19 29	26 28
3	09 54	10♋54	05 20	26 27	02 01	14 36	03 42	15 48	19 28	26 29
4	10 53	24 17	06 05	27 09	02 27	14 45	03 49	15 46	19 28	26 30
5	11 52	07♌19	06 45	27 53	02 53	14 55	03 55	15 44	19 27	26 30
6	12 51	20 04	07 21	28 38	03 17	15 04	04 02	15 42	19 26	26 31
7	13 50	02♍34	07 53	29 24	03 42	15 13	04 08	15 40	19 25	26 32
8	14 50	14 52	08 19	00♍10	04 05	15 23	04 15	15 38	19 24	26 33
9	15 49	27 00	08 40	00 58	04 28	15 33	04 21	15 36	19 24	26 34
10	16 48	09♎02	08 55	01 46	04 51	15 42	04 27	15 34	19 23	26 35
11	17 48	20 58	09 03	02 35	05 13	15 52	04 34	15 32	19 22	26 36
12	18 47	02♏51	09♏04R	03 25	05 35	16 02	04 40	15 30	19 22	26 37
13	19 46	14 42	08 58	04 16	05 57	16 13	04 46	15 28	19 21	26 38
14	20 46	26 33	08 43	05 07	06 19	16 23	04 52	15 26	19 20	26 40
15	21 45	08♐26	08 21	06 00	06 40	16 33	04 58	15 24	19 20	26 41
16	22 45	20 24	07 50	06 52	07 00	16 44	05 04	15 23	19 19	26 42
17	23 44	02♑31	07 10	07 46	07 21	16 54	05 10	15 21	19 19	26 43
18	24 44	14 49	06 23	08 40	07 41	17 05	05 16	15 19	19 18	26 44
19	25 43	27 25	05 27	09 35	08 00	17 15	05 22	15 18	19 18	26 46
20	26 43	10♒21	04 24	10 30	08 18	17 26	05 27	15 16	19 18	26 47
21	27 43	23 42	03 16	11 26	08 36	17 37	05 33	15 14	19 17	26 48
22	28 42	07♓31	02 03	12 23	08 53	17 48	05 39	15 13	19 17	26 50
23	29 42	21 49	00 48	13 20	09 09	17 59	05 44	15 11	19 17	26 51
24	00♏42	06♈34	29♎33	14 18	09 25	18 10	05 50	15 10	19 16	26 52
25	01 41	21 39	28 20	15 16	09 40	18 22	05 55	15 08	19 16	26 54
26	02 41	06♉57	27 11	16 14	09 55	18 33	06 00	15 07	19 16	26 55
27	03 41	22 16	26 08	17 14	10 09	18 44	06 06	15 06	19 16	26 57
28	04 41	07♊26	25 14	18 13	10 22	18 56	06 11	15 04	19 16	26 58
29	05 41	22 15	24 29	19 13	10 36	19 07	06 16	15 03	19 15	27 00
30	06 41	06♋39	23 56	20 14	10 48	19 19	06 21	15 02	19 15	27 01
31	07 41	20 33	23 33	21 15	11 01	19 31	06 26	15 01	19 15	27 03

NOVEMBER 2007

Date	☉	☽	☿	♀	♂	♃	♄	♅	♆	♇
1	08♏41	03♌59	23♎22R	22♍16	11♋12R	19♐42	06♍31	14♓59R	19♒15R	27♐04
2	09 41	16 59	23♎23D	23 18	11 23	19 54	06 35	14 58	19 15	27 06
3	10 41	29 37	23 34	24 20	11 33	20 06	06 40	14 57	19 15	27 08
4	11 41	11♍58	23 56	25 22	11 42	20 18	06 45	14 56	19♒16D	27 09
5	12 41	24 06	24 28	26 25	11 51	20 30	06 49	14 55	19 16	27 11
6	13 41	06♎05	25 08	27 28	11 58	20 43	06 54	14 54	19 16	27 13
7	14 41	17 59	25 56	28 32	12 04	20 55	06 58	14 54	19 16	27 15
8	15 42	29 51	26 51	29 36	12 09	21 07	07 02	14 53	19 16	27 16

NOVEMBER 2007 (Cont'd)

Date	☉	☽	☿	♀	♂	♃	♄	♅	♆	♇
9	16♎42	11♏42	27♎52	00♎40	12♋13	21♐19	07♍07	14♓52R	19♒17	27♐18
10	17 42	23 34	28 59	01 45	12 17	21 32	07 11	14 51	19 17	27 20
11	18 43	05♐28	00♏10	02 49	12 20	21 44	07 15	14 51	19 17	27 22
12	19 43	17 26	01 25	03 55	12 23	21 57	07 19	14 50	19 18	27 24
13	20 43	29 30	02 44	05 00	12 25	22 09	07 22	14 49	19 18	27 25
14	21 44	11♑40	04 05	06 06	12 26	22 22	07 26	14 49	19 19	27 27
15	22 44	24 01	05 29	07 11	12♋27R	22 35	07 30	14 48	19 19	27 29
16	23 45	06♒35	06 55	08 18	12 27	22 47	07 33	14 48	19 20	27 31
17	24 45	19 26	08 23	09 24	12 26	23 00	07 37	14 48	19 20	27 33
18	25 46	02♓39	09 51	10 31	12 24	23 13	07 40	14 47	19 21	27 35
19	26 46	16 17	11 21	11 38	12 21	23 26	07 43	14 47	19 21	27 37
20	27 47	00♈21	12 52	12 45	12 17	23 39	07 47	14 47	19 22	27 39
21	28 47	14 53	14 24	13 52	12 12	23 52	07 50	14 47	19 23	27 41
22	29 48	29 48	15 56	15 00	12 06	24 05	07 53	14 46	19 23	27 43
23	00♐48	15♉01	17 29	16 07	11 59	24 18	07 55	14 46	19 24	27 45
24	01 49	00♊20	19 02	17 15	11 50	24 31	07 58	14 46	19 25	27 47
25	02 50	15 34	20 36	18 24	11 42	24 44	08 01	14 46	19 26	27 49
26	03 50	00♋33	22 09	19 32	11 32	24 58	08 03	14 46	19 27	27 51
27	04 51	15 07	23 43	20 41	11 22	25 11	08 06	14♓47D	19 27	27 53
28	05 52	29 12	25 17	21 49	11 12	25 24	08 08	14 47	19 28	27 55
29	06 53	12♌47	26 51	22 58	11 01	25 37	08 11	14 47	19 29	27 57
30	07 53	25 52	28 25	24 08	10 49	25 51	08 13	14 47	19 30	27 59

DECEMBER 2007

Date	☉	☽	☿	♀	♂	♃	♄	♅	♆	♇
1	08♐54	08♍33	29♏59	25♎17	10♋36R	26♐04	08♍15	14♓48	19♒31	28♐01
2	09 55	20 54	01♐33	26 26	10 23	26 18	08 17	14 48	19 32	28 04
3	10 56	03♎00	03 07	27 36	10 09	26 31	08 19	14 48	19 33	28 06
4	11 57	14 56	04 41	28 46	09 53	26 45	08 20	14 49	19 35	28 08
5	12 58	26 47	06 15	29 56	09 37	26 58	08 22	14 50	19 36	28 10
6	13 58	08♏37	07 49	01♏06	09 19	27 12	08 23	14 50	19 37	28 12
7	14 59	20 29	09 23	02 16	09 00	27 25	08 25	14 51	19 38	28 14
8	16 00	02♐24	10 57	03 26	08 41	27 39	08 26	14 51	19 39	28 16
9	17 01	14 25	12 31	04 37	08 21	27 52	08 27	14 52	19 40	28 19
10	18 02	26 32	14 05	05 48	08 00	28 06	08 28	14 53	19 42	28 21
11	19 03	08♑46	15 39	06 58	07 39	28 20	08 29	14 54	19 43	28 23
12	20 04	21 08	17 13	08 09	07 18	28 33	08 30	14 55	19 44	28 25
13	21 05	03♒40	18 48	09 20	06 57	28 47	08 31	14 56	19 46	28 27
14	22 06	16 23	20 22	10 31	06 36	29 01	08 32	14 57	19 47	28 30
15	23 07	29 19	21 56	11 43	06 14	29 14	08 32	14 58	19 49	28 32
16	24 09	12♓32	23 31	12 54	05 53	29 28	08 32	14 59	19 50	28 34
17	25 10	26 04	25 05	14 05	05 30	29 42	08 33	15 00	19 52	28 36
18	26 11	09♈57	26 40	15 17	05 08	29 55	08 33	15 01	19 53	28 38
19	27 12	24 11	28 15	16 28	04 45	00♑09	08 33	15 02	19 55	28 41
20	28 13	08♉46	29 50	17 40	04 21	00 23	08♍33R	15 04	19 56	28 43
21	29 14	23 37	01♑25	18 52	03 57	00 37	08 33	15 05	19 58	28 45
22	00♑15	08♊37	03 00	20 04	03 32	00 50	08 32	15 06	19 59	28 47
23	01 16	23 36	04 36	21 16	03 08	01 04	08 32	15 08	20 01	28 49
24	02 17	08♋26	06 12	22 28	02 43	01 18	08 32	15 09	20 03	28 52
25	03 18	22 58	07 48	23 40	02 19	01 32	08 31	15 11	20 04	28 54
26	04 19	07♌05	09 24	24 52	01 55	01 45	08 30	15 12	20 06	28 56
27	05 20	20 45	11 00	26 04	01 32	01 59	08 30	15 14	20 08	28 58
28	06 22	03♍57	12 37	27 17	01 09	02 13	08 29	15 16	20 10	29 01
29	07 23	16 44	14 14	28 29	00 47	02 27	08 28	15 17	20 11	29 03
30	08 24	29 10	15 51	29 42	00 25	02 40	08 26	15 19	20 13	29 05
31	09 25	11♎20	17 28	00♐54	00 04	02 54	08 25	15 21	20 15	29 07